Sites and Sights
of the Iron Age

'This team is chosen for its skill and experience ...'

(photos: A.L. Pacitto, D. Webb)

Sites and Sights
of the Iron Age

Essays on Fieldwork and Museum Research

presented to

Ian Mathieson Stead

Edited by Barry Raftery

with Vincent Megaw and Val Rigby

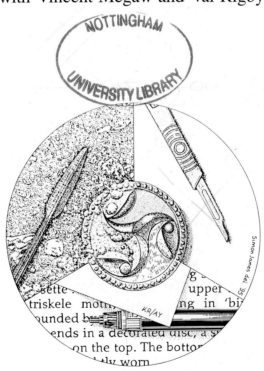

Oxbow Monograph 56
1995

Published by
Oxbow Books, Park End Place, Oxford OX1 1HN

© Oxbow Books, 1995

ISBN 1 900188 00 7

This book is available direct from
Oxbow Books, Park End Place, Oxford OX1 1HN
(Phone: 01865-241249; Fax: 01865-794449)

and

The David Brown Book Company
PO Box 511, Oakville, CT 06779
(Phone: 203-945-9329; Fax: 203-945-9468)

10007497744

Front cover: Linch-pins with matched decoration from a burial at Kirkburn (Stead 1991)
(photo: British Museum)

Back cover: Front and back views of the sheet bronze shield found at Chertsey, Surrey (Stead 1991)
(photo: British Museum)

Printed in Great Britain by
The Short Run Press
Exeter

Contents

Foreword

Some years ago, when one of us was last involved in editing a personally dedicated series of articles, he received a courteous but firm note of refusal from one who now, with the passing of time, has himself reached the age for such marks of distinction gilded with affection. 'The *Festschrift* is an outmoded institution to which I do not intend to add' commented our colleague – and then a couple of years later proved that he was wrong by himself co-editing another celebratory volume. Of course the only real purpose of the *Festschrift* is, as a strict translation of the word indicates, to celebrate, to give pleasure to the individual concerned. In that sense it may be thought that such volumes are the publisher's equivalent of the dodo, a production which can't take off and is bound to end up obsolete – or the next worst thing to obsolescence, on the bookseller's remainder table. Here we have been fortunate that David Brown has so readily agreed to take on the production of this volume, proving yet again that archaeologists make the best sort of archaeological booksellers and publishers.

Over the last twenty years one of the particular pleasures for Iron Age specialists visiting London has been the ritual visit to the Department of Prehistoric and Romano-British Antiquities of the British Museum. At least once a year there was a chance for a private view of the latest Iron Age acquisitions or material brought in for study and conservation. The viewing was often followed by discussion and the recounting of histories, sometimes worthy of the best-seller lists, over a pizza and a *vino rosso* or, if time was pressing, between a communal munching of sandwiches beside a file- and photograph-covered desk. This generosity with time and knowledge has been typical not only of Ian Stead but of the other Yorkshire Ian, Ian Longworth having, during his Keepership, maintained 'P & R-B' as a model of free access, cheerful tolerance and total co-operation which many other museum institutions could do well to copy. Indeed, for their many fans there is a concern with future chronology in the Department, chronology ADI, or, can there be life After-the-Departure-of-the-two-Ians? Of course there will be but of necessity the cramped but ever-welcoming roof-top eyrie of P & R-B will never be the same.

The selection of topics for inclusion in this tribute has been based on the Editors' desire to match material to the man. The contributions to this volume represent therefore both the geographical and temporal range of Ian Stead's professional interests. It is also only right and proper that so many of his own BM colleagues should have been eager to prepare studies – often under considerable difficulties brought about not just by the seemingly permanent state of renovation in which those who work in the British Museum find themselves but also the need to keep the recipient from knowing in advance what he was about to receive. Archaeology is an odd trade and so are most archaeologists; we have tried to mirror some of the facets of a many faceted career in a number of ways. We are particularly grateful to Simon James for the title-page vignette, many individuals including Tony Pacitto for a composite portrait of the gentleman-scholar at work and Stuart Piggott whose hitherto unpublished poem written at the beginning of his university career reminds us that we too are artefacts. Each one has portrayed the nature of the archaeological beast with prime examples of their individual creative skills while Elizabeth Fowler has continued her long association with at least one of the editors as fellow archaeologist and indexer. As to the pleasant chores of editorialising, for logistic and security reasons the heaviest burden has had to be shouldered by the Irish corner of a particularly far-reaching Bermuda triangle; if there were a dedication for this volume it undoubtedly would have been to the inventer of the fax machine.

It is certain that formal retirement for Ian Stead will simply represent an administrative irritation and not mark the end of a professional career which seems in recent years to have grown exponentially in terms of productiveness. The Bloomsbury Pizza Express will still be an essential stop-over for every jet-setting European prehistorian but it will be important to remember that behind every successful archaeologist there is – almost always – a long-suffering and no less competent partner. So, Sheelagh, this book is also a present for you. Amidst the seemingly obligatory bone-sorting and number-crunching may there remain many more years of shared, portable and totally legal antiques hunting.

VINCENT MEGAW
BARRY RAFTERY
VAL RIGBY
St Nicholas Day, 1995

I. M. Stead: An Appreciation

IAN LONGWORTH

Ian Mathieson Stead was born in York in 1936 and his up-bringing in that noblest of cities has lent colour to much of his career. After reading the Archaeology and Anthropology tripos at Cambridge where he graduated in 1958, the desire to study a topic related to Yorkshire came naturally. Bronze Age Food Vessels were quickly discarded in favour of the Iron Age for the rich burials of the Yorkshire wolds begged for further study. Following early papers in YAJ reflecting supply digging for the old Ministry of Works his doctoral thesis appeared in print in 1965 under the title *'The La Tène Cultures of Eastern Yorkshire'*, later to be reworked and extended as *'The Arras Culture'* (1979).

Already while at Cambridge Ian had established himself as a highly competent excavator and his early professional career was now to be with the Ministry of Works first as an Assistant and later from 1964–1974 as an Inspector of Ancient Monuments. Major excavations of this period included work at the Roman villas of Winterton, Rudston and Nunney, and at the Iron Age and Roman settlements of Blagden Copse and Braughing. Interspersed with these were sites more central to his own interests: Welwyn Garden City with its immensely rich La Tène burial and King Harry Lane which in turn were to lead to the search for cemeteries of Aylesford-Swarling type at Baldock. Baldock was to be excavation on the grand scale – vast areas opened by bull dozers and graders, but the extensive Iron Age cemeteries at Burton Fleming and Rudston saw a return to a more conventional approach.

This period was important for three reasons. While digging at Yearsley Ian had met Sheelagh whom he married in 1962, a highly supportive wife with whom he has shared many of the rewards and rigours of work in the field. Secondly, after the experience of Baldock, the advantages of having a regular team with whom he could dig were recognised and this became established. Known as 'the Stead circus' its members included many who were to move on to higher things – Robert Hedges to the Oxford Laboratory, Paul Buckland to the University of Sheffield and John Hinchcliff to English Heritage. It included also Val Rigby whose knowledge of pottery was to complement so admirably Ian's own interests in metalwork, and Tony Pacitto. Tony was to add a further dimension for here was a natural genius with all things mechanical, electronic and explosive (though to my knowledge the last has yet to be exploited fully in the field). A visit to the bottom of the Rudston well which Ian excavated to a depth well below the prevailing water table was made all the more memorable by Pacitto's gentle voice remarking that if the pumps failed we probably had about six seconds to get out. Together Ian and Tony were to develop geophysical techniques capable of detecting chariot burials in the field so admirably demonstrated on the Garton/Kirkburn site. A third important development was the arrival of J-L Flouest, a French school teacher with whom Ian set up an immediate rapport which was to open the door to fieldwork in France and the next phase – the search for continental origins for the Arras culture. A campaign of excavations in Champagne begun in 1971 was to last with help from the Leverhulme Trust for the following ten years.

In 1974 Ian had joined the staff of the Department of Prehistoric and Romano-British Antiquities as an Assistant Keeper, becoming Deputy Keeper three years later. Brought in to take charge of the Iron Age collections it was now possible to devote far more time and energy to his main research interests and to building up the Museum's already impressive Iron Age collections. A detailed knowledge of cart and chariot burial had already been extended to a profound knowledge of metalwork in general and not least the art that embellished it. Buckets, brooches, swords, scabbards and shields fell beneath his pen while a short guide to Celtic art published in 1985 has already sold some 22,500 copies. Yet it is a tremendous tribute that while these interests were to be pursued with spectacular results, Ian was able to produce a steady stream of final reports for excavations carried out during his former spell at the Ministry.

If the main thrust of his interest has lain in the excavation and study of Iron Age burial, Stead has always remained receptive to new ideas and new challenges.

The chance discovery of a bog body found through commercial peat cutting at Lindow Moss in Cheshire was seized upon with customary zeal. Somehow the many specialist interests involved were welded together so that publication was possible within 3 years from the time of discovery, a monumental achievement.

Lindow Man, which brought instant fame, proved to be only a beginning for a second chance discovery, this time of further finds of precious metal at Ken Hill, Snettisham, likewise evoked an immediate response. The subsequent investigations were to prove more spectacular than any could predict and were themselves to stimulate new lines of research which remain on-going.

It is a great pleasure to be able to offer thanks to a colleague whose active career still stretches out into the future, for retirement from the British Museum is surely just one milestone on the way. It was entirely appropriate that the distinction which he had won should have been recognised by election to a Fellowship of the British Academy in 1991. He had already become a Fellow of the Society of Antiquaries some 25 years previously, been made a Corresponding Member of the Deutsches Archäologisches Institut in 1976 and, to his great delight, an honorary member of the Yorkshire Philosophical Society in 1982.

Ian Stead belongs firmly to that foot-on-the-ground, trowel-in-the-earth band of British archaeologists. Never one to theorise where common sense and deduction offered a swifter more objective path, he has made and will surely continue to make contributions to our knowledge which will stand the test of time well beyond other more fashionable but essentially ephemeral approaches. The ability to see the core of a problem, to act swiftly and decisively is matched by a sensitivity which has brought new insights into the analysis of Celtic art. Above all a profound love of objects, that tangible material evidence which has come down to us from the past, illuminates his work and it is to our great delight and reward that he has chosen to share so many of his thoughts and perceptions with us both as colleague and author. I hope in turn that he may find pleasure in the essays presented here by just a few of his colleagues to mark the close of one chapter in what we all hope will remain a long and productive life.

List of the Published Works of I. M. Stead

Valery Rigby

1958   A sherd of Middle Saxon Pottery from York. *Yorkshire Archaeol. Journ.*, 39 pts 155–6: 426.

An Anglian Cemetery at the Mount, York. *Yorkshire Archaeol. Journ.*, 39 pts 155–6: 427–35.

Excavations at the South Corner Tower of the Roman Fortress at York 1956. *Yorkshire Archaeol. Journ.*, 39 pts 155–6: 515–37.

1959   The excavation of Two Beaker Burials at Staxton, East Riding, 1957. *Yorkshire Archaeol. Journ.*, 40 pt 157: 129–144.

A Chariot Burial on Foxton Moor, North Riding. *Antiquity* 33:214–6.

1961   A Distinctive Form of La Tène Barrow in Eastern Yorkshire and on the Continent. *Antiq. Journ.*, 41: 44–62.

1963   An excavation of Yearsley, North Riding 1961. *Yorkshire Archaeol. Journ.*, 41: 19–20.

1965   *The La Tène Cultures of Eastern Yorkshire.* York: The Yorkshire Philosophical Society.

The Celtic Chariot. *Antiquity*, 39: 259–65.

1966   Winterton Roman Villa: an interim report. *Antiq. Journ.*, 46: 72–84.

1967   A La Tène Burial at Welwyn Garden City. *Archaeologia*, 101:1–62.

An Excavation at Kings Square, York, 1957. *Yorkshire Archaeol. Journ.*, 42 pts 165–6: 151–164.

1968   An Iron Age Hill-fort at Grimthorpe, Yorkshire, England. *Proc. Prehist. Soc.*, 34: 148–90.

Excavations in Blagden Copse, Hurstbourne Tarrant, Hampshire, 1961. *Proc. Hampshire Field Club*, 23: 81–9.

1969   With Jones, J.D. An Early Iron Age Warrior-Burial found at St. Lawrence, Isle of Wight. *Proc. Prehist. Soc.*, 35: 351–4.

Verulamium 1966–68. *Antiquity*, 42: 45–52.

1970   A Trial Excavation at Braughing, 1969. *Hertfordshire Archaeol.*, 2: 37–47.

A Roman Villa at Whatley Combe, Nunney, Somerset. *Proc. Somerset Archaeol. and Nat. Hist. Soc.*, 114: 37–47.

1971   Yorkshire before the Romans: some recent discoveries. In *Soldier and Civilian in Roman Yorkshire* (ed. R.M. Butler). Leicester, pp. 21–43.

The reconstruction of Iron Age buckets from Aylesford and Baldock. *Prehistoric and Roman Studies* = Brit. Mus. Quarterly 35 (ed. G. de G. Sieveking). Oxford: The University Press, pp. 250–82.

Beadlam Roman Villa: an interim report. *Yorkshire Archaeol. Journ.*, 43: 178–86.

1973   With Liversidge, J. and Smith, D. J. Brantingham Roman Villa: Discoveries in 1962. *Britannia*, 4: 84–106.

1974   With Flouest, J.-L. Des tombes de la Tène II et III à Menil-Annelles et Ville-sur-Retourne (Ardennes). *Bulletin Société Archéologique Champenoise*, 67, no. 5: 59–67.

1975   The La Tène cemetery at Scorborough, East Riding. *East Riding Archaeol.*, 11: 1–11

Baldock. In *Small Towns in Roman Britain*. Brit. Archaeol. Rep., Brit. Ser. 15 (eds T. Rowley and W. Rodwell), 125–9.

A Roman pottery theatrical face-mask and bronze brooch-blank from Baldock, Herts. *Antiq. Journ.*, 55: 397.

1976   The earliest burials of the Aylesford Culture. In *Problems in Economic and Social Archaeology* (eds G. de G. Sieveking, I.H. Longworth and K.R. Wilson). Essays presented to Graham Clark. London, pp. 401–16.

La Tène Burials between Burton Fleming and Rudston, North Humberside. *Antiq. Journ.*, 56: 217–26.

Excavations at Winterton Roman Villa and other sites in North Lincolnshire 1958–67. (DoE Archaeol. Rep. no. 9).

1977   Recherches sur les cimetières de la Tène en Champagne 1971–74. *Gallia*. 35: 59–74.

Une tombe de La Tène III à Hannogne (Ardennes). *Mem. Soc. Agr. Com. Sc. Arts Dept. Marne*, 92: 55–72.

1979 *The Arras Culture*. York: The Yorkshire Philosophical Society.

Iron Age Cemeteries in Champagne: the third interim report (British Museum Occasional Paper 6).

1980 *Rudston Roman Villa*. Leeds.

1981 *The Gauls: Celtic Antiquities from France*. London: British Museum Publications.

Fouille de sauvetage à Tinqueux (Marne) 1974. *L'Age du Fer en France Septentrionale* (Mem. Soc. Archéol. Champenoise, 2): 151–76.

1982 The Cerrig-y-Drudion "hanging bowl". *Antiq. Journ.*, 62: 221–34.

1983 La Tène Swords and Scabbards in Champagne. *Germania*, 61: 487–510.

1984 Some notes on imported metalwork in Iron Age Britain. In *Cross-Channel trade between Gaul and Britain in the Pre-Roman Iron Age*. Soc. Antiq. London Occ. Pap. new series 4. (eds S. Macready and F.H. Thompson), 43–66.

Celtic dragons from the River Thames. *Antiq. Journ.*, 64: 269–79.

Cart burials in Britain. In *Keltski Voz* (eds M. Guštin and L. Pauli). Brežice: Posavski muzej, pp. 31–41.

The Linsdorf Monster. *Antiquity*, 59: 40–2.

Iron-Age Metalwork from Orton Meadows. *Durobrivae: a review of Nene Valley Archaeology*, 9: 6–7.

1985 *Celtic Art in Britain before the Roman conquest*. London: British Museum Publications.

The Battersea Shield. London: British Museum Publications.

Une tombe à char sans char. *Histoire et Archéologie*, 98: 26–7.

With R.C. Turner. Lindow Man. *Antiquity*, 59: 25–9.

1986 A group of Iron Age barrows at Cowlam, North Humberside. *Yorkshire Archaeol. Journ.*, 58: 5–15.

Iron Age chariot burials. *Illustrated London News*, 274: 60–1.

Celtic Europe. In *Seven Thousand Years of Jewellery* (ed. H. Tait). London, pp. 72–80.

With J.B. Bourke and D. Brothwell. *Lindow Man. The body in the bog*. London: British Museum Publications.

With V. Rigby. *Baldock: the excavation of a Roman and pre-Roman settlement 1968–72*. (Britannia Monograph 7), London.

1987 Lindow Man: an ancient body from a Cheshire bog, England. In *European Wetlands in prehistory* (eds J.M. Coles and A.J. Lawson). Oxford: Clarendon Press, pp. 137–143.

1988 Chalk figurines of the Parisi. *Antiq. Journ.*, 68: 9–29.

1989 With V. Rigby. *Verulamium: the King Harry Lane Site.* (English Heritage Archaeol. Rep. 12).

1990 Whitcombe, Burial 9, the Grave Goods. In Excavations at Whitcombe, 1965–1967 (eds G.M. and G.N. Aitkin). *Proc. Dorset Nat. Hist. and Archaeol. Soc.*, 112: 73–75.

1991 Many more Iron Age shields from Britain. *Antiq. Journ.*, 71: 1–35.

Iron Age Cemeteries in East Yorkshire. (English Heritage Archaeol. Rep. 22), London.

The Snettisham treasure: excavations in 1990. *Antiquity* 65: 447–65.

Somme-Bionne; The Arras Culture; The Belgae in Britain: The Aylesford Culture. In *The Celts* (eds S. Moscati, O.-H. Frey, V. Kruta, B. Raftery, M. Szabo). London: Thames and Hudson, pp. 174–5, 587–90, 591–5.

With A.P. Hartwell, J.R.S. Lang, S.C. La Niece and N.D. Meeks. An Iron Age Sword and Scabbard from Isleham. *Proc. Cambridge. Antiq. Soc.*, 70: 61–74.

1992 An Excavation near the Dominican Friary at Dunstable. *Journ. Manshead Archaeol. Soc. Dunstable*, 32: 1–4.

1995 The Metalwork. In K. Parfitt, *Iron Age Burials from Mill Hill, Deal.* London: British Museum Publications, pp. 58–111.

REVIEWS

1973 Denise Bretz-Mahler. La Civilisation La Tène I en Champagne: le facies marnien (1971). *Antiq. Journ.*, 53: 310–11.

1978 Morna MacGregor. Celtic Art in Northern Britain. *Germania*, 56: 284–6.

1982 D. N. Riley. Landscape from the Air: Studies of Crop Marks in South Yorkshire and North Nottinghamshire 1980. *Antiq. Journ.*, 62: 173–4.

1983 N. Freidin. The Early Iron Age in the Paris Basin: Hallstatt C and D. Brit. Archaeol. Rep., International Series 131, 1982. *Antiquity*, 57: 141.

1988 J-G Rozoy. Les Celts en Champagne: les Ardennes au second Age du Fer: le Mont Troté, les Rouliers. 1 Etude 2 Description. *Antiquity*, 62: 622.

1989 Ruth and Vincent Megaw. Celtic Art from its Beginnings to the Book of Kells. *Antiq. Journ.*, 69: 353

For Ian Stead: a dedicatory poem on the occasion
of his retirement

Lecturing on the Palaeolithic: Edinburgh 1946

Nostalgic in the muffs and fur
Through my mind glide Les Patineurs
As on thin glacial ice I skate
Do flints and I both patinate?

STUART PIGGOTT

A Gaul from Egypt

DONALD M. BAILEY

I am most grateful to Val Rigby for suggesting a recent acquisition by the Department of Greek and Roman Antiquities of the British Museum as a very appropriate subject for me to present to Ian Stead, a valued colleague of many years.

A terracotta figure of Egyptian manufacture, made in a two-piece mould, in typical Nile silt fabric, of a light brown clay and containing a modicum of mica, was purchased in October 1994 (fig. 1). It represents a Gaulish warrior, naked except for a substantial cloak, standing with his right hand on the hilt of his sword, which hangs at his right hip from a simple belt round his waist. To his left side he holds a large oval shield, with a vertical rib flaring at the centre, which is covered by a rectangular shield-boss. There is a wide binding-strip round the edge of the shield, and two pairs of diagonal lines, presumably decorative, cross the shield, one pair above, the other below, the boss. His hair is long and rises up from the forehead in the manner well known from classical art and literature; he does not have a moustache but his phallus is large as befits a barbarian. He is not shown wearing a torc. The terracotta is well-modelled on the front, but with only summary treatment of details on the back. His shield would not be out of place in the third or second century BC and his sword is of the comparatively short type current before the enormously long form developed in the second and first centuries BC.

The figure shows a Gaul in his full pride, arrogant and sure of himself, as one of a warrior people that had terrorised the ancient world from fourth-century Rome to third-second-century Greece and Asia Minor. This is not a defeated Gaul or a prisoner, as was so often depicted in Hellenistic art and copied by Romans. The Large Gauls and Small Gauls of the Pergamon and Athens victory monuments set up probably by Attalos I in about 220 BC, although noble, are shown dying or committing suicide in defeat (Smith 1991: 99–104), and small Roman bronzes show captive Gauls, male and female, based upon sculptural trophy groups (cf. Bieńkowski 1928: 48–57, 79). From 279 BC, various tribes of Gauls crossed from Europe into Asia Minor, causing trouble

all round and eventually settled in central Anatolia in the area to become known as Galatia. From here they raided their neighbours in various destructive ways, but were largely contained by the surrounding Hellenistic kings, the Seleucids and the Attalids. A Myrina terracotta in the Louvre shows a Galatian, with a large oval shield, trampled and gored by a war-elephant, perhaps of Antiochus I in 275 BC (Toynbee 1973: pl. 10; Scullard 1974: 121–3 and pl. VIIb), but more probably of Eumenes II, who fought Gauls in various battles in 190,

fig. 1. Terracotta figure of a Gaulish mercenary. Made in Egypt late in the third century BC. British Museum GR 1994.10–1.2.

184 and 164 BC: the terracotta has been dated to the middle of the second century BC (Mollard-Besques 1963: pl. 150d and f). The Hellenistic monarchs were, however, always in need of mercenaries, and this was a further outlet for a warlike people.

Another great Hellenistic kingdom, Ptolemaic Egypt, also employed Gauls as mercenaries. Ptolemy II Philadelphos had an unfortunate experience with them (but one that became more unfortunate for the Gauls themselves). Philadelphos's half-brother Magas, his representative at Cyrene, took advantage of the former's preoccupation with the First Syrian War with the Seleucids and marched in 274 BC on Egypt with an army. Magas had to turn back as Libyan nomads began to attack the Cyrenaica. In the mean time, however, 4,000 Gaulish mercenaries in the employ of Philadelphos, believing that Ptolemy would have his hands full with Antiochos I in front in Syria and Magas behind in the western Delta, rebelled, hoping no doubt to enrich themselves from the sack of wealthy cities and shrines in Egypt. They failed and were manoeuvered onto an island in the Sebennytic branch of the Nile where they murdered one another or died of hunger (Pausanias I, 7.2; Reinach 1910: 38).

Other Ptolemies had more positive results with Gaulish mercenaries. These, together with other soldiers of the Ptolemaic army, were amongst those settled on the land, mostly in the Fayum, to cultivate it (or lease it out to tenants), while awaiting a call to arms. On one occasion, recorded by Polybius, during the reign of Ptolemy IV Philopator, the cleruchs, as these 'sleepers' were styled, were recalled because of the threat to Egypt by the Seleucid king Antiochos III. Amongst the soldier-settlers were 4,000 Gauls and Thracians (Polybius V, 65.10; Griffith 1935: 118–19). With their help, the standing army plus 20,000 native Egyptians defeated Antiochos in 217 BC at the battle of Raphia, near Gaza (Bevan 1927: 224–9): Egyptians had been in the army of Ptolemy I Soter a century earlier when he vanquished Antigonos One-Eye at Gaza, but this was the first time that they were trained to fight in the Macedonian style. It was probably at that time that, with Gauls as heroes, the terracotta described here was made.

Gauls continued to be employed in the Ptolemaic army and are known to have been amongst the troops besieging the rebel Egyptian town of Abydos in 186–5 BC, and four of their number are named in a graffito scratched into the walls of a chapel of Horus at that place. Others are recorded as being in the garrison stationed at Hermopolis Magna late in the second century and also early in the first century BC. Gauls are named on painted funerary stelae, of third-century date, found in Alexandria, mostly in the Hadra Necropolis, and often showing depictions of the deceased, sometimes with their huge Gaulish shields; a third century Hadra hydria, a cinerary urn, from Alexandria, bears the name of a Gaul: for all these, see Reinach (1910).

Several representations of Gauls survive from Egypt and figure in its (mainly minor) art (Reinach 1910; Bieńkowski 1928: 135–9). Amongst the finest is a late third-century marble head from Giza (Smith 1991: fig. 229), but this is reminiscent of the beleaguered Gauls of Attalos I, rather than the undefeated Gaul of our terracotta. Some unique fragmentary wall-paintings said to be from Alexandria show warriors (not obviously Gauls) carrying Gaulish shields (Hanfmann 1984: pls XLVI, 1, XLV, XLVI, 1), but the author considers that they are of the late third or early fourth century AD: I suspect a case could be made for them being Ptolemaic, with mercenaries in Macedonian armour, but retaining their distinctive shields. A fine ivory carving from Oxyrhynchus in Middle Egypt, an inlay from a piece of furniture, depicts the head of a moustached Gaul in front of a public building with Corinthian columns; it is probably of the second or first century BC, and is in the collections of the British Museum (GR 1906.10–22.9; Reinach 1910: 81, fig. 17). It may represent the driving of Gauls from Delphi in 279 BC by Apollo (with a little help from the Aetolian League: Pausanias X, 23.3–6). In the same class as our Gaul, but wearing trousers, is a fine terracotta figure from Hehia once in the Fouquet Collection (Perdrizet 1921: pl. XCIII). Some well-modelled heads of Gauls, broken from terracotta figures are shown in Reinach (1910: pl. VIII). A complete figure in the Ashmolean Museum (NP 1970.1059), but rather schematically rendered, shows a fully armed Gaul, with a luxurient moustache and hair down to his shoulders, wearing mail and trousers: it must be rather later in date than ours and may not be of Egyptian origin, although I think it very probably is so (Ritchie 1985: 9). Eros, always tempted to borrow the gear of others (the club, lion-skin and drinking-cup of Herakles; the armour of Ares), could not resist the accoutrements of Gauls: a terracotta from Hermopolis Magna shows him wearing a torc, bearing a large oval shield, and holding a Celtic trumpet, a carnyx (Perdrizet 1921: pl. XCIII; for a comprehensive discussion of erotes as Gauls, see Hausmann 1984). Our Gaul, an excellent example of the Egyptian coroplasts' craft, a naked warrior full of hauteur, well armed and convinced of his invulnerability, seems a fit subject for the present volume.

Acknowledgements

The author is very grateful to Catherine Johns for discussing this paper and making very valuable suggestions; and to Helen Whitehouse for access to the Ashmolean Gaul.

References

Bevan, E. 1927. *A History of Egypt under the Ptolemaic Dynasty.* London: Methuen.

Bieńkowski, P. 1928. *Les Celtes dans les arts mineurs gréco-romains.* Cracow: Imprimerie de l'Université des Jagellons.

Griffith, G.T. 1935. *The Mercenaries of the Hellenistic World.* Cambridge: Cambridge University Press.

Hanfmann, G.M.A. 1984. New Fragments of Alexandrian Wall Painting. In *Alessandria e il mondo ellenistico-romano, studi in onore di Achille Adriani* (eds N. Bonacasa and A. di Vita), ii: 242–55. Rome: "L'Erma" di Bretschneider.

Hausmann, U. 1984. Zur Eroten- und Gallier-Ikonographie in der alexandrinischen Kunst. In *Alessandria e il mondo ellenistico-romano, studi in onore di Achille Adriani* (eds N. Bonacasa and A. di Vita), ii: 283–95. Rome: "L'Erma" di Bretschneider.

Mollard-Besques, S. 1963. *Musée du Louvre, Catalogue raisonné des figurines et reliefs en terre-cuite grecs et romains* ii, *Myrina.* Paris: Editions des Musées Nationaux.

Perdrizet, P. 1921. *Les terres cuites grecques d'Egypte de la collection Fouquet.* Nancy: Berger-Levrault.

Reinach, A.J. 1910. Les Galates dans l'art alexandrin. *Fondation Eugène Piot, Monuments et Mémoires*, 18: 37–115.

Ritchie, W.F. and J.N.G. 1985. *Celtic Warriors.* Princes Risborough: Shire.

Scullard, H.H. 1974. *The Elephant in the Greek and Roman World.* London: Thames and Hudson.

Smith, R.R. 1991. *Hellenistic Sculpture, a Handbook.* London: Thames and Hudson.

Toynbee, J.M.C. 1973. *Animals in Roman Life and Art.* London: Thames and Hudson.

'Gallo-Belgic' Coins and Britain

ANDREW BURNETT

Since the middle of the nineteenth century much of the historical framework of later pre-Roman Iron Age Britain was built upon the evidence of the coins of the period. The contribution of Evans (1864) was fundamental and began a tradition which continued to develop for well over a hundred years, culminating in the work of Allen. Given the paucity of written history, the absence of contemporary documents and the difficulties of interpreting other surviving material remains, it is not surprising that such emphasis was placed on the study and interpretation of such a systematic and apparently datable body of evidence. But after Allen, there was something of a void in the study of Iron Age numismatics, and even though there has been something of a renaissance in the study in the last few years, with the publication of a large number of valuable monographs, studies and reports of material (see the summary in Mays 1992), it seems clear that the evidence of coins has begun to play a different role. First, there is a growing realisation that, *pace* some recent publications, the coinage cannot be regarded as 'a well-ordered, well-dated series from which the clutter of old preconceptions has been totally stripped' (Cunliffe in Van Arsdell 1989; see the critical reviews of Burnett 1989 and Kent 1990). The second change has been in the way that coin evidence is now used. Few scholars would nowadays wish to use it to write the 'missing history' of Britain from Caesar to Claudius (e.g. Frere 1967), and its changed status can be seen, for example, in Collis' chapter on the Iron Age in the recent celebratory volume of the Royal Archaeological Institute (1994), where coinage has almost completely disappeared from the discussion. There has been an almost tacit abandonment of the historicist interpretation of the coinage, and hence the preferential status of coins in the study of the Iron Age: if coins lose their privileged position of being seen as a means of giving us 'history', then their study can have no intrinsic 'superiority' over the study of any other form of surviving material evidence. It is therefore no accident that recent books dealing extensively with coinage have subtitles like those of C. Haselgrove's *Iron Age coinage in south-east*

England. The archaeological context (1987) or N. Roymans' *Tribal societies in northern Gaul: an anthropological perspective* (1992).

I have no doubt that these changes in the direction of the subject are welcome, but it seems to me that a certain number of the 'old' preconceptions have survived. One could take a number of different examples to bring out this point. I have chosen the case of the 'Gallo-Belgic' coinage, partly because it illustrates the point very well, partly because of the intrinsic interest of its nature as the earliest coinage from Britain, and partly because of the occurrence of some 'Gallo-Belgic' coins at Snettisham, and the need to attempt to answer Ian Stead's questioning about their date and interpretation.

'Gallo-Belgic' is the term applied to the series of Iron Age coins whose origin seems to lie in north-east Gaul, and which are found in relatively large numbers in south-eastern Britain. They were not the only and not the earliest Continental gold coins to be found in Britain, as we know of a number of British finds of 'Philippus' imitations (made in Gaul, the Upper Rhineland and modern Switzerland) and Tarentine imitations (made in northern Gaul) (Fitzpatrick 1992). These are probably earlier than the 'Gallo-Belgic' issues discussed here, but another group of Continental coins, the 'Baiocassan' coins made in Normandy, are perhaps broadly contemporary. They have been found in parts of south west Britain, having travelled north across the Channel and are known today from a number of single finds, and principally from the hoard from Ringwood, Hampshire (Burnett and Cowell 1988: 1–4). I shall briefly return to both these groups later.

The 'Gallo-Belgic' coins were fully catalogued and classified by Scheers (1977), and since her work much attention has been paid to their interpretation, for example by Haselgrove (1987), Nash (1987: 118–22), and most recently Fitzpatrick (1992). The principal different types are labelled with letters of the alphabet, from 'A' to 'F'. Different terminologies can be, and have been, used to denote these coins, but 'Gallo-Belgic A', etc. have the merit of being well understood, without being unduly misleading inasmuch as they avoid any specific tribal ascription (see already Evans 1860: 130; more recently, Gruel 1989: 27). The different letters help to distinguish the different types, of which the two most commonly found in Britain are A, the broad flan pieces, and E, the uniface pieces. Although the distribution of the different types varies, both in Britain and on the Continent (see the maps in Cunliffe 1981), it can be argued that one should view all the main types (or at any rate A to E) as related parts of a single phenomenon. Thus, for example, C is die-linked to E, implying a continuity of time and place; B (the 'defaced' coins) seem to be made from defaced dies for A, and some of the coins of A are closely linked by style and fabric to C (Scheers 1977). This leaves D, the name given to the series of quarter staters with an abstract geometric type (the 'type au bâteau'). It seems to me that these coins may represent the smaller denomination associated with C and E. This is suggested by their metallic purity (overlapping C and E: Cowell 1992) and by the hoards from Weybourne (Allen 1971: 140) and Fring (unpublished), in which they are found with E staters. These links between the different groups, particularly the die-links, seem to me to be more significant than the minor variations in distribution patterns and to provide strong evidence for viewing all the types as part of a single whole.

Questions of chronology and interpretation are not easy to answer. First, the question of date: when were these coins made? The answer is that we do not really know. The putatively earliest issues, A, are frequently taken to be datable from their occurrence in the Tayac, Gironde hoard of 1893, but we must not cling to the view that we can date that hoard very precisely. First, we need to discard as an argument the notion that the deposition of the hoard can be associated with the migration of the Cimbri at the end of the second century BC (Haselgrove 1987: 78). Secondly, the contents of the hoard are of little help. As well as a gold torc and three gold ingots, it contained four groups of gold coins: some 65 'Gallo-Belgic' A, 78 Bohemian 'mussel' staters, and two large groups of western Celtic coins. The hoard is very unusual in the way that it is made up of coins from so many diverse origins, but we cannot use its association of these different groups to help greatly with chronology, since the chronology of none of the groups is very well fixed. The hoard is usually dated to the middle or later second century BC (Allen 1980: 73; Haselgrove 1987: 78; Boudet 1987), but Scheers, for example, has dated it to the beginning of the first century BC (1977: 44, 900). So we cannot really decide whether the hoard, and hence its different components, belong to the middle or end of the second century, or even the beginning of the first.

Little extra help can be obtained from another mixed hoard, that found in 1979 at Niederzier near Düren in the Rhineland (Göbel, Hartmann, Joachim and Zedelius 1991; Joachim 1991). In addition to a gold bracelet and two gold torcs, this hoard contained 26 'rainbow cups' and 20 'Gallo-Belgic' C staters. Rainbow cups are, like mussel staters, known from some datable German contexts. They seem to belong to the same general horizon as the mussel staters, perhaps developing out of them; at any rate the hoard has been associated with the La Tène D1 period in Germany and so dated to the first half of the first century BC (Overbeck 1987). The hoard suggests that 'Gallo-Belgic' C belongs no later than the first half of the first century BC, but no more than that.

If the date of the earlier 'Gallo-Belgic' issues is not very certain, then, I would suggest, the same is surely also true of the latest. The abundant 'Gallo-Belgic' E coinage has, since Scheers, been regularly associated with Caesar's campaigns in Gaul. She argued for an association of the E coinage with precisely 57 BC, and her connection of this coinage with Caesar has remained in place, even though Nash and Haselgrove have both suggested that it may have begun rather earlier, perhaps in about 70 BC (Nash 1987: 114; Haselgrove 1984: 4; 1987: 80–1). These variations in the dating should perhaps warn us that the chronology is by no means as sure as we might hope. Indeed it must be admitted that even the association of the coinage with Caesar's campaigns is no more than an inference: the large scale of the coinage (as clearly indicated by surviving specimens and the number of dies) is thought to 'fit' best with the historical circumstances of Caesar's campaigns, as is the pattern of hoarding and the decline in weight and purity of gold from one type to another (Haselgrove 1987: 80). But we must remember that it is only a hypothesis that these characteristics of the coinage can be explained only in the context of Caesar's Gallic War. While there certainly are well-documented cases where an increase in the level of coining is accompanied by an increase in the level of warfare, there are equally cases without this correlation. For example, Corinth produced little or no coinage in the Peloponnesian War (Kraay 1976: 80) and the detailed study of the coinage of Domitian shows no correlation between production and the German wars fought in his reign (Carradice 1983: 159–63). The same point can be made about hoards and debasement. These may accompany periods of warfare, but by no means exclusively so (Walker 1978: 106; Casey 1986: 60). Moreover, we need to appreciate that to accept the association of the 'Gallo-Belgic E' coins with the Gallic War is itself an example of the historicising approach to the interpretation of Iron Age coinage. And as we do not really know what happened in Belgic Gaul for the century or so before Caesar, there is no reason to suppose that another set of equally 'suitable' circumstances may not have obtained on some other occasion(s). One might even question the orthodox view that Gallic gold coinage as a whole did not survive the Gallic wars: is there any compelling reason to suppose that 'Gallo-Belgic' E, for example, could not have been produced afterwards?

If we confine ourselves to saying that the 'Gallo-

Belgic' coinage was probably produced from some (uncertain) time in the second century BC to some (uncertain) time in the first century BC, then we can remain on reasonably secure ground. But it seems to me that as soon as we move from this to any more precise position, particularly if we try to assign dates to the different types of 'Gallo-Belgic' coinage, then we are pretending to a knowledge which is (at the moment, at least) unattainable. How can we possibly assess, for example, the duration of 'Gallo-Belgic' A or C, or whatever? We cannot. We do not really know if 'Gallo-Belgic' coinage lasted for a period as long as a hundred years or as short a period as 30 years; and we cannot locate that period at all precisely in the second and first centuries BC.

In the light of what we can say about the date of the production of the 'Gallo-Belgic' coins, we then have to address the related but separate question of when they came to Britain. This too is not self-evident. It has often been noted that some types of 'Gallo-Belgic' coins are worn when found in Britain; Allen for example alluded to the 'worn condition ... in which they are generally found' (1960: 101). This observation is true mainly of the 'Gallo-Belgic' A coins, and the wear has been interpreted by Allen and Scheers as the result of an exceptionally long circulation of these coins in Britain, long after their import into the island (Scheers 1977: 45). Kent (1978), however, argued that these coins were imported much later with the other 'Gallo-Belgic' coins, when the coins were already worn. In his view all the 'Gallo-Belgic' coins (worn 'Gallo-Belgic' A, fresh 'Gallo-Belgic' E, etc.) came to Britain at a single time (the period of the Gallic Wars), and he supported this view with the observation that 'Gallo-Belgic' A may be found with other types of 'Gallo-Belgic' coins in British hoards in a way that they are not on the Continent, where hoards tend to comprise only one type of 'Gallo-Belgic' coin. This latter point has been reviewed by Fitzpatrick (1992: 12–14) who somewhat tentatively agrees with it. There are, however, mixed Continental hoards (Scheers 1977: 889), and the evidence for mixed hoarding in Britain is not, in fact, very strong since the 'Gallo-Belgic' coins tend to be only single pieces in larger hoards (e.g. Harpsden Wood: Burnett and Cowell 1988: 4–6). This does not seem to show a great deal other than that a few of the earlier coins were available later in Britain than they were on the Continent.

Indeed the view that the coins came later to Britain seems itself unlikely. First, if they are found in discrete hoards on the Continent, but not in later Continental hoards, then presumably they were no longer circulating there (e.g. they had been demonetised), so how could they have been available for export to Britain? A second and related point concerns the wear; if the 'Gallo-Belgic' coins are supposed to have been worn when they came to Britain, why are not worn pieces found on the Continent? If it is supposed that the coins were worn when they came to Britain, then there must have been a pool of worn coins in Gaul which could be exported. But such a pool has left no trace, and is anyway not very likely to have existed if we accept that the absence of earlier 'Gallo-Belgic' coins from later Continental hoards implies that the earlier ones had by then been demonetised and had disappeared from circulation. Both points have been made by Haselgrove (1984: 100 and 1993: 36) and seem to me to indicate that most of the coins came to Britain earlier rather than later and that most of them became worn in Britain rather than on the Continent. The likeliest conclusion at the moment seems to be that the 'Gallo-Belgic' coins came to Britain at more or less the same time as they were circulating on the Continent, but that a few of them continued to circulate longer in Britain.

The above discussion shows that these coins were present in Britain in the second/first centuries BC and so provide one possibility for the identity of the gold coins which Caesar attests to during the expedition of 54 BC, when he says that 'they [sc. the Britons] use either bronze or gold coinage or iron bars of a fixed weight instead of coins' (utuntur aut aere aut nummo aureo aut taleis ferreis ad certum pondus examinatis pro nummo: BG 5.12). Even here, however, we should remember that the text of this famous passage is not without its problems, and there are different manuscript readings. We are offered both other iron objects (aliis ferreis) and iron rings (anulis ferreis) rather than iron bars (taleis ferreis); 'nummo aereo' (bronze coinage) rather than 'nummo aureo' (gold coinage); and sometimes 'pro nummo' is omitted. However, I do not want here to discuss the question of British currency bars (Hingley 1990) or the question of bronze (does it mean bronze metal or, less plausibly, bronze coins?) and the related question of potin coins (Haselgrove 1988); but the problems of this text should warn us that the textual evidence may incorporate as many difficulties and dangers as the archaeological record.

This point reminds us that the 'archaeology' of texts needs to be treated as carefully as the archaeology of artefacts, and we need to be even more careful when we try to use the two types of evidence in combination. In the case of the interpretation of 'Gallo-Belgic' coins in Britain, for instance, Fitzpatrick (1992) has recently objected to the use of text-led explanations. Clearly we should not accept what the texts say on a subject concerning which they were not particularly well informed and obviously potentially biassed. Similarly we must acknowledge that we know about certain events in Iron Age Gaul and Britain from texts only because these particular events involved or interested Roman authors. Other events, either similar or diverse in nature, may well have happened without leaving any such trace: our total ignorance about north east Gaul before Caesar has already been mentioned as an example. Nevertheless, it seems inevitable that we may ultimately rely on textual evidence for building some alternative models for the interpretation of the material evidence, just as we may also use observations of what happens in other ancient or pre-industrial societies.

Indeed when we turn to possible explanations for the movement of the 'Gallo-Belgic' coins to Britain, we can easily see that there are a number of possibilities, and that most of them can be supported by textual evidence as well as analogies drawn from other contexts. Many such explanations have been given. Kent and Nash, for example, have used mercenaries to explain the phenomenon; Allen, famously, thought in terms of a series of migrations (1960); van Arsdell has assumed that the coins came to Britain in trade (1989); others have sought an explanation in socio-political terms (Collis 1971; Haselgrove 1993: 36). I do not want here to offer a preference for any of these alternatives or indeed anything else, but to point out that there is something to be said for all of them. But as each explanation can be supported with arguments of the same type, the conclusion can, and will subsequently, be drawn that the debate is sterile, and that different approaches should be used.

The interpretation of coin finds in terms of trade is not very fashionable at the moment, and indeed it is not easy to find examples from the ancient world where the surviving archaeological evidence points to trade as the explanation of the movement of large amounts of coin from one area to another. This is because coinage tended to stay within its own political or economic sphere of origin (e.g. most Roman coins stayed within the Roman empire), but there are a few examples of a one-way movement of coinage that seems most likely to be explained as the movement of precious metal coinage as objects of trade. Two good examples concern the movement of classical Greek silver coins to Egypt or the export of Roman denarii and aurei to India. There is no particular reason why we should not apply a similar model to Britain, even though it is often observed – and surely correctly – that Iron Age society was organised differently from a modern market or even the Roman economy and that its economic aspects were more embedded in social and political relations. Even so, we would hardly wish to deny the importance of trading activities, and we know from Strabo's famous list of grain, cattle, gold, silver, iron, hunting dogs, hides and slaves (IV.5.2), that the Romans found much to trade with Britain during the Augustan period. For all we know, some of these or other goods may have been traded between Britain and the Continent a hundred years earlier. We can use one text to give specific support to such a view, for Caesar says that the Veneti had extensive maritime contacts with Britain (BG 3.4), and this is repeated by Strabo who says that the Veneti engaged Caesar in war to prevent him crossing to Britain since they were trading with it (Strabo IV.4.1). I would have little difficulty with the view that at this period gold coins were used on occasion as objects of trade in return for other goods. That coins played this role for only one period should not be regarded as problematical, since we can

see just such a pattern in the Roman trade with India, which was sometimes carried on with coins, but sometimes without them.

A second explanation is the invasion theory. This theory originates with the discovery by Evans of the Aylesford cemetery with its cremation burials and new pottery types. The conclusion was drawn that burial rites and pottery were brought to Kent with the invasion of Belgic peoples, and it is easy to see how the same interpretation could be placed on the coins. This became the standard view, which found its fullest form in the writings of Allen and was subsequently followed, for instance, by Scheers (see also Collis 1994, for the academic context). In its most embellished form, this theory held that the arrival of successive types of 'Gallo-Belgic' coinage represented successive waves of Belgic migrants to Britain, from the second to the first century BC. Such a view was criticised by Kent (1978), and is not taken very seriously today. But, although most invasions are not associated with artefactual change, they may on occasion be. The Roman invasion of Britain in AD 43, for example, introduced Roman coinage into Britain, just as much earlier the campaigns of Alexander the Great had brought the spread of coinage from the Mediterranean to Afghanistan. In the case of pre-Roman Britain, the invasion theory might take different forms. For example, we might not, from the archaeological record, be comfortable about the idea of discrete and archaeologically discernible arrivals from the Continent, but it is still possible that large groups of people may have come to Britain, quite possibly bringing coins with them. Caesar records his view that the interior peoples of Britain claimed to be indigenous, whereas those living on the coasts were 'immigrants from Belgic Gaul who came after plunder and to make war; following their invasion they settled there' (BG 5.12). He also records in 57 BC that some of the leaders of the Bellovaci fled to Britain (BG 2.14), and the validity of some such mechanism seems to be accepted by Haselgrove for the movement of some coinage across the Channel (1987: 93).

A third type of explanation is the military or mercenary one. This has tended to dominate recent discussions. It was argued by Kent (1978), and since then has seemed to fit well into Nash's general explanation of the movement and spread of Iron Age precious metal coinages as a result of mercenary activity (1987). Warfare and the provision of mercenaries have dominated discussions of other coinages in recent years, e.g. in the Greek world. In this case, the theory holds that the 'Gallo-Belgic' coins came to Britain from Gaul in payment for help against various enemies, including Caesar. This sort of help might have taken the form of men (mercenaries), or, as a variant, it might have taken the form of supplies such as corn. Again, Caesar tells us that he invaded Britain 'because he knew that in almost all the Gallic campaigns the Gauls had received help from the Britons' (BG 4.28); specifically in the previous year (56 BC) he says that the Veneti had summoned reinforcements from Britain against him (BG 3.9). One can compare, in this context, the report that in 54 BC the relatives of Indutiomarus tried to win the support of the Germans across the Rhine by promising them money (Caesar BG 6.2).

A fourth type of explanation has seen no need for a special reason for the discovery of 'Gallo-Belgic' gold in Britain, because it can be explained by the same or similar mechanisms (whatever they were) that caused the circulation of coinage within any single Iron Age region. Although it need not depend on any political or kinship links, in its most extreme form this explanation would rely on the hypothetical existence of a single political unit in south east Britain and Belgic Gaul. This is not in itself implausible. The Channel seems more of a boundary to us than it may have seemed in the second and first centuries BC, when the real boundary surely lay much further south, namely the boundary of the Roman empire in southern Gaul. Seen in this way, the Channel can be regarded as only one natural hazard which, like a mountain range or swamp, might hinder relations between peoples on either side, but was hardly a fundamental barrier. We know from written sources of several examples of kinship and other relations between Iron Age elites on either side of the Channel, such as Commius or the Atrebates in general. In addition, according to Caesar, in the first century BC ('nostra memoria'), a certain Diviciacus, a prince of the Suessiones, was the most powerful man in Gaul and ruler of a considerable part of Britain as well as Gaul (apud eos [Suessiones] fuisse regem nostra etiam memoria Diviciacum, totius Galliae potentissimum, qui cum magnae partis harum regionum tum etiam Britanniae imperium obtinuerit: BG 2.4). Naturally this passage has not escaped modern commentators; it has been used by Rodwell (1976) as the explanation of the occurrence of 'Gallo-Belgic' C in Britain, and by Scheers (1977) as the explanation of part of 'Gallo-Belgic' A. But we have no way of knowing whether or not we should interpret the coin distribution as showing that the two areas were separate or unified. That they were unified would be a natural assumption of those who, in other cases, draw political maps on the basis of Iron Age coin finds, but this procedure is not generally justifiable. Examples drawn from other periods show that in some cases a great diversity of coinage occurs in a single political unit (e.g. the diversity of coinage made in the Roman empire) and that in other cases a distribution of a single type of coin may cover more than one political unit (e.g. Anglo-Saxon coins in Britain and Scandinavia).

We can then see that a number of different explanations can be put forward for the discovery of so much 'Gallo-Belgic' coinage in Britain. Although they are very different and one can think of objections to each one as a single convincing explanation, they all have a certain amount of plausibility and are, of course, by no means incompatible or exhaustive. There is nothing ostensibly incorrect in arguing for one or other of them or for a combination of some of them or indeed other factors, such as the exchanges, plunder, gifts, tribute and inducements mentioned by Haselgrove (1987: 191–5), or the display of status, gifts to clients, and religious payments emphasised by Roymans (1992: 131–4).

To do so, however, would not be very productive. The methodology in every case is the same, to find an analogy from another context and support its application by adducing textual evidence or further examples drawn from other periods and places. But it is not at all clear how we can, or whether indeed we should, try to argue for any particular explanation, since it is hard to see any definite or effective way of validating any particular position one might take. The conclusion I draw from this is that to do more than state the possibilities is to enter into a fruitless discussion, and that it is preferable to adopt a different approach.

Before doing so, however, I think that one further assumption underlying the debate needs to be questioned. Are we really sure that we are dealing with the export of coins from Gaul to Britain? The die-links between coins found on different sides of the Channel (Scheers 1977) show that the coins were made on one side and exported to the other, but how do we know it was from Gaul to Britain rather than the other way round? There is a natural tendency to assume that the flow must be from the Continent, since just as coinage 'spread' from the Mediterranean to central Gaul, so it then spread from Gaul to Britain. But even though we can accept that coinage was made earlier in Gaul than in Britain, this does not entail the view that the flow of 'Gallo-Belgic' coins was from Gaul to Britain. A hundred and thirty years ago, Evans thought that 'Gallo-Belgic' coins were British; they had 'a more frequent occurrence in Britain, and are therefore, in all probability, of British origin' (1860: 25). His view was not admitted by French scholars. Blanchet, for example, in his great *Traité* (1905: 369) assumed that 'Gallo-Belgic' A was made by the Bellovaci and merely alluded in a footnote with a reference to Evans that they were found in Britain. Evans has indeed been criticised for his 'mistake in attributing many uninscribed Gaulish types to Britain' (Haselgrove 1987: 5), but his point has never really been answered. Some of the 'Gallo-Belgic' coins are indeed much more common in Britain than on the Continent (e.g. staters of 'Gallo-Belgic' B are found only in Britain), and I cannot see why this is thought to have less significance than arguments based on provenance have in all other cases of the attribution of Iron Age coins. It seems to me that the question should at least be re-examined.

Whether or not the coins travelled from Gaul to Britain or vice versa (or indeed some combination of the two possibilities) does not greatly affect the different sorts of causality discussed above (one could use similar arguments in reverse) or indeed the question of whether such a discussion has any great value beyond a statement of possibilities. If we abandon such an approach, then we can try to view the distribution of 'Gallo-Belgic' coins on both sides of the Channel in a different way. This can be done in two ways. The first is to look at other coins. We can refer again to the other Gallic 'imports' mentioned towards the beginning of this article, the earlier Gallic types and the 'Baiocassan' coins. Both these cases are instances of the same phenomenon (the distribution of the same type of coins on different sides of the Channel), and they broaden the context, since they indicate that the same thing was happening both at an earlier date and in a different area. And we can contrast this pattern, as Haselgrove has (1993: 37–8), with the different, purely insular, distribution of early 'potin' coins which are probably broadly contemporary with the gold coinages under discussion. The different distribution seems striking, but only if we assume that gold and potin should be regarded as comparable. There seems no reason to suppose that they are, and it seems to me that it is no more puzzling that their distribution patterns should be different than that they should be different from any other sort of artefact or indeed settlement type, or whatever.

This leads to a second way of broadening out the discussion, which is to look at the coins in the context of other material remains. One specific approach to this would be to link the discussion of the coins more closely to that of other gold objects, principally torques, since there are clearly close associations between them. They are made of the same material and are used in similar ways, as far as we can tell from the evidence of their discovery together in hoards or their mutual absence from graves; the way that the different functions separately discussed by Roymans for gold and for gold coins overlap so much underlines the point that they should not perhaps be treated separately in this way (1992: 128–34). On a more general level, one could try to develop the coin evidence for cross-Channel cultural links with the evidence for other sorts of archaeological change, such as the development of temples, changes in the technique and types of pottery, Mediterranean imports, the introduction of cremation, etc. As Ian Stead has put it, 'whether by invasion or not, by the end of the first century BC southeastern England had developed much in common with a zone across northern France to the Rhineland' (1991: 592). Both the Aylesford culture and the coins can be seen as part of, and the results of, the long-term interaction between Britain and the Continent, rather than the consequence of specific, 'historical' events. This is the way to re-insert coinage into the study of this interaction, and, stripped of its special status as an isolated phenomenon requiring historicist explanations or enjoying a superior chronology, it can play an important and helpful role.

Acknowledgement
I would like to thank Jonathan Williams.

REFERENCES

Allen, D.F. 1960. The origins of coinage in Britain: a re-appraisal. In *Problems of the Iron Age in Southern Britain* (ed S.S. Frere). London: Institute of Archaeology Occasional Papers 11, pp. 97–308.

Allen, D.F. 1971. British potin coins: a review. In *The Iron Age and its hill forts* (eds M. Jesson and D. Hill). Southampton, pp. 127–54.

Blanchet, A. 1905. *Traité des monnaies gauloises*. Paris: Leroux.

Boudet, R. 1987. A propos du dépôt d'or celtique de Tayac (Gironde). In *Mélanges offerts au Docteur J.-B. Colbert de Beaulieu* (eds C. Bemont, C. Delplace, B. Fischer, K. Gruel, C. Peyre and J.-C. Richard). Paris: Léopard d'Or, pp. 107–19.

Burnett, A. 1989. Review of Van Arsdell 1989. *Brit. Numismatic Journ.*, 59: 235–37.

Burnett, A.M. and Cowell, M.R. 1988. Celtic coinage in Britain II. *Brit Numismatic Journ.*, 58: 1–10.

Carradice, I.A. 1983. *Coinage and finances in the reign of Domitian*. Oxford: Brit. Archaeol. Rep. International Series 178.

Casey, J. 1986. *Understanding ancient coins*. London: Batsford.

Collis, J. 1971. Functional and theoretical interpretations of British coinage. *World Archaeol.*, 3: 71–84.

Collis, J. 1994. The Iron Age. In *Building on the Past: Papers celebrating 150 years of the Royal Archaeological Institute* (ed. B. Vyner). London: Royal Archaeological Institute, pp. 123–48.

Cowell, M.R. 1992. An analytical survey of the British Celtic gold coinage. In *Celtic coinage: Britain and beyond* (ed. M. Mays). Oxford: Brit. Archaeol. Rep. British Series 222, pp. 201–33.

Cowell, M.R., Oddy, W.A. and Burnett, A.M. 1987. Celtic coinage in Britain: new hoards and recent analyses. *Brit. Numismatic Journ.*, 57: 1–23.

Cunliffe, B.W. (ed.) 1981. *Coinage and society in Britain and Gaul: some current problems*. London: CBA Research Report 38.

Evans, J. 1860. *The Coins of the ancient Britons*. London: Smith.

Fitzpatrick, A.P. 1992. The roles of Celtic coinage in south east England. In *Celtic coinage: Britain and beyond* (ed M. Mays). Oxford: Brit. Archaeol. Rep. British Series 222, pp. 1–32.

Frere, S.S. 1967. *Britannia. A history of Roman Britain*. London: Routledge.

Göbel, J., Hartmann, A., Joachim, H.-E. and Zedelius, V. 1991. Der spätkeltische Goldschatz von Niederzier. *Bonner Jahrbücher*, 191: 27–84.

Gruel, K. 1989. *Les monnaies chez les gaulois*. Paris: Errance.

Haselgrove, C. 1984. Warfare and its aftermath as reflected by the precious metal coinage of Belgic Gaul. *Oxford Journ. Archaeol.*, 3: 81–105.

Haselgrove, C. 1987. *Iron Age coinage in south-east England. The archaeological context*. Oxford: Brit. Archaeol. Rep. British Series 174.

Haselgrove, C. 1988. The archaeology of British potin coinage. *Archaeol. Journ.*, 145: 99–122.

Haselgrove, C. 1993. The development of British Iron-Age coinage. *Numismatic Chronicle*, 153: 31–63.

Hingley, R.A. 1990. Iron Age 'currency bars': the social and economic context. *Archaeol Journ.*, 147: 91–117.

Joachim, H.E. 1991. The votive deposit at Niederzier. In *The Celts* (eds S. Moscati, O.H. Frey, V. Kruta, B. Raftery and M. Szabó). London: Thames and Hudson, p. 532.

Kent, J.P.C. 1978. The origins and development of Celtic gold coinage in Britain. In *Actes du Colloque International d'Archéologie.* Rouen, pp. 313–24.

Kent, J.P.C. 1990. Review of Van Arsdell 1989. *Numismatic Chronicle* 150: 266–8.

Kraay, C.M. 1976. *Archaic and classical Greek coins.* London: Methuen.

Mays, M. 1992. Introduction. In *Celtic coinage: Britain and beyond* (ed M. Mays). Oxford: Brit. Archaeol. Rep. British Series 222, pp. i–xi.

Nash, D. 1987. *Coinage in the Celtic world.* London: Seaby.

Overbeck, B. 1987. Celtic chronology in south Germany. In *The Coinage of the Roman world in the late Republic* (eds A. Burnett and M. Crawford). Oxford: Brit. Archaeol. Rep. International Series 326, pp. 1–17.

Rodwell, W. 1976. Coinage, oppida and the rise of Belgic power in south-eastern England. In *Oppida: the beginnings of urbanism in barbarian Europe* (eds B. Cunliffe and T. Rowley). Oxford: Brit. Archaeol. Rep. International Series 11: pp. 181–367.

Roymans, N. 1992. *Tribal societies in northern Gaul: an anthropological perspective.*

Scheers, S. 1977. *Traité de numismatique celtique. II. La Gaule belgique.* Paris: Belles Lettres.

Stead, I.M. 1991. The Belgae in Britain: the Aylesford culture. In *The Celts* (eds S. Moscati, O.-H. Frey, V. Kruta, B. Raftery and M. Szabó). London: Thames and Hudson, pp. 591–5.

Van Arsdell, R.D. 1989. *Celtic coinage of Britain.* London: Spink.

Walker, D.R. 1978. *The metrology of the Roman silver coinage. Part III.* Oxford: Brit. Archaeol. Rep. Supplementary Series 40.

The Late Hallstatt Burial at Saint-Lumier-La-Populeuse (Marne) and the Problem of Jogassian Daggers

JEAN-JACQUES CHARPY

The little commune of Saint-Lumier-la-Populeuse is situated in the south-east of the Département of the Marne, in the canton of Maurupt-le-Montois, arrondissement of Vitry-le-François (fig. 2). Its territory does not seem to have been the subject of intensive archaeological research either in the nineteenth century or in the early twentieth. Emile Schmit (1926/7; 1927/8) made no mention of it in his archaeological survey. A brief note giving the circumstances of the discovery of a tomb was, however, published in 1897 (Anon 1897). It said:

> During the excavations which M. Léon Morillot caused to be carried out some time ago while constructing a road known as the Chemin du Gué de la Garonne near his property of Bussemont, some fragments of a small iron sword were unearthed, and M. Morillot immediately offered them to Monsieur Léon Morel. The latter succeeded in reconstructing the sword, which also has an iron scabbard; the exterior of the scabbard is covered with a decorative thin layer of bronze. At its extremity is the chape, also of bronze, into which the tip of the sword had been fitted. The chape gives this weapon a unique character, since it must be older than those usually found in the Marne département. It must belong to the first Gaulish period, immediately following the Bronze Age.

This notice evidently escaped Schmit's bibliographic trawl. Like many other researchers, he may have overlooked the information because it follows immediately upon the first written mention of the discovery of the Cernon-sur-Coole (Marne) cremation, then identified as a Roman tomb.

Saint-Lumier-la-Populeuse extends along the south bank of the Bruxenelle, a tributary of the left bank of the Saulx. The château of Bussemont lies at the western edge of the 238 hectare commune, and alongside a north-south road which crosses the river on the way to Blesmes. There can be no doubt that the burial, at the moment the only one known, was discovered close to this road. (fig. 3).

We are indebted to our friend Charles Poulain for unearthing, amongst the stock of illustrations in the Bibliothèque Carnegie at Reims, the two volumes containing the original watercolours and pencil drawings for the plates in Léon Morel's *La Champagne souterraine.*[1] One loose plate (leaf 74) deals with the Saint-Lumier tomb (fig. 4). According to the manuscript annotation of Henri Jadart, the manuscript became part of the collections of the Reims Library on 20 April 1909 as a gift from Morel's widow, in fulfilment of his testamentary wishes. The plates are signed, the earlier ones by Em[ile] Gastebois, the more recent by H. Jullerot. The two volumes of original plates differ from those in the 1898 publication of *La Champagne souterraine.* They contain several supplementary or unbound folios dealing with the Gaulish period; tombs at Courtavant, Saint-Jean-sur-Tourbe and Saint-Lumier-la-Populeuse as well as unprovenanced objects. The rest of the unpublished illustrations deal with the prehistoric and more especially with the Gallo-Roman and Merovingian periods. Emile Gastebois, the first illustrator, is renowned for his drawings of churches and monuments in the Marne. For his plates in *La Champagne souterraine,* Gastebois was awarded, on 28 August 1873, the bronze medal of the Société Académique de la Marne.

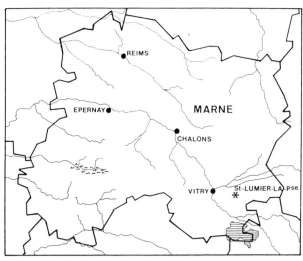

fig. 2. Geographical location of the commune of Saint Lumier-la-Populeuse in the Marne département.

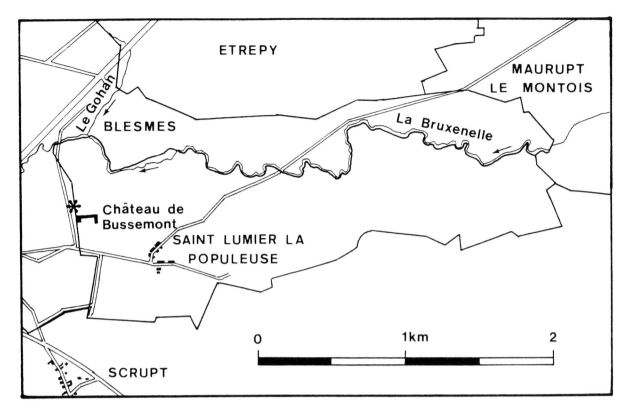

fig. 3. Geographical location of the burial within the territory of the commune of Saint-Lumier-la-Populeuse (Marne).

DESCRIPTION OF THE BURIAL AND ITS CONTENTS

We possess no further archival information about this burial and its previously unpublished[2] grave goods. A manuscript annotation by Morel on the original plate states that he informed the Ministry of the find. He must therefore have written a note which was not published by the Bulletin archéologique du Comité des travaux historiques et scientifiques. At that period only exceptional finds were published. One can assume that the burial was an inhumation. The grave goods – dagger, sword-belt and armring (fig. 4) – are in the Morel Collection in the British Museum.

The dagger (ML 2395): The weapon (figs 4, 5 and 6) is extremely corroded and survives in numerous fragments. It was originally 52.5 cm long and 3.5 cm wide at the scabbard mouth. Despite its poor condition, one can see that the iron blade is of lozenge section with a slightly raised midrib. According to the surviving drawing, the hilt, now only a small fragment, was 7.6 cm long. The scabbard has a bronze front plate generously folded back over the iron rear plate. The entry of the front plate, usually decorated on this type of weapon, no longer exists, though remaining traces indicate its campaniform outline. The suspension-loop from the drawing of fig. 7/4 is missing, and the surviving fragments of the rear plate offer no evidence of its attachment. The sword has been neither restored nor X-rayed. The anchor-shaped chape is 3.2 cm wide. It is fixed over the two scabbard-

plates and clamps them together. On its lower part is a rivet with a very well-fitted head, apparently circular on the rear but square and hammered on the front. The lowest edge of the chape displays a groove placed underneath, running along the axis of its widest point.[3] It thus joins externally the two upturned but unexpanded points of the 'anchor'. This dagger can be compared, in general shape as well as in this detail of its chape, with another example from tomb 192 at Les Jogasses at Chouilly (Marne).

The sword-belt (ML 2397–2400): According to Morel's plate, it is composed of three bronze rings (figs 4 and 5). Two have an identical exterior diameter of 16 mm, the third is larger, 19 mm. The British Museum register, however, lists four rings of virtually identical type (fig. 6). The number of iron or bronze rings in a Jogassian sword-belt is not standardised, varying between three and five. Solid bronze rings, such as those from Saint-Lumier-la-Populeuse, are generally rough castings, showing no trace of scraping or polishing and with a section which betrays the irregularities of the mould. Morel himself may have confused two similar Jogassian sword-belts, but the error could also have been made in 1901 when the British Museum acquired his collection. In any case, the unsigned drawing of these rings in the Reims library does not correspond with those in the British Museum's inventory. Since the Morel collection also contains Jogassian material originating from Heiltz-L'Evêque 'Charvais', it is possible the rings were

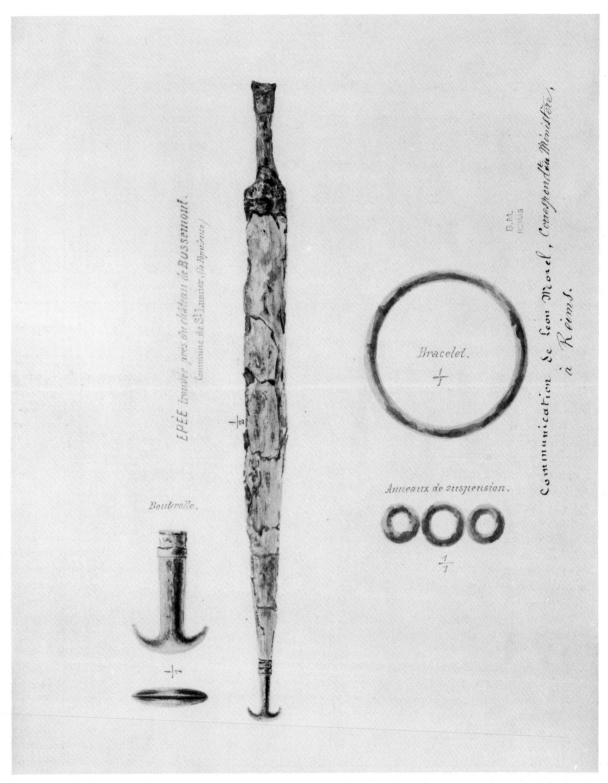

fig. 4. Watercolour plate from the original album of Léon Morel (reduced). (photo: Robert Meulle, Reims)

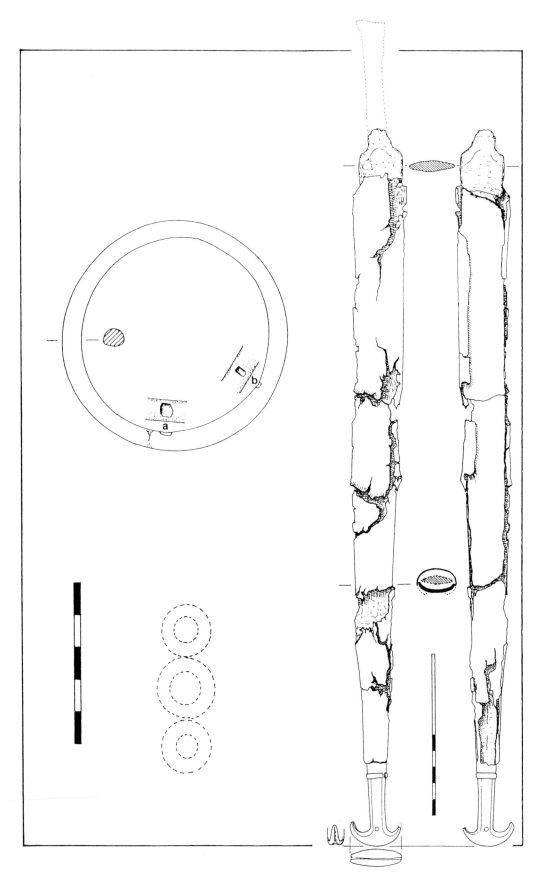

fig. 5. Grave goods from the Jogassian tomb of Saint-Lumier-la-Populeuse (Marne). Dagger, sword-belt after Morel, armring.

fig. 6. Bronze armring and sword-belt from Saint-Lumier-la-Populeuse, according to the British Museum Inventory (photo: British Museum). a, b: casting impurities

placed by mistake with the Heiltz find or with the unprovenanced material.

The armring (ML 2396): Of bronze, closed and smooth, and rectangular in section (figs 4–5). Exterior diameter 7cm, interior 6cm. Visible on the interior surface are two little hollows, possibly due to air-bubbles or, more probably, to the negative trace of impurities in the wax model (figs 5–6, a, b). The armring was not very carefully made and displays all the imperfections of the mould. This type of irregularity in manufacture is often encountered on other Jogassian objects, for example the unprovenanced dagger in the Musée des Antiquités Nationales (Marne, inv. no. 12041).

DATE OF THE TOMB

The weapon has many parallels among Hallstatt Final IIb material (Hatt and Roualet 1977) from the cemetery at Les Jogasses at Chouilly (Marne). The sword-belt, consisting of small bronze rings, is compatible with this chronological horizon. On the other hand, the presence of an armring in a male burial is quite exceptional. The only immediate comparison is tomb 192 (left burial) at Les Jogasses (Hatt and Roualet 1976: 445 and pl. 56), which not only contains an identical weapon, but also has one ring to indicate a sword-belt. In addition, this inhumation contains an iron armring which had been placed on the right arm of the dead man. It therefore

seems reasonable to consider this ensemble as credible, though with reservations about the belt-rings, which still need to be identified.

The dating of Jogassian weaponry poses real problems. Most weapons of this era either lack context (19th-century collections) or are from finds which contain only the hand-weapon and sword-belt. In the few contexts containing ceramics (Les Jogasses tomb 82), the pottery generally dates to the early fifth century BC. The arguments used in 1976 and 1977 by Hatt and Roualet to classify the arms as Hallstatt Final IIb rest mainly on the absence of any indicators permitting comparisons with finds from the Early (La Tène) period, and on the unique character of the type of vase (965 F) from Les Jogasses tomb 82: this vase is comparable only with one other (1141 F), just as isolated, and from tomb 156 of the same cemetery. In addition, the shape of these two pots is generally absent in earlier contexts. Finally, in the mid-1970s, knowledge about weapons in Champagne and its neighbouring regions was confined, after Déchelette, to the publications on Vix by Joffroy (e.g. 1960) and the monograph by Bretz-Mahler (1971).

Mapping of the burial-grounds and a wider knowledge of the Jogassian ensembles in the Marne make it possible to hypothesise an earlier date for the appearance of daggers and perhaps also of some dirks. Firstly one can note that known daggers are principally distributed along the course of the river Marne (fig. 11), in a zone occupied since Hallstatt Final IIa. Secondly, one can confirm that the deposition of pottery in Hallstatt Final IIa women's graves is exceptional. At Les Jogasses two (T. 141 and 179) out of the thirteen tombs (T. 32, 35, 42, 71, 117, 121, 130a,b, 132, 138, 141, 179) characteristic of this horizon produced one pot each: the pots are atypical forms and thus difficult to date. Finally, study of the weaponry of the Late Hallstatt to Early La Tène Ia transition period shows technological changes in the manufacture of scabbards and chapes. Notable among these are the joining of the scabbard plates, the addition of *tigettes* and of the high chape-bridge leading to the lengthening of the chape, and the gradual disappearance of wooden plates from the scabbard interior. Certainly it is the creation of the lateral gutters, a sort of clamp intended to grip the two scabbard plates, which characterised the earliest weapons of the Second Iron Age, and made wooden plates redundant. All these modifications can be seen on a series of weapons in mixed scabbards (front plate of bronze, rear plate iron) or entirely of iron, all too often without context: a selection can be seen in fig. 13 (See Bretz-Mahler 1971: pls 84/1,5,6; 85/1,6,7; 86,3,5); Ginoux (1994: pls II/3,4,5; V/1–4, 6,7) classes some of these as 'glaives' and others as long daggers. All these weapons constitute an ensemble characterised by chapes which undeniably prefigure those on Marnian fifth-century weapons. One final, determining, criterion for a slightly earlier chronology is the absence of this category of weapons from the fifth-century Marnian, for which we now have abundant evidence from, for example, Acy-Romance, Manre and Aure (Ardennes), Villeneuve-Renneville, Saint-Gibrien, Chouilly, Avize, Dormans, etc. (Marne).

THE REGIONAL CONTEXT (fig. 12)

The Saint-Lumier-la-Populeuse tomb can clearly be considered as the sole surviving evidence for a probable cemetery. It needs comparison with Dr Mougin's old and undocumented finds attributed to the adjoining commune of Blesmes (Lepage 1985: 119 fig. 95/4 and 124 fig. 99/18). The two armrings collected there are dated to Hallstatt Final I; one is ethnographically attributable to the western group defined by Louis Lepage, the other to his eastern group (Lepage 1989: 321–39: Lepage 1993: 3–27; Charpy 1991: 26–7).

The earlier Jogassian cemeteries (Hallstatt Final IIa) are mainly concentrated along the valley of the Marne. The most important known to us at present are, from west to east, Chouilly 'Les Jogasses', Bouy 'Les Varilles' and Heiltz-L'Eveque 'Charvais'. In their numerically significant ensembles we can observe the evolution of the two Jogassian phases (Hallstatt Final IIa and IIb). In IIb there is a multitude of burials over a much wider area, mostly constituting the earliest burials in the Marnian cemeteries (Charpy 1991; 1994). The distribution map of the cemeteries of the end of the First Iron Age (fig. 12) thus demonstrates a concentration in the sector which was to correspond with the fifth-century BC Marnian heartland.

It would seem, therefore, that the chalk regions of Champagne must have been progressively occupied by a succession of small groups of people: as early as Hallstatt Final I in the part south of a line joining Ecury-sur-Repos, Fontaine-sur-Coole and Blesmes (Marne) then, in Hallstatt Final IIa, a little beyond the right (northern) bank of the river Marne. We are not yet in a position to pinpoint the geographical origin of these groups, though some elements of their grave goods demonstrate close affinities with the Burgundy region (Vix) and others, especially the fibulae, more widely along the Alpine arc (Frey 1971; 1988). The earliest-occupied cemeteries are concentrated, as indicated above, along the Marne valley, which seems to have been the major axis of penetration. The most recent discoveries made in the Seine valley and as far as its confluence with the Yonne show the equal importance of this river route although, in this sector, no material has emerged to fill the gap between the discoveries dated to the end of Hallstatt Moyen/start of Hallstatt Final I (Charpy 1991: 26–7) and those of Hallstatt Final IIb (see Piette 1989: 229–41: Barray *et al.* 1994).

CATALOGUE OF JOGASSIAN DAGGERS (figs 7–10)

All the daggers come from funerary contexts with the exception of two found by dredging. The scabbards are of mixed type. The two entirely iron examples, from Les Jogasses tombs 76 and 153, have not been included in this catalogue. Even though their blades are morphologically similar to those which have mixed scabbards, their poor state of preservation allows no identification. Annexed is a table of measurements (fig. 14).

1. *Saint-Lumier-la-Populeuse (Marne)*. See above and figs 4,5 and 7/1.

2. *Saint-Denis*: dredged from the Seine (Seine-Saint-Denis) (Bulard and Degros 1980: 13–14). The weapon has since disappeared; and is known only from a cast in the Musée des Antiquités Nationales, which bears the inventory number 50364.

    Only the front plate of the scabbard and the chape remained when it was found (fig. 7/2). It is the largest of these weapons currently known to us. It is as long as the series of short swords of early La Tène Ia. The weapon is undecorated save for an incised line on its uppermost part. It was not possible to study the cast directly and we are grateful to Alain Bulard for information about it. Looking at the horizontal mouth, one might think that the scabbard is lacking its upper part which is generally campaniform on this type of weapon (see below, cat. no. 5). The slightly concave profile of the left long edge is doubtless due to the conditions of its discovery and to the wrenching off of its rear plate. If one accepts that the scabbard was undamaged, it could fit only a long cutlass, which would explain its length, its horizontal entry

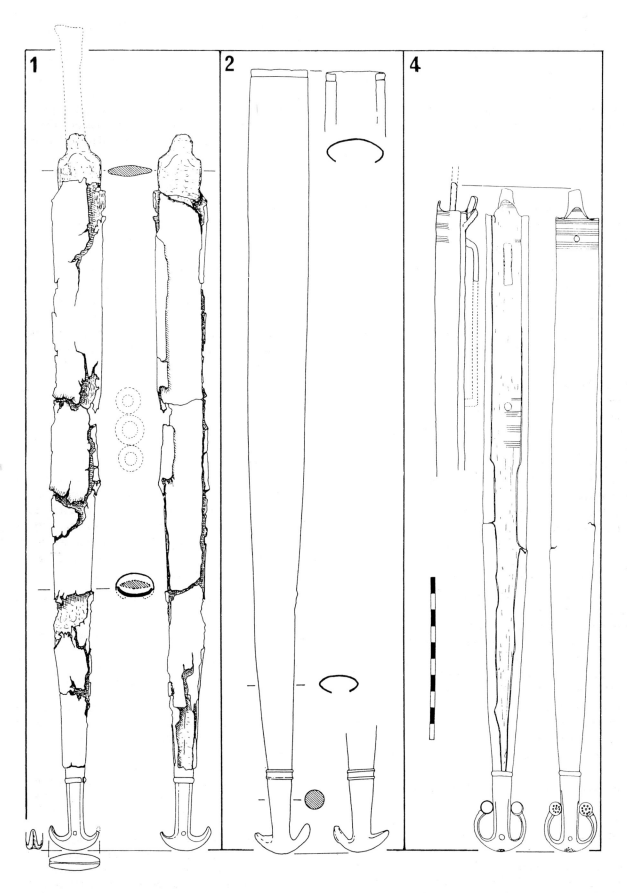

fig. 7. Catalogue of the graves containing daggers: 1. Saint-Lumier-la-Populeuse, 2. Saint-Denis (drawing: Alain Bulard), 4. Port-à-Binson.

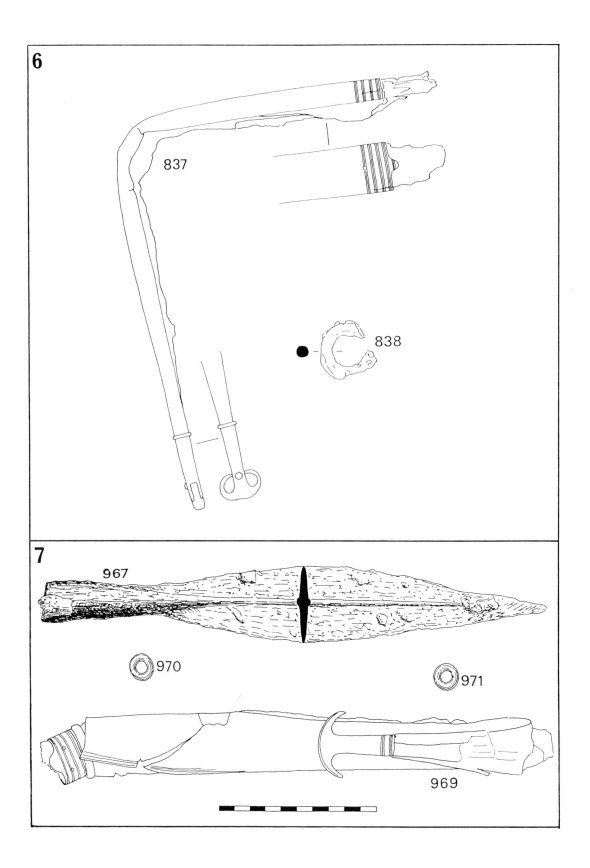

*fig. 8. Catalogue of the graves containing daggers: 6. Chouilly 'Les Jogasses' tomb 28, 7. Chouilly 'Les Jogasses', tomb 82
(drawings: Pierre Roualet)*

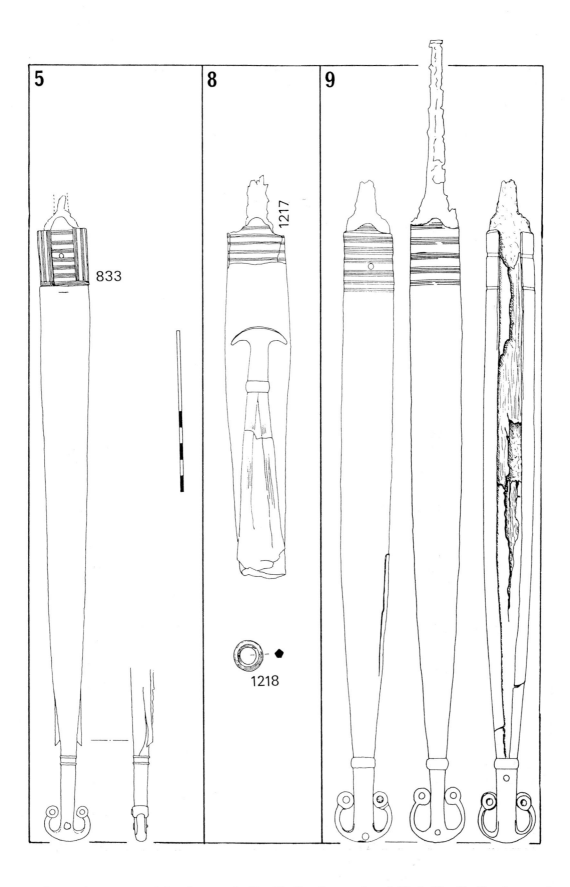

fig. 9. Catalogue of graves containing daggers: 5. Chouilly 'Les Jogasses' tomb 22, 8. Chouilly 'Les Jogasses' tomb 192, 9. Bouy 'Les Varilles' (Marne) (drawings: Pierre Roualet)

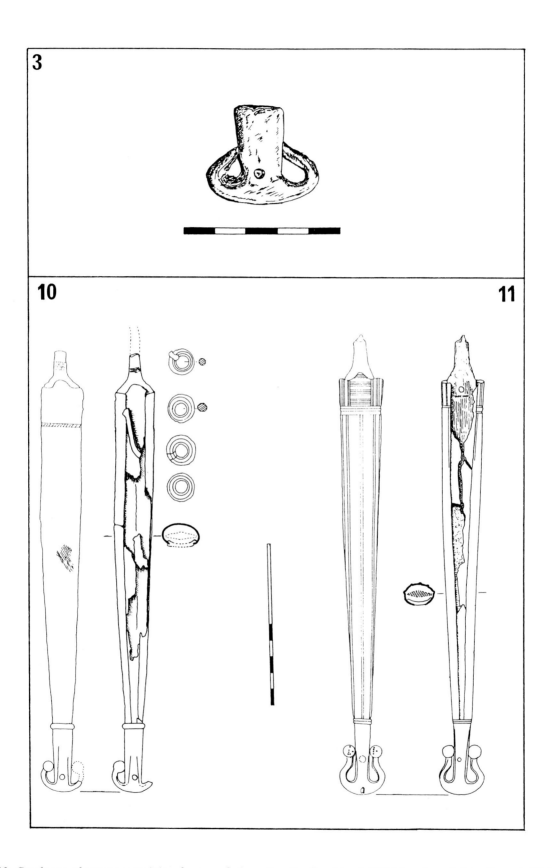

fig. 10. Catalogue of graves containing daggers: 3. Aure 'Les Rouliers' tomb 89B (drawing: Colette Rozoy), 10. Saint-Gibrien 'La Croix Mouchy' tomb 2, 11. Unprovenanced (Marne)

and the concavity of one of its sides. The close similarity of its dimensions to those of the example from Les Jogasses tomb 82 argues for its being a dagger. Knives with bronze and iron scabbards are scarce in north-eastern France and without precedent in the Paris Basin. The rare Jogassian examples are one without precise provenance (Marne, M.A.N. inv. no. 13363) and one from Bussy-le-Château (M.A.N. inv. no. 13189) (Ginoux 1994 no. 20 and pl. IV/5: no. 5 and fig. 2/6).

3. *Aure 'Les Rouliers' tomb 98B (Ardennes)* (Rozoy 1986; 1987)

   This dagger survives only as a fragment of its chape, of which Rozoy gives no detailed description (fig. 10/3). It was used as a pendant alongside other objects on a necklace from a late Jogassian woman's inhumation grave. The surviving piece is similar in type to the chape on the Saint-Lumier scabbard. It still has the hole from its fixing rivet. The two side wings of the anchor are, however, much longer and were doubtless folded to allow it to be hung.

4. *Port-à-Binson*: ford, dredged from the Marne (Marne) (Ginoux 1994: no. 22 and pl. III/2; also illustrated Charpy 1991: fig. 11/a2). In the nineteenth century the Port-à-Binson ford also yielded up a Jogassian spear, amongst other Late Bronze Age objects.

   Found in water, this dagger (fig. 7/4) was in a good state of preservation except for a missing tang. The bronze front scabbard-plate is decorated with horizontal parallel incised lines arranged in four groups of four. It is generously wrapped over the rear. On the iron rear plate one can also observe the remains of decoration similar to that on the front plate, but over a greater length, basically corresponding to the upper half of the weapon. The suspension loop, partly preserved, was riveted on to the rear plate. Restoration has revealed its precise dimensions (10.4 cm long, 0.5 cm and 0.8 cm high). The cast chape is fixed to the two plates by a rivet, positioned very low. The upward-curving wings rejoin the scabbard and end in swellings decorated with stamped circular motifs at the centre and round the edge. There is also another rivet on the front plate between the two lowest groups of lines.

5. Chouilly 'Les Jogasses' tomb 22 (Marne). Musée d'Epernay inv. no. 833 F. (Hatt and Roualet 1976; Ginoux 1994: no. 14 and pl. III/4a)

   The weapon (fig. 9/5) is in a good state of preservation and was not deliberately broken at the time of its deposition in the tomb, unlike the three other similar weapons from the same cemetery. Only the sword-tang is missing. The front of the scabbard seems to have been made in two pieces. The first is the section decorated with vertical and horizontal incisions. The crack on its left side is due to the outward pressure of corrosion on the blade, causing a break at a point weakened by a vertical incision. The overlaps of this part are emphasised by a fine incision parallel to the edges. A bronze rivet is visible on this plaque. The second part of the scabbard is smooth, but one can see, 4 mm below its upper edge, a hollow mark wider than the incisions (pre-tracing or the mark of a saw-blade). The chape is firmly

attached and kept in place by an iron rivet. The two ball-shaped terminals of its upward-curving wings are inlaid with a whitish material which could be bone. On the rear plate, one can note the start of the suspension-loop 2.8 cm below the top of the campaniform outline of the scabbard.

6. *Chouilly 'Les Jogasses' tomb 28 (Marne)*. Musée d'Epernay inv. no. 837F. Associated with an iron ring of circular section. (Ginoux 1994 no. 14 and pl. III/4b)

   The dagger (fig. 8/6) is well preserved despite its ritual deformation. The hilt is missing. The bronze front plate is in one piece, decorated by five groups of three parallel lines on its upper part. The chape, cast in one piece, is held in place by an iron rivet and retains the trace of an air-bubble or the negative trace of an impurity. The overlaps of the front plate are smooth. The iron rear plate shows no trace of a suspension loop.

7. *Chouilly 'Les Jogasses' tomb 82 (Marne)*. Musée d'Epernay inv. no. 969F. Associated with a sword-belt consisting of two bronze rings of circular section, a spear, and three pots. (Ginoux 1994: no. 14 and pl. III/4c)

   The weapon (fig. 8/7), deliberately damaged before deposition, has further disintegrated since its discovery. It has no tang. The front plate was originally in one piece and decorated on its upper part by five groups of three parallel incisions. The overlaps carry a longitudinal incision running the whole length of the scabbard. The iron rear plate retains traces of one of the attachments of the suspension loop but, in its present condition, it is not possible to locate its position precisely. The chape, cast in one piece, is riveted to the front plate. On its opposite surface at the same level as the rivet, is a dent in the bronze as if it had been hit to curb the rivet on the inside.

8. *Chouilly 'Les Jogasses' tomb 192 (Marne)*. Musée d'Epernay inv. no. 1217F. Associated with a bronze sword-belt ring, faceted and of pentagonal section.

   This dagger (fig. 9/8) was deliberately mutilated at the time of its deposition in the tomb. It is extremely fragmented and the tang is missing. The front scabbard plate is currently in three pieces. Only the top portion is decorated, with four pairs of parallel incised lines. Just below the second line of decoration one can see two fine bronze rivets. Immediately below the top section is a repoussé rib. It may have been part of what is, today, the third part of the front plate, as in the case of the Saint-Denis dagger. The fracture would therefore be due to corrosion and would have caused a tear which followed the line of folding. The lower part of the front is smooth. Along the edges of the overlaps of the front edges runs a double incision which is much more marked than on the two preceding scabbards. The chape, cast in one piece, was forcibly fitted on and is not held in place by any rivet. One can observe, however, that the chape is pierced below, presumably to hold the iron rear plate which is corroding out from this point. This is probably a type of riveting also attested on the Port-à-Binson example. Finally, on its lower edge the chape has a groove which joins its two rising extremities. It can therefore be compared with the chape of the Saint-Lumier-la-Populeuse weapon.

9. *Bouy 'Les Varilles' (Marne)*. Musée Saint-Rémi, Reims,
    no inventory number. (Nicaise 1883–4: 74–5 and pl. IV/
    4; Ginoux 1994: no. 3 and pl. III/1)

    The dagger was found in an inhumation grave con-
    taining four bodies laid out side by side. The weapon
    belonged to the second warrior from the right and was
    placed to his right. Nicaise wishes to associate it with
    the sword-belt comprising four small bronze rings and
    four spears, all of which were placed to the left of the
    body. It therefore seems that these objects had been dis-
    placed and that they cannot form part of a 'panoply'.

    This dagger (fig. 9/9) is in a good state of preserva-
    tion. The original drawing by Nicaise in the papers of
    Abbé Favret in the Musée d'Epernay gives us its precise
    dimensions at the time of its excavation in 1880. It has
    lost its sword-tang. The bronze front plate is in one piece
    and is decorated, starting from the top, by three barely
    separated groups of five incised parallel lines. These are
    followed by two groups of four and five lines with a
    bronze rivet between them. The decoration finishes with
    two groups of three lines. In the smooth spaces between
    the third and fourth group of lines from the top and then
    between the last two groups, two ribs have been created
    by repoussé work directed towards the interior of the
    scabbard. In this detail the scabbard differs from the
    examples from Saint-Denis or from Les Jogasses tomb
    22. The chape is moulded in one piece and there is red
    inlay, apparently of stone, on the terminal discs of its
    upward-curving wings: Mme Aline Bataille-Melkon, of
    the Musée de Reims, thinks it may be a semi-precious
    stone, possibly cornelian. Nathalie Ginoux (1994: 58)
    puts forward the hypothesis that there is glass or enamel
    inlay on the chape. This information is erroneous and is
    linked to observation of the cast in M.A.N. and to the
    information given by Nicaise. The left-hand stone has
    disappeared but, as on the scabbard from Les Jogasses
    tomb 22, there are traces of a black substance used to
    keep it in place. The chape is riveted on to the back
    plate. At the rear, the overlaps are decorated with a fine
    incision parallel to the edges, but only on the upper third
    of the scabbard.

10. *Saint-Gibrien 'La Croix Mouchy' tomb 2 (Marne)*. Musée
    des Antiquités Nationales inv. no. 77051a

    The cemetery of 'La Croix Mouchy' is better known
    as the 'Mauret Cemetery'. The dagger was found in in-
    humation tomb 2, excavated by Amaury Thiérot, together
    with four faceted sword-belt rings of hexagonal section.
    This weapon (fig. 10/10) is in a good state of preserva-
    tion. It has lost its tang but we know from an archival
    drawing by Thiérot that it was more complete when
    found. It is noticeably shorter that the preceding dag-
    gers. The front plate is smooth and has a simple decora-
    tion of two fine incisions, between which are fine ob-
    lique hatched lines. Half-way up the front plate some
    remains of wood are visible amongst the oxidation. The
    chape was cast in one piece and is held in place by a rivet
    which goes from front to back. The rear seems to have
    no trace of the suspension loop. The mineralised ele-
    ment which may have formed part of it, appears to be the
    remains of a leather thong from the sword belt.

11. *No provenance (Marne)*. Musée des Antiquités Nation-

ales inv. no. 13041. Purchased by Napoleon III from
Bénoni Lelaurain. (Ginoux 1994: no. 18 and pl. III/3)

    The dimensions of this dagger (fig. 10/11) are very
close to those of cat. no. 10. It is in a good state of
preservation but lacks its tang. The one-piece bronze
front plate is richly decorated. The upper part is decorated in fashion similar to the scabbard from Les Jogasses
tomb 22. On the next part, the craftsman has created, by
repoussé technique, two narrow sunken grooves, set close
together as on the Bouy scabbard. The remainder of the
scabbard, undecorated on all the other weapons in this
series, is ornamented with five vertical ridges, also produced by repoussé, but this time directed outwards. The
one-piece cast chape shows evidence of impurities and
is held in place by a rivet which runs from front to back.
At the back, the edges of the overlaps of the front plate
are emphasised by a fine incision, on the upper part
only. Near the mouth, on the rear plate, one can observe
the remains of the upper attachment point of the loop,
beneath which there is a transverse mark in the remnants
of the wood. The plate was perhaps made out of several
elements.

From the descriptions of these daggers one can draw
the following conclusions:

The bronze front plate is always generously folded back
over the rear. All the scabbards are lined inside with
wooden plates. The entry is always campaniform. Regardless of the length of the scabbards, the dimensions
of the chapes are virtually identical. The chapes are of
anchor-type, showing two variants. Variant A has its
rising terminals prolonged by a cylinder of varying thickness, always situated halfway up the chape: four out of
five of these are decorated, either with inlay or with a
stamped motif. Variant B is smooth, with a groove joining the two extremities of the anchor on half of them
(fig. 14).

The weapons can be divided into two groups according to length. The shorter ones, with a scabbard length
between 25 and 27 cm (Saint-Gibrien and unprovenanced) are less common. The longer ones have a scabbard length of 38 to 50 cm. The upper part of the scabbard is always decorated with horizontal lines, often
assembled in groups: in two cases they are framed by
vertical lines. The chape is always forcibly attached and
its dimensions are standardised. Its measurements vary
little (8 mm), regardless of the scabbard length (see fig.
14). Finally there are a number of small details which
appear on only two or three scabbards. This seems to
indicate a period of experimentation in manufacture.

COMPARISONS

The series of daggers found in the Marne département
has no typological equivalent or analogies in other regions of late Hallstatt culture. The most frequently found
weapon is the dagger with a scabbard ending in a pear-

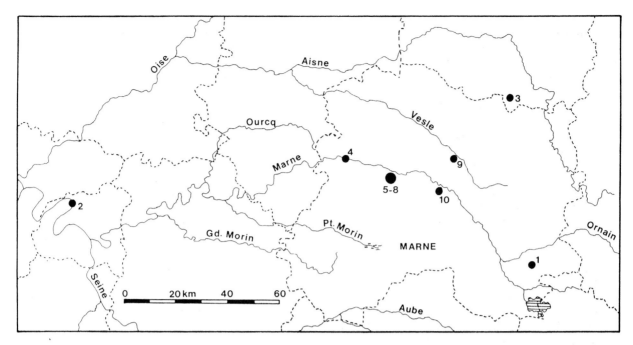

fig. 11. Distribution map of Jogassian dagger finds

shaped or globular chape, such as those from the cem- etery of Hallstatt itself, or from Hochdorf (Angeli *et al.* 1970: no. 59c and Taf. 29; Mohen, Duval and Eluère 1987: 168–9; see also Frey 1983: esp. Abb. 2). Although the slender form of the weapon seems specific to the Champagne region, the 'anchor'-shaped chape can be compared with the pelta-shapes on two knife-scabbards from Este in Italy (Fogolari nos 35, 36 and tav. 27), or with that from the dirk from Salem in Germany (Déchelette *Manuel* III, fig. 239). There is also a clear relationship between the shape of the chape represented on a stele from Villafranca in Italy (Vendryes 1914: 16, fig. 3)[4] and the chape of Saint-Lumier-la-Populeuse (vari- ant B). It therefore seems reasonable to suggest an Italic influence on the reinforcement of the lower part of the scabbards.

A one-piece anchor-shaped chape, close in form to the series from Champagne, is attached to a scabbard of organic material for an antenna-dagger from Neuenegg (Ct. Berne) (Drack 1960; 1974). These comparisons al- low us to envisage a possible route for the penetration of Italic influences, which can also be seen in the develop- ment of fibulae (cf. Frey 1971; 1988).

The general form of Variant B of the anchor-shaped chapes resembles a reduced version of the long swords of the early Hallstatt, but there is no evidence for any direct relationship. One could also make a comparison with the form of a plant-inspired motif, composed of two curved leaves cradling a shoot. This element forms part of the ornamental vocabulary of situla art, where it is used as a sequence marker in friezes of riders, fantas- tic beasts or animals, as seen on the sixth-century situlae from Vače or Providence (Fogolari 1961: tav. 30–31

and tav. E). This two-leaved sign reappears, transformed by terminals of birds' heads with hooked beaks, on the object held by one seated man on the central register of the Vače situla. The symbolic value of this sign may have been transferred to the chapes and thus provides an explanation for the re-use of one as a pendant on a wom- an's necklace from Aure (Ardennes). Such an explana- tion is identical or complementary to that which sees the short daggers of the late Hallstatt period as insignia of high social status (Frey 1983).

TECHNIQUE OF MANUFACTURE OF THE DAGGERS

Since scabbards are intended to protect and suspend the sword-blade, it is possible to attempt a reconstruction of the various phases of constructions from observation of the specimens described above.

Once the blade had been forged in a single piece, the first stage was to fit a wooden sheath,[5] consisting of joined front and rear pieces. This served several func- tions: to protect the cutting edges, to guide the weapon into its sheath and above all to ensure support for the metal plates by making the construction more rigid. Next came the making of the iron rear plate to fit the curvature and length of the wood. The rear plates of wood and iron were secured first by riveting on the two ends of the suspension-loop; see the unprovenanced dagger from the Marne, no. 11 in the catalogue, where the upper attach- ment rivet goes through the wooden plate. The bronze front plate was cut out, then formed into a cone shape with 8 to 10 mm wide overlaps to the rear. The creation of wider overlaps on the Port-à-Binson scabbard in order to fix the loop is very significant here. One might also

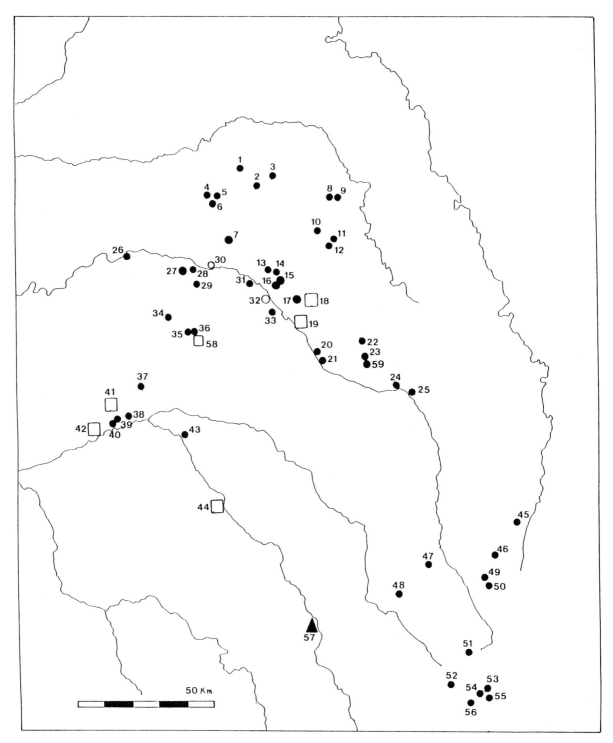

fig. 12. Distribution map of Jogassian cemeteries in Champagne-Ardenne. The concentration between Marne and Vesle foreshadows the fifth-century BC Marnian period.

1 Warmeriville (Marne)	21 Vitry-le-François "Les Marvis" (Marne)	41 Villenauxe "Eglise de Dival" (Aube)
2 Pontfaverger (Marne)	22 Heiltz-L'Evêque "Charvais" (Marne)	42 Saint-Nicolas-La Chapelle (Aube)
3 Hauviné (Ardennes)	23 Blesme (Marne)	43 Droupt-Saint-Basle (Aube)
4 Witry-les-Reims (Marne)	24 Saint-Dizier (Haute-Marne)	44 Isle-Aumont (Aube)
5 Beine "L'Argentelle" (Marne)	25 Chamouilley (Haute-Marne)	45 Nijon "La Mottote" (Haute-Marne)
6 Prosnes (Marne)	26 Dormans "Les Varennes" (Marne)	46 Essey-les-Eaux (Haute-Marne)
7 Bouzy (Marne)	27 Epernay "Rue de Bemon" (Marne)	47 Semoutiers (Haute-Marne)
8 Manre (Ardennes)	28 Chouilly "Les Jogasses" (Marne)	48 Courcelles-sur-Aujon (Haute-Marne)
9 Aure (Ardennes)	29 Avize "Les Hauts-Némerys" (Marne)	49 Vitry-les-Nogent (Haute-Marne)
10 Wargemoulins (Marne)	30 Tours-sur-Marne (Marne)	50 Dampierre (Haute-Marne)
11 Saint-Jean-sur-Tourbe (Marne)	31 Saint-Gibrien (Marne)	51 Courcelles-en-Montagne (Haute-Marne)
12 La Croix-en-Champagne (Marne)	32 Fagnières (Marne)	
13 Bouy "Les Varilles" (Marne)	33 Ecury-sur-Coole (Marne)	52 Esnoms (Haute-Marne)
14 Vadenay "L'Etau" (Marne)	34 Etoges (Marne)	53 Dommarien (Haute-Marne)
15 Cuperly "Vau-Herbau" (Marne)	35 Vert-Toulon "Le Moulin" (Marne)	54 Montsaugeon (Haute-Marne)
16 Saint-Etienne-au-Temple (Marne)	36 Vert-Toulon "Charmont" (Marne)	55 Dardenay-le-Motrot (Haute-Marne)
17 Marson "le Plat-Savard" (Marne)	37 Barbonne-Queudes (Marne)	56 Rivières-les-Fosses (Haute-Marne)
18 Le Fresne-Coupéville (Marne)	38 Esclavolles-Lurey (Marne)	57 Vix (Côte-d'Or)
19 La Chaussée-sur-Marne (Marne)	39 Courtavant "Le Crépin" (Aube)	58 Aulnizeux (Marne)
20 Couvrot (Marne)	40 Courtavant "Les Grèves" (Aube)	59 St Lumier

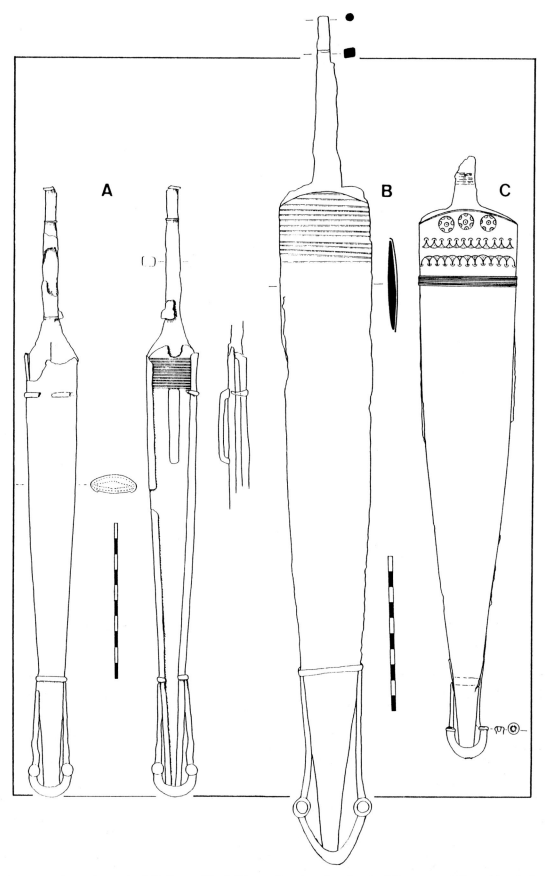

fig. 13. Weapons from the end of Hallstatt Final IIb, prefiguring the classic fifth-century BC scabbard chapes. A. Unprovenanced, M.A.N. inv. no. 13043 (Marne), B. Bergères-les-Vertus 'Les Crons', M.A.N. inv. no. 12018 (Marne), C. Bussy-le-Château 'La Croix Meunière', M.A.N. inv. no. 33279 (Marne)

SITE	TOTAL LENGTH	SCABBARD LENGTH	WIDTH OF MOUTH	VARIANT A	VARIANT B	LENGTH OF CHAPE	WIDTH OF CHAPE	DECORATION ON FRONT	DECORATION ON BACK	LENGTH OF TANG	LENGTH OF SUSPENSION LOOP
St-Lumier	52,5	43,1	3,1		X	4,5	3,3	?		<9,5	
St-Denis	48,2	<48,2	3,7		X	5,3	3,5	?			
Port-à-Bin.	40,9	39,8	2,8	X		5,0	3,4	X	X		10,5
Aure, T 89b					X	<3,2	3,5				
Jog. T 22	39,8	38,5	3,1	X		5,3	2,9	X	?		
Jog. T 28	44,5	41,5	3,1		X	4,8	2,8	X	?		
Jog. T 82	43,5	45,5	3,0		X	4,0	4,1	X	?		
Jog. T 192	40,5	38	3,7		X	4,0	3,5	X	?		
Bouy	48,5	38	3,0	X		5,2	3,6	X	?	10,5	
St-Gibrien	29	25,5	2,7	X		4,2	2,8	X			
S. origine	28,3	26	2,8	X		4,6	2,9	X			

fig. 14. Table of measurements of the daggers (in cm)

speculate that the finely incised borders along the edge of the overlaps may, in some cases, be the remains of the outline traced for cutting out the front plate. They could have been reworked with a tool to form part of the decoration (e.g. Chouilly 'Les Jogasses' grave 192). The bronze covering, between 0.6 and 0.7 mm thick, was sometimes fixed to the upper part of the wooden sheath by one or two rivets, as on the scabbards from Les Jogasses, tombs 28 and 82, Port-à-Binson and Bouy. The previously cast chape was firmly attached and secured, in some cases, by a rivet passing right through the chape.

The decoration of the front plate was created after it had been cut out, and sometimes extends to the overlaps. The solidity of the bronze part was occasionally reinforced (Bouy; Les Jogasses tomb 82; 'Marne'; Saint-Denis) by transverse or longitudinal ribs or grooves produced by repoussé.

As far as the tang is concerned one can observe the presence of wood at the socket of the grip, but also on some examples, little marks identical to those found on La Tène sword-grips and produced by small roundels of leather.

CONCLUSION

Published grave of Saint-Lumier-la-Populeuse constitutes a genuine find which allows us to consider the problem of the appearance in Champagne of a new type of weapon, the dagger with mixed bronze and iron scabbard. As has been shown above, these Jogassian weapons were all manufactured in the same technique, which probably corresponds to the production of a local workshop. All except two come from inhumation graves and are generally the only offering apart from the sword-belt. The series of daggers has no equivalent outside Champagne, while the situation is completely reversed in the case of dirks. The absence of reference contexts led Hatt and Roualet to consider them typical of their final Jogassian phase. One may put forward the hypothesis, following the argument developed above, that they should be dated slightly earlier and certainly that they appeared a little before the end of the sixth century BC. They can be classified into two groups determined by the form of their chape. These weapons vary in length, showing the lack of standardisation typical of this period as well as of the early part of the succeeding one. Finally we can assume that the form of these anchor-shaped chapes is Italic in origin and that it foreshadows, in many ways, the classic open chape of the La Tène era. The burials of the Champagne region have produced numerous models illustrating the diverse and successive experiments on the way to this final type.

Translation: Ruth Megaw

Acknowledgements
The author is especially grateful to Ian Stead and to Valery Rigby for their help and their welcome to the

British Museum, Alain Bulard for information about the Saint-Denis dagger; Pierre Roualet for his comments and to all those who have helped.

Notes

1. Léon Morel: Matériaux pour l'histoire de la Champagne souterraine, 30 ans de fouilles dans la Marne (1862-1892). Volume I, L'époque gaulois comprises 76 leaves (Reference number: Estampes et Recueils 46). Volume II, Epoques diverses contains 69 leaves (reference Estampes et recueils 47). Two collections of Gastebois' original drawings are housed in the Bibliothèque d'Epernay (Reference FC ty 7 I and II, collection Raoul Chandon). For his plates in *La Champagne souterraine,* Emile Gastebois was awarded, on 28 August 1873, the bronze medal of the Société Académique de la Marne (Société d'Agr., Com., Sc. et Art du dép de la Marne). For the biography of Morel see Stead and Rigby 1981 and esp. Vatan 1982.

2. For example, only the armring (ML 1833) from Loisy-en-Brie was published by Morel in the *Bulletin archéologique du Comité des travaux historiques et scientifiques* 1898, pp. 428-430. (For the complete find see Charpy and Roualet 1991, no. 230, pp. 184-187.)

3. Another dagger, in the Musée des Antiquités Nationales, has a chape with a similar groove (inv. no. 77051a).

4. The author refers back to a preceding article (Vendryes, Joseph 1909. Stèles funéraires gauloises en Ligurie. Revue archéologique II, 52ff, in which he summarises a contribution by M. Mazzini. One can also observe that the antennae of the hilt of the weapon represented on the stele correspond in every detail with those which used to exist, according to the original drawing by Louis Simonnet, on the dirk from Hauviné 'La Motelle-Verboyon' tomb 5 (See Charpy and Roualet 1991: no. 77).

5. This is not to suggest that the method of construction is similar to that by which the edges of situlae or large hollow bronze torcs were made as early as the 6th century BC.

References

Angeli, W., Barth, F. E., Hundt, H.-J. 1970. *Krieger und Salzherren: Hallstattkultur im Ostalpenraum* (exh. cat. 1 July-20 September 1970 Römisch-Germanisches Zentralmuseum, Mainz). Mainz, RGZM.

Anon 1897. Chronique. *Revue de Champagne et Brie,* 21, 2nd ser.: 462

Boucher, H. 1984. *Paroisses et communes de France: Dictionnaire d'Histoire administrative et démographique.* Paris: CNRS.

Barray, L., Defressigne, S., Leroyer, C. and Villemeur, I. 1994. *Nécropoles protohistoriques du Sénonais.* Documents d'archéologie française 44. Paris.

Bretz-Mahler, D. 1971. *La civilisation de La Tène en Champagne, le faciès marnien.* Supplément XXIIIᵉ à Gallia. Paris: CNRS.

Bulard, A. and Degros, J. 1980. De la préhistoire à l'histoire. In *Archéologie en Seine-Saint-Denis.* (exh. cat. La Courneuve, 25 octobre-20 décembre 1980) pp. 13–14.

Charpy, J.-J. 1991. La Champagne aux origines de la civilisation celtique. In Charpy and Roualet 1991, pp. 26–35.

Charpy, J.-J. 1994. La Haute-Marne à l'époque celtique, essai de synthèse. In *Préhistoire et protohistoire en Haute-Marne et contrées limitrophes. Colloque international du 5 septembre 1992* (eds B. Decron, L. Lepage, G. Viard). Langres: pp. 149–63.

Charpy, J.-J. and Roualet, P. (eds) 1991. *Les Celtes en Champagne: cinq siècles d'histoire.* (exh. cat. 23 June-3 November 1991, Musée d'Epernay) Epernay.

Déchelette, J. 1927. *Manuel d'archéologie préhistorique, celtique et gallo-romaine: III, Premier Age du Fer ou époque de Hallstatt.* 2nd ed. Paris: Picard.

Drack, W. 1960. *L'Age du Fer en Suisse.* Répertoire de préhistoire et d'archéologie de la Suisse, Cahier 3. Bâle (trans. J.-P. Millotte).

Drack, W. 1974. Die späte Hallstattzeit im Mittelland und Jura. In *Ur- und Frühgeschichtliche Archäologie der Schweiz* Vol. IV, *Die Eisenzeit* (ed. W. Drack). Basel: Verlag der Schweizerische Gesellschaft für Ur- und Frühgeschichte, pp. 19–34.

Fogolari, Giulia de 1961. *Arte delle situle dal Po al Danubio: (VI al IV secolo A. C.).* (exh. cat. Padua, Ljubljana, Vienna 1961–62). Florence: Sansoni.

Frey, O.-H. 1971. Fibeln vom westhallstattlichen Typus aus dem Gebiet südlich der Alpen. In *Oblatio: Raccolta di Studi di antichità ed arte in onore di Aristide Calderini.* Como: Società Archeologica Comense, pp. 355–86.

Frey, O.-H. 1983. Die Bewaffnung im Hallstattkreis. *Etudes Celtiques,* 20: 7–21

Frey, O.-H. 1988. Les fibules hallstattiennes de la fin du VIᵉ siècle au Vᵉ siècle en Italie du nord. In *Les princes celtes et la Méditerranée.* Rencontres de l'Ecole du Louvre 25–27 novembre 1987. Paris: La Documentation Française, pp. 33–43.

Ginoux, N. 1994. Les fourreaux ornés de France du Vᵉ au IIᵉ siècle avant J.-C. *Etudes Celtiques,* 30: 7–86.

Hatt, J.-J. and Roualet, P. 1976. La cimetière des Jogasses en Champagne et les origines de la civilisation de La Tène. *Revue archéologique de l'Est et du Centre-Est,* 27: 421–503.

Hatt, J.-J. and Roualet, P. 1977. La chronologie de La Tène en Champagne. *Revue archéologique de l'Est et du Centre-Est,* 28: 7–36.

Joffroy, R. 1960. *L'oppidum de Vix et la civilisation hallstattienne finale dans l'Est de la France.* Publications de L'Université de Dijon 20. Paris: Société des Belles Lettres.

Kruta, V. 1983. Deux fourreaux marniens décorés du Vᵉ siècle avant notre ère. *Etudes Celtiques,* 20: 23–41.

Lepage, L. 1984. *Les Ages du Fer dans les bassins supérieurs de la Marne, de la Meuse et de l'Aube et le tumulus de la Mottote à Nijon (Haute-Marne).* Mémoires de la Société Archéologique Champenoise, 3.

Lepage, L.1989. Bracelets du Hallstatt moyen en Champagne et en Lorraine méridionale. In *La civilisation de Hallstatt: bilan d'un recontre, Liège 1987.* Etudes et Rencontres archéologiques de l'Université de Liège no. 36 (eds M. Ulrix-Closset and M Otte). Liège: pp. 321–39.

Lepage, L. 1993. Le tumulus de Nijon et les tumulus vosgiens de la région Contrexeville-Vittel: problème des gros bracelets hallstattiens. Journées d'Art et d'Histoire, Chaumont. *Cahiers Haut-Marnais* 1993, n°. 192–3, pp. 3–27.

Mohen, J.-P., Duval, A., Eluère, C. (eds) 1987. *Trésors des princes celtes.* (exh. cat. Galeries nationales du Grand Palais 20 October 1987–15 February 1988). Paris: Réunion des Musées Nationaux.

Morel, L. unpublished. Matériaux pour l'histoire de la Champagne souterraine, 30 ans des fouilles dans la Marne (1862–1892). Volume I, L'époque gauloise (76 leaves): Volume II, Epoques diverses (69 leaves). Bibliothèque Carnegie, Reims, inv. no. Estampes et Recueils 46 and 47.

Morel, L. 1898. *La Champagne souterraine: matériaux et documents ou résultats de trente-cinq années de fouilles archéologiques dans la Marne.* Reims: Matot-Braine.

Nicaise, A. 1885. Le cimetière gaulois des Varilles. *Mémoires de la Société d'agriculture, commerce, sciences et arts du département de la Marne,* 1883–4 [1885]: pp. 73–90.

Piette, J. 1989. Le premier Age du Fer dans l'Aube: découvertes inédites ou peu connues. In *Pré- et Protohistoire de l'Aube* (exh cat.). Nogent-sur-Seine: pp. 229–41.

Rozoy, J.-G. 1986, 1987. *Les Celtes en Champagne, les Ardennes au second Age du Fer: Le Mont Troté, Les Rouliers.* Mémoire de la Société archéologique champenoise, 4. 2 vols.

Schmit, E. 1926/7 and 1927/8. Répertoire abrégé de l'archéologie du département de la Marne des temps préhistoriques à l'an mil. *Mémoires de la Société d'agriculture, commerce, sciences et arts du département de la Marne,* 2nd ser: 99–301.

Stead, I.M. with Rigby, V. n.d. [1981]. *The Gauls: Celtic antiquities from France.* London: British Museum.

Vatan, A. 1988. Histoire de l'archéologie dans la département de la Marne. *Mémoire de l'ecole pratique des hautes études,* typescript.

Vendryes, J. 1914. Notes d'archéologie et de philologie celtiques II, L'inscription celtique de la stèle de Zignano. *Revue celtique,* pp. 14–20.

Vendryes, J. 1909. Stèles funéraires gauloises en Ligurie. *Revue archéologique* 2, 50–4.

The Celtic Chariot: A Footnote

Barry Cunliffe

Thirty years ago Ian Stead published his seminal discussion of the evidence for Iron Age chariots in Europe (Stead 1965). It was an interest which had grown out of his study of the Iron Age cemeteries in Yorkshire. His continuing programme of research in Yorkshire has caused him to revisit the theme from time to time most notably in his definitive account of the Arras Culture of north-eastern England (Stead 1979) and, more recently, in a monograph detailing the results of excavations at several of the Iron Age cemeteries of east Yorkshire (Stead 1991). This 'footnote' is a tribute to a scholar whose work has inspired it.

Carts or chariots

The exact nature of the Iron Age chariot – or less evocatively, two-wheeled vehicle – raises a number of entertaining problems not least the question of whether those found in the La Tène burials of Yorkshire, were functional battle chariots, funerary vehicles or a modification of chariots for funerary purposes. The debate, so clearly and elegantly presented by Stuart Piggott (Piggott 1983: 221–5), owes much to Ian Stead's meticulous fieldwork and carefully balanced judgment. Leaving aside the subtleties of the problem, it is now generally accepted that the two-wheeled vehicle was introduced into Britain from the Continent as a component of an élite system probably in the late fifth or early fourth century BC at about the time of its initial popularity in early La Tène Europe. Two-wheeled vehicles were given particular visibility in the archaeological record because of their use, in certain restricted areas, in funerary rituals (fig. 15). Knowledge of their popularity elsewhere has had to depend on accidental discoveries of vehicle and harness fittings, anecdotal descriptions in writings of Greek and Roman historians and iconographic representations found on stelae and coins. What is tolerably certain is that the two-wheeled vehicle, as a means of élite display in daily life, warfare and death, was a widely used symbol across much of central and western Europe including the British Isles from the fifth century BC,

remaining in use, in some areas, to the time of the Roman conquest.

The dramatic nature of the burial evidence in Germany, the Low Countries, northern France and east Yorkshire has, to some extent, had a distorting effect on our perception of the use of the two-wheeled vehicle in both its ceremonial and military modes. This is particularly true in the British Isles where the picture is even more skewed by the virtual absence of inhumation rites, requiring regular cemeteries, over most of the country with the exception of the south-west peninsula and east Yorkshire. In view of this, the absence of convincing vehicle burials outside the Arras Culture region cannot be taken to imply that vehicles were not employed in funerary rituals – we simply do not know.

A more objective way to view the question of the use of the chariot is through the occurrence of horse- and vehicle-related artefacts. One has only to refer to a range of recent studies (Spratling 1972; MacGregor 1976; Palk 1984; Taylor & Brailsford 1985) to appreciate the widespread popularity of horses and vehicles in Middle and Late Iron Age Britain. Caesar's frequent references to the British war chariots which confronted his invasion force in 55 BC (*BG* IV, 24, 32, 33) and 54 BC (*BG* V, 9, 15–17, 19) leave little doubt of the highly developed nature of chariot warfare by the mid first century BC. We know from the account of Tacitus that chariots were still actively in use in warfare, at least among some tribes, at the time of the conquest (Tacitus, *Agricola* 12) and were employed during the Boudican rebellion in AD 60–61 (Tacitus, *Annals* XIV, 29–39) and even later, in AD 84, at the battle of Mons Graupius in the north of Scotland (Tacitus, *Agricola*, 36).

The question which I would like to explore here a little further is the social context in which the fighting force which opposed Caesar had developed. If Caesar is to be believed the British war leader Cassivellaunus, who led the opposition to him in the lower Thames valley, had at his disposal a very considerable native army. Towards the end of the encounter, we are told, 'Cassivellaunus ... disbanded most of his forces, keep-

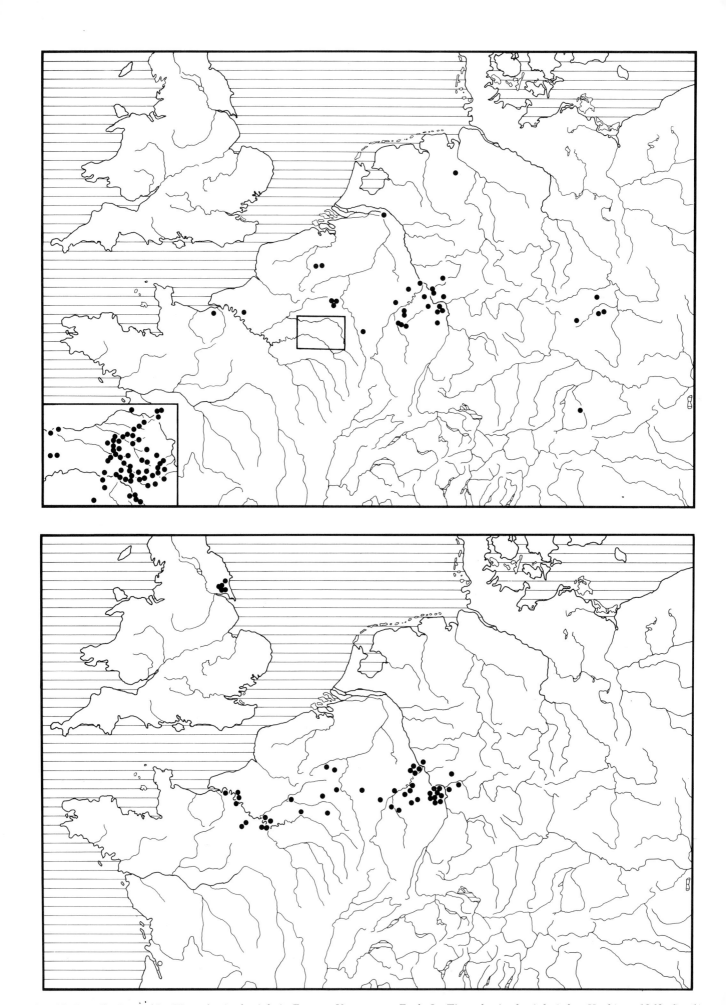

fig. 15. Distributions of La Tène chariot burials in Europe. Upper map, Early La Tène chariot-burials (after Harbison 1969: fig. 1); lower map, Late & Middle La Tène chariot burials (after Metzler 1993: fig. 1).

ing only some 4,000 charioteers' (Caesar, *BG* V, 19).
We have no way of judging the accuracy of this figure
but there is nothing inherently unlikely in it. A war leader
able to call upon the tribes of the densely-settled south-
east for support might be expected to attract the warrior
élite to the cause, eager for a share in the glory. That a
large and well-trained force was available is evident
from the reverses they were able to impose on Caesar
and from Caesar's discussion of the skill of the charioteers:

> With daily training and practice they have become so effi-
> cient that even on steep slopes they can control their horses
> at full gallop, check and turn them in a moment, run along
> the pole, stand on the yoke and get back into the chariot
> with incredible speed (*BG* IV, 33).

In his description of British chariot warfare Caesar gives
us the enthusiastic assessment of a keen military ob-
server. Written for his Roman audience to highlight his
own achievements, it is, even so, difficult to resist the
conclusion that he was impressed.

Let us then accept that in the middle of the first century BC there existed in southern Britain a large warrior
élite well-trained in the arts of chariot warfare. In what
context did they live and hone their skills? Here we
must turn to the results of recent archaeological excavations.

THE GUSSAGE ALL SAINTS FOUNDRIES

Any discussion must begin with the remarkable discovery, at the Iron Age settlement of Gussage All Saints,
Dorset, of a pit containing a large deposit of debris derived from processes involved in bronze casting (Wainwright 1979). The material has been presented and
discussed in several important studies (Wainwright &
Spratling 1973; Spratling 1979; Foster 1980; Fell 1988).
The deposit included a billet of copper alloy, bone modelling tools, crucibles, tuyères and hearth debris, iron
metalworker's tools, broken clay moulds and scrap
bronze and iron. The moulds showed that the foundry
had produced sets of vehicle fittings including linch pins,
to hold the wheels in position, terret rings and strap
unions (which Stead's work in Yorkshire has shown to
be yoke attachments (Stead 1991: 47–52)), as well as
horse tackle including loop fasteners and bridle-bits for
paired horse teams. Sufficient fragments were recovered to suggest that at least 50 sets had been produced.

The Gussage deposit presents an enormous array of
new data but it also raises a number of problems. Was
the craftsman itinerant or a member of the entourage of
the resident élite? Might he, as a man of skill, have been
'on loan' from a neighbouring élite? Were the 50+ sets
of horse gear the property of the maker, to be traded, or
the property of the resident lord to be used or distributed
as prestige goods? If distributed were they given as objects, as harness sets or as the pony and chariot ensem-

bles? Was the production a regular part of existence or
a special one-off event to meet a particular eventuality?
There are, of course, no answers but the questions must
be asked to sketch out boundaries somewhere within
which the actual interpretation may lie. In parenthesis
(since it is not particularly pertinent to the present discussion), we might query the context of the deposition.
Is it rubbish disposed of in a convenient hole or curated
material carefully deposited on the bottom of a disused
storage pit as part of an act of propitiation? – a system
we have considered in the context of related deposits at
Danebury (Cunliffe 1992).

The Gussage assemblage provides a very valuable
insight into the variety of different decorative types,
particularly among the terret rings, which could be made
in one operation probably by one craftsman. If the excavator's dating is accepted then the deposit can be taken
to indicate the types of horse gear in use in the first
century BC in central southern Britain.

GUSSAGE IN ITS WESSEX CONTEXT

Viewed in its local context the Gussage assemblage can
be seen to lie wholly within a much broader grouping of
like finds linked together in a complex network of technical and stylistic similarities. To present the full range
of data here and to argue the similarities in detail would
be to go far beyond the permitted limits of a footnote
but a few of the main threads may usefully be teased
out.

Among the terret rings manufactured at Gussage
Spratling distinguishes two groups: plain and ornate.
One of the three ornate varieties, Var. XI, he has termed
the 'Mill Plain type' after an isolated find recovered
from close to Christchurch Harbour. The characteristic
which links the two is a zig-zag petal decoration in relief running around the outside of the loop. This same
decorative feature is found on another terret said to have
been found in 'Suffolk' (Spratling 1979: fig. 100 no. 5).
The 'Suffolk' example is a fine piece with its loop further decorated with raised roundels each ornamented
with a rosette of pellets.

The second of Spratling's ornate terret varieties made
at Gussage is the Arras or lipped terret (his var. XII)
(Spratling 1979: fig. 100 nos 1–4). Terrets of identical
type are known from a number of Wessex sites (see
Appendix). They differ, however, from the Yorkshire
examples from Arras and Kirkburn in that the northern
finds have iron bars while the Wessex versions are entirely of copper alloy.

A number of mould fragments for three-link bits were
recovered from Gussage. Among the collection were at
least two fragments from the terminal bulbs of the side
links decorated in relief (Spratling 1979: fig. 105 nos 2
and 3). These are closely similar to the two three-link
bits from Ringstead, Norfolk (Clarke 1951 and more
conveniently illustrated in Spratling 1979: fig. 107) and

the three-link bridle from Hengistbury Head (Cunliffe 1987: ill. 110). The Ringstead bits have the added interest of also incorporating the 'raised roundel with rosette of pellets' motif found on the 'Suffolk' Mill Plain-type terret.

Another item of some interest in the Gussage repertoire is the bimetallic linch pin. The surviving mould fragments appear to be from bulb-headed pins with the terminal discs decorated in relief (Spratling 1979: fig. 101 no. 3). Very close parallels have been found at Owslebury, Hants. (Collis 1968) and Wigginton Common, Tring, Herts. (Ward Perkins 1941: pl. XI).

Finally we should draw attention to the mould for a strap union of the type composed of two conjoined circles with a curved bar on either side (Spratling 1979: fig. 101 no. 2) which Spratling has likened to the example recovered from Bury Hill, Hants. during the 1939 excavations (Hawkes 1940: fig. 16).

Whilst there is much more of exceptional interest in the Gussage assemblage the five threads drawn out here are sufficient to begin to create the web.

THE BURY HILL ASSEMBLAGE

It is at this point that we must introduce a recently discovered and unpublished assemblage of metalwork from Bury Hill, Hants. In 1990 the hillfort was examined by trial excavation as part of the Danebury Environs Programme directed by the writer. An area excavation within the main enclosure exposed a number of grain storage pits of normal Iron Age type. The upper filling of two immediately adjacent pits, pits 23 and 24, yielded six terret rings, three strap unions and two plain rings. Another pit (pit 57), 10 m away, produced a bimetallic linch pin while from an adjacent pit (pit 45) came a set of iron nave rings and bridle-bits together with a decorated bronze stud. The terrets, strap unions, linch pins and stud are illustrated here (fig. 16). An assessment of the ceramic evidence suggests that the occupation was short-lived and may be dated to the first half of the first century BC – that is broadly contemporary with Gussage. No evidence of on-site metalworking was found at Bury Hill but given the comparatively small size of the excavated sample the lack of evidence is without particular significance.

Two other items of bronze horse gear have come from Bury Hill, the strap link found in the 1939 excavation (Hawkes 1940: fig. 16) and the middle link of a three-link harness bit picked up recently (unpublished).

The stylistic similarities of the Bury Hill assemblage to the items discussed above are very striking. The linch pin clearly belongs to the Gussage, Owslebury, Wigginton type while the raised roundels with rosettes of pellets found on the strap union (no. 8) and the two terrets (nos 1 and 2) provide direct links with the 'Suffolk' Mill Plain-type terret and the Ringstead bridle-bits.

The ornament around the head of the Bury Hill stud (no. 11) is also identical to that on one of the Gussage terret moulds and is freely used on the Mill Plain and 'Suffolk' Mill Plain-type terrets. Less diagnostic similarities can be drawn between the lipped terrets, the strap links and the three link bridles from the two sites.

Given the very close similarities in range of types, style and dating we are, I believe, justified in defining a *Gussage-Bury Hill tradition* – the dual name providing nicely the balanced oppositions of manufacturer:user and settlement:hillfort, while the word 'tradition' is broad enough not to prejudge what we may be observing.

SOME GENERAL IMPLICATIONS

If we accept the existence of a *Gussage-Bury Hill* bronzeworking tradition focusing in central southern Britain in the early first century BC a range of intriguing possible lines of further enquiry open up. This is not the place to explore the potential exhaustively but some of the more obvious areas of interest may be outlined.

Distribution

A number of items of horse- and vehicle-related copper alloy equipment belonging to the tradition coming from other sites have already been referred to. There are others which, with varying degrees of assurance, may be linked to it. In fig. 17 and the accompanying schedule (Appendix, p. 38) we have listed those which are worthy of consideration. On detailed examination some may drop out, others will inevitably be added. At best the map and schedule are a preliminary statement.

Two things stand out: the concentration in central southern Britain; and the northern outliers in Arras Culture contexts most notably the Kirkburn linch pins and strap unions and the Garton Station terrets, all illustrated and discussed in detail by Ian Stead (Stead 1991: figs 37, 38, 39 and 41). Between the two geographical extremes intermediate finds are known, for example Tring, Hunsbury, Ulceby and Ringstead. If we can fairly relate all these pieces to the same tradition then further implications may follow (below, pp. 36–7).

Chronology

It must be admitted that the chronological limits of the tradition are imprecise but three different recent excavations, Gussage, Danebury and Bury Hill, combine to suggest a date in the first half of the first century BC. Although this might be thought to be a little late for the Kirkburn and Garton Station burials it does not contradict any of the evidence there available. Moreover certain stylistic similarities which exist with the Snettisham gold would support a first century BC dating (Wainwright & Spratling 1973: 123–4). Over what period of time items in the Gussage-Bury Hill tradition were being manufactured it is impossible to say. The Gussage find is, however, a vivid reminder of the quantity and

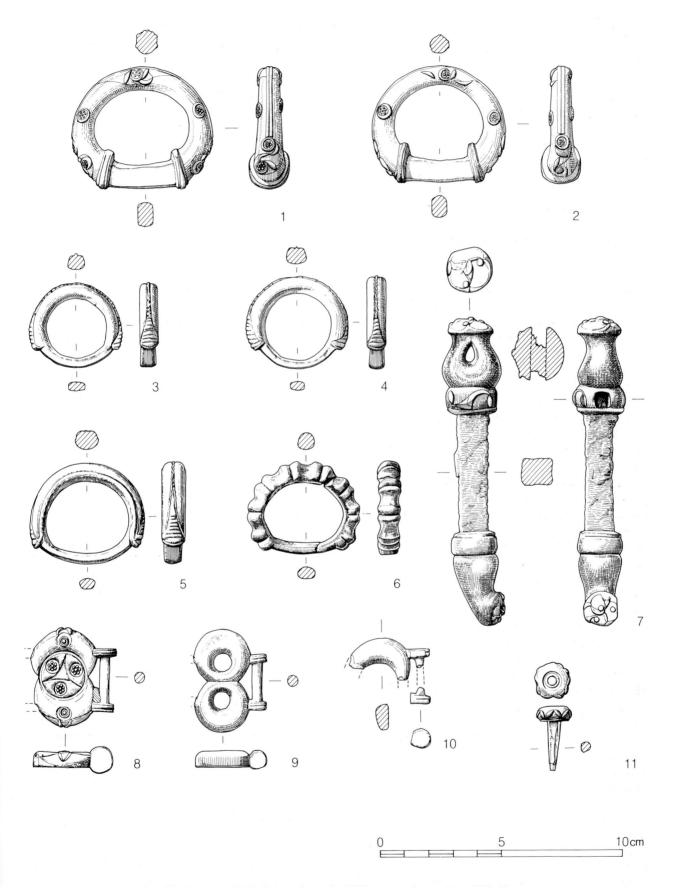

fig. 16. Bronze vehicle fittings from the 1990 excavation at Bury Hill, Hants.

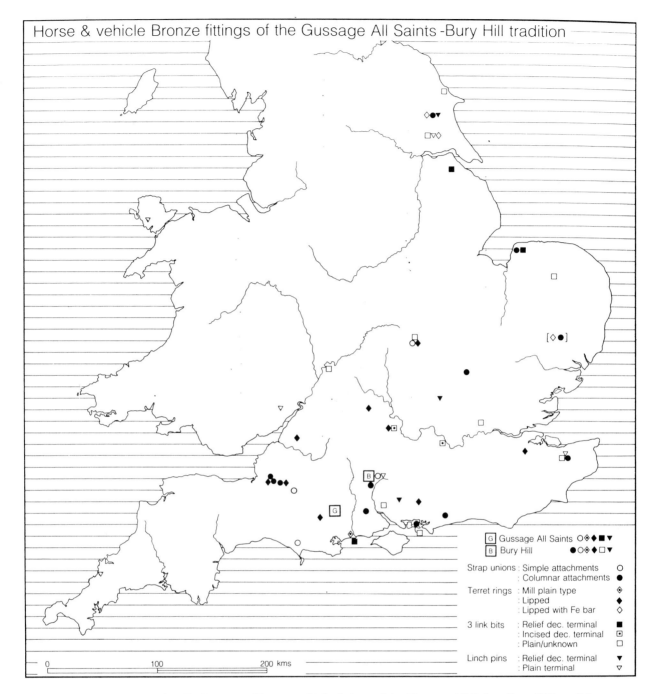

fig. 17. Preliminary distribution map of bronze vehicle fittings of the Gussage All Saints-Bury Hill tradition.

variety of material that could be manufactured, presumably by a single individual, over a very short interval. In the light of this it would not be unreasonable to take a minimalist view that all the items belonging to the tradition were made by one craftsman during his active working life. It is a possibility worth opening our minds to however unlikely it may be thought to be. A meticulous study of all the individual items may throw some further light on the question. In the meantime a date bracket of *c.* 100–50 BC seems reasonable.

Social context

Here scope for speculation is even more considerable. The Gussage All Saints excavation raises the interesting possibility that the bronze founder may have been only one of a team of craftsmen working together on the production of chariots and harness sets (Spratling 1979: 145). That ironworking was also being undertaken on a large scale is indicated by the 700 kg of slag recovered (not reported on in the published account: information from Peter Crew). The relatively large number of ma-ture horses found on the site and the virtual absence of immature beasts suggests that horses were bred elsewhere, possibly on the heathlands of the New Forest, and rounded up at the appropriate age for breaking and training. Thus the Gussage evidence would allow that completely fitted out chariots with trained pairs of horses were being produced in some quantity if only for a brief period of time.

The evidence from Bury Hill has something to add to the debate, though the full analysis of the data has yet to be completed. Here the massive defences of the later hillfort and the contemporary occupation inside appear to belong to a single brief episode in the first half of the first century BC which is broadly contemporary with the last phase of the main occupation of nearby Danebury. The exact relationship of the two forts at this stage cannot be defined but they may well have been in a state of competition, perhaps even open aggression. That there was social unrest is further suggested by the abandonment of Danebury following a massive conflagration at the entrance at about this time. What is of even more significance to the present discussion is that the animal bone assemblage from Bury Hill contains a far higher percentage of horse than was found at Danebury, which at this stage was still dominated by sheep. This, together with the unusually high number of artefacts from vehicles and horse trappings, indicates an episode in which the horse and vehicle – presumably chariots and chariot teams – were a prominent feature of the social scene.

The broad distribution of bronzes of the Gussage-Bury Hill tradition gives some indication of the areas affected (fig. 17). The schedule of sites, producing finds of this kind (p. 38), shows that, while hillforts feature large, horse and vehicle gear was also in use at non-hillfort settlements.

If we are correct in believing that this episode was focused on the early first century BC we might enquire how it came about. This raises much broader and more complex issues concerning social and economic development in central southern Britain in the Early and Middle Iron Age. These matters have been briefly considered elsewhere (Cunliffe 1994). In summary, a range of evidence combines to suggest that there may have been an increase in social stress over time culminating, in the period around about 100 BC, in clear indications of aggression and destruction. An upsurge in the use of the chariot, both as a symbol of prestige and an instrument of war, was one manifestation of this development. Against such a background it is easy to see why there were large numbers of well-trained charioteers available to rally to the call of Cassivellaunus when the Roman threat appeared. In other words the Roman incident provided the élite of the south with a new context in which to display valour and enhance their prestige. This

focus may, albeit briefly, have alleviated internal unrest.

The distribution of the Gussage-Bury Hill style of horse gear is markedly central southern British. It could be argued that this represents nothing more than the natural pattern caused by distribution from some centralized production area or a region bound by systems of élite exchange. However, the coincidence of the distribution with the hillfort-dominated zone is surely significant. The developed hillforts of this zone reflect a particular kind of socio-economic system which had begun to develop in the fifth century BC. The chariots emerge to prominence in the final, unstable, stages of this development before the system underwent a major transformation in the latter part of the first century BC.

What then of the more far-flung items – the linch pin at Trevelgue, in Cornwall and the fittings from the burials at Arras, Kirkburn and Garton Station? There is nothing inherently difficult in seeing these as a reflection of gift exchange between élites. After all if Queen Victoria could give a coach and horses to an Indian maharajah, there is nothing incongruous in suggesting that a Wessex chief might send a few chariot teams to his peers in Yorkshire and Cornwall.

Finally, our discussion of the social context of the Gussage-Bury Hill assemblages must be put in its broader chronological perspective. The tacit assumption has been that the chariot and chariot warfare were introduced into the British Isles in the fifth or fourth century BC and spread quite widely throughout the country. How widely and how intensively the chariot was in use before the beginning of the first century BC is a question worthy of a detailed consideration elsewhere and might usefuly start with a reassessment of the horse gear from Middle Iron Age contexts. Similarly the extent to which the chariot remained popular after the Caesarian episode raises intriguing questions. The various hoards of enamelled horse gear belonging to this phase (e.g. Polden, Westhall, Santon Downham, etc.) presumably represent a continuation of the tradition but they appear to be peripheral to the earlier distribution. In patterns such as this may lie an indication of the fast-changing social complexity of Britain in the century of transformation after Caesar.

This has been a somewhat longer footnote than was first intended. Its function has been simply to show that the theme of the Celtic chariot, which Ian Stead introduced to readers of *Antiquity* 30 years ago, and to which he has contributed so much in the intervening years, is one of continuing fascination. The Yorkshire burials have rightly focused our attention on these remarkable vehicles but the development of chariot warfare in Britain may well have had a very different focus.

Table 2. Terret bars from Weelsby Avenue, Grimsby

Terret bar type	Description of bar	Knob type	Illustration from below (not to scale)
Type 1	Flat rectangular section bar with straight edges Only one example	Knob meets bar at an angle	
Type 2	Flat rectangular section bar with curved edges	Knob meets bar at an angle	
Type 3	Flat rectangular section bar with curved edges and side ridges	Knob meets bar at an angle	
Type 4	Flat rectangular section bar with curved edges	Curves gracefully into terminal knob. No collar to knob	

Table 3. Terret loops from Weelsby Avenue, Grimsby

Terret loop type	Description
Type a	Plain circular section loop. Many examples. Difficult to distinguish from harness loops
Type b	Most common of the decorated terrets (Figure 7). Raised rectangular section rib around the edge of loop. Starts about 10mm from terminal knobs and has a rectangular end.
Type c	Rib starts at terminal knobs (1 example only)
Type d	Raised rib with 2 incised lines. Several
Type e	Edge of loop decorated with incised line (as GAS Var II*). Common
Type f	Edge of loop decorated with 2 incised lines (as GAS Var IV*). Common
Type g	Edge of loop decorated with central depression (as GAS Var IIIA*).1 only
Type h	Loop decorated with raised rib around side of loop rather than edge of loop

* Variety numbers follow Gussage All Saints (Foster 1980)
Table 3: Terret loops from Weelsby Avenue

moulds the features described are positive, i.e. as the bronze cast from that mould would have appeared. Plasticine is used to create a positive image, as can be seen in the photographs.

None of these bars is paralleled in the archaeological record. Rectangular bars are common but tend to be upright, not flat (e.g. Middlebie, Dumfriesshire; Macgregor 1976: nos 92–3). Only one that Spratling illustrates (from Hod Hill, no. 38) has a flat-section bar and even this is slightly curved in profile. In contrast, all the terret bars from Weelsby Avenue are flat in section. Type 4 is a particularly graceful bar (fig. 23). A similar terret is illustrated by MacGregor from Newstead (1976: no. 63), but the bar has a slightly arched "saddle" section. The Polden Hill terrets (Spratling 1972: no. 61 and no. 56) again have a superficial resemblance, but are slightly arched and far less graceful than the bars from Weelsby Avenue.

The most common loop decoration on the terrets from Weelsby Avenue (fig. 22) is also unparalleled in the archaeological record (Table 3), although it resembles a simple terret from Glastonbury (Spratling 1979: fig. 102.1). It has a raised rectangular-section rib around the loop starting about 10 mm from the terminal knobs.

Some terrets are also decorated with raised circular knobs (of rectangular section), either plain or with an incised line, or (1 example only) with a raised tear shape. These are placed on the side of the loop (fig. 24). Paral-

fig. 24. Terret moulds from Weelsby Avenue, Grimsby, with raised knobs on the loop. Length of right hand mould 28 mm. Photo Lesley Boulton.

fig. 25. Terret mould from Weelsby Avenue, Grimsby showing the casting position. Length of mould 5 mm. Photo Lesley Boulton.

lels for these raised knobs, both circular and rectangular, can be found on terrets from Scotland and Northumberland (MacGregor 1976: nos 64–66, 68–72), and Norfolk, Cambs. and Essex (Spratling 1972: 86–94), although all of these have knobs that are on the outer edge of the loop. Almost all are decorated with glass inlay by the *champlevé* technique: that is, filling recesses in the bronze with glass, usually red, sometimes accompanied by green, white, blue or yellow. These recesses were usually cut after casting (Spratling 1972: 273), using drills and gravers. It is probable, therefore, that the knobs on these terrets (and perhaps part of the loop) were decorated after casting with colours.

The terrets from Gussage All Saints were cast upside down (Foster 1980: fig. 6) with the entry coming down onto the bar, a sensible method of casting as the small jet of metal left by the gate would be easy to file away from the bar. In contrast the Weelsby Avenue terrets were cast with the entry on the loop (fig. 25). There are numerous examples of this, often for terrets with decorated loops. The piece of metal to be filed away was 16 mm by

5 mm. There were also 9 moulds for casting 2 terrets back to back in the same mould, presumably with the molten bronze poured through one gate. This arrangement would increase the likelihood of casting flaws and only a few double moulds have been found; perhaps they were an experiment.

OTHER MOULDS

Terrets form about 90% of the mould collection from Weelsby Avenue, but other items were also produced. Bridle bit moulds are present in small numbers (15 moulds). There are two types of bit represented. The first is similar to the side links from the two-link bit from Polden Hill (Palk 1984: fig 5Ac) with a collar below the ring (fig. 26). The second type are similar to side links from three link bits, as cast at Gussage All Saints (Foster 1980: fig. 8; Spratling 1979: fig. 104). Only one side link was decorated (see below).

Other items of harness were present but in small numbers. There were 19 probable linchpin moulds (fig. 27), but not of the usual types which had ring or vase-shaped bronze heads (Spratling 1972: 55ff); these from Weelsby Avenue have circular heads decorated with fine hori-

fig. 26. Mould of a bridle bit side link like that from Polden Hills, from Weelsby Avenue, Grimsby. Plasticine on the left. Length of mould 36 mm. Photo Lesley Boulton.

fig. 27. Linchpin head mould from Weelsby Avenue, Grimsby. Plasticine on right. Length of mould 63 mm. Photo Lesley Boulton.

fig. 29. Two moulds from Weelsby Avenue, Grimsby
with owl motif decoration. Plasticine in the centre from
the right hand mould. Width of motif on left hand mould
12 mm. Photo Lesley Boulton.

fig. 28. Decorated mould from Weelsby Avenue, Grimsby, similar
to a strap union but with only one strap. Plasticine on left. Length
of mould 18 mm. Photo Lesley Boulton.

fig. 30. Decorated mould from Weelsby Avenue, Grimsby, with
a ring and dot ornament. Plasticine on left. Width of plasticine
37 mm. Photo Lesley Boulton.

fig. 31. Decorated side link mould from Weelsby Avenue, Grimsby. Plasticine on right. Length of plasticine
47 mm. Photo Lesley Boulton.

zontal ridges. Three linchpin feet have domed ends like
the fragmentary example from Newstead (MacGregor
1976: no. 130). At Gussage All Saints the bronze head
and feet were cast onto iron shanks; one mould from
Weelsby Avenue has a shank 8mm square. This is much
smaller than the linchpin from Kirkburn (shank 15 mm
wide; Stead 1991: fig. 38) although in the latter case the
corroded iron could have expanded.

There are at least 12 strap union moulds all, as far as
can be determined, consisting of flat or slightly convex
plates with cut out decoration and two strap loops concealed at the back (Spratling 1972 Type II). They are
fragmentary and like Spratling's quadriolobate strap
unions (Type IIA), with curved-sided triangular cut-out

holes. All of Spratling's examples were decorated with
champlevé inlay after casting and this was probably the
case with the Weelsby Avenue ones. The most complete
mould (fig. 28) is similar to a strap union but it had only
one strap as opposed to two and no cut out decoration.
Moreover, the decoration is very unusual (see below),
being a raised ring and dot motif. This particular mould
must have been a failed casting (see below); it would not
have been possible to take the object from the mould
without breaking it further. The strap would have been
about 50 mm wide (whereas Spratling's largest strap
unions only had straps 40 mm wide).

There are a few fragments of moulds for horn caps
with a collar diameter of 55 mm. This is one of the more

enigmatic object types of the Iron Age (Spratling 1972; Stead 1984: 63), a hollow shaft with a circular collar at either end. The first mould of a horn cap was found at Beckford (Hurst and Wills 1987), comparable in size with the (few) moulds from Weelsby Avenue. Horn caps have been interpreted as parts for chariots or maceheads; this context adds to the argument about function, as almost all items cast here were connected with harness, including for example three moulds of Wild Class I button and loop fasteners (Wild 1970), especially now that these have been reinterpreted as harness. At this stage of the analysis it is not possible to identify all the objects and it is possible that some were non-harness items.

DECORATION

As at Gussage All Saints, some objects were decorated before casting and the moulds have evidence of these, rather simple, designs. There are no elaborate Celtic designs in plastic relief, but they are entirely consistent with the late Iron Age decorative tradition. One motif, which occurs 5 times, is quite unusual. This is a motif in relief (fig. 29), a circle within which are two circular bosses placed together, like the large eyes of an owl with the beak between. This owl motif occurs intermittently on La Tène art work. For example, a cat or owl appears on mirror handles (Megaw and Megaw 1989: 210–215). Superficially, the same motif can be recognized on the central roundel of the Battersea shield and on the extensions for the terminal roundels (Brailsford 1975: 26). However, if looked at in detail (e.g. Stead 1985: fig. 2) the circles on the central roundel do not touch, but are separated by curving lines. Also the "eyes" on the terminals have snouts below them (ibid. p. 16) and are therefore not intended as owls.

Stead shows (ibid. fig. 12) that the double circle motif on the Battersea shield is derived from earlier La Tène art designs, based originally on plant motifs. The simple double circles from Weelsby Avenue are a later development of this motif and again the resemblance to an owl may, or may not, have been intentional. Other superficial similarities can be traced on horse harness from Stanwick (Fox 1958: pl. 74,3), and as the central motif of the Billericay mirror (ibid. pl. 56a). Most resemblance can be found on a spearhead from the River Thames (ibid. pl. 39a), where a circle containing the double dot motif is infilled with basketry. All these examples are parallels, but none are moulded designs like those from Weelsby Avenue. Obviously a simple motif like two circles set together may recur frequently, but only the River Thames spearhead has this set inside a circle, and there it is engraved, not in relief.

The typical late Iron Age / early Roman ring and dot motif also occurs here (4 moulds), on one example incised as if a prepared ground for a glass inlay. Other items that were probably decorated with glass were some of the terrets and the strap unions, although at present it

is not clear whether this was done on site or not. The ring and dot occurs in more elaborate form on two moulds. In one the three rings are grouped around a central dot (fig. 30), like the motif of the Fulham shield boss (Stead 1985: fig. 18); here, however, the dots are set asymmetrically within the rings giving the impression of a face with its eyes crossed. The other mould is discussed above (fig. 28). The setting is broken, but probably consisted of two small rings side by side with two larger rings at top and bottom. The rings are divided by curved sided triangles.

The curved sided triangle also appears on two moulds, one a bridle bit side link (fig. 31). The decoration consists of a raised circle surrounding a curved sided triangle with the space between incised with basketry. The stop knobs on the bits from Ringstead (Fox 1958 : plate 28 a and c) are almost exact parallels.

CRUCIBLES AND FURNACE DEBRIS

Moulds and crucibles would need firing at a high temperature (Howard 1980), both to drive off moisture which might otherwise cause the clay to explode during the casting process, and also to make sure that they could withstand the melting of the metal. Production of crucibles was evidently a skilled business, probably by specialists (ibid.: 191); modern attempts to replicate and use three-cornered crucibles in casting experiments resulted in the crucibles melting before the bronze (Peter Reynolds pers. comm.).

The crucibles from Weelsby Avenue (fig. 32) are of the usual Iron Age type, triangular three-cornered and round bottomed, familiar from sites such as Gussage All Saints. The sherds occur intermingled with mould fragments as if they were discarded at the same time. The crucibles have a characteristic grey-mauve vesicular appearance, with shiny mauve deposits on the interior and slag deposits on the exterior surfaces.

The crucible illustrated here was analysed by courtesy of Paul Craddock, British Museum, by X-ray fluorescence analysis and had been used solely for melting copper, indicating not just casting of objects, but primary preparation of alloys. This is confirmed by the find of an ingot mould (fig. 33), which again was used for copper only. The width of the ingot cast was 15–20 mm, with a maximum depth of 15mm if the mould was full, but the length is unknown. A complete ingot mould carved from sandstone from Murton High Crags, Northumberland (Jobey and Jobey 1987) was of a similar size (20 mm wide, 15 mm deep) and would have produced an ingot 100 mm long.

The crucibles from Weelsby Avenue are small, with sides about 90mm long and about 30 mm deep (capacity approx. 44 cc=44ml of metal at maximum, though crucibles would never be filled to the brim), reflecting the size of the objects that were being cast at Weelsby Avenue, and indeed throughout Britain in the Iron Age.

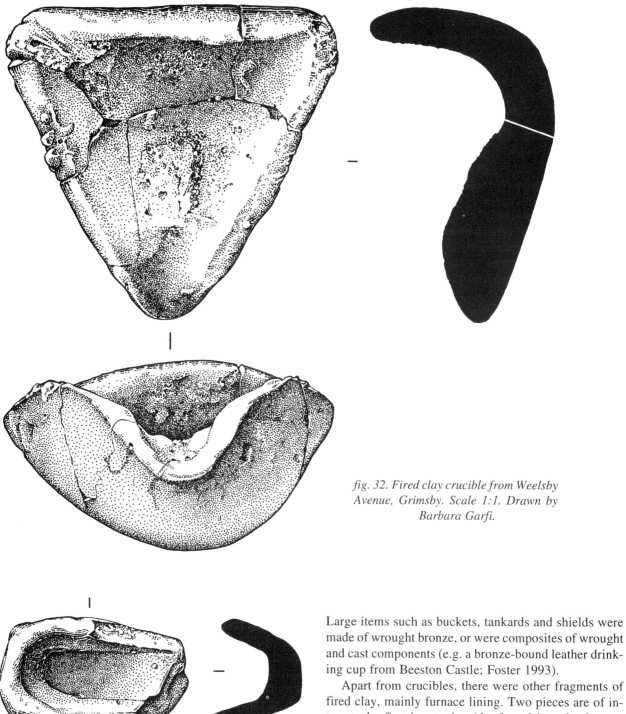

fig. 32. Fired clay crucible from Weelsby Avenue, Grimsby. Scale 1:1. Drawn by Barbara Garfi.

Large items such as buckets, tankards and shields were made of wrought bronze, or were composites of wrought and cast components (e.g. a bronze-bound leather drinking cup from Beeston Castle; Foster 1993).

Apart from crucibles, there were other fragments of fired clay, mainly furnace lining. Two pieces are of interest: the first is a tuyère (the funnel into the furnace through which air is pumped from the bellows; fig. 34). The second item is a broken slab (29 mm thick) of highly fired clay with a small hole (20 mm) through, so fired that the heat has melted the surface to a grey green glass. Possibly this is a piece of the kiln used to fire the moulds and crucibles (John Sills, pers. comm.).

CRAFTSMANSHIP

The casting debris at Weelsby Avenue was produced by professional workers, skilled in the manipulation of

fig. 33. Fired clay ingot mould from Weelsby Avenue, Grimsby. Scale 1:1. Drawn by Barbara Garfi.

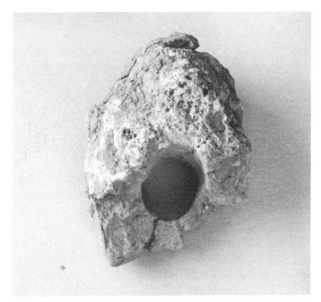

fig. 34. Tuyère from Weelsby Avenue, Grimsby, from above. Diameter of hole 19 mm. Photo Lesley Boulton.

fig. 35. Moulds of terret castings that have failed. From Weelsby Avenue, Grimsby. Length of mould bottom right 40 mm. Photo Lesley Boulton.

metals and clay. But, as at Gussage All Saints, not all the castings were successful; there were at least 11 failed castings. These moulds (e.g. fig. 35) have all the details of the object cast inside, e.g. terret terminal knobs and decorated loops, but the mould has only been partially broken open. No object could have been removed without breaking the mould; it follows therefore that the

bronze caster found part of the metal object missing. Failed castings occur because a bubble of air is trapped with the molten bronze preventing the metal from completely filling the mould. Usually this produces just a small hole or casting flaw. Flaws are common in Iron Age objects (e.g. terret from Arlington; Foster 1982) and do not seem to have been regarded as a problem; the objects were finished, decorated e.g. with enamel, and well used with the flaws apparent. On occasion, however, the casting would have been so incomplete that it was discarded and the metal remelted. Moulds can be designed with an extra hole called a riser, so that the liquid metal could flow around the moulds up the riser. At Weelsby Avenue there may have been occasional problems because the moulds had no risers, although the mould from Beckford had them. Roman craftsmen cut out casting flaws in a rectangular shape and filled with an extra piece of metal. This option does not appear to have been used in Britain in the Iron Age, although it was known from imported pieces (Foster 1986: fig. 20).

CONCLUSIONS

This group of objects reveals that there was a tradition of metalworking in north Lincolnshire that would not be suspected from plotted distributions of artefacts (e.g. Spratling 1972), which show metalwork concentrating in southern England, Yorkshire and north of Hadrian's wall. The limited repertoire of this assemblage suggests that other sites in the vicinity were producing complementary items of horse gear, the bridle bits and linchpins not made at Weelsby Avenue, and the other bronzes essential to Iron Age life: brooches, bracelets and rings, and weapon fittings, though many of the latter were wrought and not cast and would leave less evidence. It is important too that many moulds from here and Gussage All Saints are not represented by finds. The impoverished nature of the archaeological record has implications not only for distribution maps, but for the interpretation of Iron Age society. Cunliffe for example has interpreted southern British hillforts as centres of production (1991), "a move away from small-scale local production to more centralised production in the southeast as the Iron Age progresses" (1991: 454). But the evidence does not really bear this out: smelting of ores was still on a small scale up to the conquest, e.g. iron at Bryn y Castell and Crawcwellt in Wales (Crew 1979–85: 1989), and primary manufacture, as opposed to repair, of metal objects is just as evident on minor settlement sites as in hillforts, for example, Glastonbury (Bulleid and Gray 1911, 1917), Gussage All Saints (Wainwright 1979) and Weelsby Avenue. Hillforts such as Danebury (Cunliffe 1984) and South Cadbury (Freeman, Woodward and Barrett, forthcoming) have produced crucibles and waste, evidence for blacksmithing, and such small numbers of moulds that they could be explained in terms of mending rather than manufacture, though Northover suggests that this is because hillforts were producing sheet bronze items, while casting was carried out on homesteads (Northover 1987: 458). Specialist metal-workers there must have been, but there is no evidence that they were concentrated in hillforts, and, if they had centralised workshops, they have not been found.

Evidence for metalworking on the scale of Gussage All Saints and Weelsby Avenue is unusual, but small finds of slag or drips of melted bronze are common, showing that metalworking techniques were widespread. For example, in the late Iron Age at Castle Gotha, Corn-wall (Saunders and Harris 1982) stone piece moulds were used to cast brooches on a small scale (there were no crucibles for example) and hammerscale represents the repair of iron objects. Many Iron Age sites have anvils (e.g. Sutton Walls hillfort, Kenyon 1954: 23, 65, pl. XVIa); crucibles (*ibid*); droplets of molten bronze; slag and furnace linings (e.g. Trevisker, Cornwall: ApSimon and Greenfield 1972: 350–2). More recent excavations have, of course, more evidence; at Hengistbury Head there is evidence for movement of ores from a distance of at least 170km (Salter 1987: 205). Here there was probably recycling of waste materials and production of coins. But in most cases, even on larger sites, the evi-dence is for repair, both of iron and bronze, not primary manufacture, of piecemeal, individual production. This image is typified by a small rural site in Devon (Kestor Round Pound: Fox 1954), an ordinary round living house with querns and spindle whorls also contained a forging pit, a granite anvil, whetstones and hammerstones. The presence of ore and a bowl furnace suggests that iron blooms were made on a scale similar to Crawcwellt (Crew 1989). Metalworking was part of the general round of life in "these upland farmsteads, wherein could be heard the 'three sounds of increase' of an Irish Triad, the lowing of a cow in milk, the din of the smithy, the swish of a plough" (Fox 1954: 96).

Weelsby Avenue was a permanent settlement. It is difficult at present to assess the amount of objects pro-duced, although the distribution of debris suggests a longer timespan than that at Gussage (Spratling 1979: 145). It cannot, however, be assumed that the metal-workers on this site also lived there. Production in a similar economy today in the Andes shows that special-ist workers, in this case potters, travel part of the time from 200km away, producing pots, bringing their own clay but having the firing materials provided by the com-munity for whom they are making the pots. They return to the same communities about every 5 years (Lecture by Bill Sillar, Nov 94). This is obviously a sensible method of production whereby some of the effort of procuring raw materials is shared, but the important vari-able (in this case clay) is controlled by the craftsman. A similar situation may have obtained in the Iron Age with specialist bronze smiths bringing metal and formers, while the community provided wax, clay and fuel. The presence of one episode at Gussage All Saints supports

this model, although there was some evidence of metal-working from all the main phases.

This suggests, then, that the people who worked at Weelsby Avenue could have been itinerant or migrant workers. Certainly the common designs of metalwork in Britain and Ireland suggest that some metalworkers were fairly mobile, travelling at least around Britain and per-haps more widely.

Another aspect of production is the people involved. As mentioned above, Fox saw the craftsmen as Masters working in Schools, like the medieval painters. It seems that these designs were actually not restricted to one workshop. Bridle bits of two contrasting types were be-ing produced at Weelsby Avenue, while at Gussage three link bits were made in bronze, alongside steel bits of a different shape (Spratling 1979: 129). The problem is, that the archaeological record is a very sparse remainder of what was originally produced, as Spratling pointed out (1979: 141) in relation to the Gussage All Saints moulds.

Certainly Iron Age metalsmiths would not have been single workers making objects in isolation (see Cunliffe 1991: 456). Modern craftsmen work in teams; e.g. David Petersen (pers. comm.), who made a replica of the Capel Garmon firedog for the National Museum of Wales, works in tandem with three people, including appren-tices. Production on the scale at Weelsby Avenue would involve several workers, perhaps a family and not nec-essarily just men (Cunliffe 1991: 480). Some aspects of bronzeworking, such as melting temperatures, artistic design and decorative techniques like engraving and *repoussé* work, would have involved a long period of apprenticeship. But the preparation of wax originals, making and breaking of moulds, tending bees and set-ting the moulds up for pouring could easily have been done by unskilled workers.

It is interesting to look at the status of these workers within society. Cunliffe sees manufacturing in terms of patronage: "where communities were large enough to support a non-food producing specialist" (1991: 456). If this were the case workmen would have been restricted to larger centres, but this does not seem to be supported by the archaeological record. This also assumes firstly that leadership equals control of the means of produc-tion, and secondly that even if some items were pro-duced under patronage, this would apply to all Iron Age pieces. The level of skill as evidenced at Weelsby Av-enue was not high, nothing comparable with the Snettisham torc, for example (Stead 1993). The context for production here is seemingly domestic, but far from these workers being patronised by the aristocracy, I would like to suggest that the evidence in Britain points in the opposite direction, that craftsmen were in fact autonomous in their control of design and had much freedom in their methods of production.

Much of the metalwork in Britain is associated with warfare (chariots and weapons), which are seen as high status luxury artefacts. In fact, Cunliffe regards most metalwork in the Iron Age as luxury goods, including brooches, mirrors and tankards (Cunliffe 1991: 470, 479). It is true that chariots were used by only a few in society, for example, chariot burials in Yorkshire can be seen as unusual prestige burials when compared to ordinary inhumations with only an accompanying pot. The ponies that drew the chariots were also accorded an unusual status ; they were not eaten (Davies 1987) and were buried in peculiar circumstances like that of humans (e.g. at Danebury; Cunliffe 1983: 157). The terrets made at Weelsby Avenue can be seen as evidence for chariots, or two wheeled carts as Stead prefers (1991: 61; Piggott 1983: 208). There is plenty of evidence for other types of heavy vehicles, but these would have been drawn by oxen, who do not need reins but are controlled by goads and by the voice. The use of bridle bits, terrets and other harness equipment, therefore, indicates the use of horses and light vehicles. It is a wide step to assume that these vehicles were solely used "to transport privileged people" (Stead 1991: 61), but even more so to suggest that the producers were somehow privileged. There is no reason why these metal workers should have a higher status in society than, say, potters or woodturners.

To return to the artefacts at Weelsby Avenue, this site has doubled the information that we have about bronze casting in Britain in the Iron Age, although it has answered few of the questions that we should like to ask: why for example are there so few metal objects from about 800–100 BC and why should there be a sudden increase in the late Iron Age? Why should production be found on small settlements, rather than in the potentially important hillforts? However, it has reinforced some of the images we have of the Iron Age: the importance of horse equipment and the narrow range of objects that were made in metal. As at Gussage, few of the object types at Weelsby Avenue can be paralleled in the archaeological record, but the range of equipment is familiar. Here we have designs which were probably localised within a small area (e.g. a radius of 50 miles), yet are part of the tradition that obtains in the wider community of Britain and Ireland.

Acknowledgements

I should like especially to acknowledge Ian Stead for the help and encouragement he has given me; for kindling my enthusiasm for bronzes and providing the opportunity to catalogue the moulds from Gussage All Saints. After leaving Ian's employment, I have worked on many other publications and he has always freely given me the benefit of his experience.

I should also like to thank John Sills for being so patient over the last decade, and Paul Craddock for an impromptu analysis. I am grateful to my colleagues and students at the Dept. of Archaeology, Lampeter for their stimulating discussions. Barbara Garfi drew the figures and Lesley Boulton took the photographs. Finally, I would like to thank Martin Bell for his encouragement over the years, and for help with this paper particularly.

References

ApSimon, A.M. and Greenfield, E. 1972. The excavation of Bronze Age and Iron Age settlements at Trevisker, St Eval, Cornwall. *Proc. Prehist. Soc.*, 38: 302–38

Brailsford, J. 1975. *Early Celtic Masterpieces from Britain*. London: British Museum Publications.

Bulleid, A. and Gray, H. St G. 1911, 1917. *The Glastonbury Lake Village I, II*. Privately printed.

Crew, P. 1979–85. *Excavations at Bryn y Castell hillfort: interim reports*. Plas Tan y Bwlch, Gwynedd.

Crew, P. 1989. Excavations at Crawcwellt West 1986–89. A late prehistoric upland iron-working settlement. *Archaeology in Wales*, 29: 11–16.

Crew, P. and Crew, S. 1990. *Early Mining in the British Isles*. Plas Tan Y Bwlch Occasional Paper no. 1.

Cunliffe, B.W. 1983. *Danebury: Anatomy of an Iron Age Hillfort*. London: Batsford.

Cunliffe, B.W. 1984. *Danebury: An Iron Age Hillfort in Hampshire. Volume 2: The Finds*. CBA Research Report 52.

Cunliffe, B.W. 1987. *Hengistbury Head, Dorset, Volume 1: The Prehistoric and Roman Settlement, 3500 BC – AD 50*. Oxford University Committee for Archaeology Monograph no. 13.

Cunliffe, B.W. 1991. *Iron Age Communities in Britain*, 3rd edition. London: Routledge.

Foster, J.A. 1980. *The Iron Age moulds of Gussage All Saints*. British Museum Occasional Paper no. 12: London.

Foster, J.A. 1982. An enamelled bronze terret from Arlington, Sussex. *Sussex Archaeological Collections*, 120: 213–14.

Foster, J.A. 1986. *The Lexden Tumulus: A reappraisal*. Oxford: Brit. Archaeol. Rep., Brit. Series 156.

Foster, J.A. 1993. In *Beeston Castle, Cheshire. A report on the excavations 1968–85 by Laurence Keen and Peter Hough* (ed. P. Ellis). London: HBMC, pp. 50–53.

Foster, J.A. forthcoming. The copper alloy objects. In Freeman *et al.* forthcoming.

Fox, A. 1954. Celtic fields and farms on Dartmoor in the light of recent excavations at Kestor. *Proc. Prehist. Soc.*, 20: 87–102.

Fox, C. 1946. *A find of the Early Iron Age at Llyn Cerrig Bach*. Cardiff: National Museum of Wales.

Fox, C. 1958. *Pattern and Purpose*. Cardiff: National Museum of Wales.

Freeman, P., Woodward, A. and Barrett, J.C., forthcoming. *Cadbury Castle, Somerset: the Later Prehistoric and Roman Archaeology*. English Heritage Archaeological Report.

Howard, H. 1980. Preliminary petrological report on the Gussage All Saints crucibles. In *Aspects of early metallurgy* (ed. W. Oddy). Brit. Mus. Occ. paper 17. British Museum: London, pp. 189–192.

Hurst, J.D. and Wilks, J. 1987. A horncap from Beckford, Worcs. *Proc. Prehist. Soc.*, 53: 492–3.

James, D. 1990. Prehistoric Copper mining on The Great Orme's Head. In Crew and Crew 1990: 1–4.

Jobey, I. and Jobey, G. 1987. Prehistoric, Romano-British and later remains on Murton High Crags, Northumberland. *Archaeologia Aeliana*, 15: 151–198.

Kenyon, K.M. 1954. Excavations at Sutton Walls, Herefordshire 1948–51. *Archaeol. Journ*, 110: 1–87.

Lewis, A. 1990. Underground exploration of the Great Orme Copper mines. In Crew and Crew 1990: 5–10.

MacGregor, M. 1976. *Early Celtic Art in Northern Britain*. Leicester: Leicester University Press.

Megaw, R. and Megaw, V. 1989. *Early Celtic Art from its beginnings to the Book of Kells. London: Thames and Hudson.*

Northover, P. 1984. Analysis of the bronze metalwork. In Cunliffe 1984: 430–3.

Northover, P. 1987. In Cunliffe 1987: 186–90.

Northover, P. 1988. Copper, tin, silver and gold in the Iron Age. In *Science and Technology Glasgow 1987* (eds E.A. Slater and J.O. Tate). Oxford: Brit. Archaeol. Rep., Brit. Series, 196, pp. 223–34

Palk, N. 1984. *Iron Age Bridle-bits from Britain*. University of Edinburgh Dept. of Arch. Occ. Paper 10.

Piggott, S. 1983. *The Earliest wheeled transport*. London: Thames and Hudson

Saunders, A. and Harris, D. 1982. Excavation at Castle Gotha, St Austell. *Cornish Archaeol.*, 21: 109–153.

Spratling, M.G. 1972. *Southern British decorated bronzes of the late pre-Roman Iron Age.* Unpublished PhD thesis: London.

Spratling, M.G. 1979. The debris of metalworking. In Wainwright 1979: 125–53.

Stead, I.M. 1984. Some notes on imported metalwork in Iron Age Britain. In *Cross-channel trade between Britain and Gaul in the Pre-Roman Iron Age* (eds S. Macready and F.H. Thompsen). Soc. Antiq. London, pp. 43–66.

Stead, I.M. 1985. *The Battersea Shield*. London: British Museum Publications.

Stead, I.M. 1991. *Iron Age cemeteries in Yorkshire*. London: English Heritage.

Stead, I.M. 1993. Snettisham. *Current Archaeol.*, 135: 97–102

Timberlake, S. 1990. Excavations and fieldwork on Copa Hill, Cwmystwyth 1989. In Crew and Crew 1990: 22–29.

Wainwright, G.J. 1979. *Gussage All Saints: An Iron Age Settlement in Dorset.* London: HMSO.

Wild, J.P. 1970. Button and loop fasteners in the Roman Provinces. *Brittania*, 1: 137–55.

Wise, P.J. 1990. Archaeology of the Grimsby-Cleethorpes area. In *Humber Perspectives: a region through the Ages* (eds S. Ellis and D.R. Crowther). Hull University Press: pp. 213–226.

A Münsingen Fibula

F. R. HODSON

The brooch from Münsingen grave 49 (fig. 36) is one of the most frequently illustrated examples of La Tène art and craftsmanship. Since it was excavated at the beginning of the century and then published with a photograph by Wiedmer-Stern (1908), it has figured in countless La Tène studies, ranging from Reinecke (1911: fig. 3, d) through Jacobsthal (1944: no. 332) to the 'Celts' Catalogue of 1991 (Kruta 1991: 208). However, it is only the most recent restoration and study by the staff of the Bernisches Historisches Museum that have brought out previously hidden aspects of what may now be seen as a vital document to the bewildering *modus operandi* of one La Tène genius (Müller 1993). The almost microscopic procedure for shading selected motifs to contrast with others, elaborating with a further level of detail what is already a most complex but magnificently controlled composition, takes the breath away (fig. 37). A further, hitherto apparently unremarked and not so certain feature of the composition may be seen at the very centre and climax of the piece where a typically ambiguous grouping of eyes, and nose/mouths may (or may not) be construed as a mirror imaged face, peering through the strands of tortured vegetation, an excellent example of Jacobsthal's description of such ambiguities: 'One can often hesitate whether a face is intended or not' (1944: 19).

Apart from amazement, and on a more mundane level, this individual masterwork raises again the basic archaeological problem of how individual, and truly unique evidence may be brought into relationship with the more mundane and so provide a cohesive view of the whole context to which it relates. In this tribute to Ian Stead I will attempt to tackle just a few of the problems which such generalisation entails, concentrating on Münsingen and the fibula from Grave 49.

Before discussing this fibula in more detail, it is perhaps worth passing some comments on the Münsingen sequence in general since it still seems to provide the best evidence for the succession of types and styles at any one site during Early La Tène and the transition to Middle La Tène.

In republishing the grave inventories from Münsingen-Rain near Bern in 1968, I hoped to provide readier access to the finds than was given by Wiedmer's original publication, and so provide the source for a wide range of La Tène studies whether of workshop practices, art styles, the social significance of costume or, on a larger scale, cemetery structure or even the relevance of numerical methods to archaeological analysis. But following Wiedmer, the only interpretative aspect which I attempted concerned the relative chronology of the finds, an aspect that could readily be isolated and that seemed, in the absence of any other valid relative chronology of Early and Middle La Tène material, the immediate priority. This aim did not include relating a Münsingen sequence to material from other sites on the Swiss plateau or further afield, an important but a secondary and less obviously attainable endeavour and one that I was happy to leave to others. Roughly thirty years after completing the 1968 text, and after a sojourn in the realms of Hallstatt rather than La Tène, I have found it interesting to look back at some of the developments that have taken place in the interval.

A striking, if not entirely surprising feature is the continuing difficulty in dating La Tène material, especially La Tène art to limits that allow it to be related to events known and dated by the historical record. Difficulties even with such magnificent and apparently informative finds as Reinheim or Erstfeld highlight this difficulty (cf., for example, Müller 1990) and conflicting dates have in fact been assigned to this Münsingen fibula – 'soon after 400 BC' (Müller 1993: 61); 'second half of the fourth century BC' (Kruta 1991: 208). The problem has two aspects: relative and absolute. Münsingen relates to the former, and continues to occupy the centre stage, but there seems to be little agreement on either the method by which it should be approached or on the consequences.

It may be that the wealth of potential evidence itself, embracing as it does typology, horizontal stratigraphy and seriation, leads to this confusion: it is possible, for example, to arrange the Münsingen graves and types

fig. 36. The ornate fibula from Münsingen grave 49 photographed before conservation (enlarged X 11/2).

into a sequence based primarily on the evident general growth of the cemetery along a gravel ridge roughly north/south between early and late nuclei. Indeed, Wiedmer's re-numbering of the graves (see fig. 38) follows this topography closely and at one stage seems to have been considered by him to provide a ready-made chronological as well as locational progression. However, before publication (1908), he realised that this seductive evidence, although in general valid, in detail could mislead. He recognised, for example, that G101 located in a generally 'early' part of the cemetery contained two relatively late (La Tène II) fibulae and that G152, much further south than this and surrounded by 'Ic' graves was characterised by material of 'Ib'. It must be accepted, as Wiedmer himself realised, that the horizontal stratigraphy at Münsingen cannot be used to 'date' any specific grave or the material in it.

Evolutionary typology too is hardly a reliable basis for a detailed sequence: a general stylistic development of fibulae from 'Early' to 'Middle' to 'Late' is generally valid, but further general subdivisions on typology alone, such as Viollier's attempt (1916) to 'phase' Early La Tène globally into Ia, Ib and Ic stages, have appeared not only coarse grained but misleading. It is worth stressing this confusion in Viollier's methodology since, although employing Wiedmer's terminology (Ia, Ib, Ic), it masked his brilliant and fundamentally correct dating of the key material. (See, for example, how in Viollier's captions to his Plates 2 and 3, with 'Fibules de type La Tène Ib' some graves are 'dated' to Ia, most to Ic and some to La Tène II).

The primary evidence for 'dating' graves at Münsingen, then, rests not with their location or with an evolutionary typology of their contents but in the associations

fig. 37. Motif on the ornate fibula from Münsingen grave 49 drawn greatly enlarged after conservation (Müller 1993). Copyright Bernisches Historisches Museum

which some diagnostic graves provide between recognisable, discrete types ('species') and it is here that the real importance of Münsingen for relative chronology lies: in providing graves that were from the start well separated in the developing cemetery (not in re-used tumuli!) and with associations that were well recorded by the excavator. In unambiguous association had been buried whole sets of artefacts made by specialists to precise, repeated formulae but to formulae that changed to keep up with developing fashion and technology.

Should this primacy of association be doubted, the purely mechanical ordering of the graves and types by computer programmes (some 'better' than others!) has demonstrated that seriation alone can produce an order for the Münsingen graves that corresponds closely to that achieved using all traditional archaeological arguments (Hodson 1990: 41, table 7). Were horizontal stratigraphy or evolutionary typology really vital for the sequence, such a correspondence could not possibly be achieved. Of course, both traditional (unspecified) and mechanical (specified) methods of ordering depend on an adequate description of the primary data, i.e., a valid classification of the artefacts.

The uniqueness of Münsingen, then, lies in the relatively large number of graves with sets of stylistic 'species', most notably fibulae and bracelets, which were produced for short periods of time and that may be used to establish a valid seriation of cross-associated types. An additional bonus is the fact that some of these specific types were shared by males and females, allowing

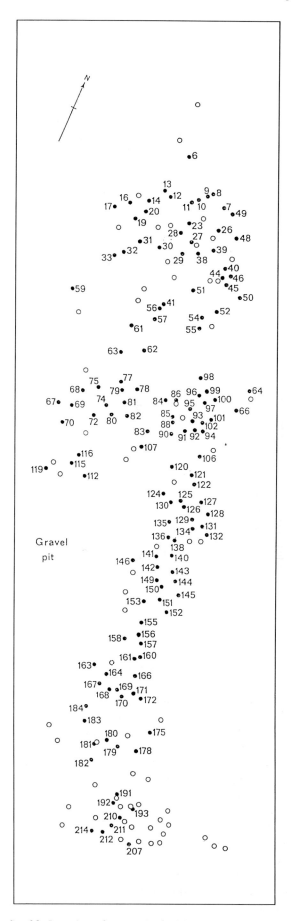

fig. 38. Location of graves in the Münsingen cemetery.

Grave	Horizons	Phases	Zeitabschnitte
	Wiedmer/Hodson 1968		*Gebhard 1989*
13	A		a
32			a
7			a
9			a
16		A = Ia	b
23			a
44			a
12			a
8a			a
8b			a
6	B		b
31	C	B/D = Ia/b	b
40	D		b
48	E		b
46			c
62			c
91		E = Ib Early	c
49			c
80			c
107			c
50	F		c
68	G		d
61		F/H = Ib Late	d
152			d
121	H		d
90			d
84			d
102	I		d
94	J		e
106		I/K = Ic Early	e
140	K		e
134			e
81	L		e
130	M		e
145	N		f
157	O	L/P = Ic Late	f
158			f
75	P		f
149	Q		f
171	R		g
170		Q/T = Ic/II	?
101	S		g
161	T		g
168	U		g
166			g
178			h
184			h
164		U = IIa	g
181			h
180			h
182			h
211			i
212	V		i
207			i
210		V = IIb	i
214			i
190			h
193			h

fig. 39. Relative chronology of key diagnostic graves at Münsingen.

the same sequence to be established for graves that otherwise include different functional types. No other La Tène cemetery has produced such an abundance of cross-associated, specific stylistic types or in other words the basis for such a detailed relative sequence.

This is not the place for a comprehensive discussion of what this sequence at Münsingen should be, but I see little evidence to change substantially the relative chronology proposed in 1968. It is only towards the end of the sequence that there is much scope for manoeuvre, and indeed the most detailed recent study (Gebhard 1989: 114–115) follows closely the phasing of graves suggested in 1968 (see fig. 39). Whether the Münsingen phases may be extended right across Europe (Gebhard *op. cit.*) is a different matter!

Once a detailed sequence of graves and types has been reached for Münsingen it is also possible to 'date' other local developments such as changes in costume over time (e.g. Martin-Kilcher 1973; Sankot 1980). It would seem illogical to attempt to reverse this procedure giving coarse-grained criteria chronological precedence over the detailed sequence of changing types that make up such costumes. Not only do these general costume changes restrict the number of possible horizons that may be defined and dissociate female and male sequences, but since they are local, they provide no possibility for inter-regional chronologies.

This sequence for graves may also be used secondarily to study the overall layout of the cemetery, including the degree to which the horizontal stratigraphy depends on factors other than time – for example on sex and age (Schaaff 1966). Potentially, also, the Münsingen sequence may be used to relate some key examples of La Tène art to each other, and it is very good news to hear that a major project of conservation and study is taking place at Bern on the Münsingen objects that bear such important examples of La Tène art. The painstaking work already carried out on the fibula from G49 shows how vital the results of this research will be. Previously, it was impossible to resolve major aspects of this decoration (cf., the photographs taken before restoration, fig. 36, with the details now revealed, fig. 37).

Mention of this masterpiece brings us back to the question posed earlier: how should it be integrated into our understanding of La Tène phenomena in general? In other words, how should it be classified?

Jacobsthal's *Early Celtic Art* (1944 = ECA) provides a good starting point where this fibula figures as no. 332. With others it was discussed in his text (1944: 129): 'Nos. 322 ff. are of later date than the preceding brooches ['mask' and related fibulae]. Many are from Münsingen – 'Münsingen fibulae' would be an appropriate name for the class ... I show a relatively large number of them because of their importance for the ornament of the Waldalgesheim style. The bow of these fibulae, wholly covered with well thought-out relief ornament is constructed symmetrically, but this is counterbalanced by the foot-finials, large, coral-inlaid disks, which spring back towards the bow and touch it.' This description fits admirably the fibula from G49 and some others from Münsingen, notably those from G50, G85 and G107 (ECA: nos 333, 334 and 337), but Jacobsthal's list also includes a rather wide range of fibulae, one (ECA: no. 340) without a characteristic foot disc, also from Münsingen G49, and one from Münsingen G62 of Certosa rather than La Tène construction (ECA: no. 339) which he himself (ECA: 207) categorises as 'one of those Certosa laggards not infrequent in Switzerland', although he unfortunately adds 'The fibula is rightly dated by Viollier (on pl. 1, 5) to his period Ic...'. As occasionally happens in ECA, Jacobsthal here is a little ambiguous. The style of decoration 'Waldalgesheim' – is clearly what interested him most with his 'Münsingen' class of fibulae but even this aspect seems a little strained since one of his listed fibulae has quite heavy curvilinear decoration that puts it well on the way to his 'plastic' style rather than 'Waldalgesheim' and two (ECA: no. 328, also from Münsingen G49 and no. 330, from Münsingen G91) lack curvilinear decoration altogether.

Nonetheless, *most* of the fibulae that he ascribes to a 'Münsingen' class bear Waldalgesheim motifs and it might not seem unreasonable to retain his definition for a Münsingen fibula 'type' even if some of his examples are excluded. His specification of coral rather than enamel for disc embellishment on these very select fibulae has been supported by more recent detailed study (Challet 1992). It is also instructive that in the next paragraph (ECA: 129) Jacobsthal distinguishes a further series of disc fibulae which he excludes from this Münsingen class: 'The last fibulae in my series illustrate some variants of interest. The accent of the decoration shifts from the bow, now left plain, to the large coral disks: nos 343–5...' (no. 343 is from Münsingen, G156).

Further relevant fibulae, some of which could be added to Jacobsthal's restricted class of Münsingen fibulae have been highlighted by Kruta (1977) who qualifies them not as 'Münsingen fibulae' but as 'fibules laténiennes à décor d'inspiration végétale'. However, since Jacobsthal, the label 'Münsingen fibula' has been extended to include a wide range of disc-footed fibulae as Pauli (1978: 125, n. 118) and Kaenel (1990: 239) have noted. While it may be useful to have a general descriptive term for fibulae with decorated disc feet as an alternative to Viollier's 'Ib' type (1916: 31; pl. 2–3), it may seem advisable to define other more specific types with a further series of labels and not to expect the 'Münsingen type' in this general sense to have a specific chronological or stylistic significance.

My 1968 classification of fibulae, which was designed primarily for Münsingen alone, attempted to follow the agglomerative polythetic and hierarchical approach to type definition which numerical experiments have helped to clarify (Doran and Hodson 1975), and I attempted to distinguish very closely related species from less cohe-

sive 'families' and 'classes' (1968: 14). (For the material from Hallstatt, I used a similar system, but to avoid possible objections to the biological analogy, I referred to 'species' as 'varieties' (1990: 20, 103). Such reservations are probably unnecessary and 'species' will be retained here). I also attempted to give descriptive labels to the types at Münsingen rather than site labels since a proliferation of such names for all levels of the hierarchy would have been incomprehensible.

In looking for a more general, non-site specific classification of Early La Tène fibulae, which could not possibly be attempted here, it would seem to me that the same hierarchical principles should still apply, and that 'species' should be distinguished from more general 'families' and given special weight.

A step in this direction was in fact taken by Champion (1985), who singled out three groups of fibulae from the total Münsingen range which occur also at sites other than Münsingen: the first, which she labelled the Münsingen-Andelfingen type, corresponds to my Column 33 species (Hodson 1968: 36 and pl. 123) within the more general class of fibulae with large bronze rivets securing a red enamel disc; the second, which she labelled 'Münsingen-Deisswil' corresponds to my 'nofinial' species, column 24 (1968: 36, pl. 123); the third, a less cohesive group 'with coral-inlaid bows and enamelled disc feet' I included in a general family of such enamel disc footed fibulae (1968: 36; column 32). These three 'types' are fine as far as they go, but include just a few of the disc-footed fibulae at Münsingen leaving the majority, among them such masterpieces as G49, still to be classified and labelled. Nevertheless, the value of defining specific types like this may be seen from the fact that the Deisswil and Andelfingen types date from different stages of the Münsingen cemetery: the latter from Münsingen Ib–Early, the former, together with the specified coral-bow variants, from Münsingen Ib–Late).

The fibula from G49 featured here is not so easy to classify. The definition suggested for a species – a group of objects as similar, or with specialised features as similar to each other as a craftsman could be expected to make them (1968: 14; 1990: 20) – is appropriate for the standardised Deisswil or Andelfingen fibulae and indeed for most prehistoric metalwork, but the craftsman's intention with the G49 fibula must have been to create a masterpiece, originally in wax, that other craftsmen could not equal and, possibly, that he himself would not wish to repeat.

In 1968 I dodged this issue, not classifying this fibula at the species level at all but including it with some other masterpieces in a *class* of 'ornate' fibulae (1968, 36, column 22 with cols 21 and 23). If *Münsingen fibula* is to continue as a general term rather than as Jacobsthal defined it, this might still seem the safest solution. The G49 fibula would then be grouped, at a general level, with the whole series of masterpieces from the Bern area, apparently produced over a relatively short space of time (in Münsingen terms, during the Ib–Early stage) and distinguished by the highest qualities of artistry and craftsmanship as well as more definable characteristics such as the preference for added coral rather than enamel, detailed attention to the catchplate, the coils and the finial and edges of the foot-disc, and a delight in curvilinear decoration with different expressions of Jacobsthal's Waldalgesheim style.

Within this large group it is possible to separate out at least two very distinctive series: in the first, the curvilinear motifs are framed by a panel on top of the bow, and a few of these share as many detailed similarities as such individual masterpieces could be expected to share. This would include ECA: nos 334 and 337 from Münsingen, no. 331, the well-known silver fibula from Schosshalde, Bern, and one of the fibulae from Deisswil (Tschumi 1953: fig. 214, 3). The ornate G49 fibula would belong to a second series where the curvilinear motifs are not framed but wrap symmetrically around the bow: ECA: no. 333, from Münsingen G50 and three fibulae from Dürrnberg, graves 20/2, 28/2 and 97 would belong (Pauli 1978: 124, fig. 15). Münsingen G50 and Dürrnberg G28/2 must surely come from the same workshop. It is these two relatively restricted but highly distinctive series of ornate fibulae that characterise the high point of fibula craftsmanship seen so emphatically at Münsingen during the Ib–Early stage there. In later phases, fibulae seem to be mass-produced and intended to impress through quantity or size rather than quality. In addition to fibulae as vehicles for La Tène art, Jacobsthal included some other Münsingen material in his study, mostly bracelets/anklets, and since a more detailed sequence for Münsingen is now accepted than that of Viollier (1916) on which he relied, it is worth recalling briefly some of the relevant ECA examples. As works of art none of these, mainly later objects bear comparison with the fibulae already mentioned nor with examples of Jacobsthal's Plastic Style from other sites, but their chronological relationship at Münsingen allows them to be seen in a sequence that is otherwise more speculative. Examples of his Plastic Style were in fact cited by him from G61 of Ib–Late (ECA: no. 281), from G135 of Ic–Early (no. 264), from G158 of Ic–Late (no. 280), and from G75 and G149 of Ic–Late and transitional Ic/II (no. 273). The first of this series, no. 281, relates to a large group of cleverly fashioned sheet bronze bracelets/anklets at first with arrow-like repoussé motifs that may be followed from the Ia/Ib stage onwards but which even after stylistic developments seem rather remote from the more typically Plastic Style seen on the cast rings, whether incipient (ECA: no. 264) or emphatic (ECA: no. 273).

But none of these Plastic Style objects bear the special, local stamp of the superb Bern fibulae. We must all wait with bated breath to see what further wonders the hand of the conservator will reveal on them.

Acknowledgements

I would like to thank colleagues at the Bernisches Historisches Museum for renewed access to the Münsingen finds and for permission to reproduce fig. 37.

References

Champion, S. 1985. Production and exchange in Early Iron Age Central Europe. In *Settlement and Society* (eds T.C. Champion and J.V.S. Megaw). Leicester: Leicester University Press, pp. 133–160.

Challet, V. 1992. *Les Celtes et l'émail*. Paris: Editions du Comité des Travaux historiques et scientifiques.

Doran, J.E. and Hodson, F.R. 1975. *Mathematics and computers in archaeology*. Edinburgh: Edinburgh University Press.

Gebhard, R. 1989. *Der Glasschmuck aus dem Oppidum von Manching*. Die Ausgrabungen in Manching 11. Stuttgart: Franz Steiner Verlag.

Hodson, F.R. 1968. *The La Tène cemetery at Münsingen-Rain: catalogue and relative chronology*. Acta Bernensia V.

Hodson, F.R. 1990. *Hallstatt the Ramsauer Graves: quantification and analysis*. Römisch-Germanisches Zentralmuseum Mainz Monographien, 16.

Jacobsthal, P. 1944. *Early Celtic Art*. Oxford: Oxford University Press.

Kaenel, G. 1990. *Recherches sur la période de La Tène en Suisse occidentale Analyse des sépultures*. Cahiers d'Archéologie Romande 50.

Kruta, V. 1977. Les fibules laténiennes à décor d'inspiration végétale au IVe siècle avant notre ère. *Etudes Celtiques*, 15: 19–47.

Kruta, V. 1991. The first Celtic Expansion: Prehistory to History. In *The Celts* (eds S. Moscati, O.-H. Frey, V. Kruta, B. Raftery, M. Szabo). London: Thames and Hudson, pp. 195–213.

Martin-Kilcher, S. 1973. Zur Tracht und Beigabensitte im keltischen Gräberfeld von Münsingen-Rain (Kt. Bern). *Zeitschrift für Schweizerische Archäologie und Kunstgeschichte*, 30: 26–39.

Müller, F. 1990. Zur Datierung des Goldschatzes von Erstfeld Uri. *Jahrbuch der Schweizerischen Gesellschaft für Ur- und Frühgeschichte*, 73: 83–94.

Müller, F. 1993. Überraschendes unter der Patina einer keltischen Fibel aus Münsingen. *Archäologie der Schweiz*, 16 (2): 60–64.

Pauli, L. 1978. *Der Dürrnberg bei Hallein III 1. Auswertung der Grabfunde*. Münchner Beitr. z. Vor- und Frühgeschichte, 18.

Reinecke, P. 1911. *Die Altertümer unserer heidnischen Vorzeit*, V. Mainz.

Sankot, P. 1980. Studie zur Sozialstruktur der nordalpinen Flachgräberfelder der La Tène-Zeit der Schweiz. *Zeitschrift für Schweizerische Archäologie und Kunstgeschichte*, 37: 19–71.

Schaaff, U. 1966. Zur Belegung latènezeitlicher Friedhöfe der Schweiz. *Jahrbuch des Römisch-Germanischen Zentralmuseums Mainz*, 13: 49–59.

Viollier, D. 1916. *Les sépultures du second âge du fer sur le plateau suisse*. Geneva.

Wiedmer-Stern, J. 1908. *Das gallische Gräberfeld bei Münsingen (Kanton Bern)*. Bern.

The Meyrick Helmet: A New Interpretation of its Decoration

RALPH JACKSON

INTRODUCTION

In 1872 Augustus Wollaston Franks presented to the British Museum two notable antiquities, a 'bronze oval British shield', and a 'bronze British helmet', both of which had formerly been in the Meyrick Collection. While the first of these – the 'Witham Shield' – was known to have come from the River Witham, near Lincoln, the place of discovery and subsequent history of the second piece were entirely lacking, and it soon became known as the 'Meyrick Helmet' (British Museum reg. no. 1872, 12–13, 2). Already by 1905, however, when Reginald Smith included it in the *British Museum Guide to the Antiquities of the Early Iron Age*, it was described as 'probably found in the north of England' (p. 95). The origin of this attribution is unclear, but probably it was based only upon the fact that much of the Meyrick Collection came from that region. As it happens, as many have observed (e.g. Fox 1958: 119; Ritchie 1968: 135 ff.; Megaw 1970: 37, 173; Brailsford 1975: 41), northern Britain is the most probable source for the helmet, given the style of its ornament.

DIMENSIONS

Weight 513.8 g. Length 302 mm. Width 171 mm. Height 167 mm. Internal diameter of cap, front-back 208 mm. Internal diameter of cap, side-side 163 mm. Internal base circumference 608 mm. Diameter of missing top knob (as disclosed by differential patina) 47 mm. Width of neck-guard 189 mm. Depth of neck-guard 89 mm. Diameter of side-plate lower rivet head 20 mm. Diameter of side-plate upper rivet head 14.5 mm. Diameter of neck-guard rivet heads 14.5 mm. Thickness of metal at break below top knob 0.3 mm. Thickness of metal at break near cap mid-point 0.2 mm. Thickness of metal at hinge notch (base thickness before rim thickening) 1.1 mm. Thickness of metal at rim of neckguard 0.6 mm (at extremity – side junction with cap – 2.3 mm).

DISCUSSION

The fullest description and consideration of the helmet, by Graham Ritchie (1968), is unpublished. Elsewhere, it is as much for its ornament – regarded as a fine example of the 1st cent AD 'school of North British art' – as for its interesting hybrid form that the Meyrick Helmet has evoked comment. The helmet is, undeniably, an artistic and technical masterpiece. It comprises a steep-sided domed cap with broad neck-guard, apparently worked up from a single sheet of bronze, to which were attached a top knob and a pair of decorative side-plates. Hammer facets are visible on the underside of the neck-guard and on the basal 3–4 cm. of the cap's inner face. As often occurs when a sheet is raised to such an extent the metal was stretched to its thinnest around the mid-point of the dome and, as on several other raised bronze helmets (see e.g. Robinson 1975: pls 6–7, 18–20, 44, 51–53 etc.), post-depositional splitting and fragmentation have occurred there (fig. 40). Despite suggestions that it was possibly lathe spun or spun finished (Ritchie 1968: 32B; Megaw 1970: 173; MacGregor 1976: 189) the helmet provides no evidence in support of these techniques, which are as yet unproven before the Medieval period (Craddock and Lang 1983).

The summit of the cap has been raised slightly above the smooth conical profile of the helmet (figs 40–41). This feature, in conjunction with a central small hole surrounded by three further rivet holes, all encompassed within a circular zone of differential patina, attest the former existence of a riveted top knob or plume/crest holder, with a base diameter of *c.* 47 mm. Its form was, perhaps, similar to the slotted, conical cast bronze crest knobs which were soldered to the top of Roman Coolus type helmets (e.g. Robinson 1975: pls 46–85).

On the lower dome of the helmet, just above and behind the right side-plate, is the lightly-scored Roman numeral II (figs 41, 42. Frere and Tomlin 1991: 44, *RIB* 2425.1, where, however, the graffito is very poorly copied). A close examination of the patina and corrosion products in this region and a comparison with the recent

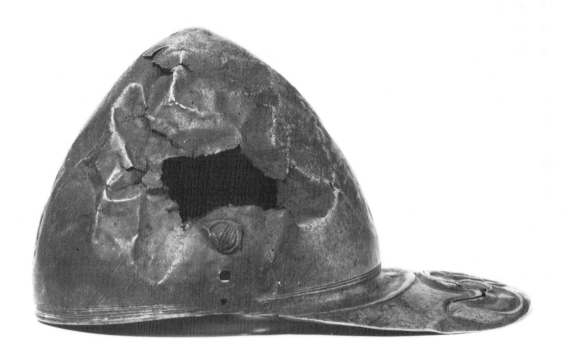

fig. 40. The Meyrick helmet, left side (Courtesy of the British Museum).

(19th century) abrasion adjacent to the right side-plate confirm the antiquity of the graffito. It has been suggested that the number relates to a temple inventory or to the listing of captured booty (Frere and Tomlin 1991: 44; Ritchie 1968: 139), but more mundane explanations are possible. For, as has been observed (e.g. Frere and Tomlin 1991: 47), numbers were not infrequently scored or punched onto pieces of Roman military equipment.

The rim of the cap, but not that of the neck-guard, is reinforced by a thickening of the metal, which varies between 2.5–4.0 mm. Immediately above the rim on the outer face of the cap is a zone of neatly cut circumferential moulding – a pair of narrow grooves on each side of a broad channel at the front of the cap, and a single narrow groove either side of a central ridge at the back. These mouldings were cut before the repoussé side-plates were attached, for they encroach onto the area originally covered by the side-plates (fig. 42). The latter were clearly envisaged, however, because the mouldings do not continue in an unbroken line across the area. As Brailsford demonstrated (1975: figs 57–58, both of which are somewhat inaccurate and idealised) the side-plates originally supported hinged cheek-pieces, and the thickened cap rim had a slot removed at that point to facilitate the functioning of the hinge assembly.

The side-plates, both of which are fragmentary, comprised a thin sheet with lobed repoussé ornament, fastened to the helmet wall by two broad-headed rivets (figs 40–42). The survival of the lower rivet on the right side and the upper rivet on the left side is fortunate, as it

reveals the original arrangement: a large-headed rivet surmounted by a slightly smaller one. A third rivet, with narrower shank and completely plain flush head, beneath the lower decorative stud, was evidently purely functional and served to anchor the back of the tab, by means of which the cheek-piece was hinged (see fig. 42, and Brailsford 1975: fig. 57), and also, perhaps, to secure a leather chin-strap or liner. The large rivet heads were ornamented with red 'enamel' (only traces remain) set in an incised cross-hatched keying. The 'enamel', more correctly termed opaque red glass, was analysed, together with 32 other examples, by Hughes (1972: 103, Table 1), who determined the percentages of lead oxide (25.6%) and cuprous oxide (11.9%) and their ratio (2.15). As Val Rigby has pointed out (pers. comm.) Spratling's re-examination and re-plotting of Hughes results (Spratling 1980: esp. fig. 1 nos. 14 and 22), which demonstrated an apparently meaningful clustering of similar values, tends to link the studs of the Meyrick Helmet with those of the scabbard of the 1st cent. AD Embleton sword (lead oxide 28.1%, cuprous oxide 11.24%).

The helmet cap is similar to that of the Coolus type helmet of the 1st cent. AD, though a little more conical. In that respect it echoes the Montefortino/Buggenum type (Feugère 1994: 79ff.; Robinson 1975: 18ff.), but the deep neck-guard is very much in line with the Coolus series, and their broad contemporaneity seems assured. The shape and breadth of the neck-guard, which exceeds only slightly the width of the helmet, is most closely paralleled by the 'partially developed' Coolus series,

fig. 41. The Meyrick Helmet, right side (Courtesy of British Museum).

fig. 42. The Meyrick Helmet, right side detail, showing rim moulding, scored graffito, fragmentary side-plate and ornamental stud (Courtesy of British Museum).

Robinson's Types D and E (1975: 40–41, figs 39–45). Like those helmets, too, the Meyrick Helmet was probably worn with the cap rim horizontal, so that the neck-guard was angled down onto the neck. In that position it would have afforded the wearer maximum protection, though whether used in Connolly's 'crouched position' (1991: fig. 68.9) or in a more upright stance cannot really be determined. Further points of similarity include the channelled moulding around the helmet rim which is occasionally present on the bronze Coolus helmets (e.g. Robinson 1975: 38, pl. 88; 41, fig. 50), but more often so on the iron helmets in the form of an applied bronze strip (e.g. fig. 45).

In addition to its functional – protective – role the neck-guard presented a broad, flat lunate field, fertile ground for the bronzesmith, who capitalised on its potential for ornamentation by filling it with a swirling repoussé design (fig. 43). This comprises a bold symmetrical arrangement, centred on the longitudinal axis of the helmet. It has been described variously as a central palmette linked to elongated trumpet-forms pointed by two enamel bosses (Fox 1958: 119), an open lyre pattern with half-moons and hatched knobs (Megaw 1970: 173), 'broken-backed' curves with enamelled bosses at nodal points (Brailsford 1975: 41) and a central palmette flanked by lobed stems and pinpointed by bosses scored for enamelling (MacGregor 1976: 189). In fact, there were probably originally three hatched 'enamelled' bosses, for the largest of the three empty rivet holes in the neck-guard, which is set at the apex of a low triangle formed by that and the two surviving hatched bosses, is the same size as the other holes made for the decorative bossed rivets on the neck-guard and side-plates. Furthermore, the 'halo' of differential patina which surrounds the hole has a diameter of 14.5mm, identical to the head size of the adjacent bossed rivets.

Components of the neck-guard ornament – high-ridged lobate curves around red-'enamelled' hatched bosses, characterised by Megaw (1970: 173) as "casket ornament', a kind of shorthand version of the Llyn Cerrig triskel' – were repeated on the side-plates (also, perhaps, on the missing cheek-pieces) providing a pleasingly integrated helmet decor. It is possible that this decor was purely abstract in intent or that it was created as an elegant vegetal patterned design. However, there is a further possibility. One of the hallmarks of Early Celtic art is the tendency for a naturalistic image to be selected and transformed into a highly devolved decorative motif, the derivation of which may, today, be hard to divine. In this case, it is contended that the craftsman who made the helmet and wrought the decoration was inspired not only by the overall shape and design of contemporary Roman helmets but also by their fittings and attachments. Such attachments, in addition to the plume/crest knob on the summit, often included a carrying handle fastened to the neck-guard, and, on the helmet wall above either ear, decorative studs or a feather- or plume-tube.

Regarded in this light the neck-guard ornament of the Meyrick Helmet bears a very striking, and surely more than fortuitous, resemblance to the carrying handles of Coolus, Imperial-Gallic and Imperial-Italic helmets of the second half of the 1st cent. AD (cf. e.g. Feugère 1994: 84; Robinson 1975: 38–39, pl. 89, 56–7, pls 126–129, 59, pl. 138 and 68, pl. 167). As a skeuomorph, it would be necessary to show the handle with its bow folded in towards the helmet dome rather than projecting over the edge of the neck-guard, as is, indeed, the case (compare figs 43 and 44). The two surviving 'enamelled' bosses would represent the domed washer and split-pin assembly on which the handle was hinged, while the looped handle terminals were rendered in a typically elaborated form, with flaring, scrolled trumpet-like finials. The postulated third 'enamelled' boss finds a parallel with a similarly decorative stud in this position on some Imperial-Gallic helmets of the later 1st cent. AD with carrying handle (cf. fig. 44, and Robinson 1975: 56–7, pls 126–7).

Robinson (1975: 47ff.) noted that helmet carrying handles were rare before the second half of the 1st cent. AD and were probably a new (though certainly not standard) feature of that period. Interestingly, they seem not to have replaced the suspension ring fastened by a rivet to the centre of the neck-guard. That rivet may also have served to anchor a leather strap, either end of which was fastened to the cheek-piece tie-straps. The two remaining rivet holes on the central axis of the Meyrick neck-guard (fig. 42) could have served a similar role. However, they are very close to the base of the cap, and in that position such a strap would probably have chafed the wearer's neck. Alternatively, therefore, they may have secured either a suspension strap or the lower end of a crest fitted to the summit top knob/crest holder, or, perhaps, both. Certainly, in size and appearance the holes are comparable to those used to fasten the top knob and those used to fix the side-plate hinge tab (figs 40–42), and a functional rather than decorative role may be assumed.

If the neck-guard decoration was, indeed, a skeuomorph of a carrying handle then the ornamented side-plates may have been intended to depict plume tubes (a possibility already noted by Ritchie (1968: 137), and the swept-back effect of the repoussé double 'comma' at least gives an impression of wind-blown feathers or plumes, albeit in a highly stylised form (fig. 42). However, the situation is even less clear-cut than with the neck-guard decoration, for some Roman helmets had ornamental rosette bosses in this position (fig. 45).

The chronological implication of a carrying handle skeuomorph – a date of manufacture in the second half of the 1st century AD – is not in conflict with other sources of evidence for the date of the Meyrick Helmet. These were most fully discussed by Ritchie (1968: 135ff.) who, as well as making comparison between the neck-guard decoration and that of the bronze panel from

fig. 43. The Meyrick Helmet, neck-guard detail (Courtesy of British Museum).

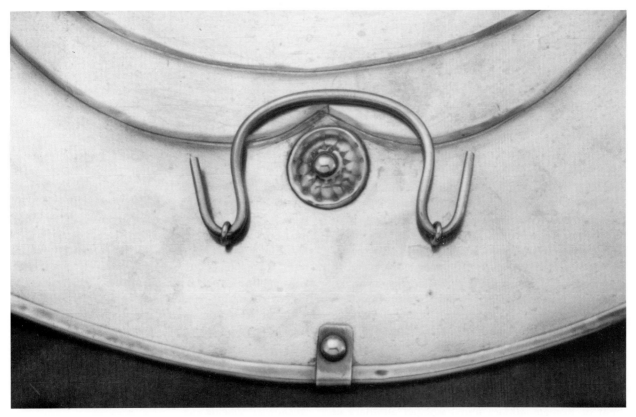

fig. 44. Carrying handle and neck-guard detail of the reconstructed helmet shown in fig. 45
(By Permission of the National Museum of Wales).

fig. 45. Reconstruction of iron and bronze Imperial-Gallic type G helmet
(By Permission of the National Museum of Wales).

Elmswell, Yorkshire, dated *c.* AD 60–70 by its associated material, also cited parallels with the late-1st century AD Polden Hills hoard. Megaw (1970: 173 and 156–7, no. 263) drew attention to the stylistic affinities between the Meyrick ornament and the upper component of the Nijmegen mirror handle (dated later 1st century AD), while MacGregor (1976: 89–90) cited the Polden Hills/Bawdrip horse brooch and a repoussé plate fragment from the Stanwick hoard. In addition to the decorative parallels, Ritchie saw as significant similarities between the form of the Meyrick Helmet and two helmets from Tongern and Mainz. In an admittedly tenuous link it was envisaged that the Meyrick Helmet emerged from contact between the Tungrian cohorts of this region and the northern British metalsmiths, when the Tungrians accompanied Agricola's army on the northern advance of the late 70's – Tungrian taste and British workmanship, perhaps, as a Tungrian auxiliary commissioned a helmet to his own particular specification. Certainly, the troubled decades in Britain which followed the upheaval of the civil wars of AD 68–9 would readily provide a variety of contexts for manufacture, use, loss etc. of the helmet and for its enigmatic graffito.

For some years now, there has been a growing appreciation of the lack of rigid standardisation of the equipment of Roman military units, whether auxiliary or legionary, in the 1st century AD. Sheer practicality would have dictated that at any one time there would be a diversity of equipment, some of which would be current or innovative – new issue – and some old, well-used, reissued pieces. In addition, as Manning has articulated (1985: 149–151), there is likely to have been a degree of latitude in, at the very least, the selection of decorative components of arms and armour. Thus, for example, the Hod Hill sword, hitherto regarded as an Iron Age weapon, has been re-interpreted as a Roman sword with 'Celtic' fittings (*ibid.*), and the Meyrick Helmet, with its combination of archaic, conservative, current and novel features, may be another manifestation of this process. Whether the owner was Fox's 'Celtic noble in Roman service' (1958: 119), Megaw's Roman auxiliary (1970: 173) or Brailsford's Roman auxiliary officer (1975: 41), the Meyrick Helmet was less likely a native piece showing Roman influence than a Roman helmet – that is to say, a helmet made for a soldier serving in a unit of the Roman army – tricked out in native style. The application of a 'carrying handle' in elaborate, if conservative, north British repoussé, was a distinctive and pleasing ornament. More than that, however, its *trompe l'oeil* effect, given the similarly 'hidden' animal faces that lurked in other contemporary Celtic ornament, was unlikely to have been lost upon those who saw it.

Acknowledgements

I am most grateful to my colleagues at the British Museum, especially Val Rigby, Ian Stead, Catherine Johns and Simon James, who discussed various aspects of the helmet with me; to Val Rigby for reading and commenting on a draft of this paper; and to Richard Brewer for very kindly supplying figs 44, 45.

References

Brailsford, J. 1975. *Early Celtic Masterpieces in the British Museum*. London: British Museum Publications.

Connolly, P. 1991. The Roman fighting technique deduced from armour and weaponry. In *Roman Frontier Studies 1989. Proceedings of the XVth International Congress of Roman Frontier Studies* (eds V.A. Maxfield and M.J. Dobson). Exeter: 358–363.

Craddock, P.T. and Lang, J. 1983. Spinning, turning, polishing. *Journ. Hist. Metallurgy Soc.* 17 (2): 79–81.

Feugère, M. 1994. *Casques Antiques. Visages de la guerre de Mycènes à l'Antiquité tardive*. Paris.

Fox, C. 1958. *Pattern and Purpose: a Survey of Early Celtic Art in Britain*. Cardiff: National Museum of Wales.

Frere, S.S. and Tomlin, R.S.O. (eds) 1991. *The Roman Inscriptions of Britain*, Vol. II, fascicule 3 (RIB 2421–2441). Oxford.

Hughes, M.J. 1972. A technical study of opaque red glass of the Iron Age in Britain. *Proc. Prehist. Soc.*, 38: 98–107.

MacGregor, M. 1976. *Early Celtic Art in North Britain*. Leicester: Leicester University Press.

Manning, W.H. 1985. *Catalogue of the Romano-British Iron Tools, Fittings and Weapons in the British Museum*. London.

Megaw, J.V.S. 1970. *Art of the European Iron Age*. Bath: Adams and Dart.

Ritchie, G. 1968. *Celtic Defensive Weaponry in Britain, and its Continental Background*. Unpublished Ph.D. thesis, University of Edinburgh.

Robinson, H.R. 1975. *The Armour of Imperial Rome*. London.

Spratling, M.G. 1980. Observations on the analysis of the composition of the opaque red glass ('red enamel') of the British pre-Roman Iron Age. In *Proceedings of the 16th International Symposium on Archaeometry and Archaeological Prospection, Edinburgh 1976* (eds E.A. Slater and J.O. Tate). Edinburgh.

The Ribchester Hoard: A Descriptive and Technical Study

R. P. J. JACKSON AND P. T. CRADDOCK

WITH CONTRIBUTIONS FROM J. LANG AND J. B. LAMBERT

INTRODUCTION

The Ribchester hoard was found in the village of Ribchester, Lancashire: in the summer of 1796 by the 13–year old son of Joseph Walton, clogmaker (Edwards 1992). He made the discovery while playing on wasteground to the rear of their house, which was the southernmost cottage on the west side of Church Street (NGR *c*. SD 651351), as it approached the bank of the River Ribble. The location of the find, 'in a hollow in the waste land at the side of the road leading to the church and near the bend of the river' was sketched (fig. 46) and recorded with some precision by the antiquary Charles Townley of Towneley Hall, Burnley, who bought the entire hoard from the Walton family on Dec. 8th 1797, and published his account of it in *Vetusta Monumenta* Vol. IV, 1800 (published in 1815).

Townley died in 1805, and the hoard was acquired by the British Museum in 1814, since when the celebrated helmet (figs 47, 48) has been almost continuously on display. Less well known is the remainder of the hoard, which comprises some thirty further complete or fragmentary objects, mostly bronzes (fig. 47). Thus, although discovered almost exactly two centuries ago very little of the hoard had been published other than the helmet (e.g. Toynbee 1962: 167; 1964: 292; Robinson 1975: 110–113), until very recently (Edwards 1992 and forthcoming). Yet it constitutes one of the more important groups of military metalwork to survive from the Western Empire, including, as it does, prestige harness trappings, chamfron fittings and *dona militaria*, and displaying within the wide typological range an equally wide range of alloys, fabrication methods and decorative techniques. The combined typological and metallurgical study of these pieces and some related material has clarified important areas of Roman metalworking practice as well as giving an insight into the whole subject of the organisation of metal supply in the Western Empire.

DESCRIPTION (RPJJ)

Although comparatively favourable circumstances prevailed in the preservation of the hoard, both before and after its discovery, a number of negative processes and events have rendered uncertain its precise form and make-up at the time of deposition. It is necessary to keep these in mind when evaluating the significance of the hoard as it survives today. Immediately noticeable is the virtual absence of iron objects or components, a surprising and most unlikely situation, which is probably to be explained by a combination of advanced corrosion and lack of recognition/interest by the finders. The presence of at least two highly corroded iron components (on cat. nos 1 and 2) and extensive iron corrosion products on several of the uncleaned bronzes, taken together with the finders' description of the hoard's soil matrix as 'a heap of red sand' (Townley 1815: 1), imply the original existence of further iron objects, probably in the final stages of decay at the time of discovery.

Secondly, there appears to have been some uncertainty as to the extent of the hoard as found. For example, although Townley believed he had acquired the entire hoard, it transpired that at least one object, described as a sphinx, had been withheld and subsequently lost (Townley 1815: 11–12). Given that Townley purchased the hoard more than a year after its discovery this is, perhaps, not so surprising. Furthermore, although the integrity of the hoard is, to a great extent, vouchsafed by the description of its context as 'an excavation in the native soil (a mixture of gravel and clay), rather less than a yard in diameter, about nine feet beneath the present surface, and filled up with fine sand' (Townley 1815: 12), and 'a heap of red sand, which formed a cube of three feet' (Townley 1815: 1) – surely implying burial in a wooden chest – there is the slight possibility that the finders incorporated in it one or more objects from adjacent archaeological strata.

Thirdly, there is a discrepancy between Townley's

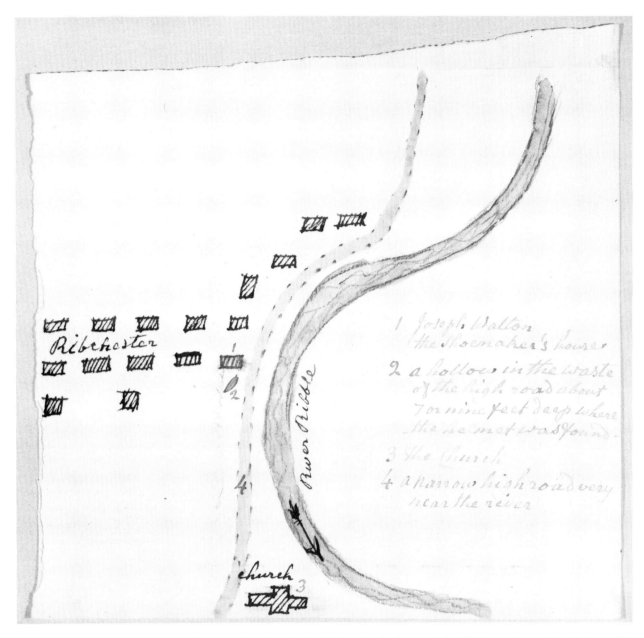

fig. 46. Charles Townley's ink and watercolour sketch pinpointing the find spot of the Ribchester hoard (marked no. 2).

published listing of the hoard and the pieces in the British Museum that can now be unequivocally identified as belonging to it. Several factors probably explain this mis-match. During the period of seventeen years in which the hoard belonged to Townley and his family some pieces, especially those of wood and leather or thin sheet bronze, may have deteriorated, or completely disintegrated, or have become separated from the other objects and thus been overlooked. Similar processes may also be invoked for the early history of the hoard in the British Museum. A standard registration system had yet to be established at this early period, and there is no contemporary record detailing the extent of the hoard as it was acquired in 1814. Furthermore, no acquisition number was applied to the objects, though at some early

stage the letter 'T' or the provenance 'Ribchester' was marked in ink upon some of them. Additionally, there were no conservation facilities, and unmarked decaying fragments of comparatively unprepossessing form would have been vulnerable to loss.

However, the uncertainty encompassed more than simply loss, and Townley's list and accompanying illustrations show a number of inconsistencies. The description of the horse eye-guards as one complete example and fragments of two others can be said to match the surviving complete example and three fragments (cat. nos 2–5), in view of the fact that two of the fragments may be from the same eye-guard. However, the same is not true of the thin sheet *phalerae* (nos 16–20) – Townley recorded four but there are, in fact, five, of consistent

fig. 47. The Ribchester Hoard, with catalogue numbers.

and distinctive form, none of which is a fragment of another. Similarly, there are at least five junction *phalerae* (nos 9–13) while Townley listed only four.

A number of unmarked pieces, in particular nos 29–33 and 35, can, with confidence, be restored to the hoard on the strength of their morphology, patina/corrosion products, and metal analysis. They have been added to the end of the catalogue as nos 29–35. No. 33 is virtually identical in every respect to nos 14–15 and is almost certainly the third of the small *phalerae* recorded by Townley. Similarly, the form and corrosion products of nos 31–32 are so close in appearance to others of the uncleaned trappings in the hoard as to leave little room for doubt, that they, also, were part of the same hoard, even though they were not mentioned in Townley's published listing. Although cleaning has removed the evidence of corrosion products from no. 35 its form, together with the composition of its body metal and inlay, is virtually indistinguishable from the remaining fragmentary junction loop on no. 7, to which it was very likely originally a counterpart. Finally, the saddle plate fragments, nos 29–30 were not specifically mentioned by Townley, and their corrosion products were mostly removed in early (and heavy) cleaning, but they were stored with other Ribchester pieces in the British Museum, and the evidence of metal analysis and general surface appearance also argue in favour of their presence in the hoard.

CATALOGUE (RPJJ)

I. Located objects in Townley's published list

Helmet (figs 47, 48)

1.   Face mask vizor helmet. 1814, 7–5, 1. Townley no. 1.
     Max. height head-piece 276 mm.
     Max. width face mask 241 mm.
     Wt. head-piece 823.5 g.
     Wt. face mask 482.1 g.

A two-piece face mask vizor helmet of brass.

a) Face mask: a finely-modelled clean-shaven male face, the naturalism of which is enhanced by a subtle asymmetry (not necessarily intentional), e.g. of the eyes, nose and cheek-bones. A little post-depositional damage has been sustained – loss of the nose tip and one ear tip, and small corrosion holes and slight fracturing near and beneath the chin – but in most places the original smooth polished surface has been preserved. Lightly punched eyebrows and eyelashes are rendered in a slightly stylised/idealised form, while the lips of the small mouth are emphasised with an incuse marginal line and textured by fine dot-punching.

Perforation of the eyes, nostrils and mouth permitted vision and the ingress/egress of air, but the ears are imperforate. The hair is especially finely-wrought, with a row of curls in high relief projecting both from the top and bottom of the ornamental crown. Further curled locks descend onto the cheeks from either side of the crown. They are intertwined with a pair of large-headed serpents. Beneath them a slender chin strap with simple punched decoration passes beneath the chin, at the centre of which is a small stylised knot.

The crown, doubtless a *corona muralis*, comprises a splayed mural base surmounted by a recessed figured frieze. The upper edge is extensively damaged and the central part of the figured zone is broken away. The wall has eight symmetrically-disposed projecting towers, a central double-portal gateway, and a single-portal gateway at each side. The coursing of the wall, surface of the gates, and windows and roofs of the towers are all rendered in detail. The figured frieze above calls to mind a sculpted pediment in that the various elements are adapted to a similarly uncomfortable space, in this case a low ellipse. The upper edge is defined by a running chevron, at each base angle of which projects a human head, eight in total (only four surviving), which correspond to the eight towers of the wall. This arcading serves to divide the frieze into a series of symmetrically arranged connecting panels. The outermost pair contains an embossed triton with twin serpentine tail. The succeeding pair contains a seated female figure, that to the left (as viewed) upon a rock, that to the right upon a mythical dog-headed sea-creature. The third pair contains a centre-facing winged victory in flight, that on the left bearing a ?palm branch and ?wreath. That on the right is now almost completely lacking, as is also the central panel, which is represented only by the remains of a vertical dividing bar on the left side.

In contrast to the smooth highly-polished surface of the face, the background of the frieze was 'stippled' with densely-packed dot-punching, giving a matt-textured backing to the embossed figures. The use of sensitive modelling, low- and high-relief embossing, incised and punched details, and shiny and dull surfaces would have provided a very striking impression, and there is no necessity to invoke the reserved silvering as some have done (e.g. Robinson 1975: 110, and pls II–III. Connolly 1988: 23). In fact there is no direct evidence at all for silvering, and if any such overlay had existed traces of it, or of the solder used to hold it in place, would have survived, as they have done on the de-silvered items, cat. nos 7/8, 9, 11–14, 17, 19 and 29–30.

Beneath each ear, just above the angle with the flanged base of the mask, is a rivet with large, flat, circular head. These were undoubtedly for anchoring to the vizor either end of an eyeletted leather fastening strap which encircled the nape of the head-piece (see Robinson 1975: pls II and III).

On the underside of the flanged base of the vizor, beneath the left ear is a *punctim* graffito read by R.P.Wright (1960: 240, no. 21) as CARΛV, but now visible only as CARᏆV. The 'setting-out dots for the top and bottom of an I' which Wright thought he saw after the V are, in fact, corrosion pitting. The more recent conjecture, by Tomlin (Frere and Tomlin 1991: 46, *RIB* 2425.6) of CARINI, though a well-attested *cognomen*, is not compatible with the visible remains.

b) Head piece: a highly ornamented bowl with high projecting peak and broad flanged neck-guard. On the bowl is a spirited combat scene between mounted and foot soldiers. The relief figures, seventeen in total (11 foot, 6 mounted), were embossed from the back and enhanced with incuse lines from the front. Apart from two confronting, but not necessarily combatant, mounted soldiers, there is nothing to suggest the cavalry component is other than a single faction. The foot soldiers, on the other hand, are shown in combat both with the mounted soldiers and with other foot soldiers. All wear the same type of helmet, and all carry in their left hand either an oval or a sub-rectangular shield displaying a variety of cover designs. The

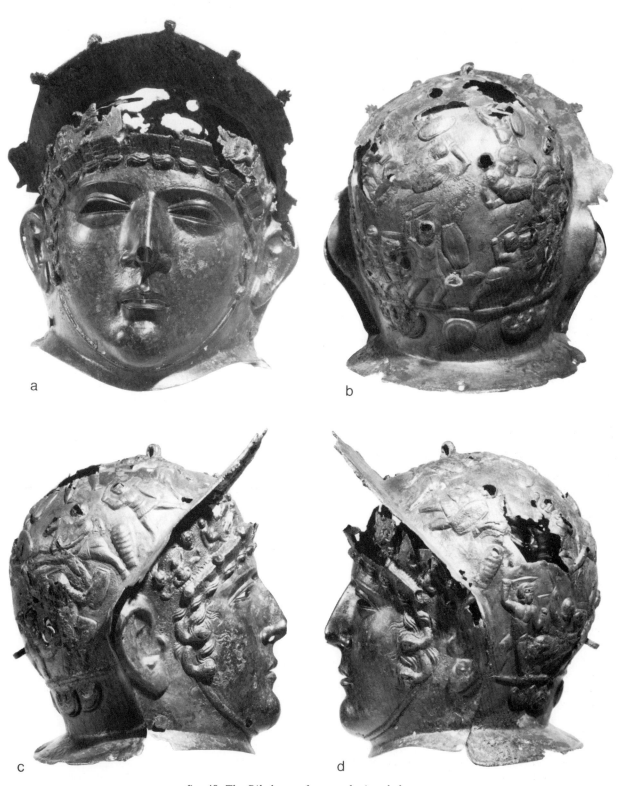

a

b

c

d

fig. 48. The Ribchester face mask vizor helmet.

mounted soldiers brandish variously a sword or spear in the right hand, while the foot soldiers are invariably equipped with a sword. The mounted warriors are all clothed whereas some of the foot soldiers are naked [*contra* Townley's engravings (Townley 1815: pls I and III, by Basire; pl. III also reproduced in Edwards 1992: 15) the naked figures do not have loin cloths. This may have been a concession to 19th century prudishness or perhaps a mis-reading of the stylized musculature of the groin]. The clothing comprises in every case a short-sleeved skirted tunic of normal military form. Pleating of the sleeves and skirt is shown, but no other detail. Cross-hatched (?quilted) saddle cloths, harness straps and *phalerae* are detailed on the mounts. Both naked and clothed foot soldiers are depicted in winning and losing situations, but the cavalry contingent, though assailed, appears supreme. Given that the helmet belonged to a cavalryman this ascendancy was surely intentional.

The scene is wrought in very competent repoussé work, in no sense inferior to the craftsmanship of the mask (and, actually very similar to the relief figures of the crown). Indeed, the adaptation to a hemispherical field of a complex scene with varied action and frequently overlapping figures in high and low relief displays a sophisticated use of space and great technical skill. However, the surface has survived less well than that of the mask so that some of the detail has been coarsened or erased, and most of the heads, which are in highest relief, have been broken away. At all events, the suggestion, variously and persistently made (e.g. Townley 1815: 5; Watkin 1883: 152; Walters 1915: pl. LXXII; Robinson 1975:113), that the mask and head-piece are non-matching, or of different date, or differing quality or by different craftsmen, is unwarranted. In fact, the metal composition of the two components of the helmet (Table 5) is so similar as to imply absolute contemporaneity of manufacture; while the style, garb and equipment of the figures are closely paralleled, *inter alia*, by the low-relief figures of soldiers on the stone column base from Mainz-Kastrich, a re-used block, probably from the *principia* or *praetorium* of the legionary fortress, and dated to the second half of the 1st century AD (Robinson 1975: pls 196–199).

The two ribbed, carrot-shaped objects, one above each ear, contrast with the rest of the repoussé decoration on the upper head-piece in that they are not integrated with the combat scene. A pair of similar objects occupies the same position on the only other two helmets in Robinson's Cavalry Sports B group (Robinson 1975: 112–113, pls 314–317, helmets from Newstead (Pit XXII) and Nicopolis). On those helmets, too, they appear unrelated to the surrounding iconography, and interpretation of the motif has for long perplexed and exercised the imagination of commentators (e.g. Curle 1911: 167; Toynbee 1962: 167; 1964: 293; Edwards 1992: 14). In fact, a mundane explanation is likely, namely that they are skeuomorphs of the plume tubes which occupied precisely this position on Roman helmets of various types (e.g. Robinson 1975: pls 33, 54, 59–61, 69–71, 84–85, 118–119, 137–140, 271). Although they are rare on cavalry helmets it is probably significant that the second of the Newstead Pit XXII cavalry sports helmets has an actual plume holder rather uncomfortably riveted in this position amongst the embossed hair locks (Curle 1911: pls XXVI, 2 and XXIX; Robinson 1975: 114, pls 318–319). Such decorative skeuomorphs are not without parallel on late Iron Age and Roman helmets, the commonest being the 'eyebrows' (cf. Robinson 1975: 42 ff.), which may,

in reality, represent projecting horns (Dr. Simon James *in litt.* who cites Diodorus Siculus V, 30, 2–3 and reliefs on the Arc d'Orange in support of this notion). A unicum, but relevant here, is the unprovenanced Celtic helmet from Britain in the Meyrick Collection (British Museum Reg.no. PRB 1872, 12–13,2) upon the neck-guard of which is what is thought to be an elaborate skeuomorph of a carrying handle (see Jackson, this volume, pp. 67–73).

The high-projecting peak or diadem has a rather rudimentarily finished forward edge, with symmetrically arranged decorative flat projections – a pair of dolphins, one at either end above the ears (that above the left ear lacking; followed by a pair of palmettes; and then three simple knops. The lower face is plain, but the upper face has a lightly-applied dot-punched design – a line and wave-crest motif at the angle with the head-piece, and a large seven-leaf palmette at the centre.

A lower register at the nape of the neck is divided from the combat scene by a plain raised cordon. It comprises a narrow zone or frieze with simple design – a central trophy of a pair of crossed spears behind a circular shield, flanked either side by a pair of overlapping peltae. At the base angle of this frieze there is punched decoration of the type found on the upper face of the diadem – a single dot-punched line, from which a repeating wave-crest or tendril motif 'laps' onto the neck-guard. The edge of the neck-guard has a neatly-finished raised rim, in contrast to the rather rudimentary cutting/filing of the rim of the diadem. There are three symmetrically-placed punched holes near the rim of the neck-guard, that behind the left ear still blocked with the corroded remains of an iron rivet. On the underside of the neck-guard are two incuse graffiti: a) near the centre a *punctim* graffito, read by R.P. Wright (1960: 240, no. 21) as CARAVI, but now visible only as CARAVI and b) towards the right ear a lightly-scored graffito, discerned for the first time: /XIII. The significance of this, presumably the number thirteen or a number in excess of that, is unclear. Scored numbers have been found on other pieces of military equipment including the cavalry helmet from Worthing, Norfolk, upon which the graffito XII was interpreted as a *turma* number (Toynbee and Clarke 1948: 20). However, as observed more recently (Frere and Tomlin 1991: 47, RIB 2425.7), *turmae* were normally signified on equipment graffiti by the name of their commander (Toynbee and Clarke 1948: 25, fn. 32).

There were originally several attachments to the head-piece, the remains of which are as follows:-

1) twin rivets behind the centre base of the diadem for securing the hooked or hinged plate, apparently of iron, but now almost entirely broken away, by means of which the mask was attached to the head-piece (for the mode of attachment see Robinson 1975: figs 130–132, pls 339–342, 359–362 etc.).
2) split spiked loops at top and base of the head-piece probably for securing a detachable crest box.
3) two pierced lugs with butted rings (one lacking) at the back of the neck, behind the ears. The exact position of the lugs was dictated by the embossed figures. Thus they were placed slightly asymmetrically in order to avoid impinging on the fore-quarters of the two horses in that region. One lug is badly damaged and has previously been overlooked, but sufficient of its base survives to confirm its presence. It is here suggested that

their purpose was to fasten a pair of detachable streamers or 'manes' of the type alluded to by Arrian (*Ars Tactica* 34.4; Toynbee 1964: 290; Webster 1969: 154–155; Hyland 1993: 72).

4) three punched holes symmetrically positioned around the rim of the neck-guard, that behind the left ear still blocked with the corroded remains of an iron rivet. They were probably for fastening a leather or textile neck pad/protector (for a wool padding bonded to the inside of the iron vizor-mask helmet from Newstead, see Curle 1911: 170).

The helmet belongs to the Cavalry Sports B group in Robinson's classification (Robinson 1975: 112–113). This group, which also includes helmets from Newstead and Nicopolis, is dated late 1st–early 2nd century AD and is especially characterised by the high projecting peak.

In Maria Kohlert's classification it is Type II (Garbsch 1978: 21), dated first quarter of the 1st century – first quarter of the 2nd century AD, and including cavalry sports helmets from Hellingen, Rapolano, Conflans, Chatalka, Newstead (2), Gaziantep, Hirchova, and Silistra.

Chamfron fittings (figs 47 and 49b)
2. Horse eye-guard. 1814, 7–5, 2. Townley no. 15–16.
   Diam. flange 148 mm.
   Diam. dome 115 mm.
   Ht. 75 mm.
   Wt. 198.8 g. (including restored section)
   Fastening perforations *c.* 3.5 mm. diam.

Intact except for a small area adjacent to a dent in the side and lower dome. The flange, lightly domed, and with a rudimentarily-cut rim, is ornamented with a single grooved line, irregularly applied, between the rim and the circle of six small, roughly-cut fixing holes. A pair of similar lines encircles the band at the base of the dome and the band at its carination. The openwork appears to have been cut from the outside. That of the lower dome has an arcaded appearance, with a row of rectangular piercings surmounted successively by single rows of circular, peltate and triangular piercings. Above the carination the piercings are set on a square grid, carefully adapted to the contours. The unpierced central square retains a lathe centre point. At the carination, where the square grid had to be accommodated to the circular band, the piercings are rhomboid and triangular, and rather irregularly cut. Three of the fixing holes are empty, one is broken, and one is blocked with corrosion. The sixth is obscured by iron corrosion products and a fragment of copper-alloy strip. These are probably part of the original strap loop fastening, and what appear to be organic remains, perhaps leather, are visible in the iron corrosion on the inside face of the flange.

Other known single eye-guards with multiple-perforated flanges have a more elaborately fretted dome (e.g. Garbsch 1978: pl. 46, nos 2–4, from Neuss and Carnuntum), but an unprovenanced example in the Römisch Germanisches Zentralmuseum Mainz (Garbsch 1978: pl. 46, no. 5) is similar to the Ribchester pieces. The Neuss and Carnuntum guards are dated 1st century AD.

Some eye-guards were incorporated in the cheek-pieces of elaborate hinged plate bronze chamfrons (e.g. Garbsch 1978: pls 4–6, 13, 47, from Straubing, Gherla and Pompeii); others were attached directly to the bridle by a set of strap loops (e.g.

Garbsch 1978: pls 45, 47, 1, from Mainz and Pompeii). A third variety appears to have been fastened to (or used in conjunction with) leather chamfrons of the kind found at Newstead and Vindolanda (Curle 1911: 153 ff., pl. XXI; Driel-Murray 1989: 283–292). The Ribchester guards, with their multiple small fastening perforations, almost certainly belong to the latter category. Thus, it is significant that the dome diameters of the two near-complete examples match exactly the eye openings of the most complete Vindolanda chamfron (I). The presence of a possible strap loop fragment on eye-guard no. 2 need not conflict with this identification as the exact method of attachment of eye-guards to leather chamfrons is uncertain and may have been by means of the underlying bridle straps (Driel-Murray 1989: 291–292). For further discussion of chamfrons see cat. no. 6, and IIIc.

3. Horse eye-guard. 1814, 7–5, 3. Townley no. 15–16.
   Diam. flange *c.* 135 mm.
   Diam. dome *c.* 110 mm.
   Ht. *c.* 73 mm.
   Wt. 114.9 g. (including restored section)
   Fastening perforation 3.5 mm. diam.

The greater part of the upper dome survives, but only about one-third of the side and one-quarter of the flange. The flange is narrow and markedly domed with a simply cut rim. A single empty fastening perforation remains, probably one of six, as on no. 2. The openwork of the lower dome has the same arrangement as no. 2, but the gap between the rectangular and circular piercings is breached. The carination is marked by a slender band with shallow groove. Above, as on no. 2, the openwork is arranged on a square grid and is similarly accommodated by rhomboid and triangular piercings at the carination. The centre of the grid in this case is set at the intersection of the bars, where a lathe centre-point is visible. Not a matching pair with no. 2, but possibly used as its partner.

4. Horse eye-guard, fragment. 1814, 7–5, 4. Townley no. 15–16.
   Diam. flange *c.* 135 mm.
   Diam. dome *c.* 110 mm.
   Wt. 38.2 g (including restoration)

In its dimensions virtually identical to no. 3, but in form and patina closer to no. 2, to which it may well have been the pair. Only about one-third of the lightly-domed flange and wall survive, together with a small segment of the arcaded openwork of the lower dome. In style and technique the openwork matches that of no. 2, as do, too, the grooved lines at the base of the dome and the edge of the flange. Two small circular fixing holes remain: one is blocked by corrosion; the other preserves an encircling groove, 8mm. in diameter, which marks the position of the rim of the rivet head which once occupied it. The fragment has, in the past, been joined to no. 5. Although the join cannot be verified it is quite likely that the two fragments are, in fact, from the same eye-guard.

5. Horse eye-guard, fragment. 1814, 7–5, 5. Townley no. 15–16.
   Length 59 mm.
   Ht. 53 mm.
   Wt. 10.1 g (including restoration)

In form, dimensions and patina very similar to nos 2 and 4. It is not the missing fragment from no. 2 and is therefore probably part of no. 4, though a certain join cannot be made.

6. ?Chamfron mount. 1814, 7–5, 6. Townley no. 6.
   Diam. 73 mm.
   Bust ht. 72 mm.
   Wt. 64.2 g.

A discoidal mount with a projecting bust of Minerva. Almost half of the plate is lacking, and the edge of the remaining part is damaged and distorted in several places. Nevertheless, two of the four fastening spikes on the back of the plate survive. They are 39 mm apart. One is broken, but the other, clenched, measures 9.5 mm from base to tip. At the front of the plate two sets of concentric paired grooves enclose the projecting bust, which has been competently, if inelegantly, formed (fig. 49b). The helmet's twin crest, cracked in the centre, and distorted forward, terminates above the forehead in a stylised griffin head. The helmet itself is plain, the grooves on the underside of the rim representing the goddess' hair. The face is of bulging triangular form, with a small chin and thick neck. The eyes, carefully depicted, incorporate lids, brows and pupils. The broad nose is slightly damaged. A pair of drilled hollows emphasise the nostrils. A similar pair of hollows marks the corners of the mouth, while a single hollow in the chin gives prominence to the lower lip. Precisely the same arrangement is followed on the *aegis*, though the nose/mouth region is less successfully rendered. The Gorgon's hair is dramatically windswept. The drapery of Minerva's *chiton* is represented by several rows of punched dashes and commas. The back of the bust is hollow, though the head is filled with mineralised remains, insufficiently dense to be lead, but probably incorporated as packing at the time of manufacture.

This could possibly have been the central mount from a horse's breast band (cf. Driel-Murray 1989: 281 ff.). More probably, however, it was the central forehead component of a composite leather chamfron and may well have formed part of the same suite of chamfron fittings as a pair of the eye-guards (cat. nos 2–5. See also IIIc below). Both of the near-complete leather chamfrons from Newstead and Vindolanda (Chamfron I) have a central circular emplacement of virtually identical size to the mount (Curle 1911: 153–155, pl. XXI; Driel-Murray 1989: 283–290, fig. 5). Furthermore, the number, size, position and spacing of the fastening spikes on the back of the mount also correspond exactly with those of the perforations in the central emplacement of Vindolanda Chamfron I, from which most of the metal trappings had been detached prior to its deposition. The style of the heads on the three remaining metal appliqués of Vindolanda Chamfron I (*contra* Driel-Murray *op. cit.* 290), which are just as likely to be Gorgon heads as Amor or Bacchus heads), displays a naivety similar to that of the Ribchester mount. Certainly, Minerva with her *aegis* was a suitably apotropaic emblem to display prominently on a chamfron, and similar projecting busts are to be found on several of the hinged plate bronze chamfrons (e.g. those from Straubing: Robinson 1975: 192–3, pls 526, 528). The context date of the Newstead chamfron (together with a second, fragmentary, example from Pit CII), all three Vindolanda examples (Driel-Murray 1989: 283), and two fragmentary examples from Carlisle (Winterbottom 1989: 330–334, figs 5–6) – late 1st to early 2nd century AD – accords well with the datable components of the Ribchester hoard.

For individual moulded circular mounts of similar form and size see Menzel 1966: 54, pl. 49, nos 111 and 113, with, respectively, Pan and Medusa as the projecting bust. More particularly, see Garbsch 1978: pls 40–42, mounts from Schwarzenacker, Carnuntum, Miltenberg and Täbris (though all much larger than the Ribchester disc), which show Minerva with *aegis* and eagle-/griffin-headed helmet. Interestingly, there are two mounts of the same size and style from Newstead, one with a lion head and the other a Phrygian-capped bust (Curle 1911: 299, pl. LXXVII, 11 and 13), though neither was found in the same pit as the chamfron.

Harness fittings (figs 47 and 49a)

7. Junction *phalera* and loop fragment. [see also no. 8] 1814, 7–5, 7. Townley no. 19.
   Diam. (excluding projections) 85 mm.
   Length, ring to ring, 108 mm.
   Width of suspension ring, ext. 24.5 mm., int. 14.5 mm.
   Width of loop bow 12.4 mm.
   Wt. *phalera* 79.8 g.
   Wt. loop 14.3 g.

An ornate, but badly-damaged, corroded, and heavily-cleaned junction *phalera*, with a convex back and dished front face (fig. 49a). The perimeter of the flat rim is ornamented with a regular series of small perforated circular projections, five between each of the three rectangular suspension rings, and one on each side of the rings themselves. Two of the rings were for strap loops, but the third held pendant no. 8 below. In the five surviving complete projections a pin of contrasting copper-alloy occupies the perforation. Although the fragmentary state of the *phalera* prevents certainty, the spacing of the circular projections argues against the fourth ring restored in Townley's drawing (Townley 1815: pl. IV, 6), and the *phalera* was probably a two-way strap junction with pendant. Two of the rings are badly damaged, but one retains its crossbar of plump D-shaped cross-section. Both plates of the surviving strap loop (Bishop's Type 5a) are broken, and one side of its bow has sheared away. Nevertheless, its rich decor is evident: the bow had an axial zone of incuse herring-bone decoration flanked by a groove and a channelled moulding, while the front plate was ornamented with a repeating sugar-loaf motif, also flanked by a groove and a channelled moulding. In one of the grooves is the last vestige of a black niello inlay (composed of copper sulphides – see below), which almost certainly originally filled the grooves and background of both decorative incuse zones of the loop (see nos 8 and 35 below). Remains of a *punctim* design or inscription can be seen on the broken end of the plate. The fine decoration of the loop and the complexity of the *phalera* are in contrast to the rough finish of its front face, where file marks on the rim and working marks on the dished surface are still plainly visible, and there is no doubt that a decorative overlay, probably including silver foil, was once attached. A silver-coloured deposit on the front face of a side bar of one of the broken rings is probably the remains of the tin-lead solder. The configuration of the edges of the torn centre of the disc imply a raised central boss *c.* 25 mm in diameter, and this is consistent with the ornamentation of the close and only known parallel piece, a complete *phalera* amongst the suite of harness fittings in Pit LV at Newstead (Curle 1911: 298–299, pl. LXXII, 9 and fig. 43), which still retains its central silver boss and

fig. 49b. ?Chamfron mount, Cat. no. 6.

fig. 49a. Junction phalera and pendant, Cat. nos 7–8.

surrounding moulded silver overlay. Its date is late 1st century AD.

8.   Pendant [for no. 7]. 1814, 7–5, 8. Townley no. 19.
      Width (excluding projections) 77 mm.
      Ht. 69 mm.
      Wt. 52.7 g.

A large horseshoe-shaped pendant belonging to junction *phalera* no. 7. (fig. 49a). Originally highly ornamented, the flat body retains several patches of a silver-coloured deposit, of tin or tin-lead solder, on its front face. The perimeter was embellished with eight evenly-spaced circular projections on either side of the suspension loop. The two surviving examples are of the same form as the *phalera* projections but are smaller and unperforated. The pendant terminals are broken across a horizontal channelled moulding. The suspension loop has a circular eye and is of the same form as the bow of the fragmentary junction loop. Its incuse herring-bone decoration incorporates at least one fragment of black niello inlay, presumably similar in composition to that identified on nos 7 and 35. On the inner edge of the pendant, below the suspension loop, is the torn base of another simpler circular loop (orig. *c.* 8 mm internal diam.), which may once have held a small secondary pendant. Cleaning of the corroded plain back has revealed a number of casting blemishes.

9.   Junction *phalera*. 1814, 7–5, 9. Townley no. 8–11.
      Diam. 90 mm.
      Wt. 121.2 g.

A cast *phalera*, with lightly convex back and shallow saucer-shaped front. Damage, corrosion and heavy, coarse cleaning have removed much detail, but the decorative scheme of the front is broadly intelligible: within the grooved rim the dished annular zone is filled with an incuse repeating stylized floral design, symmetrically disposed, consisting of four palmettes interspersed with four vine motifs. The latter comprise a pendant vine leaf set between a pair of four-fruit grape clusters. All three components are united by tendrils which, by extending to the base of the flanking palmettes, serve also to integrate the whole design. In most places the substrate brass body metal shows, but a few patches of silver-grey solder can be discerned, and just three tiny fragments of the silver foil overlay remain in position. Inlay in the punched part of the design – vine leaves, grape clusters and palmette finials – has survived very poorly. The central zone of the *phalera* is a flat recessed circle with a neatly-channelled border. In the centre is the shank of a small copper rivet which passes through to the back: it presumably once held a decorative stud, the head of which would have encompassed the whole of the central circle. There is an area of damage in the decorated annular zone, comprising a ragged hole and a split extending to the rim, and the heavy cleaning has revealed a patch of copper plugging an adjacent hole. It is not possible to determine whether this repair was to a casting flaw at the time of manufacture or to damage sustained in use, but the former is more probable, especially in view of the flaw repairs to no. 10 below. There are three rings on the rear face – Bishop's (1988) Suspension type 4a (The *phalera* does not conform to any of Bishop's Decorative types but is closest to his type 5c) 1st century AD.

10.   Junction *phalera*. 1814, 7–5, 10. Townley no. 8–11.
      Diam. 90.5 mm.
      Wt. 113.3 g.

In overall dimensions, in the profile of its rear and front faces, and in the decorative arrangement of the front face, this *phalera* is so close to no. 9 as to be regarded as a matching piece. There are four rings on the rear face (in an arrangement that does not conform exactly to Bishop's (1988) suspension typology but is closest to his type 6a/6b). As on no. 9, stripping of the patina of the rear face has revealed evidence of manufacture which would not otherwise have been noticed – an L-shaped casting flaw near the centre, and at least three more irregular-shaped blow-holes near the perimeter were patched with run-in metal of a different composition. File marks are visible at the base of the rings.

11.   Junction *phalera*. 1814, 7–5, 11. Townley no. 8–11.
      Diam. 90.5 mm
      Wt. 122.1 g.

So close to nos 9–10 as to be regarded as a matching piece. The front face is in slightly better condition than no. 10 and preserves fairly extensive patches of grey solder. The rivet is lacking from the central hole. Several repairs to casting flaws can be seen on the back face. As on no. 9 there are three rings on the rear face and in the same arrangement.

12.   Junction *phalera*. 1814, 7–5, 12. Townley no. 8–11.
      Diam. 91 mm.
      Wt. 165 g.

In overall dimensions and form similar to nos 9–11, though a heavier casting with a slightly different front face profile. The decor, too, though it incorporates the same two basic motifs palmette and vine spray – is differently contrived. Thus, its symmetry is based not upon four occurrences of each motif but on a central vine leaf and two opposed palmettes, with a freer arrangement of the vine sprays occupying the greater part of the decorated zone. The apex of the design is a large vine leaf, from either side of which springs a tendril. Side shoots, with thin leaves and grape clusters – 8-fruit and 6-fruit bunches – sprout from the main tendrils before they encompass the palmettes. The tendrils continue, with further side shoots, leaves and grape clusters, and terminate either side of a small palmette. Little, if any, of the inlay has survived, and only traces of the silver overlay/tin-lead solder can be discerned. The central circular recess, slightly smaller than that of no. 9, retains the shank of a rivet. On the rear face were two single rings and a twin ring (Bishop's [1988] Suspension type 6), but one of the single rings has broken off, and there is a repaired blow-hole immediately adjacent to the twin ring.

13.   Junction *phalera*. 1814, 7–5, 13. Townley no. 8–11.
      Diam. 87 mm.
      Wt. 112.7 g.

The same overall form as nos 9–12, but slightly smaller and with a rather more dished front face. Though damaged, the design of the annular zone is clear: it comprises four inverted palmettes interspersed with four upright examples. Filling the interstitial spaces are 8-fruit and 3-fruit grape clusters, vestigial remains of the vine spray motif. In places, though not consistently, a vine tendril encircles the palmette and unites it with the grape clusters. Tinning/solder survives over most of

the surface, and inlay is preserved in a few places – red (copper) in the fruits and grey-black (?niello) in the palmette scrolls. The central rivet hole is empty. On the rear face are three rings (Bishop's [1988] Suspension type 4a).

14. *Phalera*. 1814, 7–5, 14. Townley no. 12–14.
   Diam. 44.5 mm.
   Wt. 29.0 g.

A scaled-down version of nos 9–13, with the same profile – a lightly convex back and shallow saucer-shaped front. This example has been heavily cleaned revealing rather indistinctly the eroded decoration of the front face, a thrice-repeated stylized leaf-and-berry motif. There are extensive remains of a silver-coloured coating presumably of solder, and traces of black inlay. The central stud is lacking. On the back the broken hinge plate of a pendant is corroded in position on the pivot pin between the two hinge flanges. The two parallel flattened strap loops above would have accommodated a strap of maximum 16.5 × 5.0 mm cross-section. They are Bishop's (1988) Suspension type 2a.

A 1st century AD type, cf. e.g. Wroxeter (Bushe-Fox 1916: 30, pl. XVIII, 30) and Fremington Hagg (Webster 1971: 109–110, fig. 9, 2 (scale 1:1 not 1:2 as stated).

15. *Phalera*. 1814, 7–5, 15. Townley no. 12–14.
   Diam. 44 mm.
   Wt. 32.5 g.

Overall form and dimensions as no. 14. The ribbed rim and central stud are visible, but corrosion products obscure the decor of the front face. On the back is a pair of pierced hinge flanges, one broken across the eye, the other distorted, on which a pendant originally pivoted. Above are two flattened strap loops. They converge away from the hinge and do not, therefore, conform to Bishop's typology of suspension modes, though they broadly compare to his types 2a,2d and 2e (Bishop 1988: 94–5, 139, fig. 41). Their slot would have accommodated a strap of maximum 16 × 15.5 mm cross-section.

Dona militaria (fig. 47)

Apart from their association with several items of cavalry sports equipment there are a number of other factors – size, shape, fastening holes, and the presence of lead or tin/lead solder – which demonstrate with virtual certainty that these discs (cat. nos 16–20) were the backing plates for a set of decorative *phalerae*, one of the standard awards of the *dona militaria*. Such sets, commonly of nine discs, but also depicted in groups of seven or five, were, in combination with *torques* and *armillae*, the variety of military decorations accessible to ordinary soldiers and junior officers up to, and including, the rank of centurion. Maxfield (1981: 91ff. and fig. 11), drawing on iconographic, literary and archaeological evidence, has established the form of the *phalerae* and reconstructed the leather strap harness by which they were worn on the recipient's chest.

By the Principate the *phalerae* were of plated copper alloy and, though some may have been of quite simple appearance, the set from Lauersfort, Germany, demonstrates how rich the high-relief silver foil decoration could be (Maxfield 1981: pl. 15). The silver foil overlay of the Lauersfort *phalerae* was lapped over the edge of the backing discs in a manner reminiscent of, and consistent with, the remains seen on the Ribchester *phalerae* nos 16, 17 and 19. Much closer in appearance to the

Ribchester examples is the set of backing plates from Pit XXII at Newstead, which comprises one crescentic and eight circular discs (Curle 1911: 174ff. pl. XXXI; Maxfield 1981: pl. 16, 93–95, fig. 11). The position and form of the rivet holes used to fasten them to the strap harness is mirrored by those surviving on the Ribchester plates. If, as is probable, the Newstead *phalerae* had silver foil overlays like the Lauersfort set, then they were removed prior to deposition – it is noteworthy that two iron helmets from the same pit had certainly been de-silvered before burial (Curle 1911: 166 and 169, pl. XXVI, 1–2 and pl. XXIX). That the Ribchester discs, too, had once had a silver overlay is implied by the presence of lead or tin/lead solder on one face. [For further evidence of de-silvering see cat. nos 7–13]. The Newstead discs are all inscribed on their reverse with the lightly-scratched ownership mark DOMIITI ATTICI (Frere and Tomlin 1991: 52–3, RIB 2427.4–12). Unfortunately there is no coherence to the various graffiti preserved on the fragmentary Ribchester pieces. Unlike their counterparts, the military medals of more recent times, *dona phalerae* were probably returned to the unit on the discharge or death of the soldier who had won them (Maxfield 1981: 95). Few have been positively identified, and of those the Lauersfort set lacks a dated burial context (though stylistically the *phalerae* should date to the earlier 1st century AD), and only the Newstead discs provide a secure deposition date – late 1st century AD.

16. *Phalera*. 1814, 7–5, 16. Townley no. 21–24.
   Diam. 124 mm.
   Thickness 0.3 mm.
   Wt. 26.5 g.

A plain circular disc of thin copper-alloy sheet. There is a pair of small circular perforations near the rim, less than a third of which survives. The adjacent area is iron-stained. Dishing of the margins indicates the face from which one of the perforations was punched. On the other (back) face has been scratched somewhat off-centre a roughly equilateral triangle, with sides (partially discontinuous) of about 70 mm. Corrosion products on both faces obscure any further markings, but filed manufacture marks can be discerned around the rim. In one area of the rim margin on the back face the corrosion products, viewed in raking sunlight, can be seen to preserve what appears to be the impression of metal sheet or foil turned over from the front face for a distance of *c.* 4–6 mm from the edge. A similar feature is also discernible on nos 17 and 19. and may be compared with the folded-over silver foil overlays which still survive on the Lauersfort *phalerae* (see e.g. Maxfield 1981: pl. 15b).

17. *Phalera* 1814, 7–5, 17. Townley no. 21–24.
   Diam. 104 mm.
   Thickness 0.3-0.4 mm.
   Wt. 22.5 g.

Another, smaller, example retaining two small perforations near the rim, almost a half of which is intact. As on no. 16 the direction of punching of the perforations is evident. On the front face is a dot-punched centre point and at least two scratched lines. More significantly, a silvery coating (the remains of a lead or tin-lead solder) is visible beneath the corrosion products over most of the face and can be seen to extend a distance of *c.* 5–6 mm onto the back face in the one section clear of corrosion products. Raking light across the back face reveals a set of three parallel scratched lines 12.5 mm and 10 mm apart, extending for a distance of at least 55 mm, and with the hint of a *punctim* inscription between.

18. *Phalera*. 1814, 7–5, 18. Townley no. 21–24.
    Diam. 115 mm.
    Thickness 0.3 mm.
    Wt. 12.5 g.

Another example, which preserves only two arcs of its cut rim, and no certain perforations. What remains of the disc is in good condition with a brown-golden patina, and the dot-punched centre-point is visible on one face.

19. *Phalera*. 1814, 7–5, 19. Townley no. 21–24.
    Diam. 124 mm.
    Thickness 0.2-0.3 mm.
    Wt. 11.8 g.

Another example retaining two small perforations (one in a fold-damaged section of the edge), and little more than a quarter of its rim. As on nos 16–17 the direction of punching of the perforations is evident. The dot-punched centre-point is visible on the back face upon which can also be discerned several incised lines and hints of a *punctim* inscription. A silvery coating (the remains of a lead or tin-lead solder) is visible over most of the front face and on a small section of the back face edge.

20. *Phalera*. 1814, 7–5, 20. Townley no. 21–24.
    Diam. *c*. 95 mm.
    Thickness 0.3-0.4 mm
    Wt. 7.6 g.

Another example, patina as no. 18, with a lunate segment cut from one edge, as evidenced by the reverse curve of its centre base section. Rather less than a quarter of the convex rim survives, retaining only one perforation which is blocked with corrosion. Nothing other than a pair of short scratched lines is visible on the front face, but on the back face, as on no. 17, there is a series of three parallel lines, 8 mm and 9 mm apart, running a distance of at least 32 mm with a possible transverse line at one end. There are a number of punched dots within this zone.

For similarly shaped discs in the *phalera* sets of *dona militaria* from Newstead and Lauersfort see Maxfield 1981: pls 15a and 16a.

Amulet (fig. 47)

21. Boar's tusk amulet. 1814, 7–5, 21. Townley no. 25.
    Length across chord 93 mm.
    Perimeter length 148 mm.
    Wt. 19.8 g.

Desiccation since discovery has caused the outer and inner face to contract differentially resulting in the splitting of the tusk into two pieces. Additionally, exfoliation has destroyed part of the surface of the convex face. At the broad end green-staining of the cut edges attests to the former presence of a copper-alloy mount.

On account of its warlike nature and virility the wild boar was a potent symbol frequently associated with the military. The tusks – the essence of the animal – were often perforated or

mounted as amulets as, for example, at Segontium (Casey and Davies 1993: 202–3, fig. 10.19, 451: perforated), Richborough (Bushe-Fox 1949: 141–2, pl. XLVI, 173–4: two examples with bronze mounts) and North Wraxall (*Archaeol. Journ.* 18, 1861: 146–147; a pair of tusks with central bronze mount). For a boar's tusk set in an ornate bronze pedestalled mount terminating in a boar's head and foreparts, unprovenanced; and for a similar example, lacking its tusk, from Frenz, Germany, see Menzel 1986: 173–4, pl. 147 nos 480 and 481. Both are regarded as wagon parts (yoke attachments), while the simpler mounted variety and those made entirely of bronze (e.g. Menzel 1966: 112–113, pl. 84, no. 274, from Trier) were primarily intended as horse amulets, as was, probably, the present example. For representations of boars' tusks on chamfrons from Eining and Straubing see Garbsch 1978: fig. 5, A6, B18, B19, pl. 5.2; and Dixon and Southern 1992: pl. 31.

Vessels (fig. 47)

22. Bath saucer. 1814, 7–5, 22. Townley no. 2.
    Bowl diam. 133 m.
    Length with handle 232 mm.
    Depth 37 mm.
    Wt. 242.8g.

Complete, except for parts of the wall and chips in the rim. Patches of corrosion, quite extensive on the interior base, have etched into and pitted the metal, but in many places the original surface, now a dull golden-brown, is visible. The small slender handle is plain except at the terminal where, on the upper face, there is a simple grooved moulding and a finial in the form of a small knob on a pedestal. Beneath is a 'keyhole' slot for suspension. The finely-profiled bowl has punched arcaded decoration on the horizontal inner ledge and a simpler segmented motif on the outer wall of the rim: both are slightly irregularly applied. In conformity to the type (non-culinary) there is no evidence of tinning of the interior. A lathe centre point is just visible within a corrosion patch. The integral base has a low flared footring enclosing two finely-worked concentric raised rings and a central knop. Working marks are most evident on the underside of the rim. A silvery deposit on the inner surface adjacent to two of the damaged wall areas may be the remains of ancient soldered repairs.

A 1st–early 2nd century AD type. Cf. Willers 1907: 72–3, fig. 42 for the type, notably from Pompeii. Also den Boesterd 1956: 14–15, no. 39. Other examples from British sites include Wheeler 1930: 117–118, fig. 40, no. 3 (of iron) from London; Bosanquet in Wheeler 1926: 107–111, fig. 53, from Brecon fort, handle only, of L. Ansius Epaphroditus, in a late 1st century AD context; and Eggers 1966: 106 no. 38, 136, fig. 36 from Chesterford.

23. Bath saucer. 1814, 7–5, 23. Townley no. 3.
    Bowl diam. 158 mm.
    Length with handle 265 mm.
    Max. surviving depth 28 mm.
    Wt. 223.6 g.

As no. 22 but a little larger and less well preserved: the rim is fractured and slightly sprung, the base is lacking, and corrosion products adhere to much of the surviving surface. The slender handle, quite plain and rather rudimentarily finished, has a 'keyhole' slot for suspension (blocked with iron corrosion products) and a knobbed finial with adjacent moulding of the upper surface. In contrast to the rather indifferent workmanship of the handle finial, the rim of the pan is finely profiled and has a neatly-applied incuse decoration on the horizontal inner ledge and on the outer wall. The latter, an arcaded (or developed ovolo) motif, shows signs of wear. Flaws in manufacture are present both on the handle and the pan. The majority are tiny insignificant blowholes. A split below the rim coincides with a slight dent and was probably the result of ancient damage.

1st–early 2nd century AD. For references see no. 22.

24. Saucepan. 1814, 7–5, 24. Townley no. 4.
    Pan diam. 192 mm.
    Length with handle 348 mm.
    Max. surviving depth 33 mm. ⎫
                                   ⎬ see no. 25
    Wt. 378.1 g.   ⎭

The handle and rim are damaged, and only fragments of the thin pan wall are still attached. For the pan base and wall fragment, which once belonged but are now separate, see no. 25. Corrosion products on the upper face of the handle at its junction with the pan appear to have derived from another copper-alloy object corroded to the pan, perhaps one of the bath saucers nested into the vessel and touching at that point. Otherwise, the original surface is generally intact and clear of corrosion and accretions. The underside of the large handle is plain. A close examination revealed no trace of a punched ownership mark. The margin of its upper face is embellished with a deep incuse groove, which tapers away onto the pan rim and merges with the peripheral groove of the discoidal handle end. The faintly impressed stamp near the handle end is set in a rectangular cartouche running axially towards the pan. Neither end is now visible, but the reading]CONP[can be made out. As R.P. Wright observed (*Britannia* 1,1970: 311, no. 23) there is no name starting with these four letters in Kajanto's *Cognomina*, and the stamp is still a unicum. However, a saucepan handle from Oberhof, Thüringen is stamped COM[(Willers 1907: 90, no. 171). The handle disc has a worn corded border and a large circular eye. One side is badly eaten by corrosion. Below the lightly convex overhanging rim is a band of punched decoration on the bulging pan wall. The design, a row of small rings above a broad palisade, is the same as that found on some of the pans stamped by P.Cipius Polybius (see e.g. Willers 1907: 77, fig. 44, no.1). Tinning of the inner wall face extends over the rim and a corresponding distance onto the handle.

A 1st–2nd century AD type. Cf. Willers 1907: 77–78, figs 44–45, for the type, notably from Pompeii. Also den Boesterd 1956: 10–11, nos 25–29, esp. no. 27 (pl. II, 27), probably from Nijmegen, 1st–2nd century AD, which den Boesterd regards as Capuan (xx–xxi and 10–11). For other examples from Britain with the same palisaded decoration see Eggers 1966: 109, no. 76, 127, fig. 22 esp. b, from the Lamberton Moor, Berwickshire hoard; Eggers 1966: 107, no. 54, 131, fig. 28a, from the Sittenham, Yorkshire hoard. Also from South Shields, Kingsholm, and Whitehill, Berwickshire (Eggers 1966: 108–9, no. 66, 122, fig. 15; 104, no. 26, 157, fig. 58, no. 26; 109, no. 74, 161, fig. 62, no. 74).

25. Saucepan base. 1814, 7–5, 25. Townley no. 5.
    Base diam. 112 mm.
    Max. surviving diam. of pan 196 mm.
    Max. surviving depth 63 mm.   ⎫
                                          ⎬ see no. 24
    Wt.300.9 g. [after removal of thin section] ⎭

The flat, deeply-ringed base (part lacking) and part of the lower wall of saucepan no. 24. Corrosion of the base is advanced, heavy and extensive. Nevertheless, the original fine workmanship is evident. A simple moulded channel separates the flared base from the strongly-bulging, plain wall. The interior surface of the wall and lightly omphaloid base preserve large areas of tinning.

26. Mortarium. 1814, 7–5, 26. Townley no. 17.
    Diam. 324 mm.
    Max. height 99 mm.
    Wt. 2787 g.

A complete example, now a creamy-brown colour, with the clearly impressed stamp of Boriedo on the flange to one side of the pouring spout. Both the base and interior show signs of heavy/prolonged usage, and the remaining grits in the interior are worn smooth. Small patches of copper-alloy corrosion products are present in four places on the underside but are nowhere visible on the interior surface. Four short parallel incised lines on the rim (at 11 o'clock, with the spout as 6 o'clock), which appear to have been cut intentionally, may have signified the number IIII.

Kay Hartley writes:

'A complete mortarium in micaceous, fine-textured fabric, intended to be cream but very badly discoloured. The upper surface of the flange has some concentric scoring combined with tiny fragments of flint, pinkish and transparent quartz, opaque red-brown material and rare flecks of galena. The whole of the internal surface would originally have been treated in the same way but heavy wear has removed all but the last vestiges just below the bead.

The single potter's stamp, impressed diagonally across the flange, clearly reads **BORIEDO F** with **DO** ligatured, for Boriedo *fecit*. Another stamp of his has been recorded from Castleford in a first-century context (publication forthcoming). Boriedo was one of several contemporary potters making similar mortaria, who were active in Gallia Belgica in the second half of the first century; the optimum period for Boriedo is probably c. AD 60–90.'

Analysis by Michael Hughes (British Museum Dept. of Scientific Research):

'In view of the extensive series of spectrographic analyses of Romano-British mortaria by Richards and Hartley (1960) and Hartley and Richards (1965), and the more recent neutron activation analyses by Rush (1993), it was felt to be of interest to analyse the Ribchester example and compare it with the reference analyses already available.

A sample of the body material was obtained with a diamond-embedded abrasive wheel used on a broken edge of the mortarium, and the sample was then weighed and prepared for analysis using the lithium metaborate fusion technique described by Hughes, Cowell and Craddock (1976). A Perkin-Elmer Model 306 atomic absorption spectrometer was used for the analysis and this showed that it contained 14.9 % Al_2O_3, 1.28 % TiO_2, 2.06 % total Fe_2O_3, 0.014 % MnO, 0.58 % MgO, 0.61 % CaO, 1.98 % K_2O, 0.295 % Na_2O, 0.0082 % Cr_2O_3 and 0.0015 % NiO. The analytical precision for all these elements (except manganese, chromium and nickel) is about 3–5% relative, but for the latter elements is about 10% because of their low concentration.

Rush (1994) has analysed Roman mortaria by neutron activation analysis: his results for mortaria from Gallica Belgica all show the presence of 9.9–18.2% calcium, in contrast to the Ribchester example which contains less than 1% calcium. It is extremely unlikely that burial conditions for the Ribchester mortarium have allowed the almost complete leaching of a high calcium content without destroying the fabric. Mortaria from production centres in Britain did produce low-calcium fabrics (Rush 1993) but the analysis of the Ribchester mortarium does not at present throw any light on its place of production. The discrepancy between the analysis result and archaeological assignment to Gallia Belgica has no obvious explanation.'

Unidentified objects (fig. 47)

27. ?Mount. 1814, 7–5, 27. Townley no. 18.
    Stem diam. 26 mm.
    Ht. 24 mm.
    Wt. 36.6 g.

A heavily mineralised brass fragment from a decorative and composite object. The remains comprise a splayed, capital-like hollow component with circular-sectioned stem, twin-ridge moulded decoration and a broken scalloped edge (nowhere complete), secured to a fragmentary umbonate sheet by a central rivet. The rivet has a burred-over head on the sheet side, but its shank is broken at the other end. Tiny fragments of gold overlay (confirmed by analysis) are visible within the corrosion products of the decorative component.

Townley suggested that this piece, together with no. 28, was part of the stem of a candelabrum, but it could equally well have been part of an ornamental horse trapping.

28. ?Terminal. 1814, 7–5, 28. Townley no. 18.
    Rod diam. a) 14 mm. b) 16 mm.
    Reel diam. a) 24 mm. b) 25.5 mm.
    Reel ht. 17 mm.
    Wt. 55.3 g.

A copper-alloy and lead fragment from a decorative composite object. The remains comprise a cast, copper-alloy, moulded, reel-like ring or collar held on a circular-sectioned rod of lead encased in thin copper-alloy sheet. Both components are tapered, and one end of the rod is certainly broken, but the marked splaying of the casing at the other end and the apparently unbroken surface of the lead core imply a terminal or junction at or near that point. Townley regarded this as part of the stem of a candelabrum, but it is too fragmentary for certainty.

II. *Located objects not in Townley's published list*

Saddle and harness fittings (fig. 47)

29. Saddle plate. 1814, 7–5, 29.
    Width/length 113 mm.
    Diam. of perimeter rib 96.1 mm.
    Thickness *c*. 0.9 mm.
    Wt. 58.1 g.

The greater part of what was almost certainly originally a square plate, although with only parts of two adjacent sides surviving absolute certainty is not possible. Symmetrically placed within the plain edges of the square is a repoussé low umbonate disc with a raised perimeter rib and an omphaloid centre. Still corroded in position is a hollow-domed stud (head diam. 17 mm), apparently of iron, with a fragment of iron plate corroded to its head. A silver-grey coating, probably the remains of a lead or lead-tin solder, which evidently originally covered the whole front face of the plate, is still extensively preserved. In several places are remnants of the silver foil which it bonded. No identifiable rivets or rivet holes survive on the edges of the plate.

The plate is Bishop's (1988) Type 3b. For similar plates from Doorweerth see Brouwer 1982: pls 8–9, esp. pl. 8, no. 195. For their use see *ibid*. pl.11, no. 3; Bishop 1988: 115, fig. 31; and Connolly 1988: 26. In all cases the side of the saddle cloth is decked with a pair of large plates (like nos 29 and 30), each flanked top and bottom by a smaller, rectangular, plate with a pair of small repoussé discs. Examples of the latter type were found at Newstead (Curle 1911: pl. LXXII). They were from Pit LV, which also yielded the closest parallel to junction *phalera* no. 7 above. For the likely mode of attachment of saddle plates see Bishop 1988: 110, fig. 28. Both the Doorweerth and Newstead examples date to the late 1st century AD.

30. Saddle plate. 1814, 7–5, 30.
    Width/length of plate, if square, *c*. 113 mm.
    Diam. of perimeter rib 96.1 mm.
    Thickness *c*. 0.9 mm.
    Wt. 20.6 g.

A corner fragment from a plate of identical form and dimensions to no. 29, and very probably its pair. This, example: however, has the addition of an engraved arc within the perimeter rib and traces of ?niello decoration in the silver foil. (It is likely that no. 29 also had niello decoration which is no longer discernible in the very fragmentary foil). There are also hints of punched graffiti on the two surviving edges. Two simple rivets or fixing pins survive on one edge. They are 34 mm apart, and the ?complete one is 7.5 mm long.

31. *Phalera* and pendant. 1814, 7–5, 31.
    Diam. of *phalera* 43.2 mm.
    Width of pendant 55.2 mm.
    Wt. 59.2 g.

Form and dimensions of the *phalera* as nos 15, 32 and 33. The upper part is broken (not necessarily in antiquity), and corrosion products obscure the front face, but the ribbed rim and prominent domed head of the central stud are visible. The front face of the large trifid pendant is also encrusted with corrosion products, but the hanging acorns, midrib of the central oak leaf, and traces of silver overlay can be discerned. Of the strap loops on the rear face of the *phalera* only the basal stubs flanking the flanged pendant hinge remain. Their rangement, nonetheless, would appear to have conformed to that on *phalera* nos 15, 32 and 33. The pendant is Bishop's (1988) Type 1. For its Neronian-Flavian dating and distribution see Oldenstein 1985: 86–88 and fig.1.

32. *Phalera* and pendant. 1814, 7–5, 32.
    Diam. of *phalera* 42.9 mm.
    Width of pendant 52.9 mm.
    Wt. 76.8 g.

Although the trifid pendant is a little smaller than that of no. 31, this *phalera*/pendant set is otherwise virtually identical in every respect and was undoubtedly part of the same suite of trappings. As on no. 31, corrosion products obscure most of the front face of both components, but elements of the foliate design can be discerned in places. The pendant is Bishop's (1988) Type 1.

33. *Phalera*. 1814, 7–5, 33.
    Diam. 44 mm.
    Wt. 23.9 g.

Form and dimensions as nos 15, 31 and 32. Heavy corrosion products cover the front face, but the ribbed rim and relatively large domed head of the central stud are visible. On the back face the thin strap loops are corroded, broken and distorted, as are the pierced hinge flanges for the missing pendant. The arrangement of the strap loops is as no.15.

34. Junction *phalera* and loops. 1814, 7–5, 34.
    Diam. 85.6 mm.
    Length of complete loop 62 mm.
    Wt. 136.9 g. (includes loops).

The same overall form and condition as nos 9–12, but in size and decor very similar to no.13. The design of the annular zone comprises four inverted palmettes symmetrically interspersed with four upright examples. Filling the interstitial spaces are 8–fruit and 5–fruit clusters, vestigial remains of the vine spray motif. All eight palmettes are linked by a sinuous encircling vine tendril which unites them with the fruit clusters. Only slight traces of solder and inlay survive. A flat-headed copper rivet remains corroded in the central hole. It shows that the now missing applied central disc was a maximum of 2.5 mm. thick. On the rear face are two single rings and a twin ring, in an arrangement similar to no. 12 and Bishop's (1988) Suspension type 6. Junction loops of Bishop's type 6a remain in three of the rings – a complete example in one of the single rings, and two fragmentary examples in the twin ring. Solder survives on the decorated front face of all three, and silver overlay on one, but there is no trace of inlay in the impressed foliate design. The two rivets which secured the plain, thin back plate to the front plate remain in position and evidence a strap thickness of 3.5 mm.

35. Junction loop. 1814, 7–5, 35.
    Width of loop bow 12.7 mm.
    Width of loop front plate 21.2 mm.
    Wt. 27.0 g.

Both front and back plates are fragmentary, the latter also distorted, and the bow is slightly damaged. However, sufficient survives to show that the loop was virtually identical to the loop of junction *phalera* no. 7, except that the bow interior was much larger. Like no. 7 and no. 8 the bow has an axial

zone of incuse herring-bone decoration flanked by a groove and a channelled moulding, while the front plate was ornamented with a compressed running-scroll motif, also flanked by a groove and a channelled moulding. A niello inlay (of copper sulphides) survives partially in the herring-bone and grooved decoration and extensively in the running scroll. The loop is Bishop's (1988) Type 5a.

Although the size and decoration are slightly different to those of the loop on no. 7, it is quite possible that both belong to the same *phalera*. No. 35 certainly fits the suspension rings of no. 7.

III. Unlocated objects in Townley's published list

a) Large bronze dish. Townley no. 7:-
'The remains of a bason, twelve inches in diameter and three inches deep. From its similarity to ancient basons, which were appropriated to religious uses, this probably had the same destination'. Watkin (1883: 151), who describes it as 'Portions of a bronze basin, which, when entire, has been of the annexed form' shows a large flat-based dish with steep wall and simple everted rim. A sheet metal vessel, evidently already incomplete at the time Townley acquired it, would have been very vulnerable and it was probably reduced to fragments before or after it passed to the British Museum.

b) Piece of wood with mortise. Townley no. 20:-
'A piece of wood ten inches long, which has a mortice, and may have been part of a chair, or the handle of an utensil' Neither Townley nor Watkin illustrated the piece, which, without effective conservation, would probably have deteriorated quickly. Many possible identifications present themselves, not least part of a wooden box or chest in which the hoard might have been contained, but with such a tantalisingly brief description speculation is fruitless. Edwards (1992: 24) has recorded details of a second missing wooden fragment supposedly from the hoard.

c) Piece of leather with perforations. Townley no. 26:-
'A piece of leather, which, by the many perforations it has in regular lines, appears to have been a lining fastened with small nails.' There is no illustration of this fragment which is likely to have suffered the same fate as b). Speculation as to its identification is equally fruitless. However, the presence of eye-guards and a probable chamfron fitting in the hoard, together with the similarity between Townley's description of the numerous fastening holes, and the appearance of the studded leather chamfrons from Newstead and Vindolanda, make an identification as part of a chamfron a distinct possibility. Edwards (1992: 21) has noted a second possible chamfron discovery at Ribchester.

COMPOSITION (PTC)

Almost all of the major items of copper alloy from Ribchester were quantitatively analysed (Tables 4 and 5). Where composite, (the helmet, and trappings cat. nos 7/8/31 and 32) each component was sampled, and both of the two major surviving fragments of saucepan no. 24/25 were also analysed. The mainly unpublished analyses of some other relevant bronzes found in Britain have also been reported (Table 6), together with a re-publication of the analyses of the trappings from Fremington Hagg (Craddock *et al.* 1973, supplemented by an additional analysis) (Table 6).

Phalerae cat. nos 16–20 and the saddle plates cat. nos 29–30 are of thin sheet metal that was clearly in a very corroded state when found and was subsequently rigor-ously cleaned. One face of each piece had been soldered to hold silver foil, traces of which have survived. All of these factors meant that it would have been impossible to have obtained a sample that reflected the original composition of the sheet metal itself and, thus, only qualitative analysis by energy dispersive X-ray fluores-cence spectrophotometry on the conserved surfaces was performed, to determine the main alloy type of the body metal, solder and overlay.

The metal was sampled with a modeller's drill mounted with a size 60 (one mm) diameter hardened steel bit. Approximately 10 mg of uncorroded turnings were collected for each analysis. The analyses were per-formed by atomic absorption spectrophotometry, details of which method are given in Hughes *et al.* (1976). The analyses have a precision of ± 2% for the major ele-ments, and approximately ± 30% for the minor and trace elements, the error rising sharply as the detection limit is approached. The detection limit for all the elements quoted in the Table is 0.01 weight % in the metal, except for arsenic and tin for which the limit was of the order of 0.05%. Note that for items 25 (saucepan), 4 (eye guard), 35 (junction loop) and 7 (junction *phalera*) gold and arsenic were not determined.

There is a wide range of composition, although some consistency within types is displayed.

A. *The Vessels* (Table 4)

The cast saucepan and bath saucers are all of leaded bronze. The now separate rim/ handle and base of sauce-pan 24/25 were both analysed and show some variation in both major and trace element composition even though they should belong to the same casting. A series of these pans and other cast vessels or casseroles principally from the forts of the Limes in the Netherlands, now in the G.M. Kam Museum, Nijmegen (den Boesterd 1956), has been analysed (den Boesterd and Hoekstra 1965). Other examples from Britain have been analysed, including a previously unpublished patera handle, believed to date from the first century AD, in Peterborough Museum (Table 4), some bowls from Wales (Boon 1970) and another example found recently at Ormsthorpe, Notts., also of first century date (Bishop and Freeman 1993). The latter example had about 20% of tin but only traces of lead. Although these cast vessels show considerable variation in their tin and lead content, the combined tin and lead content is usually in the region of 20–25%. In

general terms these are high values, although Roman cast bronzes often have a high lead content (Craddock 1985 and forthcoming).

The *Mappae Clavicula*, compiled in the early Medi-eval period but which retains very clear echoes of Ro-man practice, contains many insights into classical met-allurgy, including one which seems relevant to the composition of the Ribchester vessels. Recipe 79 con-cerns an alloy known as *caldarium*, that is for cooking vessels. This was made up from one part lead to five parts bronze (Smith and Hawthorne 1974: 38). Pliny (*Natural History* 34.94; Rackham 1952: 197) merely remarks that *caldarium* is brittle and only suitable for making castings, which, of course, would be true with that composition. The alloy would have been very fluid when molten with a long freezing range, and thus would have facilitated the casting of the thin-walled vessels by ensuring that the metal completely filled the narrow space between the mould walls before setting. The lead would also act as an internal lubricant in the metal, making the casting much easier to machine, although in the case of the Roman *patera* this seems to have been confined to minor turning of the sides and polishing on the lathe (see below).

B. *The Military Brasses* (Tables 5 and 6)

The remainder of the metal items from the hoard are of brass, that is an alloy of copper and zinc, in this instance usually with some lead, and minor quantities of tin. The majority of the trappings, with the exception of cat. no. 7/35 have rather similar compositions, around 15% of zinc, 1–3% of tin, 7–10% of lead, and broadly similar, although quite unexceptional trace element contents. The lead content is significantly higher than that found in any of the other comparable trappings from Britain (Tables 5 and 6) or from Xanten in Germany (Jenkins 1985). The compositions are sufficiently close to suggest, that with the exception of trapping no. 7/35, the pieces were made from the same stock of metal. This is not to argue that trapping no. 7/35 does not belong to the Ribchester group as a whole. Its composition is very similar to that of the helmet, the analysed eye guard (no. 4), and, perhaps more significantly, to the small hammered loop on trap-ping no. 34, the cast roundel of which is of the leaded brass alloy of the remainder of the trappings.

It is perhaps significant that the postulated chamfron mount (cat. no. 6) is of the same alloy as the trappings, and this provides additional evidence that the Ribchester metalwork originates from one set of equipment.

The analysed trappings from Fremington Hagg and from Xanten also show a close internal compositional consistency. The trappings from Fremington Hagg (Table 6) have similar zinc and tin contents to those from Ribchester, but much less lead and the Xanten trap-pings have more zinc and only traces of lead or tin. This consistency of composition amongst the variously

Table 4. Composition of Cast Vessels from Ribchester etc.

Cat. No.	Description	Cu	Zn	Pb	Sn	Fe	Sb	Ni	Au	Ag	As	Bi
Ribchester												
22	bath saucer	77.5	.1	10.90	9.40	.06	.15	.035		.050		
23	bath saucer	74.5		20.30	5.20	.10	.15	.030		.060	.10	.030
24	saucepan handle and rim	74.0		12.20	12.20	.10	.15			.070	.10	.010
Peterborough Museum												
	patera handle	77.5	2.8	11.30	8.90	.25	.16	.025		.035	.05	.030

The analyses have a precision of ±2% for the major elements and approximately ±30% for the minor and trace elements, the error rising sharply as the detection limit is approached.

The detection limit for the elements quoted in the table is 0.01 weight % in the metal, except for As and Sn for which the limit is of the order of 0.05%.

analysed groups is of some help in resolving the problem of the extra trappings 29–35 which, although they do not appear in Townley's published list, have always been associated with the find. Trappings 32, 34 and 35 were analysed, and the main, cast parts of each except 35 was of the same leaded brass alloy as the unambiguous Ribchester pieces. Junction loop no. 35 is of brass with very little lead or zinc and is stylistically very similar to the loop on junction *phalera* cat. no. 7, which is certainly part of the hoard. That they do indeed belong together is confirmed by the almost identical composition of cat. no. 35 and the two analysed components of cat. no. 7. The loop on trapping no. 34 is also of pure undiluted brass with only traces of other metals, but as explained above this is a hammered component, where the lead content would have been detrimental. The general appearance, especially the distinctive corrosion on the other uncertain pieces, cat. nos 31 and 32, are very similar to the analysed pieces and leaves no serious doubt that they too belong with the rest of the trappings from the hoard.

The eye guards, the helmet and trapping no. 7/35 have the highest zinc content but only traces of other metals, and are broadly similar to some other specifically military items such as the Hawkedon gladiator's helmet (Painter 1968/9 and Table 6). There was some adulteration of the brass with lead and scrap copper alloy in the majority of the trappings, but the compositions are largely determined by the Roman method of making brass.

The technology of Roman brass making has been discussed at length elsewhere (Caley 1964; Craddock 1978; Bayley 1990) but can be briefly restated here. The familiar alloy of copper and zinc probably first became popular in the Roman world at just about the beginning of the Imperial Age. Indeed the first large scale use of brass was for the *dupondii* and *sestertii* of the reformed coinage of Augustus in 23 BC, which were themselves derived from issues current in parts of Asia Minor through the previous half century (Craddock *et al.* 1980; Burnett *et al.* 1982). Zinc is extremely volatile, and its isolation as a metal in classical antiquity must have been exceedingly rare, certainly there are very few surviving pieces (Caley 1964; Craddock 1990; Fellmann 1991 and Rehren forthcoming). There are no extant contemporary descriptions of brass making, even from amongst the alchemists, but from later descriptions and the surviving material, notably the brasses themselves it is possible to piece together the process with some confidence. Brass was made by reacting copper metal with zinc ore directly in a solid state process, known as cementation, and this method was to persist in the west through to the 19th century (Day 1990; Galon 1764; Percy 1861: 612–18). The finely divided copper was mixed with charcoal and calcined zinc carbonate ore, $ZnCO_3$ (traditionally called calamine, but now often known as smithsonite, especially in America), and placed in a crucible. The lidded crucible was heated to temperatures in the region of 1,000°C. Carbon monoxide generated from the charcoal reduced the zinc ore to zinc, which at 1,000°C was a vapour. This dissolved in the exposed surfaces of the copper forming the brass. The temperature was critical. It had to be above the boiling point of zinc, 919°C, or no zinc vapour would form, and the absorption of zinc was facilitated by increased temperature. However, if the temperature rose too high the forming brass would melt before it had the chance to absorb more than a small percentage of zinc (Pure copper melts at 1,083 °C, a brass with 20% of zinc begins to melt at about 1,000 °C at atmospheric pressure). Molten brass would sink to the bottom of the crucible leaving only a much reduced surface exposed to the zinc vapour and

　　　　　R. P. J. JACKSON AND P. T. CRADDOCK

Table 5. Composition of Military Brasses from Ribchester.

Cat. No.	Description	Cu	Zn	Pb	Sn	Fe	Sb	Ni	Au	Ag	As	Bi
Helmet												
1	face mask, crown	78.0	20.5	.10	.50	.20	.10	.010		.025		
1	face mask, neck flange	78.5	18.8	.17	.80	.45	.05	.010		.025		
1	headpiece, diadem	78.5	20.3	.10	.50	.23	.05	.015		.025		
Horse eye-guards												
2		80.0	18.4	.10	.50	.56	.10	.015		.030		
4		86.0	14.1	.00	.90	.77		.060		.060		
Harness trappings												
6	Minerva mount	74.5	13.2	8.10	3.20	.34	.10	.020		.040		
9	phalera, large	72.0	19.7	7.40	.40	.30	.07	.010		.035		
11	phalera, large	73.0	18.3	7.70	.70	.25	.05	.010		.045		
12	phalera, large	77.0	10.6	8.80	2.20	1.10	.09	.015		.080		
15	phalera, small	76.5	12.7	8.80	1.20	.35	.08	.015		.060		
14	phalera, small	72.0	15.0	11.10	1.30	.40	.10	.015		.080		
32	phalera, small	72.0	13.1	11.70	1.50	.40	.05	.015		.060		
32	pendant	76.0	10.7	10.15	1.40	.44	.08	.015		.065		
7	phalera, large	77.5	19.9	.20	.30	.30	.05			.030	.03	
7	junction loop	78.5	20.5	.30	.40	.23	.10	.012		.046		
35	junction loop	78.0	20.8	.65	.70	.45	.10	.015		.330		
34	phalera, large	74.0	13.8	9.50	1.70	.33	.07	.015		.065		
34	junction loop	78.0	20.0	.20	.20	.23	.07	.014		.018		

The analyses have a precision of ±2% for the major elements and approximately ±30% for the minor and trace elements, the error rising sharply as the detection limit is approached.

The detection limit for the elements quoted in the table is 0.01 weight % in the metal, except for As and Sn for which the limit is the order of 0.05%.

Table 6. Composition of selected Military Brasses from elsewhere in Britain.

Reg. No.	Description	Cu	Zn	Pb	Sn	Fe	Sb	Ni	Au	Ag	As	Bi
Hawkedon, Suffolk												
PRB 1966, 6-5, 1	gladiator helmet	73.5	25.6	.13				.030		.060	.50	
Fremington Hagg, North Yorkshire												
Harness trappings												
PRB 1880, 8-2, 152	phalera, large	82.0	13.3	2.15	1.70	.38	.20	.020		.080	.20	
PRB 1880, 8-2, 150	phalera, large	81.0	13.6	2.66	2.15	.70		.030		.250	.20	
PRB 1880, 8-2, 150	pendant	78.5	15.2	3.10	1.50	.70	.10	.015		.100		
York.Mus.H.141.19	phalera, small	81.0	14.7	2.52	1.96	.34	.10	.020		.110	.20	
Lincoln												
Harness trapping												
PRB 1875, 6-25, 2	pendant	79.5	9.0	3.10	5.20	.33	.15	.025		.075		
Brough, Westmorland												
Harness trapping												
PRB 1874, 12-28, 30	phalera, small	80.0	17.4	3.40		.15	.03			.003	.15	
Hod Hill, Dorset												
Harness trapping												
PRB 1892, 9-1, 855	phalera, small	79.0	18.2	2.20	.40	.18	.12	.008		.060	.15	.005

The analyses have a precision of ±2% for the major elements and approximately ±30% for the minor and trace elements, the error rising sharply as the detection limit is approached.

The detection limit for the elements quoted in the table is 0.01 weight % in the metal, except for As and Sn for which the limit is of the order of 0.05%.

further absorption would be considerably reduced. Thus the brass makers were seeking the maximum temperature that would retain the forming brass in the solid state until almost the end of the process.

The earliest detailed accounts of the true solid state cementation process date only from the 16th century, in such well known accounts as those of Biringuccio (Smith and Gnudi 1942: 70–6) or Ercker (Sisco and Smith 1951 254–7). The Medieval account of brass making given in the *de artibus* of Theophilus (Hawthorne and Smith 1963: 142–4) differs significantly from the later descriptions. In particular the forming brass was melted in the crucible, and additional calamine was stirred in with an iron rod to encourage further absorption. Strictly speaking that is not a cementation process at all. In fact the description seems rather improbable, as the lid would have had to have been removed during the stirring and most of the zinc vapour would have evaporated and oxidised. Possibly Theophilus was just describing the steps taken at the end of the process immediately prior to pouring the brass from the crucible in order to minimise loss. However, the detailed description does not read like that and Theophilus was normally well informed and reliable. Thus it is not clear from the literary evidence whether the Romans also allowed the metal to melt as part of the process or carried out a true cementation.

As noted above there are no classical accounts of brass making, but Pliny (*Natural History* 34.4; Rackham 1952: 129) notes that certain types of copper absorb zinc ore, *cadmea* better than others, to form *orichalcum*, which suggests a process involving metallic copper and zinc ore (see below for the comments of Dioscorides and Galen on the sublimation of zinc oxide from the ores).

Similarly, little physical evidence for Roman brass making has yet been recognised apart from a series of small crucibles that have been claimed as cementation crucibles (Bayley 1984, 1990; Zwicker *et al.* 1985). These are of a distinctive fabric and seem to have all been lidded. The inner surface of the walls is always massively impregnated with zinc minerals together with some copper, and Bayley has suggested that these crucibles were used for brass making. If so, they were of small capacity, capable of holding only a few hundred grams of metal at most. It is possible they were used for melting brass, the lids being useful in reducing the evaporation of zinc from the molten alloy. It is perhaps significant that a crucible of this type (Bayley 1990: 28d) has been found in the recent excavations at Ribchester (Edwards and Webster 1985 etc.). The earliest unequivocal cementation crucibles so far recognised are from Dortmund, Germany of 12th century date (Rehren *et al.* 1993), and are somewhat larger than the putative Roman examples.

The other main source of information is the brasses themselves, and a surprising amount can be elucidated from their composition. Experiments performed by Haedecke (1973; Werner 1970) showed that at temperatures of 1,000 °C and atmospheric pressure, the maximum zinc content of a forming brass would be 28%. This compares very well with the figures quoted by brass makers in the past, such as Nehemiah Champion who made brass in Bristol in the early 18th century and who claimed 28% was the maximum penetration of zinc that he could achieve (Day 1973: 61–2); and also with the 29.5% claimed by Ercker (Sisco and Smith 1951: 257) in the 16th century. Later developments by Champion and others raised the maximum level to about 33% (Percy 1861: 616). The maximum zinc content of Roman brasses approaches 28%, but none of the thousands of analysed pieces ever exceeds this figure (Bayley 1990; Craddock 1978 and forthcoming). The majority of the fresh cementation brasses, unadulterated with scrap bronze, as evidenced by their tin content, seem to contain about 20% of zinc, as is the case with the helmet, the eye guards and trapping no. 7/35, reported here. This might suggest a rather inefficient process, operating at below the maximum temperature, or allowing substantial losses of zinc vapour from the crucible during the process or during subsequent remelting and casting operations.

Lead and tin in the copper severely limit the absorption of the zinc, principally by reducing the melting point, and thus later brass makers were at pains only to use pure copper (Day 1973: 55), and inspection of analyses of Roman brasses show that the highest zinc contents occur in brasses that are substantially free of lead or tin. It will be noted, however, that lead is quite prevalent in the Ribchester brasses, and this metal could have a variety of origins.

Lead and zinc ores are always associated together, and thus cementation brass always contains a little lead, sometimes no more than traces, as exemplified by the helmet, but often amounting to several percent, arising from the ore itself. Additional lead may well have been added to the alloy to improve its casting properties, and some lead may have been present in any copper alloy added to the brass.

As well as lead the brass of the Ribchester trappings contain small amounts of tin. Where the tin content is much below one percent then the tin was probably in the copper used in the cementation process and the smiths were almost certainly unaware of its presence. The tin probably came to be in the copper through small amounts of scrap bronze, as tin in any quantity is rare in copper ores. Some of the brasses have several percent of tin in the alloy and these probably originate from scrap bronze added to the brass after it had been made. It is noticeable that there is a very approximate inverse proportional relationship between the tin and zinc contents, that is those with more elevated tin contents tend to have substantially less zinc. This is a general trend in Roman brasses (Craddock 1978 and forthcoming). Thus, for example, the composition of trapping no. 12 could have arisen by the dilution of a cementation brass containing 20% of zinc with equal quantities of a bronze containing about 5% of tin and 15% of lead, although some of the lead could already have been present in the brass, or represent a separate addition.

The four analyses of the very comparable trappings from the Fremington Hagg group (Webster 1971) show a similar relationship between the tin and zinc (Craddock *et al.* 1973: Table 3), but the trappings from Xanten have only traces of tin and zinc contents in the range of 18%-23%, suggesting that pure cementation brass was used (Jenkins 1985).

The iron content of the Ribchester brasses is notably higher than in the bronzes and this is true of Roman brass, and indeed other cementation brasses, generally. The enhanced iron originates in the small quantities of iron minerals that are always found with the calamine and no matter how carefully the ore is beneficiated some would enter the cementation crucible along with the zinc ore. There it would be reduced to metallic iron and on melting the freshly made brass at the end of the process some could dissolve in the molten metal. The freshly made cementation brass could sometimes contain several percent of iron and this would have a deleterious effect on the working properties of the metal. These 'hard and knotty places, arising from iron in the metal' were noted in the cementation brass of later times (Day 1973: 124), and are additional evidence that the Roman brasses from Britain and the rest of the western Empire were produced by cementation of the calamine ores without the pretreatment carried out in the Middle East. (The possible places where the brass for the Ribchester trappings etc. could have been made are discussed in more detail below).

In the Middle East calamine seems not to have been common and a different technology had to be evolved to pretreat the sulphidic zinc ore (principally sphalerite, ZnS) to remove the sulphur. In the process described by Dioscorides (Gunther 1934; Riddle 1985) and referred to by Galen (Walsh 1929), the ore was burnt in a tall chamber creating dense clouds of zinc oxide. This sublimate was condensed on the upper walls of the chamber, or onto a framework of iron rods suspended above the burning ore. This sublimation very effectively separated any involatile minerals, notably those of iron, and to a lesser extent lead, from the zinc, and thus the zinc mineral entering the cementation process was much purer. This purity is reflected in the composition of the brass. For example, the brass coins minted through the first century BC in the Near East generally have lower iron contents than the slightly later brass coins of the general reform of the currency in 23 BC (Craddock *et al.* 1980).

Over a thousand years after the descriptions of Dioscorides and Galen, almost identical processes were still current in the Middle East and described by Islamic writers (Allan 1979: 39–45), and remains of the process are still to be found in Iran (Barnes 1973). This provides an interesting example of a regional variation in a technical process which endured through many centuries.

Fabrication (PTC)

A. *The Vessels*

The Ribchester pans belong to a large group of Roman vessels with complex recessed annular patterns on their base. The manner in which the vessels, and in particular the rings, were made has long been the subject of debate (see anon 1970, for example). The vessels in the G.M. Kam Museum in Nijmegen were examined by a working bronze-founder, Mr. D. Grosman from Arnhem, who was reported to be 'inclined to think that some of the specimens were cast thin and then spun and others were made out of a flat sheet (cast and beaten?) of bronze and then spun. But all of them were then turned on the lathe' (den Boesterd 1956: XX); Mutz (1970 and 1972), followed by Brown (1976) and many others, believed the deep concentric rings had been carved out of the bronze whilst the cast vessels were turned on the lathe. This question has been previously addressed by two of the present authors (Craddock and Lang 1983) and by Hermans (1970), and to some degree there is a problem of terminology. Thus it is necessary to define the terms used before evaluating the evidence as to how the vessels were made.

Spinning is a very specific process for forming vessels whereby a disc of metal spinning on a lathe is pressed against a former. The method is quick compared to hand raising and suitable for producing large numbers of similar shapes. As such it came to prominence during the Industrial Revolution, but the earlier history of the technique is very uncertain, not least because the process leaves few obvious and unique distinguishing marks on its products. It does require a powerful continuous action lathe with a cranked action, for which there is little evidence prior to the Medieval period (Woodbury 1961), and it is perhaps no coincidence that the earliest pieces so far confidently recognised are Medieval Islamic (Craddock and Lang 1983, Atil *et al.* 1985).

Lathe turning is a process for cleaning up a casting etc., or cutting deep grooves by mounting the piece on the lathe and removing metal with a chisel. This method is of greater antiquity than spinning, but for really deep carving like that on the pan bases once again a powerful continuous action lathe is necessary, as Mutz found when he tried to deep carve replicate bronze bowls.

Finally, any piece of metal of circular profile can be cleaned up and polished on a lathe, and this method has been employed since at least the Iron Age. The diagnostic features are the parallel annular scratch marks on the metal and the distinctive hollow pip in the centre of the piece, where it was mounted on the lathe. The pip can also originate from marking out designs on the piece. Too often the pip has been taken as evidence of spinning or turning where in fact nothing more drastic than polishing had been carried out.

The claims of Mutz that the deeply carved annuli on the bases of the Roman vessels had been turned on the

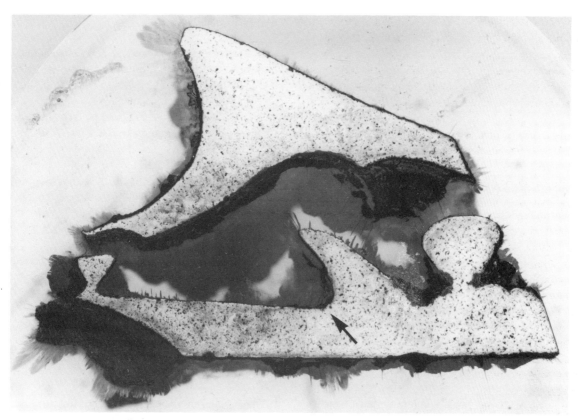

fig. 50a. Two pieces of the section cut through the saucepan base, Cat. no. 25, mounted and etched with ferric chloride. The position of the area covered by 5b is indicated by the arrow.

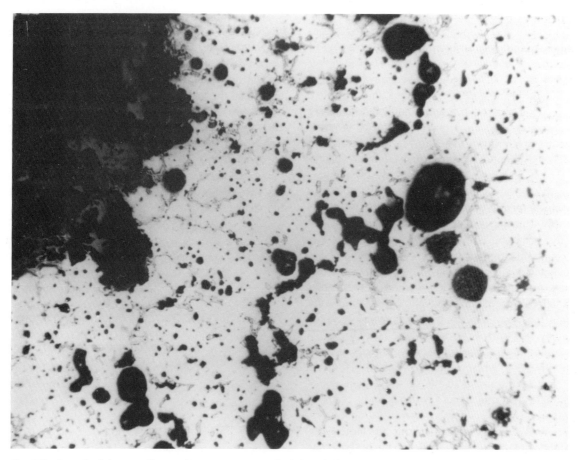

fig. 50b. Detail of the metallographic section, typical of the whole section, showing the metal in an as-cast state with no distortion of the structure even at the surface. The black globules are of lead.

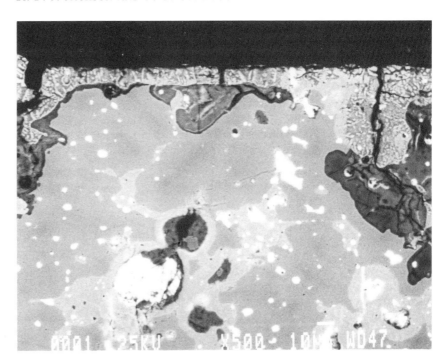

fig. 51. SEM micrograph of section through wall of saucepan Cat.no.25 showing remains of tinning on inner wall. The tinned layer is not of tin alone but of the delta phase alloy containing 32% tin, 68% copper. This was deliberately induced by heating the tinned metal until the desired alloy had formed in situ on the surface. The dark grey or black areas in the body metal are corrosion or voids, and the white blobs are lead.

lathe seemed worthy of investigation, not least because he had been unable to replicate this using intermittent action lathes powered by a bow string, such as were used in antiquity and shown in some contemporary depictions, or even the medieval pole lathes (Woodbury 1961). These lathes are also of low power and intermittent action and are completely unsuited to the deep carving of metal.

To carry out the investigation a wedge was cut from the fragmentary pan base 25, extending from the edge to the centre. This was polished and examined both before and after etching (fig. 50). The section showed the typical structure of a leaded bronze in as-cast condition. The dark areas are globules of lead, which is almost insoluble in copper and its alloys and thus always remains separate. It can be seen that the globules of soft lead display absolutely no trace of distortion even at the surface. It seems inconceivable that large quantities of metal could have been gouged from the surface without some distortion or smearing of the lead.

If the rings were not cut out of the metal then they must have been present on the mould, and from their 'turned' appearance it is likely that the deep rings were turned on the wax. This is also the conclusion of the study made by Poulsen (forthcoming). There are modern parallels for this amongst the brass smiths of India (Mehta 1960: 34), where it is observed that 'To cast a vessel, first a solid model of the vessel is made out of clay and when dry it is covered with a layer of prepared wax, fitted in a lathe, and turned.' After casting the vessels were finished on the lathe, and this was almost certainly done with the Roman vessels, no matter how they had been formed.

The Ribchester vessels seem to be substantially in an as-cast condition. They are rather corroded but cat. no. 24/25, in common with many similar vessels from elsewhere, is noticeably silvery on the inside. Such vessels are often variously described as tinned, silvered or just plated. However, as many of the alloys are very rich in tin and/or lead they would be prone to the phenomena known as sweating. This occurs in alloys where there is a great difference in the melting point of the components, and the melt is allowed to cool slowly. Thus with leaded bronzes, a copper-rich metal freezes first and finally just before the whole alloy sets, the remaining tin-rich bronze and the lead is squeezed to the surface giving the appearance of deliberate plating (Meeks 1993). With these considerations in mind the vessel was examined by N.D. Meeks (British Museum Dept. of Scientific Research) who reported as follows:

'The inner surface of vessel no. 24/25 has both dark and silvery grey areas. Small samples were taken from both, mounted and polished for metallographic examination in the scanning electron microscope. There is no evidence of lead sweat to the surface which suggests the metal cooled swiftly in the mould. The body structure shows the presence of the euctectoid intermetallic copper tin compound. This is hard, brittle and silvery. However, much tin is held in solid solution in the metal and also indicates rapid cooling of the metal after casting.

The microstructure shows the inner surface is tinned, and the two samples show different tin-copper compound structures, both characteristic of hot tinning (Meeks 1986 and 1993). Analysis showed the compound present at the surface to be the ∂ phase (32% tin, 68% copper). The darker sample indicates that this part of the bowl reached a temperature in excess of 520°C while the lighter area reached

about 450ºC. These temperatures are higher than are necessary for simple tinning but it has been shown (Meeks 1986,
1988, and 1993) that Roman metalsmiths regularly heated
their tinned surfaces to develop hard, silvery and corrosion
resistant surfaces after the first application of the tin by
wiping or dipping.

    Final polishing would produce a fine silvery-grey sheen
on the inner tinned surface of the bronze bowl.'

In addition taper sections were polished on the sides
of vessels 22 and 24/25. These showed the structure was
basically cast with some evidence of working but no
annealing. These apparently worked structures probably
resulted when the sides were reduced by turning.

B. The Military Brasses

This category includes the helmet, eye guards, *phalerae*
and saddle plates as well as the harness trappings. As
they are different in composition as well as fabrication
technique they will be considered separately.

– Helmet and eye guards, cat. nos 1–5. These items
have all been raised from sheet metal with frequent
annealing which has resulted in fine-grained micro-
structures, as revealed by metallographic examination of small samples removed from damaged or
inconspicuous areas.

    The sheet metal of the helmet is very thin – much
thinner than, for example, the Hawkedon gladiator's
helmet (Painter 1968/9) – and confirms its status as
parade armour. The face piece of the helmet was
shaped by the repoussé technique, with the brass sheet
set in some yielding but firm medium such as pitch or
lead, and hammered out from the back. Some of the
details may have been chased in from the front after
it had been released from the medium. Edwards (1992)
suggested that the figures on the head-piece could
have been struck from dies. This is certainly possible
although it would have been difficult on the complex
curves of the helmet's inner surface. Several of the
figures overlap and this would have created additional
problems if dies had been used. It should also be
noted that amongst the 17 figures there are no repeats
and thus on balance we believe that they are more
likely to be repoussé work.

    Sections from eye guards nos 2 and 4 revealed
extensive working and annealing, showing that the
metal had been raised. A lathe pip survives on no. 2
where the raised hemisphere had been held on the
lathe during turning or polishing operations. The rectangular and triangular holes were then chiselled out
from the front. Some distortion to the rectangular holes
near to the edges suggests a little further raising was
necessary after the holes had been cut.

– *Phalerae*, cat. nos 16–20. These are of hammered
and smoothed sheet. Qualitative XRF analysis of nos
16 and 17 showed the body metal to be of copper

with some zinc and tin. One face on each plate had an
enhanced lead content which is almost certainly the
remains of soft solder either of lead-tin or of lead
itself, which originally held some now lost component.

– Saddle plates, cat. nos 29–30. The two fragmentary
saddle plates are of thin sheet metal that has suffered
extensive corrosion. Qualitative XRF analysis showed
that they are of copper with some tin and zinc and
traces of lead. A pin on no. 30 was also analysed and
found to be of copper with some zinc, and traces of
lead. The grey metal on one face of each plate was
found to contain more tin and lead than the underlying body metal, suggesting that a solder of tin/lead or
possibly just lead had been applied to hold a silver
foil, traces of which survive in a few places.

– Harness trappings, cat. nos 6–15 and 31–35. Taper
sections were polished on *phalerae* and loops nos 6,
9, 11, 12, 14, 15, 7/35 and 34 for metallographic
examination, which showed that they had been cast
to shape, including the suspension rings and hinges at
the rear: the broken ring on the back of *phalera* 12
has a dendritic structure, which shows that it was cast
in place and was thus part of the original casting.
There is no evidence for annealing on any of the
pieces, suggesting that the subsequent post-casting
work was relatively minor. This would have included
the carving of the face to hold the inlays. The castings
in the sections examined were of very poor quality
with gas porosity being prevalent, and there are some
quite major faults. On some of the trappings there had
been some attempt to repair the more serious of these
holes either by pouring more metal into the hole (nos
10–12) or, in one case (no. 9), by letting a piece of
solid copper into the hole. Qualitative XRF analysis
of the filler metal cast into the holes in the original
casting of *phalera* 10 showed that it contained much
more lead and less zinc than the surrounding metal.

The decorative schemes on the *phalerae* were broadly
similar to those on other and better preserved trappings,
as exemplified by Fremington Hagg (Craddock *et al.*
1973) and Xanten (Jenkins 1985). These have a symmetrical stylised floral pattern, inlaid with copper and
niello, which was set into an overlay of silver. The evidence for the silver overlays and inlays is not extensive
on the Ribchester trappings: the silver overlay only survives in a minority of the pieces, and its identification
was proved by surface analysis on a small area on *phalera*
9 and on the junction loop of *phalera* 34. Copper inlay
was only positively identified on some of the stylised
grapes on *phalerae* nos 9 and 11. It seems that the silver
was deliberately and quite thoroughly removed from all
of the silvered pieces prior to burial. Note that silver was
detected by XRF on the surfaces of several of the cleaned
trappings. The origin of this silver is very uncertain, it

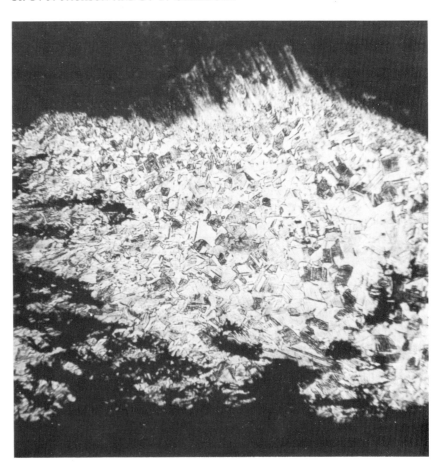

fig. 52. Section through eye guard, Cat.no.4, showing small grain size with much twinning, indicative of heavy working and annealing.

could be the remains of a corroded overlay, or it could originate in an unrecorded silver oxide conservation treatment. The majority of the faces (but not the backs) of the Ribchester trappings are rich in tin, and but for the surviving areas of silver overlay on trapping 9 etc. it would not be certain that this was not tinning, such as is found on the interior of vessel no. 24/25, rather than a solder to hold the overlay. However enough metallic silver foil survives on trappings 9 and 34 etc. to show the technique must have been very similar to that found on the Fremington Hagg trappings. First a thin sheet of silver was soldered onto the front face with a soft solder. This was quite a common method of silver plating in the Roman world, and it became popular again in the early nineteenth century when it was known in Britain as close plating (La Niece 1990 and 1993). Tin and silver-tin alloys were quite frequently used as silver solders in the Roman period, and do, in fact, make very satisfactory solders for silver (Lang and Hughes 1984), although lead or lead-tin solder was used on the *dona militaria* (cat. nos 16–20). The designs would then have been lightly drawn on the overlay (and can still be seen on some of the Fremington Hagg pieces), and then chiselled out, where appropriate, through the overlay and into the underlying body metal, keying the surface where necessary to hold the niello inlays.

On the Ribchester trappings very little inlay survived in those areas that held niello on comparable pieces from elsewhere. However, the niello still in place on the two fragmentary junction loops nos 35 and 7 was sampled for X-ray diffraction analysis, and the copper sulphides, djurleite, $Cu_{1.96}S$ and covellite, CuS were identified, but no silver sulphides. In her major study of ancient niello, La Niece (1983) showed that almost invariably the composition of Roman niello reflected the composition of the metal in which it was set. Thus, a copper sulphide niello would be set in a bronze and a silver sulphide niello in silver. Most of the niellos from the other trappings, notably Xanten were of silver sulphides, although those from Fremington Hagg were of a mixed copper-silver sulphide, which is presently unique for the early Roman period. Thus, were it not for the few small surviving areas of silver foil, the copper sulphide niello on the Ribchester junction loops could have been taken as evidence that the Ribchester pieces were tinned rather than overlain with silver.

Conclusions, scientific (PTC)

There is a very clear difference in composition between the vessels and the military metalwork from Ribchester, and this difference is quite typical of other similar vessels and trappings from elsewhere. The causes of this consistent difference in alloying practice are likely to be complex, but the two most obvious factors are geography and typology.

The vessels were almost certainly made in Italy as attested by the makers' marks cast on many of them, whereas the trappings seem to be specifically western. The prevalence of brass has been noted in some other specifically western metalwork such as the Hemmoor buckets (den Boesterd and Hoekstra 1965). The source of the zinc in the Roman brass has always been thought to be from the Stolberg deposits near Aachen (Willers 1907), and more recent work has confirmed Roman activity in these deposits. Some studies have associated the Hemmoor buckets directly with Stolberg (Holtz 1992).

Similarly, analytical studies on Roman metalwork from France have shown that the locally-made pieces tend to be of brass while only the more important pieces of art metalwork, imported from the Mediterranean, were of bronze (Beck *et al.* 1985). This is reinforced by the examination of crucibles and other metalworking debris from the sites of some Roman workshops in France (Rabeisen and Menu 1985). Taken together the evidence does seem to suggest a prevalence of brass over bronze in the north west of the Empire.

The Ribchester brasses are predominantly military and decorative, artifacts for which brass seems to have been favoured, at least in the West. Whereas only about 10% of Roman copper alloys could be considered as having significant zinc content (over 5%), this rises to about 30% for decorative metal such as fibulae and brooches (although with great variation between different types: Bayley 1990), and to over 90% for the specifically military trappings etc. (Craddock forthcoming). Furthermore many of the military pieces, exemplified by the helmets from Ribchester and Hawkedon (Table 6), and the trappings from Xanten etc., are 'fresh' brass undiluted by scrap bronze, whereas this is rare amongst civilian brasses with the exception of some specific types such as the Hemmoor buckets. Thus one could argue that brass was disseminated through the western Roman provinces through the reuse of old military equipment, with a component coming from the brass coins, which were still usually made of unalloyed brass through the first century (Craddock *et al.* 1980).

However, there are specific ingots of brass, such as the large inscribed sheet, with 26.8% of zinc and only traces of other metals, found in the civilian industrial area of Sheepen at Colchester (Musty 1975), and the Roman bun ingot found at Claydon Pike, in the Upper Thames Valley which contains 20.6% of zinc and 0.9% of lead (Bayley 1990).

There are also the small lidded crucibles discussed above, which, if they are for brass making, demonstrate that at least some of the brass was produced locally. Significantly almost all of these crucibles are from military sites. The Ribchester crucible might suggest the brass for the military metalwork was made locally, or at least that the trappings were cast locally. This would be supported by the rather poor quality of the trappings compared to those from Xanten or Fremington Hagg.

CONCLUSIONS, ARCHAEOLOGICAL (RPJJ)

Provenance

After the passage of almost two centuries it is difficult to pinpoint the exact provenance of the hoard. We are very fortunate to possess Townley's original sketch map and written description which localise the findspot to the area immediately behind the houses at the S.W. end of Church Street. However, it is uncertain whether the Walton's house corresponds to any existing building, and because Townley's map was only a sketch (he has, for example, mis-orientated the church) it cannot be used for the measurement of distances. This is unfortunate, because the potential findspot falls within an area which straddles the N.E. defences of the fort. Thus, the hoard might have been buried immediately outside the fort, in or beneath the rampart, or just inside the fort. In fact, probability suggests the latter, if only because at this point the line of defences passes very close to the rear wall of the properties on Church Street (Edwards and Webster 1985: fig. 1; *ibid*. 1987: fig. 29), leaving little scope for either an extra-mural or a rampart context. Therefore, assuming the fort to have had a regular layout, the most likely point of burial of the hoard would have been midway along the N.E. side of the north quadrant of the fort, a short distance within the rampart. This position was usually occupied by the sides/ends of barrack blocks fronting the intervallum road.

Date

Cat. nos 6, 21 and 27–28 are not closely datable, but all the other pieces in the hoard can be dated within the bracket later 1st-early 2nd century AD, implying a probable deposition date within the first few decades of the 2nd century. It may be more than coincidence that this date mirrors that of a number of coin hoards from the region, a phenomenon that suggested to Shotter 'some uncertainty in the 120's, which might in its turn not be unconnected with a temporary loosening of control in the Ribble Valley area' (in Edwards and Webster 1985: 89). More specifically the low proportion of Trajanic coins from Ribchester has been taken to imply a break of occupation at the fort, albeit short-lived. Archaeologically this is perhaps represented by the 'radical replanning' of the fort defences and interior that followed the end of phase 1a/phase A in the 120's AD (Edwards and Webster 1985: 22 and 38), and the contemporary demolition and clearance of *vicus* buildings to the north and north-west of the fort (Edwards and Webster 1987: chapters 2 and 8, esp. 113 ff.). This dislocation may well have been connected to the redeployment northwards of its garrison, the Ala II

Asturum. This unit, which was raised from the Astures of N.W. Spain, was brought to Britain by Cerealis and is attested at Ribchester on an altar (RIB 586: undated, but probably 2nd century) set up by one of its decurions. By the later 2nd century it is attested at Chesters, where it was to remain for the 3rd and 4th centuries (Holder 1982: 107; Jarrett 1994: 39). A tenuous link between the unit and the hoard is provided by the helmet inscriptions: if the personal name Caravus is correctly read then the best parallels to this so far unique occurrence are both from Spain – a place name and a female *cognomen* (Wright 1960: 240, fn. 27).

Purpose

Had there been unequivocal proof that the hoard had been found outside the fort defences, then its identification as the (rich) contents of a grave would have been conceivable (for cavalry sports equipment in graves, but also in forts, *vici* and other contexts, see Garbsch 1978: 45–88). However, even allowing that the absence of human remains (at this period most likely to be cremated bone) could be explained away as a failure of recognition by the finders, the composition of the hoard is more suggestive of an official/semi-official military context than of a private, civilian context. The hoard comprises predominantly cavalry sports equipment, including a set, or part-set, of military awards, but also three bronze vessels (originally four – see cat. III, a), a mortarium, and a few uncertain fragments, as well as a number of now missing organic items. The similarities in composition, style, condition and date (though not burial context) to the still richer group from Pit XXII at Newstead (Curle 1911: 121–122) is most striking. As is evident from the catalogue, the Ribchester hoard is composed of a) some pieces that were apparently complete and intact on burial b) some pieces that had been de-silvered prior to burial, and c) some pieces that appear to have been buried in a worn, damaged or broken state. Such a mixture suggests the hoard was a miscellaneous assortment of equipment, some functional and some not, which was being stored for future use or for re-use as scrap. In view of the evidence which hints at its burial in a wooden box or chest (*supra*) it is postulated that the hoard, which may be interpreted as the parade equipment of a single cavalry trooper of Ala II Asturum (but is not necessarily so), was placed in sub-floor storage beneath a barrack block prior to the re-deployment of the unit, was forgotten, for some reason, and was not re-located by the subsequent incoming garrison.

Acknowledgements

The authors are grateful to Kenneth Painter who initiated work on the hoard in 1973; to Ben Edwards who generously shared with us his thoughts on the hoard and its discovery in advance of his own publication of the find in the *Ribchester Excavations* series; to Catherine Johns, Val Rigby and Peter Shorer for help and advice; and to Robert Bailey who re-located cat. no. 21. All photographs courtesy of the British Museum.

References

Allan, J.W. 1979. *Persian Metalworking Technology 700–1300 AD.* London: Ithaca Press.

Anon. 1970. Meeting on Roman Bronze Vessels at Rijksmuseum G.M. Kam, 20–23 April 1970.

Atil, E., Chase, W.T. and Jett, P. 1985. *Islamic Metalwork.* Washington: Smithsonian Institution.

Barnes, J.W. 1973. Ancient Clay Furnace Bars from Iran. *Bull. Hist. Metallurgy Group,* 7, 2: 8–17.

Bayley, J. 1984. Roman brass-making in Britain. *Journ. Hist. Metallurgy Soc.,* 18, 1: 42–3.

Bayley, J. 1990. The Production of Brass in Antiquity with Particular Reference to Roman Britain. In Craddock (ed.) 1990: 7–28.

Beck, F., Menu, M., Berthoud, Th. and Hurtel, L.-P. 1985. Metallurgie des bronzes. In *Recherche gallo-romaines* 1. Réunion des musées nationaux (ed. J. Hours). Paris, pp. 69–140.

Bishop, M.C. 1988. Cavalry equipment of the Roman army in the first century AD. In *Military Equipment and the Identity of Roman Soldiers. Proceedings of the Fourth Roman Military Equipment Conference.* Brit. Archaeol. Rep., Int. Series, 394 (ed. J.C. Coulston). Oxford, pp. 67–195.

Bishop, M.C. and Freeman, P.W.M. 1993. Recent work at Osmanthorpe, Nottinghamshire. *Britannia,* 24: 181.

den Boesterd, M.H.P. 1956. *The Bronze Vessels in the Rijksmuseum G.M. Kam at Nijmegen.* Nijmegen.

den Boesterd, M.H.P. and Hoekstra, E. 1965. Spectrochemical Analyses of the Bronze Vessels. *Oudheidkundige Mededelingen uit het Rijksmuseum van Oudheden te Leiden* 46: 100–127.

Boon, G. 1970. Roman Bronze vessels in Wales. In Anon (1970).

Brouwer, M. 1982. Römische Phalerae und anderer Lederbeschlag aus dem Rhein. *Oudheidkundige Mededelingen* 63: 145–199.

Brown, D. 1976. Bronze and Pewter. In *Roman Crafts.* (eds D. Strong and D. Brown). London: Duckworth, pp. 25–41.

Burnett, A., Craddock, P.T. and Preston, K. 1982. New light on the origins of *orichalcum,* In *Proceedings of the 9th International Congress of Numismatists* (eds T. Hackens and R. Weiller) Association Internationale des Numismatistes Professionels. Publication 6: 263–268.

Bushe-Fox, J.P. 1916. *Third Report on the Excavations on the Site of the Roman Town at Wroxeter, Shropshire 1914.* Soc. Ants. Res. Rep. IV. Oxford.

Bushe-Fox, J.P. 1949. *Fourth Report on the Excavations of the Roman Fort at Richborough, Kent.* Soc. Ants. Res. Rep. XVI. Oxford.

Caley, R.E. 1964. *Orichalcum and Related Ancient Alloys.* The American Numismatic Society. New York.

Casey, P.J. and Davies, J.L. 1993. *Excavations at Segontium (Caernarfon) Roman Fort, 1975–1979.* C.B.A. Res. Rep. 90. London.

Connolly, P. 1988. *Tiberius Claudius Maximus, the Cavalryman.* Oxford.

Craddock, P.T. 1978. The Origins and Early Use of Brass. *Journ. Archaeol. Science*, 5,1: 1–16.

Craddock, P.T. 1985. Three Thousand Years of Copper Alloys. In *Application of Science in Examination of Works of Art* (eds P.A. England and L. van Zelst). Museum of Fine Arts. Boston: pp. 59–67.

Craddock, P.T. 1990. Zinc in Classical Antiquity. In Craddock (ed.) 1990: 1–6.

Craddock, P.T. (ed.) 1990. *2,000 Years of Zinc and Brass*. British Museum Occasional Paper 50: London.

Craddock, P.T. (forthcoming). *Roman Non-ferrous Metallurgy*. British Museum Occasional Paper 100: London.

Craddock, P.T. and Lang, J. 1983. Spinning, Turning, Polishing. *Journ. Hist. Metallurgy Soc.*, 17, 2: 79–81.

Craddock, P.T., Lang, J. and Painter, K.S. 1973. Roman Horse Trappings from Fremington Hagg, Reeth, Yorks. *Brit. Mus. Quarterly*, 37, 12–2: 9–17.

Craddock, P.T., Burnett, A.M. and Preston, K. 1980. Hellenistic copper-base coinage and the origins of brass. In *Scientific Studies in Numismatics* (ed. W.A. Oddy). British Museum Occasional Paper 18. London, pp. 53–64.

Curle, J. 1911. *A Roman Frontier Post and its People. The Fort of Newstead in the Parish of Melrose.* Glasgow: James Maclehose.

Day, J. 1973. *Bristol Brass*. Newton Abbot: David and Charles.

Day, J. 1990. Brass and Zinc in Europe from the Middle Ages until the 19th century. In Craddock (ed.) 1990: 123–150.

Dixon, K.R. and Southern P. 1992. *The Roman Cavalry from the First to the Third Century AD*. London.

Driel-Murray, C. van. 1989. The Vindolanda chamfrons and miscellaneous items of leather horse gear. In C. van Driel-Murray (ed.) *Roman Military Equipment: The Sources of Evidence. Proceedings of the Fifth Roman Military Equipment Conference.* Brit. Archaeol. Rep., Int. Series 476, Oxford: 281–318.

Edwards, B.J.N. 1992. *The Ribchester Hoard.* Preston: Lancashire County Books.

Edwards, B.J.N. and Webster, P.V. (eds) 1985, 1987 and 1988 *Ribchester Excavations* Pts. 1–3. Cardiff: Dept. Of Extra Mural Studies, University College.

Edwards, B.J.N. forthcoming. The Ribchester Hoard. In *Ribchester Excavations* 4, forthcoming.

Eggers, H.J. 1966. Römische Bronzegefässe in Britannien. *Jahrbuch des Römisch Germanischen Zentralmuseums Mainz*, 13: 67–164.

Fellmann, R. 1991. Die Zinktafel von Bern-Thormebodenwald und ihre Inschrift. *Archäologie der Schweiz*, 14: 270–3.

Frere, S.S. and Tomlin, R.S.O. (eds) 1991. *The Roman Inscriptions of Britain*, Vol.II, fascicule 3 (RIB 2421–2441). Oxford.

Galon, M. 1764. *L'Art de convertir le Cuivre Rouge ou Cuivre de Rosette en Laiton ou Cuivre Jaune.* Descriptions des Arts et Métiers. Academie Royale des Sciences: Paris. Reprinted and edited A.P. Woolrich and A. den Ouden. nd. Der Archäologische Pers. Eindhoven.

Garbsch, J. 1978. *Römische Paraderüstungen*. Munich.

Gunther, R.T. (ed.) 1934. *The Greek Herbal of Dioscorides* (from the translation of John Goodyer 1655). Oxford: Oxford University Press.

Haedecke, K. 1973. Gleichgewichtsverhaeltnisse bei der Messingherstellung nach dem Galmeiverfahren. *Erzmetall*, 26: 229–233.

Hartley, K.F. and Richards, E.E. 1965. Spectrographic analysis of some Romano-British mortaria. *Bull. Inst. Archaeol.*, 5: 25–43.

Hawthorne, J.G. and Smith, C.S. 1963. *On Divers Arts: The Treatise of Theophilus.* Chicago: Chicago University Press.

Hermans, H. 1970. The Craft of Metal bowl making in Roman times: A Theory. In *Anon 1970.*

Holder, P.A. 1982. *The Roman Army in Britain*. London.

Holtz, F. 1992. *Von Erzen, Sagen und Geschichten.* Herausgegeben vom Heimat- und Handwerksmuseum. Stolberg.

Hughes, M.J., Cowell, M.R. and Craddock, P.T. 1976. Atomic absorption techniques in archaeology. *Archaeometry*, 18, 1: 19–37.

Hyland, A. 1993. *Training the Roman Cavalry*. Stroud.

Jarrett, M.G. 1994. Non-legionary Troops in Roman Britain: Part One, The Units. *Britannia*, 25: 35–77.

Jenkins, I. 1985. A Group of Silvered Horse-Trappings from Xanten. *Britannia*, 16: 141–164 (with appendix by P.T. Craddock and J. Lambert on the composition).

Lang, J. and Hughes, M.J. 1984. Soldering Roman Silver Plate. *Oxford Journ. Archaeol.*, 3: 77–107.

La Niece, S. 1983. Niello: An Historical and Technical Survey. *Antiq. Journ.*, 63, 2: 279–97.

La Niece, S. 1990. Silver plating on copper, bronze and brass. *Antiq. Journ.*, 70, 1: 102–14.

La Niece, S. 1993. Silvering. In *Metal Plating and Patination* (eds S. La Niece and P.T. Craddock). Oxford: Butterworth Heinemann, pp. 201–10.

Maxfield, V.A. 1981. *The Military Decorations of the Roman Army*. London.

Meeks, N.D. 1986. Tin-rich surfaces on bronze- some experimental and archaeological considerations. *Archaeometry*, 28: 2. 133–62.

Meeks, N.D. 1988. A technical study of Roman bronze mirrors. In *Aspects of Ancient Mining and Metallurgy: Acta of a British School at Athens centenary Conference* (ed. J. Ellis Jones). Bangor, pp. 66–79.

Meeks, N.D. 1993. Surface characterization of tinned bronze, high-tin bronze, tinned iron and arsenical copper. In *Metal Plating and Patination* (eds S. La Niece and P.T. Craddock). Oxford: Butterworth Heinemann, pp. 247–275.

Mehta, R.J. 1960. *The Handicrafts and Industrial Arts of India*. Bombay: Taraporevala.

Menzel, H. 1966. *Die Römischen Bronzen aus Deutschland, II, Trier.* Mainz.

Menzel, H. 1986. *Die Römischen Bronzen aus Deutschland, III, Bonn.* Mainz.

Musty, J. 1975. A brass sheet of first century AD date from Colchester (Camulodunum). *Antiq. Journ.*, 55, 2: 409–11.

Mutz, A. 1970. Verbindungstechniken an zweiteiligen römischen Bronzegefässen. In *Anon 1970.*

Mutz, A. 1972. *Die Kunst des Metalldrehens bei den Römern.* Basel: Birkhäuser.

Oldenstein, J. 1985. Manufacture and supply of the Roman army with bronze fittings. In *The Production and Distribution of Roman Military Equipment* (ed. M.C. Bishop) *Proceedings of the Second Roman Military Equipment Research Seminar.* Brit. Archaeol. Rep., Int. Series 275, Oxford: 82–94.

Painter, K.S. 1968/9. A Roman bronze helmet from Hawkedon, Suffolk. *Brit. Mus. Quarterly*, 33, 2: 121–30.

Percy, J. 1861. *Metallurgy of Copper, Fuel, etc.* London: John Murray.

Poulsen, E. forthcoming. Remarks on Roman bronze casseroles with deep grooves under the bases. In *Proceedings of the 1992 Bronze Congress Nijmegen.* Nederlandse Archeologische Raporten 18.

Rabeisen, E. and Menu, M. 1985. Métaux et alliages des bronziers d'Alésia. In *Recherches Gallo-romaine* I. Paris: Ministère de Culture.

Rackham, H. 1952. *Pliny; The Natural History*, 9. Loeb edition. London: Heinemann.

Rehren, T. forthcoming, A Zinc Tablet from Bern, Switzerland. *Proc. Archaeometry '94 Conference.* Ankara.

Rehren, T., Lietz, E., Hauptmann, A. and Deutmann, K.H. 1993. Schlacken und Tiegel aus dem Adlerturm in Dortmund. In *Montanarchäologie in Europa* (eds H. Steuer and U. Zimmermann.) Sigmaringen: Jan Torbecke, pp. 303–14.

Richards, E.E. and Hartley, K.F. 1960. Preliminary spectrographic investigation of some Romano-British mortaria. *Archaeometry*, 2: 23–25.

Riddle, J.M. 1985. *Dioscorides on Pharmacy and Medicine.* Austin: University of Texas Press.

Robinson, H.R. 1975. *The Armour of Imperial Rome.* London.

Rush, P. 1993. *The economics of Roman mortaria production: ceramic production and distribution in southern Roman Britain.* Unpublished Ph.D. thesis. University of Bradford.

Sisco, A.G. and Smith, C.S. (eds) 1951. *Lazarus Ercker's Treatise on Ores and Assaying.* Chicago: Chicago University Press.

Smith, C.S. and Gnudi, M.T. 1942. *The Pirotechnia of Vannoccio Biringuccio.* New York: Basic Books.

Smith, C.S. and Hawthorne, J.G. 1974. *The Mappae Clavicula. Trans. American Philosophical Soc.*, 64, 4. Philadelphia.

Townley, C. 1815. Account of Antiquities discovered at Ribchester. *Vetusta monumenta quae ad rerum Britannicarum memoriam conservandam societas antiquariorum Londini sumptu suo edenda curavit* IV: 1–12.

Toynbee, J.M.C. 1962. *Art in Roman Britain.* London.

Toynbee, J.M.C. 1964. *Art in Britain under the Romans.* Oxford: Oxford University Press.

Toynbee, J.M.C. and Clarke, R.R. 1948. A Roman decorated helmet and other objects from Norfolk. *Journ. Roman Studies*, 38: 20–27.

Walsh, J. 1929. Galen Visits the Dead Sea and the Copper Mines of Cyprus (166 AD). *Bull. Geog. Soc. Philadelphia*, 25: 93–110.

Walters, H.B. 1915. *Select Bronzes, Greek, Roman and Etruscan, in the Departments of Antiquities.* London.

Watkin, W.T. 1883. *Roman Lancashire.* Liverpool.

Webster, G. 1969. *The Roman Imperial Army of the First and Second Centuries AD.* London.

Webster, G.A. 1971. A hoard of Roman military equipment from Fremington Hagg. In *Soldier and Civilian in Roman Yorkshire* (ed. R.M. Butler). Leicester: 107–125.

Werner, O. 1970. Über das Vorkommen von Zink und Messing im Altertum und im Mittelalter. *Erzmetall*, 23: 259–269.

Wheeler, R.E.M. 1926. *The Roman Fort near Brecon.* London.

Wheeler, R.E.M. 1930. *London in Roman Times.* London.

Willers, H. 1907. *Neue Untersuchungen über die Römische Bronzeindustrie von Capua und von Niedergermanien.* Hannover and Leipzig.

Winterbottom, S. 1989. Saddle covers, chamfrons and possible horse armour from Carlisle. In *Roman Military Equipment: The Sources of Evidence* (ed. C. van Driel-Murray) *Proc. Fifth Roman Military Equipment Conference.* Brit. Archaeol. Rep., Int. Series 476, Oxford, pp. 319–336.

Woodbury, R.S. 1961. *History of the Lathe to 1850.* Cambridge, Ma: MIT.

Wright, R.P. 1960. Roman Britain in 1959, II. Inscriptions. *J. Roman Studies*, 50: 236–242.

Zwicker, U., Greiner, H., Hofmann, K-H. and Reithinger, M. 1985. Smelting, Refining and Alloying of Copper and Copper Alloys in Crucible Furnaces. In *Furnaces and Smelting Technology in Antiquity* (eds P.T. Craddock and M.J. Hughes). British Museum Occasional Paper, 48. London, pp. 103–115.

Mounted Men and Sitting Ducks:
The Iconography of Romano-British Plate-Brooches

Catherine Johns

Romano-British fibulae and other brooches have long been the focus of extensive typological research, and the native, non-Classical elements which are obvious in the form or decoration of many types have frequently been commented upon, but comparatively little attention has been paid to the choice of animals and inanimate objects represented in so many of the small plate-brooches, except by the late Richard Hattatt (1982; 1987; 1989). Possibly the subject has been seen as too art-historical for real archaeologists, or the brooches have simply been regarded as too trivial and common for iconographic study.

Visual symbolism is complex and meanings may vary according to the viewer's knowledge, the context and even the occasion. Though we can never hope to reach total understanding of the iconography of a past culture, an aberrant pattern should at least engage our interest. When the range of animate and inanimate subjects depicted in plate-brooches is compared with those common in Roman and Romano-Celtic iconography generally, an unexpected picture emerges: many creatures and objects which were frequently illustrated in the art of Roman Britain and the other northern Roman provinces are rare or even apparently absent amongst the brooches, while some which we do not recognise as meaningful in that art appear repeatedly.

Geographical distributions are unlikely to be of great importance in the present state of knowledge. Certain areas of Britain are particularly popular for metal-detecting, and have produced correspondingly large quantities of metal finds. Furthermore, we can seldom say with any confidence where specific brooches or types of brooches were made. Representational enamelled plate-brooches are found in other Celtic provinces, not only the adjacent regions of Gaul and the Rhineland, but as far afield as Pannonia, and many Continental types were undoubtedly imported into Britain. What is important is that they were bought and used in Roman Britain.

The approximate numbers of brooches of various types quoted below are based on a combination of two sources, Hattatt's publications (1982; 1987; 1989) and Donald Mackreth's index of Roman brooches, a copy of which he has kindly allowed to be housed in the Prehistoric and Romano-British Department of the British Museum. It is important not to lose sight of the element of chance in loss and rediscovery: the brooches which were lost in antiquity rather than recycled, which have been found again, and in recent times rather than the distant past, and which above all have been made known in the archaeological literature, must represent only a tiny proportion of the brooches which were in use in antiquity. Nevertheless, the relative frequency or rarity of recorded types should still have some significance, and where a given type seems to be standardised as well as numerous, it is fair to assume that it was made in some quantity.

This paper is not intended to be a comprehensive survey of types or of interpretation, merely a first step in a line of research which may be of interest. Modest contribution though it may be, I am glad to be able to offer these thoughts on a distinctive class of Romano-Celtic objects to Ian Stead, in the hope that, as a connoisseur of artefacts generally, and brooches in particular, he will find it of some interest.

FUNCTION OF PLATE BROOCHES

Ancient brooches, though often highly decorative, were essentially functional items intended as fasteners for clothing. However, there is good reason to suspect that Romano-Celtic plate-brooches were worn primarily for visual effect, like their modern counterparts. The simplest plate-brooches are small enamelled discs, often as little as 2 cm in diameter. The pin on a brooch of this size will be able to pick up a section of cloth only about 1 cm wide, since allowance has to be made for the space occupied by the hinge lugs (or more rarely, the spring) and the catchplate. The clearance between the pin and the plate may be 0.5 cm or less, and therefore the fabric also has to be fairly thin, which implies either a double layer of finely-woven wool or linen, or a single layer of a more robust over-garment. The majority of the zoomorphic plate-brooches are of comparable dimensions. A penannular brooch of this diminutive size is able to take up a considerably wider and thicker piece of woven textile, as can a miniature fibula. The largest disc brooches are around 5.5 cm diameter, and have pins as long as those on a medium-size fibula, though they still provide much less space for a thick pleat of cloth than a bow-brooch. Large disc-brooches are less common than the small specimens. The average dragonesque brooch, a distinctively Romano-British type which is usually classified as an aberrant plate-brooch, is clearly the functional equivalent of a fibula, and will not be discussed here (for a full typological discussion, see Johns 1996: *forthcoming*). Combined with the fact that the enamelled inlay which is found on so many disc- and plate-brooches is often colourful to the point of gaudiness, their limited efficacy as fasteners leads one to infer that these artefacts were intended less for use than ornament.

Trends in modern fashion (non-precious) jewellery can be inspired by sources as frivolous or transitory as cartoon characters or specific advertising campaigns. They result in designs which would be incomprehensible to anyone lacking a full and detailed knowledge of contemporary popular culture: consider, for example, brooches or pendants based on the cartoon animals Snoopy or Garfield, or the fleeting popularity of gold coffee-bean earrings and pendants inspired by a particular television commercial for instant coffee in the early 1990s. Even allowing for the fact that twentieth-century mass media can disseminate popular knowledge of such ephemeral images in a way which could not even remotely be approached in antiquity, there may be a parallel. A widely-known fable, parable or saying, a famous architectural or natural feature of an important place, a symbol associated with some popular game or activity, could all give rise to a symbol which would work well as a badge, and would have clear meaning to others in the same society. Likewise, a specific religious cult or site, or a group of people with related interests, might be identified by a badge: again, modern and indeed medieval parallels (e.g. pilgrim-badges) come readily to mind.

If this is so, and some plate-brooches in Roman Britain and other Celtic provinces are decorative souvenirs and badges which reflect the tastes, beliefs and interests of sections of the population who were not necessarily the wealthiest members of society (who were wearing gold and silver jewellery of Graeco-Roman designs indistinguishable from those found throughout the Empire), their iconography clearly deserves serious study, even allowing for the difficulties of interpretation referred to above.

ANTHROPOMORPHIC BROOCHES

With the exception of the horse-and-rider brooches described below, anthropomorphic brooches, whether depicting human or divine characters, are extremely rare.

The image of a god or goddess engraved on a gemstone set in a ring, though a Classical introduction, was not an unusual possession in Roman Britain: in principle, therefore, it would not be surprising to find small plate brooches depicting Classical deities such as Mars or Minerva, or Celtic ones such as the trio of Mother Goddesses. Apparently they do not exist.

An enamelled brooch in private ownership (fig. 53) shows a standing male figure holding the large Roman legionary shield; the rectangular shape of the shield, quartered with orange and blue enamel (the latter colour almost lost), is the main part of the brooch, with bearded profile head above and probably the feet, now lost, below. This brooch is so far unique. Whether it is intended to evoke an ordinary legionary soldier or a warrior god, it is clearly a romanised concept. Another anthropomorphic brooch, allegedly from Colchester, was seen some years ago and is precisely paralleled at Augst, Switzerland (Riha 1979: no. 1708). It is a standing draped figure, without enamel, wearing a large crescentic headdress. Classical interpretations are possible, Luna being the most obvious, but the style is unfamiliar, and a Celtic element seems very likely.

The one anthropomorphic (or deomorphic?) type which is well-known and very standardised in Britain is

fig. 53. Anthropomorphic enamelled brooch depicting a bearded warrior with a shield. H. 3.8 cm. Photo: British Museum

the horse-and-rider brooch. Around forty of these have been recorded from Britain, so the real number must be substantially higher, making them a fairly common brooch-type. Most are very similar; around 2.5–3 cm long, they present a highly stylized and simplified image of a prancing long-tailed horse with upstanding mane. The head and torso of the rider are seen above the animal's back, and in some, but not all, his leg and foot projects below the horse's belly. The enamel inlay is disposed in simple shapes, usually three main cells following the form of the body. On a few of the more elaborate examples, it is possible to make out what may be a sword in the hand of the rider (the 'baton' described in Hattatt 1982: 162 and Hattatt 1987: 232). They face to the right, like the great majority of zoomorphic brooches. Hattatt (1982: 160–1) explains this by pointing out that a wearer would prefer the head of the animal, rather than its hindquarters, to be slightly raised above the horizontal. Assuming that the average wearer was right-handed, and given that the point of the pin is always at the head end, the animal would need to face to the right. This is so, but it still does not explain why the pin should always point towards the head. One published horse-and-rider brooch from Kirkby Thore is illustrated facing to the left, but since the publication is a fairly early one, there is a possibility that the reproduction from an engraving was reversed (Smyth 1846: 284).

Horse-and-rider brooches appear to be far more common in Roman Britain than in other provinces, and they seem, moreover, to be concentrated on certain sites which are known to have had Romano-Celtic temple precincts, e.g. Hockwold-cum-Wilton, Norfolk. This distribution implies that the image of a mounted warrior is linked with the Romano-Celtic rider god who was occasionally represented in sculpture and small bronze statuettes in Roman Britain, and who was evidently a manifestation of Mars conflated with a native, Celtic deity (e.g. Johns 1990: 446–452). If the connection exists – a possibility which has frequently been suggested, (e.g. Mackreth 1986) – the pilgrim-badge analogy from the Middle Ages could be a very close one, as the brooches may well have been souvenirs which could be purchased at the appropriate temples and worn as a proof of a visit to the shrine.

ZOOMORPHIC BROOCHES

Horses alone feature in a substantial number of zoomorphic brooches, many of them quite similar in appearance to the mount of the rider-god, though generally more detailed and elaborate. A few are embellished with coloured spots of enamel, and there are also horse-brooches without enamel inlay. Horses feature in Classical art principally as mounts for human riders. The horse as an animal attribute of a deity is effectively absent in Graeco-Roman iconography, and it is noteworthy that the goddess Epona, who was widely adopted by the Roman cavalry throughout the Empire, was a deity of Celtic, not Classical, origin. Though the suggestion is not susceptible of any kind of proof, it seems likely that horses meant more symbolically to Celts than to Romans.

Hunting was an important preoccupation in both native and Roman culture and at many different levels of society, so it is not surprising that images evoking the hunt are extremely widespread in provincial Roman art. They cannot be classified as specifically native or Roman. The subject-matter of many of the animal-brooches may be accounted for by the interest in the chase, and indeed, there are some designs which specifically depict a hunted animal overtaken by a predator.

Running hound brooches, of which at least 20 are recorded from Britain, together with many others from other northern provinces, are no doubt intended to depict hunting dogs: we may note the well-known fact that hounds were one of the prized exports from Britannia to the rest of the Empire. They are often enamelled in a single colour, blue or red, with spots of a contrasting hue. It can be difficult to distinguish hares from hounds; the latter are shown with longer tails, but both are depicted with very long ears. Hounds are frequently shown wearing collars in representations in sculpture or more humble media such as decorated pottery, but this detail, which makes it possible to separate the hounds from the hares, has not so far been noted on jewellery.

In Classical art, dogs appear not only in simple representations of hunting and indeed in their other rôles as watchdogs, herding dogs and simply as companions (Merlen 1971) but also on occasion as attributes of deities. Hunter gods such as Silvanus and Diana are often depicted with their hounds, but the dog was also associated with healing and indeed with chthonic symbolism. The principal god of healing, Asclepius, was frequently accompanied by a dog. In Celtic religion, too, the animals would seem to have had a link with healing shrines, most famously at the Romano-Celtic temple of Nodens at Lydney, Gloucestershire (Wheeler and Wheeler 1932: 40–41; Henig 1984: 55; Green 1986: 159–160 and 175–6).

In many of the hare-brooches the animals are crouching rather than running, and there is one variety in the form of a compact sitting hare with two smaller hares enamelled within its body, presumably to suggest a female with young (Hattatt 1989: 170, nos 1632–1633). Another variant is a hare brooch with stripes applied not in enamel but in black niello; there is an example from London and a virtually identical one from Luxembourg (in the Museum of London and the Musée d'Art et d'Histoire, Luxembourg respectively); these are plated in white metal, probably tin but possibly silver. A third example, in rather poor condition, is noted by Hattatt (1987: no. 1192). There is some indication that hares might have had religious significance in Celtic society, but it is at best tenuous (Green 1986: 185).

An exceptional brooch from Baldock, Hertfordshire,

represents a young hare seized by a predator (Stead and Rigby 1986: fig. 49, no. 152). The theme of a hound running down a hare is found in all kinds of small decorative items, but brooches of this design are not common, and no example has yet been noted from Britain. However, the Baldock brooch is more remarkable still, because the predator is not the usual hound but a cat. It has stripes, originally defined with niello rather than enamel. This object is not only a unique brooch but is also the only known representation of a cat from Roman Britain. The European wildcat (*Felis silvestris silvestris*) was native to Britain, but it is likely that the domestic cat, which probably evolved principally from the North African species *Felis silvestris libyca,* was first introduced in the Roman period. Of course it is impossible to say whether the Baldock brooch represents a wild animal or a domestic one: any cat, the European wildcat, the North African wildcat, or the domesticated species *Felis cattus*, is equally capable of chasing and killing a small animal such as a young rabbit or leveret. Whether the Baldock brooch was made in Britain or another northern province, it would seem to owe more to direct observation than to artistic tradition.

Red deer feature regularly as hunted animals in Roman and provincial Roman art, but in spite of its impressive appearance, the stag was not common in Celtic iconography, and it would seem that the species was not of major importance in the religious or mythological symbolism of either culture. Deer were not common subjects for zoomorphic brooches, though some examples are known, and those which have been found vary a good deal in appearance. The existence of a standardised type, as in the case of the horse-and-rider brooches and many of the hares and hounds, would seem to imply large-scale production.

It is somewhat surprising that other large and powerful male animals were evidently not especially popular as subjects for zoomorphic brooches. Bulls, wild boars and rams are all found with some frequency in both Celtic and Roman iconography, for different reasons, but they are rare or as yet absent in the known repertoire of the craftsmen who made enamelled brooches. There are no known bull or ram brooches, and very few boars. The lions and leopards which are ubiquitous in Roman art are occasional, sporadic occurrences amongst the zoomorphic brooches.

Leopards (panthers) and tigers were associated with Bacchus and were consequently very widespread images, but although there is a distinctive leopard-brooch type, it is not common and appears mainly on the Continent (Hattatt 1987: 243, no. 1196). It depicts the spotted body of the leopard in profile facing right, like most other animal brooches, but the head is raised and turned towards the viewer, rendered three-dimensionally which produces the effect of a reclining beast. All the more bizarre, therefore, is the rare variant in which a human figure, down to the waist, has been riveted onto the body

of the panther. This gives the gruesome effect of a man rising from the belly of the animal, but it is almost certainly intended to evoke the image of Bacchus riding on the panther. The fact that it is a rare and very clumsy adaptation of a standard type rather than having been designed as a coherent image in itself supports the view that conventional Classical iconography was not foremost in the minds of the craftsmen who made enamelled brooches.

Dolphins were also Bacchic animals, and were associated too with the marine Venus. As a shorthand visual image referring to the sea and the marine *thiasos* of Bacchus, they occur in Classical art from the earliest times, continuing into the late-Roman period and indeed into Christian art. In addition to their symbolism, underlined by their dual nature (sea-creatures, and yet not fishes), they are decorative, and either with or without fanciful embellishments such as multiple serpent-like coils or triple, leaf-like tail-flukes, they might be expected as obvious subjects for these colourful brooches. They are almost wholly absent from the enamelled brooch repertoire. A tiny silver dolphin-brooch from London (without enamel) is not unique, but it is the only one of its kind from Britain (Brailsford 1951: fig. 12, 45). Fishes are far more common subjects than dolphins, a reversal of the position in Roman iconography generally. They occur both as fish-shaped ornaments and as rectangular plaques with a fish rendered in enamel. The importance of some fishes, notably salmon, in Celtic imagery is indicated by the Medieval literary evidence, but we cannot exclude the possibility that these designs were liked simply for their attractive appearance. Cryptic Christian iconography is unlikely in the Middle Empire period in question here.

ORNITHOMORPHIC BROOCHES

When we turn to birds, the same slightly unexpected distribution of species is seen. Eagles and peacocks both occur, the former sometimes depicted in the act of devouring a hare, and there are two or three strutting cockerels in profile and a considerable number of unidentifiable flying birds seen from above, perhaps pigeons or doves. Eagles, peacocks and cockerels all have specific connections with major Roman deities, Jupiter, Juno and Mercury, while doves are connected with Venus. All were widespread and familiar in Roman art. By far the most common bird amongst the brooch menagerie, however, is a three-dimensional representation of a stylized duck, its back decoratively enamelled and the pin attached beneath its hollowed body (Hattatt 1989: 360, fig. 219). The pose calls to mind a bird sitting on a nest, but is obviously intended to represent a swimming, rather than a sitting, duck. Ducks and other water birds were apparently important in Celtic mythology, though it is difficult to define their significance precisely (Green 1986: 186–7). Images of aquatic birds can be found in northern European prehistoric art from the Bronze Age onwards. The heads of ducks or swans were also used ornamentally in many classes of Hellenistic and Roman bronze and silver tableware, for example on the attachments which join the handle of a metal pan to its body, and in the distinctive class of fourth-century spoon which features a short, coiled handle terminating in the head of a water-bird, such as those in the major late-Roman treasures from Thetford and Hoxne (Johns and Potter 1983: Bland and Johns 1993). The duck imagery might therefore have had both Celtic and Roman origins and resonances.

Almost as common as the ducks are sitting chickens designed and decorated in exactly the same way. They have curved tails, and have therefore been described with good reason as cockerels, but their heads and the sitting pose are more suggestive of a broody hen than a cock (Hattatt 1989: 360, fig. 219). The tails always have a small perforation which was presumably intended for the attachment of a chain or cord. Although these birds have little in common with the standard representation of a strutting cockerel which often accompanies Mercury, a link with this god seems likely. His worship was widespread in the Celtic provinces.

One bird-brooch illustrated by Hattatt (1987: no. 1156) might well depict a parrot, an exotic species which is found in Roman art because it was linked with the Indian travels of Bacchus.

BROOCHES IN THE FORM OF OTHER LIVING CREATURES: REPTILES, AMPHIBIANS, INSECTS AND MYTHICAL AMIMALS

Amongst the creatures which might have been expected to feature regularly as zoomorphic plate-brooches are snakes. In Classical symbolism, snakes were connected with the Underworld and with healing and resurrection; from Hellenistic times onward they were frequently represented in high-quality gold jewellery as rings and bracelets, to which their sinuous form made them well suited. There was evidently nothing in Celtic mythology to contradict the fortunate symbolism of snakes (it was left to Christianity to effect a radical change in their significance) but their occurrence was certainly more usual under Roman influence than earlier. No serpentiform plate-brooches have been recorded.

Snake-like or reptilian heads are found as terminals of a different brooch-type, Hattatt's 'Equal-ended' type (Hattatt 1987: 202, figs 64–5), but the zoomorphic terminals found on these ornaments seem unlikely to have been designed specifically as snakes. Rather they evolved independently from the form of the projections as generic animal-heads.

A few examples of the Classical sea-serpent, the *ketos*, have been noted however; one from London is typical, with an S-shaped body, dolphin-like tail, fins and a crested (or properly, eared) snake head (Jones 1991: no.

343); another example is illustrated by Hattatt (1987: no. 1206). This is an undeniably Graeco-Roman image which has no counterpart in the native cultures of northern Europe. Classical mythology was populated with a wide range of monsters, many of them strangely beautiful, and if Roman values and decorative appearance were the major criteria in the choice of subjects, we might expect to see many of them reproduced as personal ornaments.

A few hippocamps and capricorns are known, but the winged horse Pegasus and the griffin, a mythical creature so completely accepted in Roman art that it regularly appears alongside natural species in hunting scenes, have yet to be noted in the enamelled plate-brooch repertoire.

Frog-brooches existed, as did some in the form of insects (Hattatt 1987: fig. 1204; 1989: 1638). Many enamelled brooches carrying a representation of a fly or similar insect are in fact fibulae, variants of the common trumpet-brooch type, rather than plate-brooches. The winged shape was probably suggested by the form of the moulding in the centre of the bow.

SKEUOMORPHIC BROOCHES

(NB. Hattatt employs the term *skeuomorphic* for object-shaped brooches: though this is not the traditional archaeological definition of the word, which is normally used to refer to imitation of one material in another, it seems justified by the entymology, and is more convenient than the English equivalent, 'object-shaped').

Many inanimate objects come to mind which are decorative shapes well suited to the design of brooches and which would have carried protective and apotropaic symbolism for wearers in Roman provincial society. For example the cantharus, evoking Bacchus, the club of Hercules, Mercury's caduceus, the steering oar and cornucopia appropriate to Fortuna, and the thunderbolt of Jupiter are all familiar in Roman decorative arts and would seem obvious subjects for personal ornament.

It comes as something of a surprise, therefore, to discover that the most common object-shaped enamelled brooches in Roman Britain were apparently those in the form of a pointed and hobnailed shoe- or sandal-sole (e.g. Jones 1991: no. 341). They are usually enamelled in one colour, often blue, with spots of another colour inset direct in the background enamel, presumably to suggest nail heads. Brooches of this variety were equally popular in other Celtic provinces, but it is very difficult to know why. Like all of the brightly coloured trinkets in this class, they would have looked attractive pinned onto a fabric of a soft and subtle shade, but why a shoe-sole? There was surely a reason for their considerable popularity which escapes us. There could conceivably be a military link, or the nailed sole could be connected with the idea of travel, and thus with protection from the dangers of travel, but there might be some much more

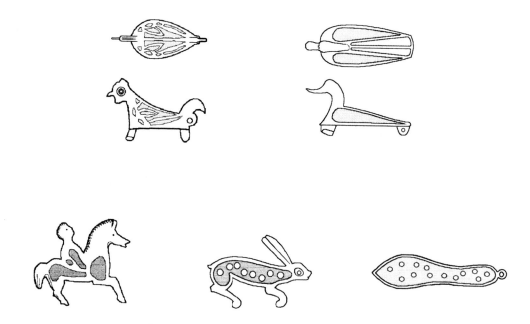

fig. 54. Diagrammatic drawings of some plate-brooch types: chicken, duck, horse-and-rider, hare, sandal-sole.
No common scale.

obscure concept to which we have no key at all. The footprint name-stamps which occur on mass-produced Roman pottery (terra sigillata and lamps) are unlikely to be connected: apart from the fact that they represent the prints of bare feet rather than shoes, they belong to the early Empire, and were principally of Italian manufacture.

A characteristically Celtic shield-shape, including the central boss, is found in a number of plate-brooches, mostly enamelled but a few without added colour (Jones 1991: nos 342, 442). Some are so stylized that their interpretation as shields depends on knowledge of other, more certain examples. The Celtic shield was a type known throughout the Roman Empire, and it undoubtedly carried clear symbolic messages. In general, though, weaponry and armour were rare subjects, though some sword- and dagger-shaped brooches are known. Miniature bronze axes and other tools form an important class of votive bronzes found at temple sites, and it is likely that the brooches of the same form are connected (Hattatt 1989: 358, fig. 217). The pilgrim-badge analogy suggested for the horse-and-rider brooches could well apply to axe-brooches, which are sometimes of quite complex and decorative design.

Double-handled pedestalled vases, ubiquitous as an attribute of Bacchus, are not a standard brooch type; brooches which depict a one-handled flagon are more common, and their significance is unknown.

Wheel-brooches were made in large numbers and in a complex variety of forms. The significance of wheels in both Celtic and Roman religious symbolism has often been discussed, and spoked circles feature in certain standard types of Roman gold jewellery. Unfortunately it is virtually impossible to define wheel-shaped brooches precisely, because a radial design on a circular field is such a basic geometric form that many 'wheels' may be no more than geometrically patterned discs. The combination of crescents and wheels is a standard one in Roman jewellery, the two forms representing respectively the sun and the moon. Crescentic enamelled plate-brooches have also been noted.

CONCLUSIONS

It would seem that the subjects favoured by the manufacturers and purchasers of enamelled plate-brooches made in the shapes of animals or inanimate objects raise a number of questions about meaning and use. They may be more significant than has previously been imagined. The range of representations (fig. 54) suggests something other than a simple predilection for colourful ornaments, but it is clearly not related in a straightforward way to the symbols of the standard Graeco-Roman cults. We are probably justified in seeing a fairly strong Celtic preference at work, not only in Britain but throughout the Celtic provinces.

Acknowledgements
I would like to record my thanks to Val Rigby for many long discussions on the subject of this paper and for sharing her extensive knowledge of Iron Age and Romano-British brooches, to Don Bailey, and to S. W. Bragg.

References

Bland, R. and Johns, C. 1993. *The Hoxne Treasure; an illustrated introduction*. London.

Brailsford, J.W. 1951. *Guide to the Antiquities of Roman Britain*. London.

Hattatt, R. 1982. *Ancient and Romano-British Brooches*. Sherborne.

Hattatt, R. 1987. *Brooches of Antiquity*. Oxford.

Hattatt, R. 1989. *Ancient Brooches and other Artefacts*, Oxford.

Henig, M. 1984. *Religion in Roman Britain*. London.

Johns, C. 1990. Romano-British statuette of a mounted warrior god. *Antiq. Journ.*, 70: 446–52.

Johns, C. 1996: forthcoming. *Jewellery in Roman Britain*. London.

Johns, C. and Potter, T. 1983; *The Thetford Treasure*. London.

Jones, C. 1991. Romano-British Jewellery, In *Treasures and Trinkets; Jewellery in London from pre-Roman times to the 1930s* (ed. T.Murdoch). London.

Mackreth, D.F. 1986. Brooches. In *Settlement, Religion and Industry on the Fen-edge: Three Romano-British sites in Norfolk* (ed. D. Gurney). East Anglian Archaeol., no. 31.

Merlen, R.H.A. 1971. *De Canibus: dog and hound in antiquity*. London.

Riha, Emilie 1979. *Die römischen Fibeln aus Augst und Kaiseraugst*. Augst.

Smyth, W. H. 1846. On some Roman Vestigia recently found at Kirkby Thore, in Westmoreland, *Archaeologia*, 31: 279–288.

Wheeler, R.E.M. and Wheeler, T.V. 1932. *Report on the Excavation of the Prehistoric, Roman,and Post-Roman Site in Lydney Park, Gloucestershire*. Soc. Ant. Res. Rep. 9: Oxford.

A Gold Finger-Ring Found at Arras, Gone Missing Long Since

Martyn Jope

This gold finger-ring was found by the Revd E. W. Stillingfleet during his excavations in Sept. 1816 of what he called 'The Queen's Barrow' in the large cemetery at Arras in S.E. Yorkshire (Greenwell 1906: 25; Stead 1979: 8ff., 86, 114). The ring was exhibited at the York Meeting of the Royal Archaeological Institute in 1846, but it never subsequently reached the Yorkshire Museum with other finds that fell to Stillingfleet's share when his collections passed to that Museum in 1865 (Stead 1979: 8). The ring, though lost, can nevertheless still be very informative through the drawing (fig. 55) made for Greenwell about 1905–6 from "a full-sized drawing, apparently an accurate one," of the ring in Stillingfleet's excavation notes of 1816 (Greenwell 1906: 249). Greenwell presumably took away these notes, for they are no longer traceable (Stead, pers. comm.). The metal was at least confirmed as of "very nearly standard gold, in weight 3 dwts. 21 grs." (Greenwell 1906: 249).

'The Queen's Barrow', A4 in Stead's composite plan (1979: 9, pl. 2a) was a mound almost 3 ft (90 cm) high covering a shallow grave about 1 ft (30 cm) deep, the skeleton crouched ("her feet gathered up") head to N., a distinctively native tradition. No specific report on the skeletal material is given, however, to indicate sex or age, as Hawkes was quick to note (Hull and Hawkes 1987: 144). Sex is to be inferred presumably from the funerary goods (and perhaps lack of weapons), but there is no definitive evidence for age. Other items in the burial (mainly the elaborate brooch) give a fair indication of date (third century BC; Hull and Hawkes 1987: 144–6), cultural milieu and social standing of her funerary attire (see below, fig. 57; cf. Hodson 1990).

The gold ring may be described in some detail from the drawing made for Greenwell from the scale drawing in Stillingfleet's excavation notes (Fig. 55; Greenwell 1906: 250). It is of graceful, economical and logical design. A continuous loop of gold wire of about 0.7 mm gauge, some 90 mm across, had been squeezed together (and presumably hard-soldered) to make a double strand for about two-thirds of its length. This double strand divides towards each end, the strand thinning slightly to about 0.5 mm, and opening into a reversed Ω-loop, the feet of each loop butted together to close the ring (fig. 55) to fit a fully adult finger (20 mm). On each side a gold ball about 1.0 mm across has been inserted between the two strands as they open apart, and another such ball (about 1.2 mm) has been set in the central focal space. The soldered join between the two strands has been covered along its length by a cross-ribbed wire neatly stopped at each end by the gold balls set between the diverging strands; this tectonic device adds to the finished and substantial look of the ring (cp. ECA: pl. 52, no. 83; from Marson – but here the cover is of sheet gold). The Arras ring is a most logically conceived design, very restrained and in excellent taste, and not at all flamboyant like the fine rings in Celtic Europe which followed from Etruscan models (e.g. that from the rich 5th century burial at Rodenbach in the Rheinpfalz, ECA: no. 72, pp. 106, 135, 212).

Another gold finger-ring of simple good taste worth comparing here, is from Tomb 12 at Münsingen near Berne (Hodson 1968: 43, pl. 8, 721; ECA: no. 77), a burial of around 400 BC (Hodson 1968; pers. comm.); this ring has a serpentine, but has not the interest of the inserted gold balls. By comparison, the gold ring from Tomb 9 at Filottrano near Ancona (ECA: no. 76) does its best – it has a hint of inserted gold balls, but has much

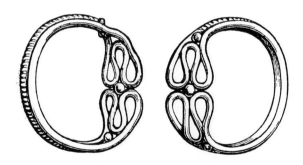

fig. 55. "The Queen's Barrow", Arras (A4), Yorkshire: lost gold ring taken (1906) from original (lost) drawing of 1816. Scale 3:2.

disfigurement from solder-flooding (see below); it is rather cobbled work, not very artistically conceived.

This little gold ring from Arras in Yorkshire is now carrying us deep into the complex intermixing of Italo – Celtic life and craft practices in the 4th century BC, and earlier, and reveals complex Celto-Italic-Etruscan inter-relations (cf. Echt and Thiele 1995; Megaw and Megaw 1989: 86ff.). Finger-rings such as we have been considering may be seen in relation to a strigil from Bologna which is signed ΟΛΛΟΩΡΩ, and on which some ornament seems to have been taken from a Celtic signet; ΟΛΛΟΩΟΡΩ must indeed have been a Celt who made strigils for Celtic customers (Brizio 1887: pl. V. 31; Montelius 1895: pl. 111.1; ECA: 125, 145). In its art, the rich gold ring, already noted, from a wealthy tomb at Rodenbach (Rheinpfalz) tells a similar story (ECA: pl. 52 no. 72; 106, n. 3; 135, 212; Echt and Thiele 1995). Jacobsthal furthermore would see the mëander-step pattern on the back of an Etruscan tombstone at Montefortino as 'an old-fashioned Celtic symbol set shyly and shamefacedly on the back of an otherwise deeply Etruscanized tombstone' (ECA: 75, 144; pl. 52).

It is such a milieu that must have fostered the emergence of the Waldalgesheim intertwining manner in the 4th century BC. But the stylistic purity spread so evenly between all the bronze-work and gold in the primary material of the Waldalgesheim grave itself in the Rheinpfalz (ECA: nos 43, 55, 156; Jope 1963), complete with the Campanian bucket as exemplar for some of the ornament, surely points to a master and his atelier at the immediate command of the Waldalgesheim élite away to the north in the Rheinpfalz lands. And it is the Waldalgesheim neckrings which show canonic purity of ornament while the equivalent from the southerly milieu of Filottrano tomb 2 shows bungled stuffing of flowers backwardsway-on into the pseudo-axils (Jope 1963; Landolfi 1991: 286; cf. Echt and Thiele 1995: 439). For further mixings, note Megaw and Megaw 1989: 86ff.

TECHNIQUES

The skills used in making the Arras ring can also be inferred to some extent from the drawing, fig. 55. Of the hot-bonding techniques, Celtic craftsmen themselves probably by their experimentation contributed much towards the development of hard-soldering and brazing from the 6th century BC onwards (Echt and Thiele 1995: 435, 449). But 'reaction soldering', the essential part of the 'granulation' process probably used for inserting the gold balls, was of Etruscan (and ultimately Near Eastern) derivation (Echt and Thiele 1995: 435–37); it is in fact the earliest hot-bonding skill known to have been used by Celtic craftsmen working in gold, in the 6th century BC, in e.g. Burgundy and Alsace (Eluère 1987, 1989; Echt and Thiele 1995: 440–42), and must have been learnt from Etruscan craftsmen (Echt and Thiele op. cit. 435ff.).

Wire had been made by drawing in the Near East probably since the 6th century BC or earlier, but only for wire up to about 0.2 mm gauge; to draw wire of 0.7 mm gauge for this ring would have needed powered drawing equipment, which was not developed until the 15th century AD (Maryon and Plenderleith 1954: 755–7; Maryon 1956: 481–3, 655; 1959: 41–2, 135ff.). Gold wire such as needed for this ring would have been made by hammering thin strip, a procedure inferred from some of the Snettisham gold-work (Clarke 1954; Brailsford and Stapley 1972: 228–34; Stead 1991b: figs 2, 4, 9). Soldering and 'Granulation': The drawing (fig. 55) made from that in Stillingfleet's notes seems to show hints of solder-flooding round the contact points where wires and convolutions have been joined, but not round where the gold balls have been inserted. This suggests that a different process was used for fixing the balls, part of the 'granulation' process in which the balls are set in place with a glue containing a little copper salt which is reduced to finely divided metallic copper as the glue is carbonised on heating (cf. Echt and Thiele 1995: 437 – a process now called 'reaction soldering') and probably of Etruscan (and ultimately Near Eastern) derivation (Plenderleith and Maryon 1954: 654–9; Maryon 1959: 8, 9; Echt and Thiele 1995: 435–40). I once, in a back room of the old British Museum laboratory, showed this drawing of this ring to Herbert Maryon when working with him on metal bowl-making methods in the early 1950s. Intrigued, he produced some gold wire, and a few small rods of wood, and in no time produced the gold frame. Three gold balls were soon made by rolling and stuck in place with glue from his copper-glue-pot (Echt and Thiele 1995: 437); a little gentle heating and he handed the result – "Spec' that's how they made it!" came from a mouthful of bits and pieces. But understanding of the 'granulation' (reaction soldering) trick was essential; the disfiguring effects of solder-flooding can be seen on a gold ring from Filottrano Tomb 9 (ECA: pl. 52 no. 76, pl. 73 (use a hand-lens)). It must have been among the craftsmen of this kind of Celto-Italic milieu such as that of the Senones around Ancona in the 4th-early 3rd centuries BC that Celtic craftsmen learnt ingenious southerly tricks and probably carried them north to the craftsmen of Celtic Europe; Megaw (in lit.), for instance, draws attention to very relevant gold-work in grave 115 in the cemetery at Mannersdorf-an-der-Leitha, Lower Austria (Neugebauer 1992: 60–1); the gold balls here seem soldered, not very skilfully, for they are only fixed at two points of contact. But botched work could evidently be seen in the south – and equally, clear understanding of canonic ornament in the Celtic north (e.g. Waldalgesheim: Jope 1963; Joachim 1991; for techniques see Echt and Thiele 1995).

But even though the apparent lack of solder-flooding on the gold balls of the Arras ring points to a background of Etruscanized skills, the simple purity, the tasteful lack of ornateness do not suggest it as a straight-

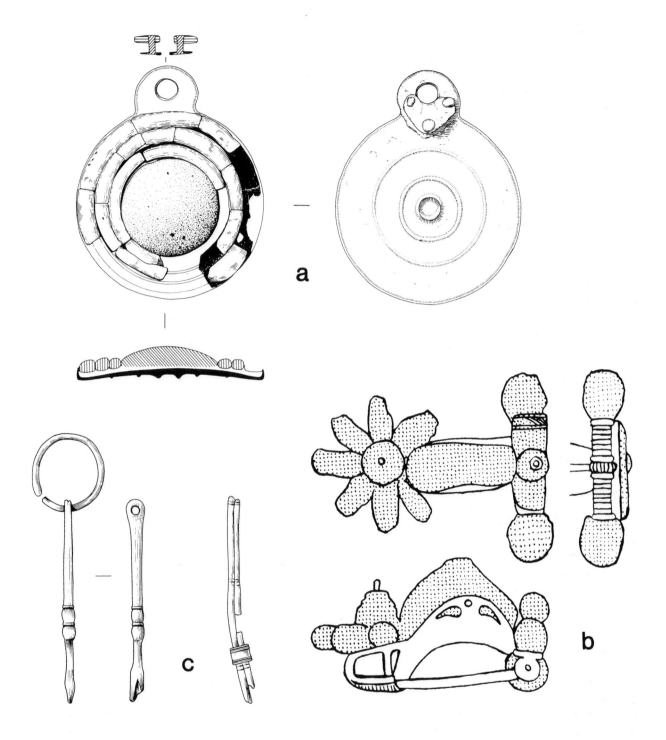

fig. 56. "The Queen's Barrow", Arras (A4), Yorkshire: items from female burial; a, bronze pendant, with 'red enamel' and local stone settings; b, bronze brooch, encrusted with pale pink coral (reconstruction); c, bronze toilet set. Scales 1:1. For other items from burial, see Stead 1989.

forward product of this Etrusco-Celtic world. Now dramatically Stead's recent excavations at Snettisham might provide a very attractive alternative origin for this Arras ring. In this great, ordered, Treasury deposit (over 30 kg of gold items: Stead 1991b: 450–5), the cage-terminal torcs of Hoard L show a craft-milieu in which the frame design of the Arras ring could have been conceived

(Stead 1991b: fig. 9, pl. VIII; note tiny gold balls in figs 1.5 and 9). So at once we see that the Arras ring might after all have come from the great workshops only 70 miles away to the south, as perhaps a bridal gift. The new Snettisham finds make it clear that the craft was hard at work making this great treasury from at least the 3rd century BC onwards; and its sheet-gold style was evidently worked up out of the new confident British relief style in beaten bronze, as best seen in the Wandsworth 'mask' shield of the later 3rd century BC (note stylistic comparisons between Stead 1991b: figs 11, 12, pls VIII, X and the Wandsworth 'mask' shield, Jope 1976: 171, fig. 3 and ECABI pls 70–76). But behind that there might have been ultimately a Continental Celtic background also (cf. ECA: pls 48.61, 51.70, 52.74; Clarke 1954: 42–51, pls V–VI; Furger-Gunti 1982: 23ff.).

Hence now we see that this ring, worn by the lady of the 'Queen's Barrow' at Arras in the 3rd century BC, might after all have come from the hands of craftsmen hard at work producing the gold-work of the Snettisham Treasury, the ring perhaps a simple bridal-gift with a bride from a neighbouring tribe; and the whole material culture milieu falls in place as the provincial but fairly prosperous and well connected Yorkshire of the 3rd–2nd century BC (Stead 1991a; Dent 1985; Jope 1995). But still the skill which would set in the gold balls without solder-flooding is exotic, with ultimate Etruscan roots, reminding us once again of the craft skills being picked up by, for example, the Senones around Ancona in the 4th century BC, and gradually disseminated through the workshops of early Celtic Europe. It will be of the greatest interest to see where the craft-roots of the Snettisham gold-masters lay as the technological study of the Great Treasury unfolds in the coming years in the hands of Ian Stead and his colleagues in the British Museum Laboratory (see already Northover 1992 passim).

The fruits of gold analysis are only just beginning of course – and much ought to come from this. The Iron Age coin-makers clearly understood pretty well what they were doing with making alloys and maintaining a gold standard (as always, progressively lowering it).

FUNERARY ATTIRE

We must see how the lady possessor of so valuable and tasteful a gold ring in Yorkshire of the 3rd century BC was attired for her funerary rites (fig. 57: not of course necessarily quite the same as for her daily life). This can be done to some extent from the co-finds and what Greenwell tells us from Stillingfleet's notes. We have to remember that Stillingfleet saw this as a crouched burial ("with her feet gathered up"), and that some items in the mid-body area may have been bunched up together a little.

Most conspicuous would have been the 100 and more sizeable decorative vitreous beads (mostly 10–18 mm across; Greenwell 1906: 46; Guido 1978; Henderson pers. comm.) "near the head and neck" (Greenwell 1906: 46); this seems a lot of bulky beads to be a necklace only, and the variety of bead designs and mention of 'head' might suggest possibly a head decoration as well (cf. Deal: Stead 1995). True, the 140 beads in tomb 12 at Münsingen-Rain were fairly clearly a necklace only, but

most of the beads were much smaller (Martin-Kilcher 1923: 26, fig. 1; Hodson 1968: 43). Beads are otherwise rare in these Yorkshire graves.

A thick amber ring 42 mm across outside, with 12 mm central hole, lay " in front of the chest and close by were a brooch and pendant ornament" (Greenwell 1906: 47). The new drawing of the pendant (Stead 1979: 85) shows from the rivet detail that it was fixed to a host some 3 mm thick (presumably leather), and apparently hung fairly centrally; this is a very thick leather for any kind of capelet or neck-strap, but the ordinary waist-strap seems precluded by the precisely noted high position. Everything seems very crowded in this area, especially with the mass of beads. The pendant (fig. 56a), like the brooch, is a product of the very skilled Yorkshire craftsmen of this time; the domed central setting is of local sandstone, the concentric boss of 'coral' set in a "black resinous substance" (cf. the bedding of the opaque red vitreous settings on the Battersea shield of the 2nd century BC (Stead 1985; Henderson pers. comm.).

The brooch (fig. 56b), with its profuse settings of 'coral', is crucial, for it gives a firm dating (early 3rd century BC: Hull and Hawkes 1987: 144–45), and its central placing also suggests a garment held somewhere across the chest (rather than on the shoulder) and designed to hold gathered folds of cloth about 7 mm thick. The whole impression is of symmetrically conceived attire rather than a cloak clasped on one shoulder

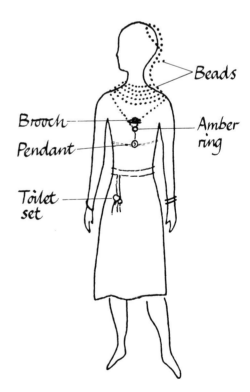

fig. 57. Reconstruction of burial attire of female in "The Queen's Barrow", Arras, Yorkshire. Note element of frontal symmetry.

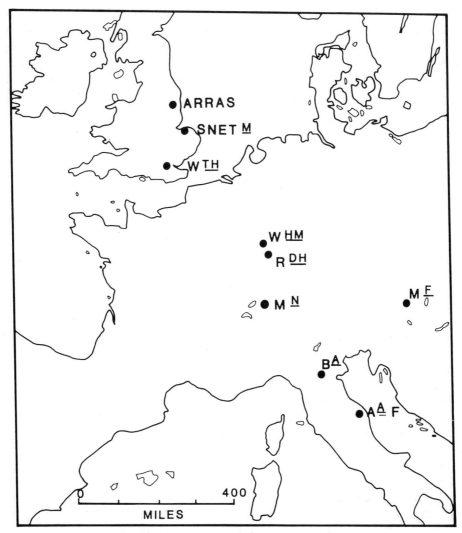

fig. 58. Location map of places mentioned in text.

ARRAS	Yorkshire		
AAF	Ancona-Filottrano, Italy	RDH	Rodenbach, Rhineland, Germany
BA	Bologna, Italy	SNETM	Snettisham
MF	Mangersdorf, Lower Austria	WHM	Waldalgesheim, Rhine Palatinate,
MN	Münsingen-Rain, Switzerland	WTH	Wandsworth, London

(Hawkes 1982); it therefore seems in line with Continental Celtic practice of the time (e.g. Martin-Kilcher 1973: 33, fig. 10). She perhaps had in fact a simple belt, from which the toilet-set (Stead 1979: 85; Greenwell 1906: 249) would have hung (fig. 56c).

The lady had two armlets, one of twisted bronze bar, the other of iron rod flashed with bronze and a third penannular with flattened circular ends (Greenwell 1906: 248–9; Stead 1979: 72–3, 75–6). Of anklets there is no mention; though frequent in both male and female burials in Celtic Europe, they have rarely been observed in Britain. She compares in attire with a burial of this time at Trevone on the N. Cornish coast, with two (differing) brooches centrally placed about 15cm below the chin, and two bracelets (Dudley and Jope 1965: 18).

The impression is thus of frontally-symmetrical attire (fig. 57). Otherwise, in spite of her precious gold ring, she seems set up rather frugally, only one brooch compared with the profusion so often seen by then in Celtic Europe (e.g. Martin-Kilcher 1973: 33), and seeming in fashion a little provincial (cf. Stead 1991a *passim*).

GOLD IN BRITAIN: 7TH – 1ST CENTURIES BC

This little gold ring from Yorkshire proves to be vital towards our understanding of gold in Iron Age Britain and is unusual in another respect – it seems to be the only item of gold we know from a burial in Britain (or indeed almost from any context, except the new finds from Snettisham) between the cessation of Irish gold-work in the 7th century BC (Hawkes and Clarke 1963; Northover 1992: 239–41) and the later 2nd century BC when for about six decades we have a certain amount of work in Snettisham 'classic' manner scattered over Britain. In Celtic Europe this is five centuries of rich but gradually declining gold display. Note use of gold-surfaced-work on iron (e.g. Agris) – but in Britain suggestions of mercury gilding have sometimes been disproved (Stead 1985: 49; but see Northover 1992: 275–6).

And now in Stead's new excavation we seem to have a carefully organised and concealed Treasury being built up from at least the 3rd century BC onwards (Stead 1991b; cf. Jope 1978), and yet almost no gold elsewhere in Britain for almost a century. What could this mean? Are there other tribal Treasuries concealed and stored equally carefully in other parts of Britain (e.g. Ipswich, Needwood-Glascote, Hengistbury, Clevedon etc.)? If not, then how is it – why *was* it – that an overweening power abrogated to itself nearly all the gold in Britain and hoarded it so systematically and secretly that it remained hidden till now from the probings of modern technology? It might suggest supra-tribal political power reaching out through the whole land – a High King in effect since the 3rd century BC. Here is a view of pre-Roman Iron Age Britain to be worked out in the coming few decades as Ian Stead and his colleagues unfold the study of the great new Snettisham Treasury. Any supply of gold to Britain in 3rd – 2nd BC must have been largely Continental (Cauuet 1995; Waldhauser 1995; Northover 1992). And from the earlier-mid second century BC, coinage and then coin-making, introduced for largely mercantile reasons, assume an ever increasing part in the use of gold in Britain (Northover 1992; Burnett in Stead 1991b) This brings us to consider emblems of regality, crown (= *Helm* or *Casque*) of state, and emblems of succession (the Agris helmet was in a grotto; Cerrig-y-Drudion had no real evidence of a burial: Stead 1995; Jope 1995).

In this lost ring we have here almost the only piece of gold known from a British burial of this age (c. 600–0 BC), worn by a lady who seems straightforwardly part of a reasonably prosperous and technically well skilled, but very solidly provincial milieu in Britain of the 3rd century BC And there do not seem to be among these known Yorkshire burials (Dent 1982, 1985; Stead 1991) any persons that are much more élite, let alone regal. If there were loftier people at that time in Britain (as clearly there were in Celtic Europe), how were their bodies disposed of post mortem – perhaps riverine (Jope 1961; Bradley and Gordon 1988).

Even this little note makes it clear how much Ian Stead's carefully programmed researches, in both field and museum, are contributing to our understanding of prehistory. Long may this continue!

Acknowledgements

I am most grateful to the following for discussions and help in various ways: Prof. F. R. Hodson, Dr. C. A. Ralegh Radford, Dennis Britton, Dr. Peter Northover, Dr. John Taylor, Dr. R. Ivens, Dr. J. Henderson, and of course I.M.S. himself.

References

Abbreviations

ECA   P. Jacobsthal, *Early Celtic Art*. Oxford 1944.
ECABI   E.M. Jope and P. Jacobsthal, *Early Celtic Art in the British Isles*. (in press, Oxford).
Celts   Moscati *et al.* (eds), 1991. London: Thames and Hudson.

Bradley, R. and Gordon, K. 1988. Human skulls from the River Thames, their dating and significance. *Antiquity*, 62: 503–09.

Brailsford, J.W. and Stapley, J.E. 1972. The Ipswich Torcs. *Proc. Prehist. Soc.,* 38: 219–234.

Brizio, E. 1887. *Tombe e necropoli galliche della Provincia di Bologna.* Atti Mem. Bologna, 119–234.

Cauuet, B. 1995. Celtic Gold Mines in West Central Gaul. In Morteani and Northover (eds) 1995.

Clarke, R.R. 1954. The Early Iron Age treasure from Snettisham, Norfolk. *Proc. Prehist. Soc.*, 20: 27–86.

Dent, J. 1982. Cemeteries and Settlement patterns of the Iron Age in the Yorkshire Wolds. *Proc. Prehist. Soc.* 48: 437–57.

Dent, J. 1985. Three cart-burials from Wetwang, Yorkshire. *Antiquity*, 59: 85–92.

Dudley, D. and Jope, E.M. 1965. An Iron Age Cist Burial with two brooches, from Trevone, N. Cornwall. *Cornish Archaeol.*, 4: 18–23.

Echt, R. and Thiele, W.R. 1995. Sintering, Welding, Brazing and Soldering as Bonding Techniques in Etruscan and Celtic Goldsmithing. In Morteani and Northover (eds), 1995: 577–596.

Eluère, C. 1987. L'orfèvrerie. In *Trésors des Princes Celtes*. Galeries nationales du Grand Palais 20 octobre 1987 – 15 février 1988. Paris, pp. 27–44.

Eluère, C. 1989. A "Gold Connection" between the Etruscans and Early Celts. *Gold Bull*. 22: 48–55.

Furger-Gunti, A. 1982. Der Goldfund von Saint Louis bei Basel und ähnliche keltische Schatzfunde. *Zeitschrift f. Archäologie und Kunstgeschichte*, 39: 1–47.

Greenwell, W. 1906. Early Iron Age Burials in Yorkshire. *Archaeologia*, 60: 251–324.

Guido, M. 1978. Glass Beads of the Prehistoric and Roman Periods in Britain and Ireland. Soc. Antiq. London Res. Rep. 35: London.

Hawkes, C.F.C. 1982. The Wearing of the Brooch: Early Iron Age Dress among the Irish. *Studies on Early Ireland: Essays in Honour of M.V. Duignan* (ed. B. G. Scott). Belfast, pp. 51–73

Hawkes, C.F.C. and Clarke, R.R. 1963. Gahlstorf and Caister-on-Sea : two finds of Late Bronze Age Irish Gold. In *Culture and Environment: essays in honour of Sir Cyril Fox:* (eds I.Ll. Foster and L. Alcock) London: Routledge and Kegan Paul.

Hodson, F.R. 1968. *The La Tène Cemetery at Münsingen-Rain*, Acta Bernensia 5.

Hodson, F.R. 1990. *Hallstatt: the Ramsauer Graves.* Bonn: Habelt.

Hull, M.R. and Hawkes, C.F.C. 1987. *Corpus of Ancient Brooches in Britain*. Brit. Archaeol. Rep., Brit. Series 168, Oxford.

Joachim, H.E. 1991. The Waldalgesheim Tomb. In *Celts*, 294

Jope, E.M. 1961. Daggers of the Iron Age in Britain. *Proc. Prehist. Soc.*, 27: 307–43.

Jope, E.M. 1963. The Waldalgesheim Master. In *The European Community in Later Prehistory*. Studies in honour of C.F.C. Hawkes (eds J. Boardman, M.A. Brown and T.G.E. Powell). London: Routledge and Kegan Paul, pp. 165–180.

Jope, E.M. 1976. The Wandsworth Mask Shield and its European Stylistic Sources of Inspiration. In *Celtic Art in Ancient Europe* (eds P.-M. Duval and C.F.C. Hawkes) London: Seminar Press, pp. 167–184.

Jope, E.M. 1978. The Southward Face of Celtic Britain 300BC-AD50. *Quaderno Accademia Nazionale dei Lincei*, 237: 27–36. Rome.

Jope, E.M. 1995. Social Implications of Celtic Art: 600BC to AD600. In *The Celtic World* (ed. M. Green). London: Routledge, pp. 376–410.

Landolfi, M. 1991. The Filottrano Settlement and Cemetery. in *Celts*, 286.

Martin-Kilcher, S. 1973. Zur Tracht- und Beigabensitte im keltischen Gräberfeld von Münsingen-Rain: *Zeitschrift f. Schweizerische Archäologie u. Kunstgeschichte*, 30: 26–39.

Maryon, H. 1956. Metalwork and Enamelling. In *Hist. Technol.* I (eds C. Singer and E. J. Holmyard). Oxford.

Maryon, H. 1959. *Metalwork and Enamelling*. London: Chapman and Hall.

Maryon, H. and Plenderleith, H.J. 1954. Fine Metalworking. In *Hist Technol.* I (eds. C. Singer and E. J. Holmyard). Oxford.

Mays, M. (ed.)1992. *Celtic Coinage: Britain and Beyond*. Eleventh Oxford Symposium on Coinage and Monetary History. Brit. Archaeol. Rep., Brit. Series. Oxford.

Megaw, R. and Megaw, J.V.S. 1989. The Italian Job. *Mevit. Archaeol.* Adelaide, 2.

Montelius, O. 1895. *La civilization primitive en Italie depuis l'introduction des metaux*, I. Stockholm: Imprimerie royale.

Morteani, G. and Northover J.P. (eds) 1995 *Prehistoric gold in Europe*. Dordrecht: Kluwer Academic Publishers.

Moscati, S., Frey, O.-H., Kruta, V., Raftery, B., Szabó, M. (eds) 1991. *The Celts*. London: Thames and Hudson.

Neugebauer, J.W. 1990. *Die Kelten im Osten Österreichs*. St. Pölten: Niederösterreichisches Pressehaus.

Northover, J.P. 1992. Materials issues in the Celtic Coinage. In Mays (ed.) 1992: 235–299.

Northover, J.P. 1995. Bronze Age gold in Britain. In Morteani and Northover (eds) 1995, pp. 515–532.

Raftery, B. 1983. *Catalogue of Irish Iron Age Antiquities*. Marburg: Kempkes.

Stead, I.M. 1979. *The Arras Culture*. York: The Yorkshire Philosophical Society.

Stead, I.M. 1985. *The Battersea Shield*. London: British Museum Publications.

Stead, I.M. 1991a. *Iron Age Cemeteries in East Yorkshire*. London: English Heritage.

Stead, I.M. 1991b. The Snettisham Treasure: Excavation in 1990. *Antiquity* 65: 447–64.

Stead, I.M. 1995. The Metalwork. In K. Parfitt, *Iron Age Burials from Mill Hill, Deal*. London: British Museum Publications, pp. 58–111.

Waldhauser, J. 1995. Celtic Gold in Bohemia. In Morteani and Northover 1995, pp. 577–596.

A Metallographic Examination of Eight Roman Daggers from Britain

J. Lang

Introduction

Weapons often incorporate the more advanced technical achievements of their day. Iron Age swords (Lang 1984) and Roman swords (Lang 1988) have already been investigated metallographically. The latter study showed that the Roman smiths were capable of producing sound metal with few inclusions, selecting suitable pieces and welding them together, shaping by forging and filing, and also carburising and quenching to harden the metal. They may have employed tempering to reduce excessive hardness and improve the toughness of some items.

The eight daggers were examined as part of this continuing metallurgical study of ferrous bladed weapons from the collections of the Department of Prehistoric and Romano-British Antiquities in the British Museum (fig. 59). The daggers are described in the Catalogue of the Romano-British Iron Tools Fittings and Weapons in the British Museum by Manning (1985). A typological discussion is provided in the same publication by Scott (1985) and military daggers of the 1st century AD are described at greater length in another paper by Scott (1985).

Making bladed weapons

A satisfactory bladed weapon, such as a sword or dagger, should be sharp enough to cut through metal, leather, wood, flesh and bone, but at the same time, it needs to be able to withstand blows without shattering and therefore must be tough as well as hard. Ferrous metal can provide an ideal material if it is suitably selected and fabricated. In the Iron Age and Roman periods, iron and steel were used with varying success. Unlike bronze, iron could not be cast to shape. After extracting the metal from the ore, it then had to be made suitable for use by removing most of the impurities (mainly slag entrapped during extraction). Hot forging at this stage helped to expel the majority of the slag, weld up any cavities and homogenise the structure. If much slag was retained, the metal would be brittle and difficult to forge, as the slag particles act as stress raisers. The metal could be carburised at this stage or later by packing it closely in charcoal and heating for several hours. Iron which contains 0.2% or more carbon may be considered to be steel.

A sword or dagger blade can be made from one or more pieces of metal (fig. 60). The Iron Age smiths often made their blades from several strips laid one on top of the other and forge-welding them together (edge-to-edge structure). Another method was to lay strips down side by side, so that the joins, instead of running across the blade from cutting edge to cutting edge, were from one surface of the blade to the other (surface-to-surface). Harder iron (containing more carbon) might have been selected for the cutting edges. Unless the structure has been very thoroughly homogenised by work and heat treatment, the joins can be identified in a metallographic polished section and often on radiographs. How the metal was selected for the Iron Age and Roman weapons is not known: if any simple tests were carried out, which is likely, we have no direct knowledge of them.

After the sword or dagger was forged to shape, grooves were sometimes made in the surface, either by forging or by grinding. Afterwards the surface and especially the cutting edge might have been carburised to increase the hardenability. The hardness depends on the carbon content and the heat treatment (Samuels 1980).

In order to harden the metal, the blades would have been first heated to above 723°C when iron and steel transform to austenite (the high temperature iron-carbon phase: 723°C is the transition temperature from the lower temperature phase pearlite to austenite) and then quenched by rapid cooling (ie. plunging into water). In a steel, a completed quench normally produces martensite (a very hard metastable iron-carbon quenching product, formed by cooling rapidly from above 723°C). If cooling is interrupted so that the transformation takes place at a somewhat higher temperature, either bainite (a eutectoid transformation product) (450°C – 300°C) or fine pearlite (a eutectoid transformation product, consisting of alternate fine bands of iron carbide and ferrite, nearly pure iron) is formed. All of these structures are encountered in early blades.

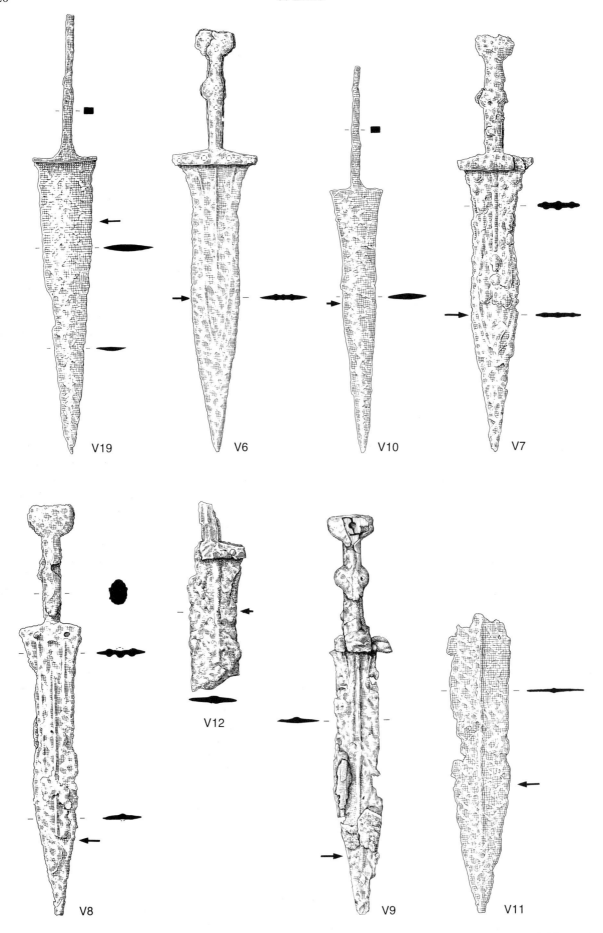

fig. 59. The Roman daggers from Britain. The location of the samples is shown. (Philip Compton, British Museum).

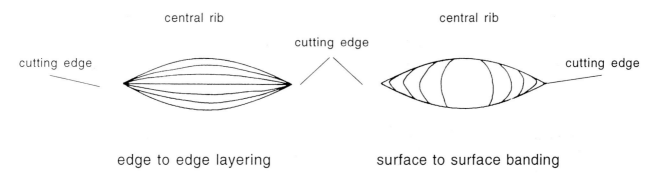

central rib   central rib

cutting edge

cutting edge   cutting edge

edge to edge layering   surface to surface banding

fig. 60. Schematic cross sectional drawing of the edge-to-edge and surface-to-surface methods of blade construction.

To ensure that the blade was tough rather than brittle, it might have been tempered, which relieves structural stress and reduces the hardness slightly. This could have been achieved by withdrawing the blade from the quenching medium before the centre of the blade had cooled to 250°C or below (a process known as auto-tempering), by using a less rapid quench medium (e.g. oil), by allowing the blade to remain in the hearth at 250°C for some time or by reheating to between 250°C and 600°C again after quenching and allowing to cool slowly. Pliny (Rackham 1968) discusses quenching into water and also, to avoid brittleness in small objects, quenching into oil. Tylecote (1986: 18) also mentions gradient quenching, in which the part of the blade which is to be tough rather than hard, is protected during quenching by an envelope of clay.

Toughness is improved with a fine structure. This is achieved by controlling the conditions of working and heat treatment to promote the formation of small grains and discouraging grain growth by avoiding high temperatures or long soaking periods at elevated tempera-

tures. On heating, the metal is allowed to transform to austenite at the lowest temperature possible (that is, just above 723°C, the transition temperature from pearlite to austenite) and for the minimum period of time. This process can be repeated several times to achieve a small austenitic grain size.

A summary of the information available about each dagger is given in Table 7.

EXAMINATION

Metallurgical samples were removed from the blades by cutting a section from the cutting edge to the central rib in a suitable area which was determined by visual inspection and radiography. A corresponding position was chosen on each blade as far as possible. The samples were mounted in cold setting resin, polished and examined by optical and scanning electron microscopy (SEM), and analysed using the energy dispersive X-ray analyser in the SEM (EDX). X-ray fluorescence analysis and microhardness tests were also carried out (Vickers dia-

Table 7

Reg no.	Provenance	Cat.no	Sample no.	Date	Tang/handle	Blade
1892,9–1,1211	Hod Hill	V8	1002	mid 1st AD	I	B
1892,9–1,1213	Hod Hill	V12	1003	mid 1st AD	I	A
Col.22 1938	Colchester	V9	1004	1st AD	I	B
1819,2–10	Kingsholm	V11	1005	mid 1st AD	–	A
1870,10–13,28	Kingsholm	V19	1006	mid 1st AD	–	–
1888,7–19,37	unprovenanced	V6	1007	1st AD	I	B
1810,2–10,11	Kingsholm	V10	1008	mid 1st AD	II	C
1892,9–1,1210	Hod Hill	V7	1009	mid 1st AD	I	B

The typology of the daggers was outlined by Scott (Manning 1985:153–4):

Tangs: Type I. Flat with its edges following the outline of the handle.
         Type II. Simple and straight.

Blades: Type A. Broad, simple midrib, not tapered as B or C. Associated with tang Type I.
         Type B. Deep grooves defining the mid rib; a marked waist and long tapering point. Tangs may be Types I or II.
         Type C. Narrower than A or B, only slightly waisted. Associated with tang Type II.

mond pyramid with a 100g. wt). The sections are referred to by their metallurgical sample number in the following discussions.

Results

(i) Composition

The results of the EDX analyses of the inclusions carried out in the SEM are summarised in Table 8.

A few inclusions in each blade contained phosphorus (usually less than 1%). Some of the blades had a few inclusions with sulphur (less than 1%). The silicon content was quite variable but it did not seem to be especially associated with the joining areas, so that there is no evidence for silica being used as a welding flux except possibly in 1006.

Several of the blades had been made with surface-to-surface bands and consisted of a cutting edge area and a central (rib) area (1005, 1007, 1009). Comparisons were made of the inclusions in the three blades between those in the central rib area and those in the cutting edge area: small differences can be detected between the manganese contents of the two areas in 1005 and 1007, as well as in the magnesium content. Number 1005 also shows differences in the potassium and calcium contents. The only difference in the two areas of 1009 is in the calcium content. The light and dark etching areas of 1002 show small differences in the manganese, magnesium, potassium and calcium contents. It might be suggested that the metal for the two sections in 1002, 1005 and 1007 could have come from different sources.

(ii) Metallographic examination

The metallographic examination was carried out before and after etching with nital. The unetched examination revealed the distribution of the inclusions, mainly of slag, while etching revealed the metallographic structure of the metal. This information, taken with the results of the hardness tests, enabled some conclusions to be drawn about the construction and heat treatment of the metal. In most of the blades containing pearlite and ferrite grains, areas of Widmanstatten morphology indicated that the blades were cooled rapidly at least to about 650°C from the austenite region. The results are given briefly below and summarised in Table 9. Schematic representations of the metallographic structure and hardness values are shown in figs 61a, b.

Sample 1002

Sample 1002 consists of two portions: the cutting edge section which is completely corroded and the central rib section. This has very few inclusions; most are single phased, elongated and aligned parallel to the surface. Etching reveals a diagonal change from a ferrite-rich to a pearlite-rich area in the central rib section indicating an increase in the carbon content. There are also light etching bands at the broken and corroded edge which suggests that there was a transverse join. The dark etching metal is very fine pearlite with some areas of martensite which are extremely hard and do not readily respond to the etch.

Sample 1003

Sample 1003 has broken in two at the groove. Both pieces have large quantities of two phased inclusions. Some of these inclusions have rough rather than smooth outlines and appear to be breaking up. Etching revealed that 1003 had a ferritic structure and appears to have little or no layering. Because it contained carbon in the form of carbides in the grain boundaries and dispersed within the grains, it is harder than the other ferritic sample, 1008 (fig. 62). The grain size varied with smaller grains near the cutting edge. The hardness decreases from the central rib to the break at the groove while the remainder of the blade is twice as hard. Probably the abrupt change in hardness, exacerbated by inclusions, induced a stress concentration which resulted in fracture.

Sample 1004

Sample 1004 has very few inclusions; most are single phased and elongated parallel to the surfaces. Etching reveals a dark etching structure. A ferrite-rich band runs from the central rib which divides to make a Y shape, outlining the wedge of carbon-rich material which forms the cutting edge. This consists of rapid etching martensite which is tempered. It was hard (690 HV) which indicates that the carbon content was probably greater than that of 1007, although it looked metallographically similar.

Sample 1005

The inclusions in 1005 are elongated and lie parallel to the surface. Some are associated with transverse joins but do not show any distinctive compositional characteristics. There are both single and two phased inclusions. Etching shows between five and seven strips of alternating light and dark etching metal making a transverse join between the lower carbon central rib areas and the higher carbon cutting edge section (fig. 63). It is possible that ferritic or soft iron strips were used to facilitate the welding process. The cutting edges contain more carbon and have a very fine structure which could only be identified in the SEM as martensite.

Sample 1006

Sample 1006 contains more inclusions than 1005; most are aligned parallel to the surface, with a number concentrated in one band. SEM(EDX) analysis of a large, triangular two phased inclusion (fig. 64), located at the join between a transverse band at the central rib and the edge-to-edge bands of ferrite and low carbon pearlite which form the rest of the blade, showed that it consisted mainly of iron, with a little silicon. It is probably iron oxide, introduced during the welding process and

Table 8

Sample		Mn	Ti	S	Mg	Al	Si	P	K	Ca
1002	light	2 –14	0.2	0–0.3	1–7	0–3	8–36	0–8	0– 0.4	2–16
	dark	0.2–5	0–0.7	0–0.5	0–2	0–7	9–47	0–0.2	0.3–5	5–23
1003	ce	3–6	0.1–0.4	0–0.3	1–3	3–7	9–25	0–0.3	2–4	3–7
	cr	1–4	0–0.3	0–0.5	0.5–2	3–9	4–21	0–0.8	2–6	3–9
1004		0–5	0–0.9	0–0.2	0–3	0–10	3–52	0–1.5	0–7	1–20
1005	ce	3–4	0.4–1	–	3–7	5–8	38–61	–	3–4	12–25
	cr	1–10	0.1–1	0–0.4	1–3	4–13	24–52	–	3–8	6–13
1006	ce	0–0.3	0–0.2	0–0.7	0.4–2	1–7	13–27	0–7.8	0.1–5	1–5
1007	ce	1–15	0–0.4	–	0–16	0–3	13–51	0–0.8	0–3	1–22
	cr	1–5	0–0.2	0–0.2	0–3	0.3–6	1–22	0–2	0–4	1–33
1008		0.3–0.8	0.2–0.3	0–0.3	–	2–4	14–22	0.4–4	1–2	2–4
1009	ce	1–3	0.2–0.7	–	2–3	4–6	27–54	–	1–3	8–29
	cr	1–6	0.1–0.6	–	2–5	3–7	26–55	–	1–3	8–28

light – light etching area, dark – dark etching area, ce – cutting edge, cr – central rib area

Accuracy limits:	major elements 100% – 20%	±1% absolute
	Minor elements 20% – 1%	±0.5%
	Traces (detection limit 0.2%)	±0.2%

Table 9

No	Construction	Hardness rib	Hardness edge	Unetched	Etched (2% nital)	HT
1002	groove; +1 component; diagonal join	300	800	small incl. ‖ surface; more in dk etch area	lt+dk diagonal; fine P;M; Widman.; α at priory (large)	Q
1003	groove; 1 component	260	300	variable incl. some large; ‖ surface	α, variable size; carbide in grain boundaries	Q
1004	plane; +1 component; ? separate ce	250	690	few incl. ‖ surface	lt Y-shaped band encl. ce; rem.dk, irres.P + dk M at ce	QT
1005	groove; 2+ components; transverse join	200	600	many incl. ‖ surface; transv. group at join	lt cr, dk ce;lt and dk bands at join; fine P, dk M at ce	QT
1006	3 layers; transverse join at cr	160	215	oxide at weld; many incl.; ‖ surface	α and P banding	RC
1007	groove; 2 components; transverse join	160	450	small incl.in ce; large in cr; ‖ surface	α-rich cr; P-rich ce; Widman; banding	QT
1008	slight groove; 3 layers	190	190	many incl. various sizes; ‖ surface	α, α+P banding; Widman.; more C at 1 surface	RC
1009	groove; 2 components; transverse join	240	470	more incl. in cr; ‖ surface	v.fine P ; dk M at ce	QT

Construction:	the presence of a groove or channel is indicated, together with the number of component layers and any transverse joins.
Inclusions:	the quantity, size and orientation are indicated.
Etched structure:	the phases present and their distribution are given.
Heat treatment (HT):	the structure indicates the heat treatment.

Key to Table 9:

HT: heat treatment, Q: quenched, QT: quenched and tempered, RC: rapid cool (with little carbon, martensite is not produced), ce: cutting edge, cr: central rib area, incl.: inclusion, ‖: parallel, α: ferrite (almost pure iron), lt: light etching – in contrast with – dk: dark etching (areas containing more carbon etch more rapidly than ferritic areas but sometimes light etching is due to arsenic, dissolved oxides or other impurities), P: pearlite, Widmann.: Widmanstatten (which is characterised by pearlite with acicular ferrite spikes forming at the prior austenite grain boundaries), M: martensite, dk M: dark etching martensite (martensite etches rapidly after it has been quenched), irres. P: extremely fine pearlite, C: carbon, γ phase: austenite (stable above 723 °C and can contain up to 2% C, as the temperature drops below 723 °C, ferrite and pearlite or martensite form, depending on the rate of cooling).

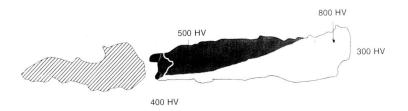

V8/1002   Hod Hill

V9/1004   Colchester

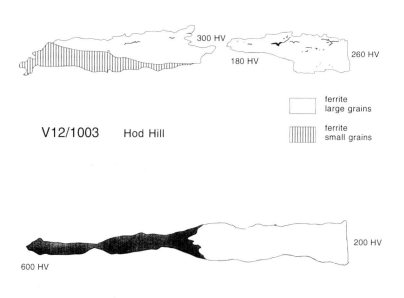

V12/1003   Hod Hill

V11/1005   Kingsholm

*fig. 61a. Schematic representation of the metallographic structure of sections of the blade sections, with hardness values.
(Tony Simpson, British Museum).*

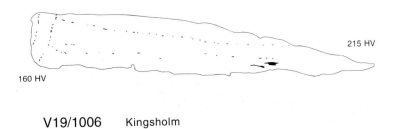

215 HV

160 HV

V19/1006 Kingsholm

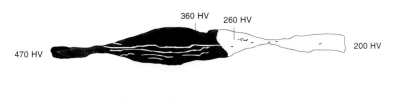

360 HV 260 HV

470 HV 200 HV

V6/1007 unprovenanced

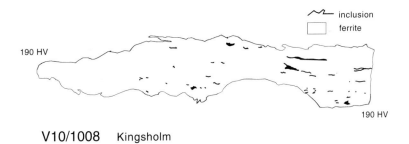

inclusion
ferrite

190 HV

190 HV

V10/1008 Kingsholm

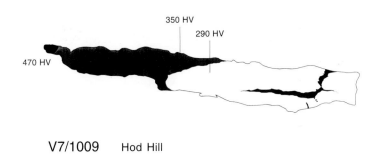

350 HV

290 HV

470 HV

V7/1009 Hod Hill

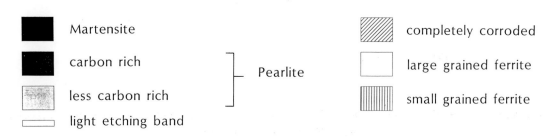

Martensite · completely corroded

carbon rich · large grained ferrite

less carbon rich · Pearlite · small grained ferrite

light etching band

fig. 61b. Schematic representation of the metallographic structure of sections of the blade sections, with hardness values.
(Tony Simpson, British Museum).

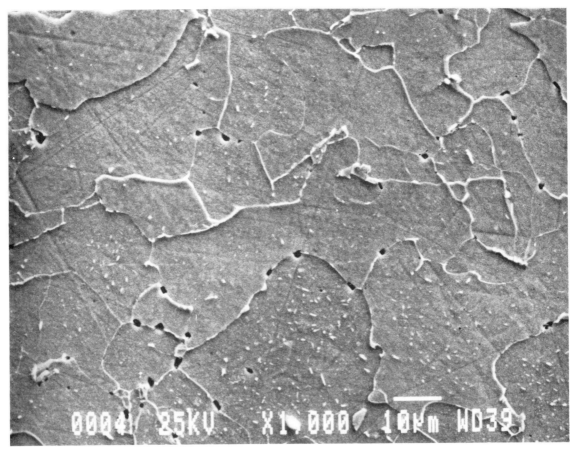

fig. 62. Sample 1003. Ferrite grains with carbide inclusions in the grain boundaries and within the grains (the cavities in the grain boundaries probably originally contained carbides). Scale bar 0.001mm.

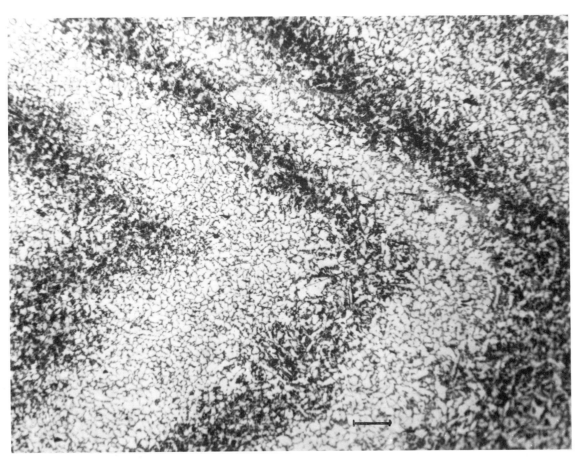

fig. 63. Sample 1005. Transverse weld areas, showing carbon rich bands (dark) and ferrite rich bands (light). Scale bar 0.07mm.

the presence of silicon might suggest sand was used as a flux. The grain size was small. Some pearlite formed long bands of linked single grains: this was probably associated with the welding process.

Sample 1007

There are a number of elongated inclusions parallel to the surface in 1007 and also some are associated with a transverse join. Etching shows less carbon and bigger grains on the central rib side of the light etching weld (fig. 65). There is some banding in the cutting edge section and the edge itself is tempered martensite.

Sample 1008

There are large quantities of two phased inclusions. Some have rough rather than smooth outlines and appear to be breaking up. Etching reveals a ferritic structure with slightly more carbon at one surface. It has a sandwich construction, with a thinner band at each surface enclosing a thicker band. The grain size is varied with smaller grains near the cutting edge. This is the only blade which shows no indication of hardening.

Sample 1009

There are both single and two phased inclusions. Some of the latter are quite large. Inclusions are associated with a transverse join. The central rib area has more slag inclusions and a deep corroded crack. The structure of the cutting edge has transverse bands of light and dark etching material and is mainly pearlitic with a fine grain size.

DISCUSSION

Bladed weapons of the 1st century AD

Iron Age swords have been examined by Pleiner (1993) and Lang (1984) amongst other workers. The general conclusions are that the quality of the blades is extremely variable. The construction may be plain (that is with no apparent layering) or composite, with either edge-to-edge or surface-to-surface layers. Composite structures appear to have been popular with Iron Age smiths. This may have been because it was easier to produce sound metal in small quantities which could be forge-welded together, or possibly because the striations, often visible on the surface after surface-to-surface welding, were considered to be decorative or significant in some way. Although the blades were usually cooled rapidly in their final heat treatment, because their carbon content was lower, they rarely achieved the hardness exhibited by the Roman swords.

Few Roman swords have been studied, largely because not many have been found. Three swords from the 1st century AD were examined by Lang (1988). They did not show transverse banding. The swords had relatively homogenised structures, hardened cutting edges and few inclusions. Three slightly later swords, which were examined in the same study, however, show more obvious banding and a deterioration in quality in every way. They have more inclusions and lower carbon contents and consequently lower hardness. This trend towards composite construction and decreased quality seems to be borne out by other studies. A sword from Whittlesey examined by Tylecote (1986: 164–7) and dated to the late 1st or early 2nd century AD, consists of three edge-to-edge layers. Hardness tests appear to have been carried out only at the centre of the blade, yielding the maximum value of about 200 HV. Williams (1977: 77–87) examined a 1st to 2nd century AD gladius from the Rheinisches Landesmuseum in Bonn which does not appear to have a markedly banded structure: surface hardness is 240 HV. The Vindonissa sword (Vindonissa Museum, Brugg Inventuar. 1938) is described by Biborski (1986: 45–80) as having a ferritic core encased in an outer layer which had a higher carbon content: however, the cutting edge (216 HV) had not been effectively hardened. It is later, in the 2nd to 4th centuries AD, especially in the Romano-Barbarian regions, such as Nydem, Nijmegen and Illerup, that the piled structure (usually considered to consist of a number of layers: Pleiner 1993) becomes common and develops into pattern welding. An early example might be the Roman spatha dated to the 2nd century AD (120–200 AD) found at Canterbury which exhibits proto-pattern welding (Watson *et al.* 1982: 188–190).

The Roman daggers in this study

In the present study, the dagger blades were constructed in a variety of ways and it is clear that a multilayered structure was preferred. Only one of them (1003) has little or no layering. The other blades have either an edge-to-edge construction or transverse piling, the exception being 1002, which appears to have a diagonal join but may also have a transverse one. These features are also found in the blades of Iron Age swords (Pleiner 1993), although few have as neat and elegant an arrangement of transverse strips as 1005. In his typological study, Scott (1985: 165) says that it was unclear (without radiography, presumably) which daggers have what he calls piled cores. He describes a blade with a piled core as having "a core that has been built up and the edges apparently welded to it" (1985: 182). He does not positively indicate which daggers he considers to have piled cores although he concludes that the daggers from Vindonissa, Chester and Augsberg-Oberhausen do not. The sample 1005, for example, shows a rather featureless core joined by a multilayered surface-to-surface strip to the cutting edge, which exhibits some traces of edge-to-edge banding. It is clearly a piled structure and the surface of the dagger blade shows banding, running down the blade. This is also visible on the radiograph. Surface striations can often be seen on the surface of piled or pattern welded blades which was probably part of the reason why they were constructed in this fashion in order to make a decorative finish (Lang 1989: 109–110). Care must be taken in interpreting the surface appearance, of course: Wyss (1968) has shown, by comparing cross-sections of swords with the corresponding grooves on the surface, that the welds in the section do not always correspond with the surface grooves.

Most daggers in the present study show a high degree of hardness which was achieved by heat treatment. The metal itself was of reasonably good quality although occasionally the welding left something to be desired, as for example, in 1006, where a triangular mass (of side 0.1–0.2 mm) of iron oxide clearly marks a junction between the transverse and horizontal layers near the central rib.

It appears that the practical aspects of carburising were understood. Not only was carbon-rich iron used for the cutting edge, but also 1008 appears to have been surface carburised. A carbon-rich section may have been used to make the cutting edge of 1004 for example; the single light etching band divides to enclose a carbon rich wedge which forms the cutting edge.

Primarily the blades would have been shaped by forging, but grinding and filing were also employed in the later stages. The edge-to-edge bands, which can be seen in some sections lying parallel to the short axis of the blade, terminate at the surface, rather than being compressed and following the surface contours towards the cutting edge. This is the result of grinding and filing. Forging compresses the bands as exemplified by an Iron Age sword from Waltham Abbey (Lang 1975: 203), which has a banded structure and is grooved. The microsection shows that the layers have been compressed by forging to make a groove. The light etching bands on 1007, for example, do not appear to be much compressed at the groove and are cut by the surface.

The heat treatment for every blade included at least part-quenching. The small grain size in most of the blades suggested that the final treatments were carried out at a relatively low temperature and perhaps repeatedly. Probably the final quench was from just above 723°C. All the quenched blades were also tempered, except for 1002. A similar finding was made by Tylecote (1986: 17) who examined a few Romano-British knives and reports that those with martensitic structures had been tempered.

A correlation seems to exist between the outward appearance of the blades and the metallurgical quality. Two of the blades (V10/1008 and V19/1006) appear to be rather basic in appearance as they do not have any grooves on the surface. The microsections show that they have low carbon contents, no transverse welds and their hardness is low. On the other hand, the more decorated weapons (V6/1007, V7/1009, V8/1002 and V9/1004) have higher carbon contents, more sophisticated construction and heat treatment and they are harder. The broken blade (V11/1005) falls into this group while the

other fragment (V12/1003) is anomalous: this may be because as the blade was broken, it was sampled from an area much closer to the hilt than the other blades.

The makers of the Roman daggers

Having discussed some of the technical aspects of the daggers, it remains to consider who made them and where, why there was a difference in the style of construction and to assess the quality of Roman ironwork.

The question of who made the equipment is a somewhat disputed one. There are several possibilities: the work might have been carried out by civilians or by legionaries (specialised or not) working in a fabrica, or by civilians working inside the camp. MacMullen (1960) supports the first suggestion, saying that the main source of supply for arms in the earlier Empire was small shops and dealers. A number of helmets and swords are known (MacMullen 1960) which are inscribed with the name of the individual maker. On the subject of private production, Bishop comments (1993: 186) "A few items do hint at it: inscriptions on sword scabbards from Vindonissa (Ettlinger 1984) and Strasbourg (CIL XIII, 10027, 197), and on a dagger sheath from Oberammergau (Ulbert 1971), name Roman citizens as the producers of the individual pieces. The first two actually name the place of production (LVGV and AD ARA). However the fact that these were citizens' names means we cannot rule out the possibility of military production or perhaps more likely, manufacture by veterans. "Some swords are stamped on the tang and a case might be made that these are also maker's stamps as there would be little point in having the owner's name concealed under the hilt. It seems unlikely that these blades would have been name-stamped if they had been made by legionaries in the fabrica, otherwise, why are the majority of blades not stamped?

Robinson suggests that some work was carried out by the legionaries, but that highly skilled jobs were probably carried on outside the camps. His opinion (1975) was that "It is not known for certain whether the fabri or specialist craftsmen of a legion actually made armour or only repaired it. No doubt many of them were capable of making it in times of emergency, or when a legion was stationed in newly conquered territory far away from production centres, but had manufacture been their fulltime occupation there surely could not have been any need for private firms to manufacture arms of any kind... I would suggest that maintenance of equipment and the production of javelin heads, arrows and the like were the main tasks assigned to the average military workshop."

Bishop (1993) concluded that almost all the work was done by the army itself and summarised his view of the production of military equipment for the Principate (Imperial) forces thus: "... the extended services of armies in the West led to increased production by the military Principate forces in the north-west, beyond areas of

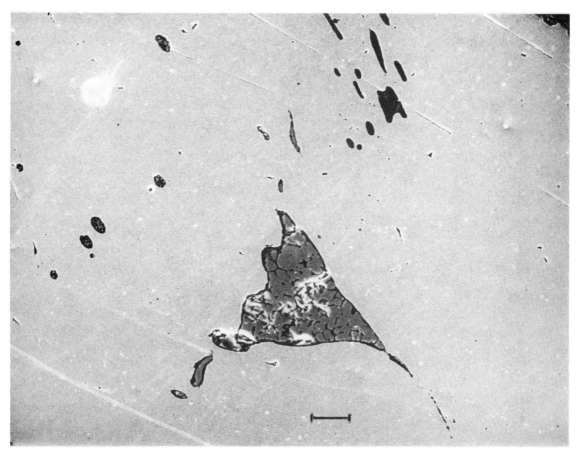

fig. 64. Sample 1006. Large inclusion at a join, mainly iron oxide, the result of incomplete welding at the join of three pieces of metal. Scale bar 0.03 mm.

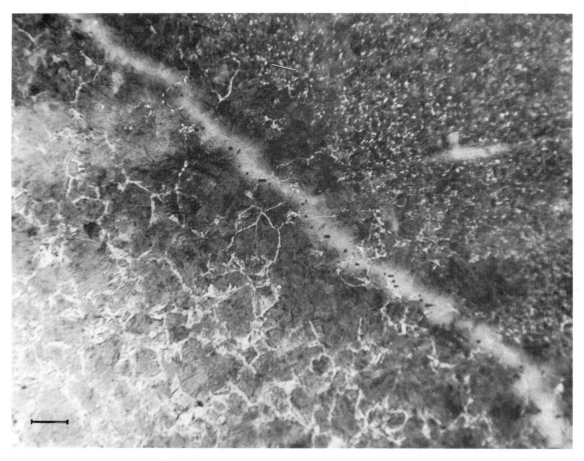

fig. 65. Sample 1007. The weld line (with some slag inclusions) between the fine grained cutting edge section and the coarser grained central rib section. Pearlite with grain boundary ferrite. Scale bar 0.02 mm.

Principate forces in the north-west, beyond areas of Mediterranean urbanisation, which were self sufficient, relying on their own fabricae." He based his views on archaeological and textual evidence. The archaeological evidence seems to suggest that most of the military equipment which has been excavated on Roman military sites (and military equipment has been found at almost all military sites of the 1st century AD) was discarded as scrap by the time it entered the archaeological record (1985: 8). Oldenstein (1977) has shown that military equipment was produced on the German limes of the 2nd and 3rd centuries AD. Raw materials, crucibles and moulds have been found in the region and Oldenstein has pointed out that scrap metal evidently played an important part as a resource. Bishop (1985: 8) suggests that when a fort or camp was abandoned, all the scrap which could be transported was taken away. Any remaining was buried; in Britain this seems to have happened at Inchtuthil (Taylor 1961) and possibly at Newstead (Curle 1911) while on the limes, the finds from Augsburg-Oberhausen and Vindonissa are well known. The waste products of working were certainly found at Hofheim (Ritterling 1904, 1913), Oberstimm (Schönberger 1978), Wiesbaden (ORL nr. 31), Rheingönheim (Ulbert 1969) and Exeter (Bidwell 1980), amongst other sites. Even a fortlet, like Martinhoe (N. Devon), only occupied over a short period (AD 55–70), mainly in summer, has a forge and metalworking debris (Fox 1965). Bishop follows Oldenstein in concluding that, as virtually every military site has yielded military equipment (he implies in the form of a deposit), this suggests that production was widespread. It could also be suggested that the scrap was normally collected and sent off to more centralised fabricae for recycling and not necessarily used on the spot: however, the layers of deposit from different legions found at Vindonissa may be regarded as support for Bishop's view.

Vegetius is used by Bishop (1993: 42) as an important textual source for the early Empire. The text was compiled in the 3rd to 4th centuries AD but included material from earlier texts (Parker 1932). The origins of many parts of the text are considered to have been identified by scholars as contemporary with the early Empire. Vegetius (II, 11) says that a legion had smiths and craftsmen in their winter quarters and that "they even had workshops for shields, cuirasses and bows, in which they fashioned arrows, missiles, helmets and all sorts of weapons. For this was a principal concern: that whatever they saw was necessary for the army, was never missing from the camp." This clearly suggests that most or all equipment was produced by the legions at their winter bases. Bishop concluded that the text "does not appear to leave much room for the private arms industry under the Principate (the early Empire)."

On the available evidence, it seems probable, therefore, that a large amount of equipment was made by the army for its own use, but at the same time, the practice established in the Republic of buying equipment from a well-reputed dealer or workshop continued.

However the production was organised, whether by private or military production (or a mix), it is clear that some blades were made by smiths who specialised in blade making. The evidence of the metallography of the Roman swords and daggers from Britain in the British Museum collections shows the skill of the smiths who were working in the 1st century AD. Certainly Manning (1979: 55) considered that "the Roman army was superbly equipped: an examination of the tools from Newstead leaves little doubt not only of the range available to the military craftsmen but of their sheer quality." While there is little or no information about the independent workshops, more is known about the fabricae. There is evidence that the legionary workshops in the 1st century AD were manned by specialist workers. The Vindolanda tablets (Tab. Vindol. II, 160, Tab. Vindol. II, 184), although fragmentary, list fabri by century and mention scutarii and possibly gladiarii, showing that there were craftsmen soldiers (Bowman 1994). The craftsmen were assisted by a daily detail of legionaries and possibly others. A later (2nd or 3rd century AD) papyrus P. Berlin inv. 6765 (Bruckner 1979) records auxiliaries, camp servants and (interestingly) civilians with guards working in the legionary workshop in a document which describes the activities in a fabrica over two successive days. On the first day, amongst other things, ten swords were made. This is an impressive total, especially if the hilts and grips had to be made as well. It is more probable that the basic units were readily available and that these were assembled and finished. However it hints at a possible reason for the decline in the quality of the blades as shown by the later swords. If these had been produced in large numbers without adequate supervision the results are unlikely to have been satisfactory. The swords of the 2nd century AD examined by the present author (Lang 1988) were not of particularly good quality and could have been made relatively rapidly. The dagger from Brancaster (Tylecote 1986:144), (probably 2nd century AD or later) is ferritic and has a low hardness (119 HV), which is consistent with the contemporary swords. The present study does not include any daggers later than the 1st century AD. However, it might be mentioned that the craft of quenching and tempering was being used to produce tool tips at the quarrying site at Mons Claudianus (Egypt) during the 2nd – 3rd centuries AD. Records show that smiths, bellowsmen, hardeners and hammermen were employed in making quenched and tempered points for quarrying tools (Peacock in press).

The smithing was not standardised, however, even in the 1st century AD, when it appears to have been most successful. Although presumably the craftsman (gladiarius) knew about the selection of suitable iron, forging, welding, carburising, heat treatment and finishing, it is significant that there are differences in construction between all the blades and also some differences in the operation of the heat treatment and carburising processes. Some blades were fully hardened, while others were also tempered.

There is a distinction to be made between the construction of the 1st century AD Roman swords and the daggers. These were possibly made by different craftsmen, but there seems to be no evidence for this. It would be far-fetched to suggest that civilian Celtic metalworkers, perhaps in slave-labour camps (Bishop 1993:184) made the daggers, but the method of construction is closer to the piled structures favoured by the Celtic smiths of the time (although more skilfully carried out) than the more straightforward Roman sword construction of the 1st half of the 1st century AD.

Another possibility is that the daggers were a product of the recycling policy which Bishop (1993) considers to be central to military arms production. Off-cuts and broken blades could be reconstituted to make small but very effective weapons. Because the blades were short, it would be somewhat easier to make a sound blade from several component strips. This might encourage experiment and versatility. It would be possible to produce a more individualised weapon by piling. Highly decorated dagger scabbards are well known (Bishop 1993: 77): the use of patterned blades would be consistent with the formalised display aspects of daggers. The frequently occurring texture or pattern on the blade may have been considered prestigious or to have special properties. Certainly the blade of the Velsen dagger (buried about AD 28 with a soldier in a well) has flowing lines on either side of the central rib. It also has a splendid sheath. In discussing the find Morel (1989: 187) suggests that the decorated dagger sheaths were an addition to the standard issue, perhaps even in the character of an officially sanctioned distinction. He continues: "It may be significant that other than the dagger and the fibula, no metal equipment accompanied the soldier. He was not buried in his uniform: helmet, sword and armour are absent. This emphasises the personal nature of the dagger, which might otherwise have been withheld at burial."

If the daggers were made, at least partly, from recycled material (as Oldenstein's work (1977) suggests they could have been), then it may be an argument in favour of their being made in the military workshops. They might have been made by the proto-immunes, but it seems likely that whoever made the blades was well aware of the Celtic piled structure blades. If civilian workers were being escorted into the fort by guards (P. Berlin, inv. 6765) at a later period, a similar policy might have prevailed in the West in earlier times, with Celtic smiths. Alternatively, the impetus might have come through the auxiliaries. The better quality dagger blades are unlikely to have been made by Celtic smiths outside the Roman influence partly because of the shapes, but also because they were effectively quenched and tempered, a final process that the Celtic smiths do not appear to have used on a regular basis.

Tylecote (1986: 199) has said "When we come to look at the Roman scene in Britain one is appalled at what the Romano-British customer is willing to accept.... In many cases the Roman smith gave the user a piece of steel but for some reason was unwilling or unable to heat treat it." While this might present an accurate view of the state of the later Roman blades, the present study and the previous work on 1st century AD swords shows clearly that the contemporary smith was perfectly capable of carburising, grain refining, quenching and tempering, although later these skills appear to have been forgotten or ignored in the military context.

To summarise: the majority of the daggers were skilfully made from several strips. On the available evidence, it seems likely that they were fabricated in the legionary workshops, but with some allowance either for non-standard materials or for individualism by the smith. The use of piled structures hints at a Celtic influence, with a practical Roman adaption for the production of a decorative, possibly prestigious weapon from recycled scrap. The simpler daggers were considerably less sophisticated in every way and perhaps intended for a different market. In the wider view, the daggers and the swords of the 1st century AD compare favourably in technical aspects to the contemporary Iron Age and post-1st century AD weapons.

Acknowledgements

The author would like to thank her colleagues Ralph Jackson (Department of Prehistoric and Romano-British Antiquities) and Paul Craddock (Department of Scientific Research) for helpful advice and comment, Tony Simpson (Department of Scientific Research) for the drawings and also Ian McIntyre (Department of Conservation) for cutting the samples from the blades.

References

Bennett, P., Frere, S.S. and Stowe, S. 1982. *Excavations at Canterbury*, 1. Gloucester.

Biborski, M., Kaczanowski, P., Zedierski, Z. and Stepinski, J. 1986. Ergebnisse der metallographischen Untersuchungen von römischen Schwertern aus dem Vindonissa-Museum Brugg und dem Römermuseum Augst. *Gesellschaft pro Vindonissa, Jahresbericht 1985*. Brugg: Vindonissa-Museum.

Bidwell, P.T. 1980. *Roman Exeter: Fortress and Town*. Exeter: 31–5.

Bishop, M.C. 1985. The military *fabrica* and the production of arms in the early principate. In *The Production and distribution of Roman Military equipment*. Proceedings of the Second Roman Military Equipment Seminar, Brit. Archaeol. Rep. S275. Oxford.

Bishop, M.C. and Coulston, J.C. 1993. *Roman Military Equipment*. London: Batsford.

Bowman, A.K. and Thomas, J.D. 1983. Vindolanda: the Latin Writing Tablets. *Britannia Monograph Series no. 4*. London.

Bowman, A.K. and Thomas, J.D. 1994. *The Vindolanda Writing-Tablets (Tabulae Vindolandenses II)*. London: British Museum Publications.

Bruckner, A. and Marichal, R. (eds) 1979. Chartae Latinae. *Antiquiores* Part X. Germany1. Zurich. pp.6–7.

Cavenaile, R. 1958. *Corpus Papyorum Latinarum*. Wiesbaden. 189.

CIL *(Corpus Inscriptionum latinorum)* XIII, 10027: 197.

Curle, J. 1911. *A Roman Frontier Post and its people*. Glasgow: James Maclehose, pp. 113–5.

Ettlinger, E. and Hartmann, M. 1984. Fragmente einer Schwertscheide aus Vindonissa und ihre Gegenstücke vom Grossen St Bernhard. *Jahresbericht der Gesellschaft pro Vindonissa*: 5–46.

Fox, A. and Ravenhill, W. 1965. Old Burrow and Martinhoe. *Antiquity*, 39: 253–8.

Harrauer, H. and Seider, R. 1977. Ein neuer lateinischen Schuldschein: P. Vindob. L 135. *Zeitschrift für Papyrologie und Epigraphik*, 36: 109–20.

Herrman, F.-R., 1969. Der Eisenhortfund aus dem Kastell Künzing. *Saalburg Jahrbuch.*, 27: 129–141.

Lang, J. 1984. The technology of Celtic iron swords. In *The Crafts of the Blacksmith* (eds B.G. Scott and H. Cleere). Belfast, pp. 61–72.

Lang, J. 1988. Study of the metallography of some Roman swords. *Britannia*, 9: 199–216.

Lang, J. and Ager, B. 1989. Swords of the Anglo-Saxon and Viking Periods in the British Museum: a Radiographic Survey. In *Weapons and Warfare in Anglo-Saxon England* (ed. S. Hawkes). Oxford University Committee for Archaeology. Monograph No. 21. Oxford, pp. 85–123.

Lang, J. and Williams, A.R. 1975. The hardening of iron swords. *Journ. Archaeol. Science*, 2: 199–207.

MacMullen, R. 1960. Inscriptions on armor and the supply of arms in the Roman Empire. *American Journ. Archaeol.*, 64: 23–40.

Manning, W.H. 1979. Native and Roman Metalwork in Northern Britain: a question of origins and influences. *Scottish Archaeol. Forum*, 11: 52–61.

Manning, W.H. 1985. *Catalogue of the Romano-British Iron Tools, Fittings and Weapons in the British Museum*. London.

Morel, J.-M.A.W. 1989. An Early Roman burial at Velsen I. In *Roman Military Equipment: the sources of evidence.* (ed. C. van Driel-Murray). *Proceedings of the Fifth Roman Military Equipment Conference*. Brit. Archaeol. Rep., Int. Series 476, Oxford.

Oldenstein, J. 1977. Zur Ausrüstung römischer Auxiliareinheiten. *Bericht der römisch-germanischen Komission*, 57: 49–366.

Oldenstein, J. 1977. Zur Buntmetallverarbeitung in den Kastellen am obergermanischen und rätischen Limes. *Bulletin des Musées Royaux d'Art et d'Histoire*, 46: 185–196.

ORL *Der obergermanisch-raetische Limes des Römerreiches*. Nr. 31. 34.

Parker, H.M.D. 1932. The antiqua legio of Vegetius. *Classical Quarterly*, 26: 137–49.

Peacock, D.P.S. (in press) Excavations at Mons Claudianus.

Pleiner, R. 1993. *The Celtic Sword*. Oxford: Clarendon Press, pp. 134–154.

Pliny. *Natural History* 26. Trans. H. Rackham. Loeb, London 1968. 233–5.

Ritterling, E. 1904. Das frührömische Lager bei Hofheim i.T. Ausgrabungs- und Fundbericht. *Annalen des Vereins für nassauische Altertumskunde*, 34: 1–110, 397–423.

Ritterling, E. 1913. Das frührömische Lager bei Hofheim i.T. *Annalen des Vereins für nassauische Altertumskunde*, 40: 1–416.

Robinson, R. 1975. *The Armour of Imperial Rome*. London: Arms and Armour Society.

Samuels, L E, 1980. *Optical Microscopy of Carbon Steels*. American Society for Metals, 352.

Schönberger, H. 1978. *Kastell Oberstimm: die Grabungen von 1968–1971*. Berlin: 304.

Scott, I.R. 1985. In Manning 1985.

Scott, I.R., 1985. First century military daggers and the manufacture and supply of weapons for the Roman army. In *The Production and distribution of Roman military equipment*. (ed. M.C. Bishop). Brit. Archaeol. Rep., Int. Series 275: 160–213.

Suetonius, *The Twelve Caesars*. Trans. Robert Graves, 1965: 37–8.

Tacitus *Annales*. Trans. C.H. Moore, J. Jackson. Loeb. 1992.

Taylor, M.V. and Wilson, D.R. 1961. Roman Britain in 1960. I Sites explored. *Journ. Roman Studies*. 51: 157–91.

Tylecote, R.F. and Gilmour, B. 1986. *The Metallurgy of Early Ferrous Edge Tools and Edge Weapons*, Brit. Archaeol. Rep. 155: 164–7.

Ulbert, G. 1969. *Das frührömische Kastell Rheingönheim*. Berlin: 113.

Ulbert, G. 1971. Gaius Antonius: der Meister des silbertauschierten Dolches von Oberammergau. *Bayerische Vorgeschichtsblätter*, 36: 44–9.

Williams, A.R. 1977. Roman arms and armour: a technical note. *Journ. Archaeol. Science*, 4: 77–87.

Wyss, R. 1968. Belege zur keltischen Schwertschmiedkunst. In *Festschrift für Rudolf Laur- Belart* (eds E. Schmid and L. Bürgin). Stuttgart, pp. 664–81.

Youtie, H.C. and Winter, J.C. 1951. Papyri and Ostraca from Karanis. *Papyri in the University of Michigan Collection*. vol. 8: Ann Arbor. 2.

Note. An interesting report by D. Horstmann (Max-Planck-Institut für Eisenforschung) of the metallographic examination of two quenched and tempered high quality early 1st century AD daggers from Haltern and Oberaden in the *limes* in Communication 55, Comité pour la Sidérurgie Ancienne (ed. R. Pleiner, Prague 1995, 335) came to the author's notice too late to be discussed in this paper

Ritual or Refuse: The Harrow Hill Enclosure Reconsidered

W. H. MANNING

The small sub-rectangular enclosure, measuring 60 ×
52 m (Holleyman 1937: 231), which stands on the summit of Harrow Hill (fig. 66), high on the Sussex Downs,
6 km north of Angmering (fig. 67), was partially excavated by G. Holleyman in 1936. Although often referred
to as a small hillfort (e.g. in Holleyman 1937: 230), the
site is better described as enclosed rather than defended.
Both the bank and ditch are relatively slight; the average
height from the bottom of the ditch to the top of the
rampart being no more than 1.5 m, and, as Holleyman's
sections make clear, the ditch can never have been more
than 1 m deep and 2 m wide with a correspondingly
slight bank. Neither the ditch, which varied in its cross-
section from a wide U-shape to one with a flat bottom,
nor the bank would have presented a serious obstacle to
any attacker.

Of the two entrances shown on Holleyman's plan (fig.
68A), only that on the western side is likely to have been
original. Excavations showed that originally there had
been a timber structure within it carried on four posts,
one pair on each side, with "palisade trenches" running
between the posts of each pair, probably to hold posts
revetting the ends of the banks (fig. 68B). Below the
centre of the bank was a row of relatively close-set post-
holes. The report is silent on whether the posts had run
through the body of the rampart, as Cunliffe suggests
(1991: 37), or had preceded it. The published section
(Holleyman 1937: pl. II, C–D) suggests the latter (fig.
68D), but the reality is probably that, given the nature of
the rampart material, it was impossible to tell. In another
cutting through the bank (Cut III) the excavators found
two rows of post-holes which they identified as the remains of the timber revetment of a Hollingbury style
rampart (fig. 68C). However, the small size of these post-
holes (only 7.5 cm in depth), and their irregular spacing
in two converging lines, makes such an identification
unlikely. More probably the front line is a continuation
of those found near the gate, while the others are the
remains of some structure predating the bank. Given the
relatively slight nature of the bank, it is probably best to
see the main row of post holes as the remains of a pali-

sade set in the bank, as Cunliffe suggests, rather than
evidence for an earlier palisade.

The entrance is of a type which is known at other
sites, perhaps most notably at Little Woodbury where it
was associated with the palisade which formed the first
phase of that enclosure (Bersu 1940: 46, fig. 8).

A series of small cuttings was made in the interior,
almost at random to judge by the published plan, but
they failed to detect any signs of structures. However,
given what we now know of the slight nature of many
Iron Age huts, the absence of evidence for huts in
trenches of this type cannot be taken as proving a genuine absence of such huts. More significant was the failure to find either pits or more than a minimal amount of
pottery, "not more than half a pound weight" (Holleyman
1937: 244, figs 11–13). The little which was found was
diagnostic of "Early Iron Age A ware" (fig. 68E), and it
is this which provides the suggested sixth century date
for the site (Drewett *et al.* 1988: 96), although an earlier
date within the general late Bronze Age/early Iron Age
continuum is not impossible, hence Cunliffe's more general suggestion of an early first-millennium date (Cunliffe
1991: 37).

Given the inevitable limitations of small scale excavations undertaken sixty years ago, it would be easy to
dismiss Harrow Hill as a typical Late Bronze Age or
Early Iron Age enclosure in which the excavators had
failed to locate the huts, were it not for the strange nature of the animal remains from the site. These consisted
of two teeth and part of the shin bone of a sheep, the
mandibles of some thirteen or fourteen oxen and the
loose lower and upper teeth of oxen, together with two
fragments of limb bones. (J.W. Jackson in Holleyman
1937: 248).

These details are slightly expanded by the excavator
who states that the total number of animals represented
by the mandibles and teeth "must number between fifty
and one hundred from our small cuttings alone. This
would mean, at a very conservative estimate, that the
whole earthwork must contain the remains of well over
a thousand heads." (Holleyman 1937: 250). The possi-

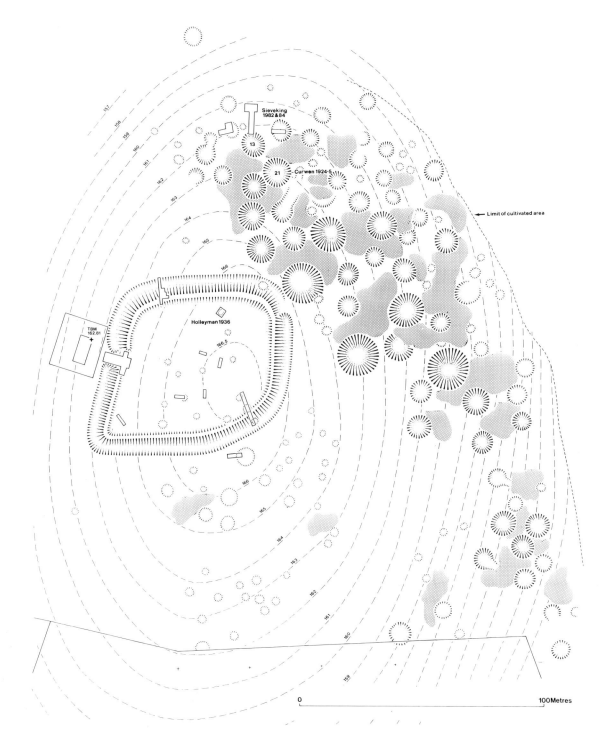

fig. 66. Harrow Hill, the site. Survey by Fred Aldsworth, 1986.

bility of a ritual explanation for this strange assemblage was tentatively advanced: "One is tempted to theorize about sacrificial offerings by mass slaughterings to propitiate mysterious Celtic deities, but this is beyond the scope of this paper" (1937: 250).

Later writers have noted the oddity of the bone assemblage, but have treated the suggestion of ritual with some caution. Cunliffe, who discusses the site at some

length, notes this possibility, but also suggests that the site could have been used for the slaughtering of surplus stock at certain times of the year, "the worthless parts of the carcase, including the heads, being discarded before the rest was carried off", adding that the two explanations are not mutually incompatible (Cunliffe 1991: 37). Drewett and his collaborators prefer the latter explanation and suggest that the bones "perhaps indicate that the

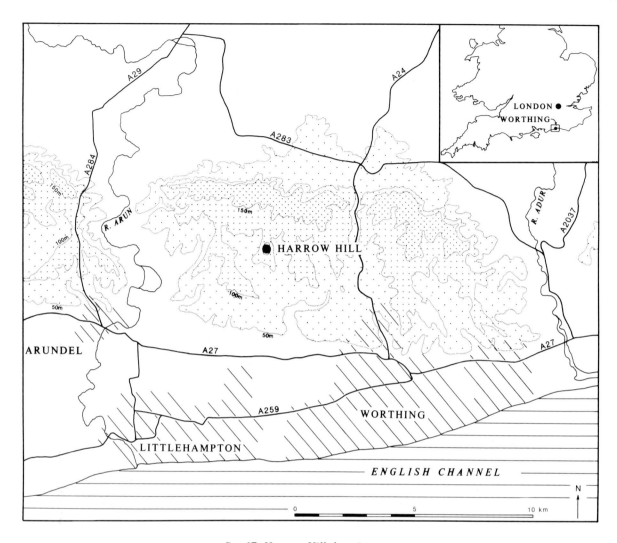

fig. 67. Harrow Hill, location map.

processing of animal products was at least one activity which took place on this site." (Drewett *et al.* 1988: 96).

The purpose of this paper is to suggest that the bone evidence does suggest ritual behaviour, and that there is one other piece of evidence which, although well known, has not been linked before with the possibility of ritual activity at Harrow Hill.

Although one cannot totally deny the possibility of sites being specially constructed for slaughtering animals, it does not seem logical to construct such a site on top of the South Downs rather than conveniently close to the settlements where the meat would have been consumed. Nor is it immediately obvious why, if the animals were butchered at Harrow Hill, all of the bones should have been removed save for the lower jaws. If the butchery was taken to an advanced stage, which it must have been for the upper and lower jaws to have been separated, other bones such as the feet and rib cage could equally well have been discarded; while if the butchery was mainly preliminary, to enable the carcase to be more easily transported, one would have expected the head, which contains two large delicacies, the tongue

and brains, to have been removed in one piece. On these grounds alone it may be thought that the alternative hypothesis – that the mandibles were taken to Harrow Hill rather than all parts of the beasts save the mandibles removed from it – must be considered as being more probable.

The argument against this, of course, is why should anyone want to carry the lower jaw of a cow, let alone of several hundred cows, to a hilltop enclosure? To which the most reasonable answer would seem to be – as ritual offerings.

Clearly if this explanation is correct, there must have been a reason for the choice of Harrow Hill as a ritual site. Normally the reason for any site being chosen as a religious centre in the Iron Age is likely to remain a mystery, but that may not be so in the present case. As is well known, Harrow Hill is one of the major flint-mining sites in the south of England. Even today the remains of some one hundred and sixty mine shafts are visible (Drewett *et al.* 1988: 49), and others have been so completely levelled as to be invisible on the ground. Three such were located in the excavation of the enclosure, and, given the small scale of the work, more probably exist within it. In the first millennium BC the remains of these mines will have been far more obvious than they are today, and while their original function had probably been forgotten, the fact that they were the remains of large and deep shafts must have been evident. One of the few clear facts about Iron Age religious customs is that throughout the Celtic world shafts and pits were linked with cult practices. In Britain the Wilsford shaft shows that this practice had begun by the early to middle Bronze Age, and it continued through the Iron Age to the end of the Roman period (Manning 1972). The most striking examples are those shafts which were sunk for no apparent reason other than for cult purposes. Such shafts were discussed at length by Ross (1968), and even if her more questionable examples are eliminated, an impressive number remain (Wait 1985). Similar shafts are known on the Continent, where those found in some of the rectangular earthworks known as Viereckschanzen in Germany are probably most familiar to English readers (Piggott 1968: 77ff.; Green 1986: 132ff.) More recent has been the recognition of the fact that many of the storage pits found on Iron Age sites in the south of England had ritual deposits placed in them before they were refilled. Danebury is probably the site where this is most clearly seen, but it is equally common at other settlements. The nature of the offering may vary, but the commonest form seems to have been a cow's head.

The most obvious reason for the digging of the deep shafts which appear to have no functional explanation is that it was thought that they gave the worshipper contact in some way with deities dwelling below the earth. Similarly the offerings placed in storage pits which had fulfilled their purpose and were about to be refilled, can most logically be identified as thanks offerings to the chthonic deities who had safeguarded the grain stored in the pit, and who, it was no doubt hoped, would guard that put in any new pits.

It is this aspect of late Bronze Age and Iron Age ritual which suggests that it was the existence of considerable numbers of very large and deep pits on Harrow Hill, an area of otherwise smooth downland, which made the site in some way sacred early in the first millennium B.C., and which led to the construction of a small enclosure within which the cult was celebrated with the type of offerings which were commonly made to the chthonic deities of Iron Age Britain, namely ox-heads. The use of rectangular or sub-rectangular enclosures to define a temenos is common in the Celtic world (Piggott 1968: 60ff.; Woodward 1992: 33, fig. 19; Woodward and Leach 1993: 305ff., fig. 210). Indeed, the need to define and enclose sacred space is characteristic of classical as well as Celtic cults, and undoubtedly reflects a fundamental aspect of much religious practice. In Britain the Iron Age shrines which preceded the Romano-Celtic temples at Colchester, Harlow, Hayling Island, Lancing Down, and Uley all lay within enclosures, which were associated with palisades in several cases. At Hayling Island the enclosure was a regular rectangle, at Uley sub-rectangular, at Lancing Down and Colchester almost circular, and at Harlow an unusually large oval (Woodward and Leach 1993: 305ff.) In this respect Harrow Hill would be in no way exceptional as a sacred site, although probably rather earlier in date than most of those just cited.

In recent years the Belgic areas of northern Gaul have produced a number of sites which are of outstanding interest and importance for the study of Celtic religious practices. Almost all of these were set in dominant positions, often on the highest points of plateaux. The best known is Gournay-sur-Aronde where a rectangular enclosure delineated by a ditch in the early La Tène period, underwent a series of changes before its eventual ritual closure in the first century BC (Brunaux 1988: 13ff.) The original enclosure, which was 45 × 38 m, was defined by a ditch 2.5 m wide and 1.8–2.0 m deep. Later a palisade set in a low bank was built inside the ditch with an additional ditch on its inner side. In its first phase the interior appears to have been devoid of structures, but in the third century BC a group of sacrificial pits was dug at its centre, and these, in their turn were superseded, firstly by an oval temple and subsequently by two successive rectangular ones. Throughout all of these changes, however, a central pit was retained within the buildings to serve as the main sacrificial point of the complex. The chosen victims were usually relatively old cattle. However, the most striking aspect of the site was the vast mass of sacrificial material which had been deposited in the enclosing ditch. In all it produced some 2,000 weapons, most of which had been ritually broken or distorted, and some 3,000 animal bones. Some of these bones represented the remains of the cattle which had been sacrificed, and these were concentrated in the ends of the ditch flanking the entrance to the enclosure where cattle skulls were particularly common. These bones showed no signs of knife marks, suggesting that they had not been butchered for food, but the remains of the other animals in the ditch, mainly young lambs, pigs and some dogs, did show such marks and were interpreted as the remains of ritual feasts which had taken place within the enclosure. The material in the ditch had accumulated throughout the life of the enclosure and probably represents the ritual disposal of offerings originally made within it; a situation which may be analogous to the burial of accumulations of figurines and other offerings of no intrinsic value within the temenos of a Greek cult site.

Although of a far more spectacular nature than Harrow Hill, there are a number of points of similarity between the two sites. The use of an enclosing ditch with a palisade set in a bank is one, as is the emphasis placed on a relatively elaborate entrance structure. The symbolical importance of the entrance into a sacred area is obvious; as Brunaux remarks, it is the point of commu-

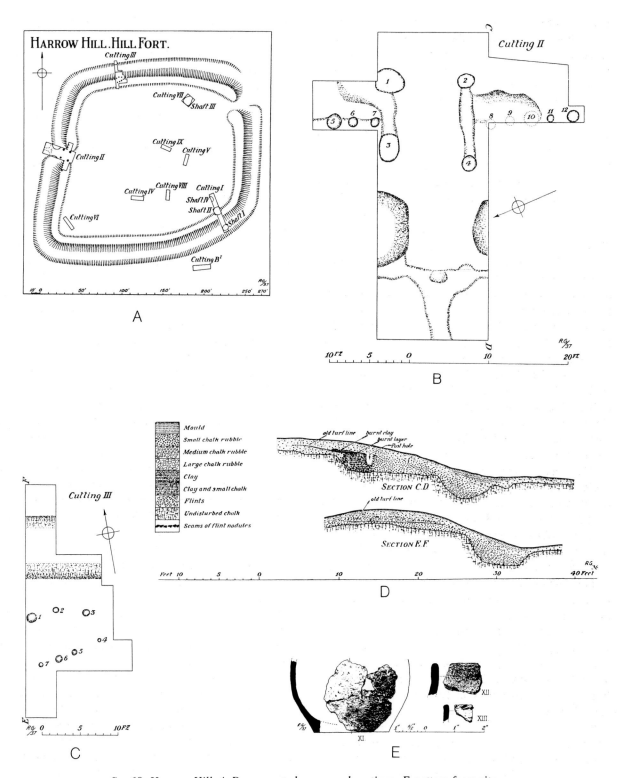

fig. 68. Harrow Hill. A-D, excavated areas and sections; E pottery from site.

nication between the worlds of the sacred and profane, and the elaboration of such entrances is characteristic of sanctuaries throughout the ancient world. The choice of cattle for the sacrificial beasts is another point of similarity, as is the emphasis on the sacrificial pit, which probably provided a point of contact with chthonic deities (Brunaux 1988: 120). Another possible similarity is

the fact that, as Brunaux notes (1988: 8), the actual sacrifices did not take place on the cult site itself but somewhere else, presumably in the settlement, which at Gournay was adjacent to the sacred enclosure, and only selected parts of the beast were then taken to the shrine; a fact which is made clear by the absence of certain bones from the ditch deposits.

Although Gournay is the best known of these sanctuaries, it is only one of an increasing number, most of which show marked similarities to it in the use of enclosing ditches and palisades, within which a wooden shrine was built at a relatively early stage in the history of the site. In most cases the ditches were the final repositories of masses of offerings represented by pottery, metalwork and animal bones (Brunaux 1988).

Although these points of resemblance do not prove that Harrow Hill was a Celtic sanctuary, they do show that many of the structural features noted there are paralleled in more certain sanctuaries in Britain and in the adjacent parts of northern Gaul, and thus strengthen an argument which only excavation can finally prove or disprove. Whether such an excavation would show the presence of a timber shrine is another matter. Although the precise date of the construction of Harrow Hill is far from clear, it must be relatively early in the Iron Age, and the evidence from both Gaul and Britain tends to suggest that most shrines were relatively late in date, although, and possibly significantly, those in Gaul could be constructed within pre-existing sacred enclosures.

It may be some memory of the sacred nature of the site which led to the deposition of two coins of Domitian in the top of one of the shafts late in the first century AD (Holleyman 1937: 236), and to the Anglo-Saxon name of the site, which most probably derives from "Hearg", meaning a heathen temple (Curwen 1922: 27ff.).

Acknowledgement

I would like to thank Dr. Robin Holgate for providing the new site plan and Mr. Fred Aldsworth for permission to reproduce it; Mr. Howard Mason for preparing the location map, and Mr. John Morgan for copying the original plans and sections.

References

Bersu, G. 1940. The Excavations at Little Woodbury, Wiltshire, Part I. *Proc. Prehist. Soc.*, 6: 30–111.
Brunaux, J. L. 1987. *The Celtic Gauls: Gods, Rites and Sanctuaries.* London: Seaby.
Cunliffe, B. 1991. *Iron Age Communities in Britain.* London: Routledge.
Curwen, E.C. 1922. *Sussex Archaeol. Coll.*, 63: 27ff.
Drewett, P., Rudling, D. and Gardiner, M. 1988. *The South-East to AD 1000.* London: Longman.
Green, M. 1986. *The Gods of the Celts.* Gloucester: Alan Sutton.
Holleyman, G. 1937. Harrow Hill Excavations, 1936. *Sussex Archaeol. Coll.*, 78: 230–52.
Manning, W.H. 1972. Ironwork Hoards In Iron Age And Roman Britain. *Britannia*, 3: 224–250.
Piggott, S. 1968. *The Druids.* London: Thames and Hudson.
Ross, A. 1968. Shafts, Pits, Wells – Sanctuaries of the Belgic Britons? In *Studies in Ancient Europe* (eds J. Coles and D.D.A.Simpson). Leicester: Leicester University Press, pp. 255–85.
Wait, G.A. 1992. *Ritual and Religion in Iron Age Britain.* Brit. Archaeol. Rep., Brit. Series 149: Oxford.
Woodward, A. 1992. *Shrines and Sacrifice.* London: B.T. Batsford/English Heritage.
Woodward, A. and Leach, P. 1993. *The Uley Shrines. Excavations of a Ritual Complex on West Hill, Uley, Gloucestershire: 1977–9.* London: English Heritage in association with British Museum Press.

An Unprovenanced La Tène Linchpin with 'Vegetal' Decoration in the British Museum

J. V. S. AND M. RUTH MEGAW

Amongst the shrewd but at first sight less spectacular acquisitions made on Ian Stead's recommendation for the Department of Prehistoric and Romano-British Antiquities at the British Museum is the iron and bronze linchpin which is the subject of this note (figs 69; 70:1 71:1). Its small size and, frankly, present display in the Iron Age art gallery at the Museum – to change when a new Iron Age gallery opens in 1996 – dictates that only the keenest visitor gives it even a passing glance. Its purchase, however, marks a welcome addition to the inventory of the Museum's collection of examples of the so-called 'Waldalgesheim' or 'Vegetal' style of Continental La Tène art conventionally dated to the late fourth to third centuries BC. Heretofore, the Museum has owned only a handful of objects in this style whose evolution came about as the result of a fusion of the early phase of La Tène art with elements of contemporary Italo-Greek plant-based ornamental motifs. While the actual region where the new style developed remains the subject of debate, it is clear that the immediate stimulus was the expansion south of the Alps of La Tène groups and subsequent movements both north and south (for summaries see Jacobsthal 1944: esp. 94ff.; Kruta 1974; *id.* 1982; Frey 1976; *id.* 1986; *id.* 1991; Castriota 1981; Peyre 1982; Verger 1987; Megaw and Megaw 1989: 106–21).

Other examples of the 'Vegetal' style in the British Museum[1] include a cast bronze brooch from Prosnes, Marne, part of the collection of antiquities made in Champagne by Léon Morel, purchased by the British Museum in 1901 and currently the subject of a catalogue in preparation by Ian Stead and Val Rigby (see brief history of the collection in Stead and Rigby 1981:13). The brooch exhibits on its bow and foot a variation of the continuous wave-tendril which is the hall-mark of the 'Vegetal' style. The brooch type is to be compared with the more southerly examples of the so-called 'Münsingen-Duchcov horizon', type fossils for the fourth century period of expansion (Morel 1898: Album pl. 24, fig. 25; Kruta 1977: 26 and fig. 4:2; *id.* 1979; Stead and Rigby 1981: no. 242; Verger 1987: 307 and fig. 18:2). Also from the Morel collection but without any firm indica-

tion as to provenance is a circular bronze strainer plate, presumably originally from a wine sieve, decorated with a four-armed 'vegetal' whirligig (Jacobsthal 1944: no. 400; Stead and Rigby 1981: no. 243; Megaw and Megaw 1989: ill. 176 – for a discussion of La Tène and Etruscan sieves north of the Alps see most recently Geiss-Dreier 1991).[2] A third piece from the Morel Collection is a pedestalled vase from Prunay, Marne, one of a series of wheel-turned and painted pots whose decoration is related to the developed 'Vegetal' style (Morel 1898: Frontispiece (centre); Jacobsthal 1944: no. 408 – the decoration is invisible on the published photograph!; Megaw 1970a: no. 154; Rowlett 1968: fig. 10; Stead and Rigby 1981: no. 241; Rigby *et al.* 1989: Corradini 1991: esp. 115 and fig. 5).[3]

THE BRITISH MUSEUM LINCHPIN AND ITS TYPOLOGICAL PARALLELS

The linchpin, inv. no. 1989.1.7.1, has a maximum height of 107 mm and width of 55 mm. Following examination by the British Museum Department of Research, it has been established that the pin is mainly of iron with the addition of decorated strips of bronze which were attached to the iron by projections from the underside of the bronze (fig. 73) which fit into holes and grooves in the iron. The terminal to the pin is very close fitting and only a few millimetres thick; it could have been made by casting the bronze around the iron or by separately casting a hollow cap and hammering it to fit tightly. There are signs of wear, the top plate in particular has lost a small part of its vegetal design and the 'cable edging' has worn smooth in several places (fig. 69b).

As to the history and provenance of the pin, it was purchased in 1989 from the London dealers, Erasmus and Co. of Cork Street, who had in turn obtained it through the antiques market some five years previously. The dealer's own records give no indication of its possible origin although it may be noted that the same source has a considerable amount of material not from Morel but from another nineteenth-century collector in the

a   *b*

c

fig. 69a–c. Unprovenanced iron linchpin with bronze flashing. Photos: British Museum.

Marne region, Charles-Louis-Auguste Nicaise (Stead: pers. comm.; see also MacGregor 1987: esp. 11). But for reasons that should become clear, not too much credence can or should be placed on such slender evidence.

On the other hand, that the piece under discussion is most likely to be a linchpin, originally one of a pair used to keep the free-running wheel of a cart or chariot on the axle, is simply to follow the normal interpretation given to this and a number of other examples, several first briefly discussed as a group by Jacobsthal (1944: 120). The following linchpins with rectangular heads are the most important for our purposes:

1–2. *Brežice, grave 6, Slovenia.* Pair of iron linchpins with rectangular bronze heads from a La Tène C1 chariot grave, one decorated with a diamond-shaped lozenge and concentric circles and the other with one surface with raised parallel ridge and pierced for ?binding thong; both have knobbed terminals to the pin. Length 124 mm. (Guštin 1984: 115, 119 and T.3(1–2))

3–4. *Danes Graves, barrow 43, Humberside, England.* A pair of iron linchpins with flat square – rather than rectangular – head; the complete example of the pair ends in a circular disc. Length of complete pin 130 mm. (Stead 1965: 34 and fig. 15:2; *id.* 1979: 45 and fig. 14:3).

5. *R. Erms bei Urach, Kr. Reutlingen, Germany.* Iron pin with head covered in embossed bronze. Surviving length 107 mm. (Jacobsthal 1944: no. 159; Fischer 1979: 108–10 and Abb. 49: 2; Bittel *et al.* 1981: 196–9 and Abb. 109)

6. *Grossdraxdorf, Kr. Greiz, Germany.* Iron pin with knobbed terminal and bronze-covered head, decorated with a human face set against a dotted background; the piece appears to have been lost in World War II. Length 110 mm. (Kaufmann 1966: 209 and Abb. 3; Megaw 1970a: 105)

7–8. *'Malkata Mogila', Mezek, Bulgaria.* Pair of cast bronze and iron linchpins with knobbed terminals. Length 121 mm. (Jacobsthal 1944: no. 164; Megaw 1970a: 112; Egami *et al.* 1979: no. 385; Domaradski 1984: 1245-6 and obr. 34)

9. *'Mont-de-Marne', Condé-sur-Marne, Marne, France.* Iron pin and head of plano-convex cross-section, the curved face inset with three D-sectioned cast bronze strips alternating with two rows of coral beads fixed with bronze pins. Jacobsthal (1944: no. 202), when publishing two fragments of iron encrusted with carved coral which are now missing, did not illustrate or mention the linchpin and overlooked the precise source of the find, an early La Tène chariot burial discovered by labourers in a sand-pit in 1907. Length 97 mm. (Stead 1965:34 and fig. 16:4) – drawn before cleaning; Verger 1987: 287; Legendre and Gomez de Soto 1990: esp. 297, fig. 1:1 and Taf. 40:3) (fig. 72b)

10–11. *Manching, Kr. Ingolstadt, Germany.* Two linchpins of iron with flat cross-sectioned rectangular heads, square cross-sectioned pins and knobbed ends. The first example has a single raised ridge on one face and the second three raised lines. Length 117 and 115 mm (Jacobi 1974: esp. 218–9, no. 854–5 and Taf. 56)

12. *Nanterre, Seine, France.* Iron linchpin with ring below bronze head which has a 'Maltese cross' setting filled with enamel. There is also a knobbed end to the pin. From a La Tène C chariot grave; Jacobsthal (1944: no. 174a–c and p. 120) in discussing material from this chariot grave, comments that it is 'later than the others'. Length 150mm. (Hubert 1902: esp. 67 and fig. 1 on p. 72;[4] Van Endert 1984: esp 53 and Abb. 16:4; Haffner and Joachim 1984: esp. 75 and Liste 4:22).

13. *Niederweis, Kr. Bitburg, Germany.* Cast bronze pin with decorated knobbed terminal and rectangular head of plano-convex section. Immediately below the head is a small loop or ring similar to that on no. 11–12. Length 94 mm. (Jacobsthal 1944: no. 161; Megaw 1970a: 86, 102, 104)

14. *Pipinsburg, Kr. Osterode, Germany.* Iron linchpin with bronze rectangular head flat on one surface and tapering on the other to a semi-circular profile to match that of the pin which has a bronze knobbed terminal. Length 108 mm. (Claus 1958: Abb. 9 :12)

15. *Prunay, Marne, France.* Iron pin with flat rectangular head found with two iron brooches and other iron fittings, probably the remains of a La Tène A chariot grave. Length 130 mm. (Rowlett 1969: fig. 19; Stead 1979: 45)

16. *? Seine, Paris, France.* Iron pin with cast bronze head, flat at back. Surviving length 55 mm, width 85 mm. (Jacobsthal 1944: no. 163; Megaw 1970a: no. 166; Stead and Rigby 1981: no. 251)

17–18. *Toarcla, jud. Braşov, Romania.* Two iron linchpins, one flat and undecorated, the other with a rectangular head of plano-convex cross-section and with three bronze strips, one brazed onto the upper surface and two onto the curved outer face. From a La Tène B2 warrior cremation grave with chariot fittings and horse harness. Surviving length 96 mm. (Horedt 1941–44: esp. 191–2, no. 7 and Abb. 1:6; Zirra 1971: 182–9; Crişan 1973: esp. 64 and 66; Végh 1984: 109) (fig. 72c–d)

19–20. *Waldalgesheim, Kr. Mainz-Bingen.* From the chariot grave of a wealthy woman, the type-site of the La Tène B1 'Vegetal' phase of early Celtic art; two iron linchpins, both lost during World War II; the more ornate of the two had a knobbed end and head of plano-convex section which from the surviving drawing and photograph appears to have had a rectangular bronze plate brazed onto the front, the plate being decorated with a curvilinear design and apparently coral inlay.[5] Length 101 mm. (aus'm Weerth 1870: esp. Taf. 5–6, fig. 15; Jacobsthal 1944: no. 156g; Driehaus 1971: 107) (fig. 72e–f).

The fullest discussion of linchpins and especially those with rectangular heads remains that by Jacobi (1974: 216–21). Apart from stray finds or those of uncertain origin, (nos 5–6, 10–11, 13), one comes from a hill-fort (no. 14) and the balance are from chariot graves or are associated with other pieces of chariot and/or harness-fittings. Several pins have loops or rings below the heads which are interpreted as being to take leather thongs to secure the pins onto the axle shaft. As to the genesis of the form, Pingel draws attention to – but does not illustrate – a curious iron sword-scabbard, probably a ritual deposit, found on the Alpe Matta, Balzers, Liechtenstein (Wyss 1958–9). Here the front of an otherwise unexceptional piece of La Tène B2 date has been decorated with an appliqué plaque which in outline certainly looks not unlike our particular form of linchpin (fig. 72a).

Of the examples listed, the form of our linchpin, made in iron with a rectangular head of plano-convex section, additional bronze plates and knobbed end to the pin, is best matched by nos 9, 17 and 19. Where datable or stylistic associations exist, the earliest linchpin in our list (no. 15) is another object from the Morel Collection in the British Museum.[6] The iron brooches with which the Prunay linchpin is associated date to the end of La Tène A, while other linchpins date to La Tène B1 (nos 9, 19–20) and several to La Tène C1 or even possibly later (nos 1–2, 10–12). Nos 5, 7–8 and 16 are best attributed to Jacobsthal's 'Plastic' style (i.e. 'Sculpted or '3-dimensional') or what we have termed the 'Disney' style (Megaw 1970b; Megaw and Megaw 1989: 135–44). On the basis of such finds as those from Mezek (nos 7–8), discovered with other chariot fittings as a secondary burial in a Hellenistic tholos tomb with painted cupola, it is possible to associate objects decorated in this style with the period of Celtic migration into the Balkans in the early third century BC or La Tène B2. And one must not fail to note the pair of linchpins from Danes Graves discussed by Stead himself in his reconsideration of the evidence for the so-called Arras culture and its possible French antecedents (Stead 1979: 26–29, 45; 1984: 39).

But, as observed at the outset, it is the very different style exhibited on the bronze plates of our unprovenanced linchpin which is the key to placing it in the development of what, unrepentantly, we continue to refer to as early Celtic art (Megaw and Megaw 1994).

STYLISTIC AFFILIATIONS

Since Jacobsthal's first analysis of what, following French practice, we shall call here the 'vegetal style', the significance of plant-based ornamentation of ultimately classical origin has been regarded as a key to the style's development. Kruta (1982; 1991), in particular, has placed a strong emphasis on Italy itself as the catalyst for this development, transmitted through the agency of La Tène settlers in the north of Italy maintaining contact with their northern homeland. Frey, on the other hand, has continued to refine the distinctions between the largely static and again classically-inspired motifs of the Early Style – the rich art of the fifth- and earlier fourth-century princely graves, centred on the Middle Rhine – and the flowing, intertwining vegetal patterns (Frey 1979). Verger (1987), among others (e.g. Castriota 1981), denying the primacy of Italy, looks to a development from the Early Style within the Champagne area itself, particularly of chains of triskels, forming what he terms 'le Premier style continu'. Most recently Frey has taken a middle position, looking to a coalescence of Marnian and Italian stylistic elements.[7]

Our linchpin offers two of the most characteristic vegetal motifs. First is the 'S'-chain (fig. 70:1), which in the Early Style was carefully constructed with the aid of compasses; later it becomes freer and more three-dimensional or 'plastic' in character. On the front of the pin, the chains of 'S's on the bronze strips are in fact constructed from four contiguous elements. Comparable designs may be found on metalwork from the end of La Tène A (Jacobsthal 1944: no. 376; Müller 1989: Grundmuster D: 54–55, fig. 2:2, 4–5) and on La Tène B1 stamped pottery (Schwappach 1971; id. 1973) (fig. 70:3). Amongst the earlier material, the sheet bronze crescentic mounts from a warrior's burial at Étrechy near Châlons-sur-Marne, with their combination of 3–part whirligigs and fat S-curls, are of particular interest as representing precursors to the continuous patterns which are a key feature of the true 'Vegetal' style.[8]

The more complex and assured design on the top of the linchpin is a pattern described by Jacobsthal, following Riegl (trans. 1992), as an 'intermittent wave tendril', the central feature of which is really a spread-out triskel or whirligig (Jacobsthal 1944: esp. 93) (fig. 71). The building up of patterns by means of various combinations of the two key elements, the S-curl and the triple-armed whirligig, is a key feature of much of the expansion period. Pairs of confronted 'S's become a lyre or simplified palmette which, when repeated, turns into a continuous chain or stack. As such, it occurs both on metalwork and, again in various combinations, also on La Tène B stamped pottery (Schwappach 1971: esp. 161 and Taf. 10). The wave tendril or 'sprung palmette' can be either a continuous pattern (Megaw 1970a: nos 138–9 – two finger-rings, one in gold from the Dürrnberg, Ld. Salzburg, grave 28 (fig. 71:7) and the other in silver from Deisswil, Kt. Bern, grave 8–15) or, as on our linchpin, a single, closed, design reversed laterally around a central point. The relative chronological position of both finger-rings is clear enough, especially with regard to that from the Dürrnberg which comes from a warrior's grave with an ornate cast bronze brooch with a coral setting on its foot-disc, which belongs to the general 'Münsingen-Deisswil' class (Pauli 1978: 123–5, 170–3, Abb. 15:4 and Taf. 25:A3). As Roy Hodson (above p. 66) indicates, 'such relatively restricted but highly distinctive series of ornate fibulae' which occur in the Münsingen, Kt. Bern cemetery itself, are typical of a relatively early stage of La Tène B1/Ib.

It is the second or 'closed' variant of the tendril design which gradually transmogrifies into the 'Cheshire-cat' (or, occasionally, a more definitely human) face characteristic of La Tène B2 (Frey 1971: 92 and Abb. 8; Lenerz-de Wilde 1982). In this sequence, stylistically our pin must have a fairly early position. The nearest parallel, however, for this closed design is to be found on one of two similar sheet-bronze mounts (?shield mounts) from a warrior's inhumation burial at Brunn-am-Schneebergbahn, Wiener-Neustadt, grave 10; this was originally dated as late as La Tène C although it is more likely to be La Tène B2 (Willvonseder 1937–38: 244–6, 255–9 and Abb. 12–13; Jacobsthal 1944: no. 377; Frey 1971: Abb. 8:2; Neugebauer 1992: 107 and Abb. 43, 1; fig. 71, 2). Both of our key motifs can also be found, with variations, on the *Scheibenhalsringe* of the Middle and Southern Rhineland (figs 70, 4–5; 71, 3). These torcs, often inlaid with enamel or occasionally coral, range in date from La Tène B1 to La Tène C and are occasionally found as imports not only in Champagne but as far afield as Romania and Hungary. The extremely worn condition of many of the easternmost examples suggests that they may have been brought as dowry by new groups of settlers (Müller 1989: 85–88).

ORIGIN AND DATING

Determining where the linchpin might have been manufactured is more difficult than demonstrating its stylistic relationships. Recent work in central and eastern Europe has established two factors; firstly, that there is a much

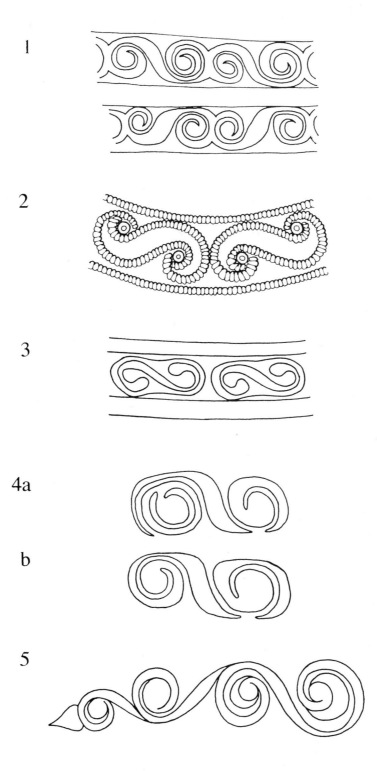

fig. 70. 'S' tendril patterns. 1 British Museum linchpin. Detail of decoration on side of head; 2 Étrechy, Marne. Detail of bronze ?shield mount; 3 Hidegség, Sopron m. Detail of pot stamp on double vase; 4a-b Ammerbuch-Pfäffingen, Kr. Tübingen. Detail of decoration on bronze Scheibenhalsring; *5 'Dammelberg', Trebur, Kr. Gross-Gerau. Detail of decoration on* Scheibenhalsring. *Various scales. Drawings: Karen Hughes and Andrew Noble.*

fig. 71. 'Closed' tendril patterns. 1 British Museum linchpin. Decoration on top of head; 2. Brunn an der Schneebergbahn, Gem. Wiener-Neustadt, grave 10. Decoration on sheet bronze mount; 3 Schönenbuch, Kt. Basel. Detail of decoration on bronze Scheibenhalsring; 4 Waldalgesheim, Kr. Mainz-Bingen. Detail of rolled-out decoration on pair of bronze bracelets; 5 Filottrano, S. Paolina, Ancona, grave 22. Detail of decoration on bronze sword scabbard; 6 Waldalgesheim, Kr. Mainz-Bingen. Detail of rolled-out decoration on gold neck-ring; 7 Dürrnberg-bei-Hallein, Ld. Salzburg, grave 28/2. Detail of rolled-out decoration on gold finger-ring; 8 'Giegenpeter', Dietikon, Kt. Zürich, grave 6. Detail of rolled-out decoration on silver finger-ring. Various scales. Drawings: Karen Hughes and Andrew Noble.

fig. 72. (a) Alpe Matta, Balzers, Liechtenstein. Detail of iron sword and scabbard. Width 58 mm. Photo: Schweiz.
Landesmuseum, Zürich; (b) 'Mont-de-Marne', Condé-sur-Marne. Iron linchpin with bronze flashings and coral insets.
Width of head 50 mm. Photo: Musée municipal, Châlons-sur-Marne; (c-d) Toarcla, jud. Braşov. Iron linchpin with bronze
flashings. Width 42 mm. Photos: J.V.S.Megaw; (e–f) Waldalgesheim, Kr. Mainz-Bingen. Iron linchpin with bronze flashing
and ?enamel inlay (now lost). (e) engraving as published by aus'm Weerth in 1870; (f) as photographed pre-World War II.
Width 60 mm. Photos: Rheinisches Landesmuseum, Bonn.

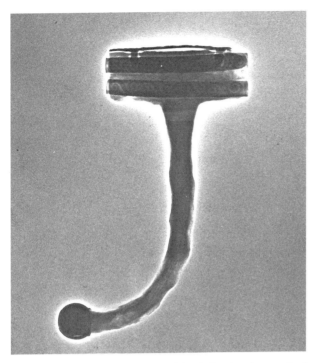

fig. 73. X-ray of unprovenanced linchpin showing method of attaching bronze strips to the iron pin. Photo: British Museum.

more easterly extension than used to be thought of the early phases of early Celtic art, i.e. La Tène A (Megaw, Megaw and Neugebauer 1989, Neugebauer 1992; Szabó 1992) and secondly that the genesis of the Sword-style sub-groups lies firmly in an eastern spread of the 'Vegetal style' and its subsequent developments (Szabó and Petres 1992; Rapin *et al.* 1992). It is obvious that the Vegetal Style or the use of continuous plant-based designs extends well into La Tène B2 or even La Tène C1 as can be seen from material from cemeteries in northwestern Romania (e.g. Zirra 1971: Abb. 12; Németi 1993: fig. 2:4, 8, 6 (O1); Rapin *et al.* 1992: esp. 40–52). In this context, the linchpin from Toarcla is significant; it was found in 1885 in a grave with the cremated bones of a warrior with iron sword, scabbard with open chape of so-called Hatvan-Boldog type (q.v. Petres and Szabó 1986; Charpy 1987) and sword-chain, together with fragments of a disc-terminalled brooch. While there has been some discussion both as to date and as to whether all the pieces were found as part of the same grave (Zirra 1971: 182–9; Crişan 1973: 62–3, 66), it seems most probable that they come from an in-urned La Tène B2 cremation associated with a chariot burial.

As to our two other closest typological parallels, the linchpins from Condé-sur-Marne (no. 9) and from Waldalgesheim (no. 19–20) (fig. 72b, e–f), both come from graves containing objects decorated in characteristic 'early' Vegetal style, the former, regarded by Legendre and Gomez de Soto (1990: esp. 297–300) as definitely La Tène B1 in date and with vegetal patterns

cut with extraordinary precision on coral settings of various chariot- and/or harness-mounts. While it is now obvious that a strict equation is no longer possible between the style and a limited La Tène B1/2 time frame, the context of these pins supports an early date. As just noted, the style of the decorative panels on our pin is suggestive of an earlier rather than a developed phase of the 'Vegetal' style, or in other words no later than La Tène B2. But while the natural tendency is to regard its place of origin as western Europe, it may just as well have come from much further to the east. Only further time, probably spent not so much in the field but rather in museum collections, may give further refinement to this, at present, all too inconclusive an opinion.

Acknowledgements

Over the last ten years we have been able to study at first hand almost all the material mentioned here in the course of preparation of a Supplement to Jacobsthal's *magnum opus,* a work still in progress and for which the essential funding has come from the Australian Research Council. We should like to thank our many friends and colleagues in the British Museum itself and on the Continent of Europe in particular Jean-Pierre Ravaux of the Musée municipal, Châlons-sur-Marne and Petre Munteanu Beşlau of the Muzeul Brukenthal, Sibiu as well as our driver and expert guide during a whirl-wind tour of northwestern Romania in October 1994, Vlad Vintila Zirra of the Institutul de Arheologie, Bucharest. Dr René Wyss kindly supplied us with a photograph of a strange piece indeed which we had sighted nearly thirty years ago and Professor H.-E. Joachim of the Rheinisches Landesmuseum, Bonn, editor of the forthcoming complete publication of the Waldalgesheim find, looked in vain for us for the linchpins from the site while Professor Emeritus Otto-Herman Frey kindly allowed us to read his own latest thoughts on the 'Vegetal' style which are to appear as a contribution to this long-awaited volume. But of course it was Ian Stead who gave us access to the British Museum linchpin even if he didn't know where, when or how it was first to be published.

Notes

1. The most obvious 'Waldalgesheim' or 'Vegetal' style pieces in the British Museum might seem to be the gold torc and pair of bracelets purchased in Belgium in 1930, objects which Jacobsthal himself compared with the similar set of neck- and two armrings from the type-site, the woman's chariot grave of Waldalgesheim, Kr. Mainz-Bingen (see Jacobsthal 1944: nos 45, 56 and nos 43, 55). The Waldalgesheim grave is dated to the late fourth century and includes one linchpin of particular significance for our concerns (see our list no. 19–20 and fig. 72–f). But there has for a long time been a question-mark as to the authenticity of the 'Belgian' rings, a doubt which should be settled once and for all as the result of technical

investigations which are being undertaken by the British Museum Research Laboratory as this paper goes to press.

2. To bronze sieves listed by Geiss-Dreier following Wolfgang Dehn, add the example in silver now in the Kunsthistorisches Museum, Vienna and found in 1858 in an early La Tène princely grave at Hradiště, okr. Písek, southern Bohemia, together with the well-known Etruscan *Schnabelkanne* and bowl; the latter are in the Národní Muzeum, Prague (q.v. Michálek 1977: esp. 638 and obr. 1:1).

3. As pointed out by Corradini (1992: 115) there is no proof for the alleged association of the Prunay vase with the remains of a possible chariot burial (q.v. Rowlett 1969 and here List no. 15).

4. The illustration of the linchpin in Hubert is referred to on p. 67 of his article as 'fig. 4' and on p. 72 is erroneously numbered 'fig. 1' (*recte* 'fig. 11').

5. Since the decorated linchpin is now lost, there is no certain evidence for the statement made by Legendre and Gomez de Soto (1990: 297), in comparing the Waldalgesheim and Condé-sur-Marne linchpins (our list no. 9, 19–20), that the former is 'orné ... de corail'; indeed, the nineteenth century engraving makes it much more likely that the inlay was in enamel (compare the Basse-Yutz flagon stoppers for the early use of 'enamel' in a complex design (Megaw and Megaw 1990: 39–43).

6. As pointed out in n. 3 above, the metal objects in the Morel Collection, inv. nos ML 2910–27, are not to be associated with the fine painted pedestalled vase from the same commune. On the other hand, there are undoubtedly other linchpins from north-east France which could be cited here and it is to be regretted that it has not been possible for us to refer to Stéphane Verger's recently completed doctoral thesis on chariot-burials in France.

7. In his analysis of the art of the Waldalgesheim type-site (Frey: in press)

8. It was Ian Stead (1968: esp. 173–8 and fig. 17) who first identified the Étrechy crescents as shield mounts *contra* Jacobsthal's firm statement that 'Morel's assumption that the crescents from Étrechy, no. 376, belong to shields is unfounded' (Jacobsthal 1944: 115, n. 6).

References

aus'm Weerth, E. 1870. *Der Grabfund von Wald-Algesheim = Bonner Winckelmannsprogramm. Bonn: Rheinisches Landesmuseum.*

Bittel, K., Kimmig, W. and Schiek, S. (eds) 1981. *Die Kelten in Baden-Württemberg.* Stuttgart: Konrad Theiss.

Castriota, D. R. 1981. Continuity and innovation in Celtic and Mediterranean ornament: a grammatical-syntactic analysis of the processes of the reception and transformation in the decorative arts of antiquity. Doctoral dissertation. Columbia University. [University Microfilms 1982]

Charpy, J.-J. 1987. Les épées laténiennes à bouterolle circulaire et ajourée des IVe et IIIe siècles avant J.-C. en Champagne. *Études Celtiques,* 24: 43–102.

Claus, M. 1958. Die Pipinsburg bei Oserode am Harz. In *Neue Ausgrabungen in Deutschland* (ed. W. Krämer). Berlin: Gebr. Mann, pp. 161–74.

Corradini, N. 1991. La céramique peinte à décor curviligne rouge et noir en Champagne. In *La céramique peinte celtique dans son contexte européen = Mém. de la Soc. Archéol. Champenoise,* 5 (eds J.-J. Charpy, R. Neiss and A. Patrolin), pp. 109–42.

Domaradski, M. 1984. *Keltite na Balkanskiya Poluostrov* Sofia: Nauka i Iskustvo.

Driehaus, J. 1971. Zum Grabfund von Waldalgesheim. *Hamburger Beiträge z. Archäol.,* 1(2): 101–13.

Duval, P.-M. and Kruta, V (eds) 1982. *L'art celtique de la période d'expansion: IVe et IIIe siècles avant notre ère = Actes du colloque au Collège de France à Paris du 26 au 28 septembre, 1978.* Geneva/Paris: Librairie Droz.

Egami, N., Tanabe, K. Hori, A. and Gotoh, T. (eds) 1979. *Thracian Treasures from Bulgaria.* Nagoya: The Chunichi Shimbun.

Fischer, F. 1979. *Der Heidengraben bei Grabenstetten: Ein keltisches Oppidum auf der Schwäbischen Alb bei Urach = Führer zu archäol. Denmälern in Baden-Württemberg* 2 (2ed). Stuttgart: Konrad Theiss.

Frey, O.-H. 1976. Du Premier Style au Style de Waldalgesheim: remarques sur l'evolution de l'art celtique ancien. In *Celtic art in ancient Europe: five protohistoric centuries* (eds P.-M. Duval and C.F.C. Hawkes). London: Seminar Press, pp. 141–63.

Frey, O.-H. In press. Das Grab von Waldalgesheim: namengebend für eine Stilphase des keltischen Kunsthandwerks. In *Das Grab von Waldalgesheim* (ed. H.-E. Joachim). Bonn: Rheinisches Landesmuseum

Frey, O.-H. and Schwappach, F. 1973. Studies in early Celtic design. *World Archaeology,* 4: 339–56.

Geiss-Dreier, R. 1992. Stamnos und Sieb. In *Hundert Meisterwerke keltischer Kunst: Schmuck und Kunsthandwerk zwischen Rhein und Mosel = Schriftreihe des Rheinischen Landesmuseums Trier* 7(eds R. Cordie-Hackenberg, R. Geiss-Dreier, A. Miron and A. Wigg), pp. 99–103.

Guštin, M. 1984. Prazgodovinski grobovi z vozovi na ozemlju Jugoslavije. In Guštin *et al.* 1984: 111–32.

Guštin, M. and Pauli, L. (eds). 1984. *Keltski Voz = Posavski muzej Brežice* Knjiga 6.

Haffner, A. and Joachim, H.-E. 1984. Die keltischen Wagengräber der Mittelrheingruppe. In Guštin *et al.* 1984: 71–87.

Horedt, O.K. 1941–44. Zwei keltische Grabfunde aus Siebenbürgen. *Dacia,* 9–10, 1945: 189–200.

Hubert, H. 1902. Sépulture à char de Nanterre. *L'Anthropologie,* 13: 66–73.

Jacobi, G. 1974. *Werkzeug und Gerät aus dem Oppidum von Manching = Die Ausgrabungen in Manching* 5. Wiesbaden: Franz Steiner.

Jacobsthal, P. 1944. *Early Celtic Art.* Oxford: Clarendon Press (reprinted with corrections 1969).

Kaufmann, H. 1966. Der Maskenarmring von Pössneck. *Jschr. mitteldt. Vorg.,* 50: 205–22.

Kruta, V. 1974. Remarques sur l'apparition du rinceau dans l'art celtique. *Études Celtiques* 14: 21–30.

Kruta, V. 1977. Les fibules laténiennes à décor d'inspiration végétale au IVe s. avant notre ère. *Études Celtiques,* 15, 1976–77: 19–46.

Kruta, V. 1979. Duchcov-Münsingen: nature et diffusion d'une phase laténienne. In *Les mouvements celtiques du Ve au Ier siècle avant notre ère* (eds P.-M. Duval and V. Kruta). Paris: CNRS, pp. 81–115.

Kruta, V. 1982. Aspects unitaires et faciès dans l'art celtique du IVe siècle avant notre ère: l'hypothèse d'un foyer Celto-Italique. In Duval and Kruta 1982: 35–49.

Kruta, V. 1991. The first Celtic expansion: prehistory to history. In Moscati *et al.* 1991: 192–213

Legendre, R. M. and Gomez de Soto, J. 1990. La tombe à char de Mont-de-Marne, Condé-sur-Marne (Marne). *Archäologisches Korrespondenzblatt*, 20: 285–303.

Lenerz-de Wilde, M. 1982. Le 'style de Cheshire Cat': un phénomène caractéristique de l'art celtique. In Duval and Kruta 1982: 101–14.

MacGregor, A. (ed.) 1987. *Antiquities from Europe and the Near East in the collection of the Lord MacAlpine of West Green.* Oxford: Ashmolean Museum.

Megaw, J. V. S. 1970a. *Art of the European Iron Age: a study of the elusive image.* Bath: Adams and Dart.

Megaw, J.V.S. 1970b. Cheshire Cat and Mickey Mouse: problems in the analysis of the art of the European Iron Age. *Proc. Prehist. Soc.*, 35: 261–79.

Megaw, (M.) R. and Megaw, (J.) V. (S.) 1989. *Celtic art: from its beginnings to the Book of Kells.* London: Thames and Hudson.

Megaw, J.V.S. and Megaw, M.R. 1990. *The Basse-Yutz find: Masterpieces of Celtic art = Society of Antiquaries Research Report*, 46.

Megaw, J. V. S. and Megaw, M. Ruth 1993. Cheshire Cats, Mickey Mice, the new Europe and ancient Celtic art. In *Trade and exchange in prehistoric Europe = Oxbow Monographs* 33 (eds C. Scarre and F. Healy). Oxford: Oxbow Books for the Prehistoric Society and the Société Préhistorique Française, pp. 219–32.

Megaw, J.V.S. and Megaw, M. Ruth. 1994. Through a window on the European Iron Age darkly: 50 years of reading early Celtic art. *World Archaeol.*, 25(3): 287–303.

Megaw, J. V. S., Megaw, M. Ruth and Neugebauer, J.-W. 1989. Zeugnisse frühlatènezeitlichen Kunsthandwerks aus dem Raum Herzogenburg, Niederösterreich. *Germania*, 67: 477–517.

Michálek, J. 1977. Knížecí mohyly z časné doby laténské u Hradiště okr. Písek. *Archeologické rozhledy* 39 (6): 634–43.

Morel, L. 1898. *La Champagne souterraine: matériaux et documents ou résultats de trente-cinq années des fouilles archéologiques dans la Marne.* Reims: Matot-Braine.

Moscati, S., Frey, O.-H., Kruta, V., Raftery, B. and Szabó, M. (eds) 1991. *The Celts.* London: Thames and Hudson.

Müller, F. 1989. *Die frühlatènezeitlichen Scheibenhalsringe.* Römisch-Germanische Forschungen 46.

Németi, J. 1993. Necropola Latène de la Pişcolt, jud. Satu Mare, IV. *Thraco-Dacica* 14 (1–2): 117–29.

Neugebauer, J.-W. 1992. *Die Kelten im Osten Österreichs.* Wissenschaftliche Schriftenreihe Niederösterreich, 92–94. St Polten and Vienna: Niederösterreichisches Pressehaus.

Pauli, L. 1978 *Der Dürrnberg bei Hallein III = Münchner Beiträge zur Vor- und Frühgeschichte*, 18(1). München: Beck.

Petres, É. F. and Szabó, M. 1986. Notes on the so-called Hatvan-Boldog type scabbards. In *Actes du VIIIe colloque sur les Ages du Fer = Aquitania* suppl. 1 (eds A. Duval and J. Gomez de Soto). pp. 257–72.

Peyre, C. 1982. Y a-t-il une contexte italique au style de Waldalgesheim? In Duval and Kruta 1982: 115–35.

Rapin, A., Szabó, M. and Vitali, D. 1992. Monte Bibele, Litér, Rezi, Pişcolt: contributions à l'origine du style des épées hongroises. *Comm. Archaeol. Hungariae*, 1993: 23–54.

Riegl, A. 1992. *Problems of style: foundations for a history of ornament* (trans. E. Klein, annotated D. Castriota). Princeton, NJ: Princeton University Press (first published 1895. *Stilfragen: Grundlegungen zu einer Geschichte der Ornamentik.* Berlin: G. Siemens Verlag).

Roska, M. 1915. Kelta sirok s egyéb emlékok Balsárol. *Dolgazatok Kolozsvár*, 6: 18–48

Rowlett, R.M. 1969. Une tombe à char de Prunay (Marne). *Bull. Soc. Archéol. Champenoise* 62: 12–17.

Schwappach, F. 1971. Stempel des Waldalgesheimstils an einer Vase aus Sopron-Bécsidomb (West-Ungarn). *Hamburger Beiträge z. Archäol.*, 1(2): 85–100.

Schwappach, F. 1973. Frühkeltisches Ornament zwischen Marne, Rhein und Moldau. *Bonner Jahrb.*, 173: 53–111.

Stead, I.M. 1965. *The La Tène cultures of eastern Yorkshire.* York: The Yorkshire Philosophical Society.

Stead, I.M. 1979. *The Arras Culture.* York: The Yorkshire Philosophical Society.

Stead, I.M. 1984. Cart-burials in Britain. In Guštin *et al.* 1984: 31–41.

Stead, I.M. with Rigby, V. n.d. [1981]. *The Gauls: Celtic antiquities from France.* London: British Museum Publications.

Szabó, M. 1992. *Les Celtes de l'Est: le second Age du Fer dans la cuvette des Karpates.* Paris: Éditions Errance.

Szabó, M. and Petres, É. F. 1992. *Decorated weapons of the La Tène Iron Age in the Carpathian Basin.* Budapest, Magyar Nemzeti Múzeum, Inventaria Praehistorica Hungariae 5.

Van Endert, D. 1984. Keltische Wagenbestattungen in Frankreich. In Guštin *et al.* 1984: 43–60.

K.-Végh, K. 1984. Keltische Wagengräber in Ungarn. In Guštin *et al.* 1984: 105–10.

Verger, S. 1987. La genèse celtique des rinceaux à triscèles. *Jahrbuch des R-G Zentralmuseums Mainz*, 34: 287–339.

Willvonseder, K. 1938. Das Latène-Gräberfeld von Brunn an der Schneeberg-bahn. *Prähist. Zeitschr.*, 28–9 (1937–8): 233–65.

Zirra, V. 1971. Beiträge zur Kenntnis des keltischen La Tène in Rumänien. *Dacia*, N.S. 15: 171–238.

The Conundrum of Irish Iron Age Pottery

BARRY RAFTERY

INTRODUCTION

R.A.S. Macalister, writing some sixty years ago in the first modern synthetic work on Irish archaeology, expressed the view that the pottery of the Iron Age "so far as we know, differs little from the rude pottery of the preceding Bronze Age". He did, however, regard the fine, lidded vessel from Danesfort, Co. Kilkenny as "the highest attainment of the iron age potters in Ireland" though he conceded that "the pattern does not suggest to the mind the special characters of La Tène ware; the vessel may be even later than that period" (1928: 159). In passing, he noted the total absence of pottery from his then recent excavations at Uisneach in Co. Westmeath, a site which he believed to belong to the Iron Age.

Some years later, in a second monograph, Macalister returned to the absence of pottery at Uisneach and other sites (as he believed) of the Iron Age in Ireland. "From every point of view" he wrote "this fact is inexplicable". He went on to state "It is difficult to see how so elementary an art, freely practised during the Bronze Age, could have become lost: it is difficult to imagine what substitute could have been found to take the place of the pottery vessels for cooking and feeding" (1935: 98–9). His 1949 revised version of the 1928 work saw no advance on this uncertain situation.

Macalister in 1935 had touched on an important problem in Irish Iron Age studies though the impact of the difficulties was somewhat lessened by his inclusion as "Iron Age" of crannóg ware, which we now know to be much later than the Iron Age, and also of the Danesfort pot which is today universally accepted as a funerary vase of the Early Bronze Age (Ó Ríordáin and Waddell, 1993: 117, no. 537).

J. Raftery (1951) was more tentative than Macalister in assigning coarsely made pottery, such as that from Ballintoy, Co. Antrim, Lugg, Co. Dublin and elsewhere, to the Iron Age (*ibid*. 188) but he, like Macalister, took the Danesfort pot to belong to this period (*ibid*. 186) and he did state that pottery was "definitely known" in the Iron Age (*ibid*. 208).

It was more than a quarter century before another synthetic work on Irish prehistory was published (Herity and Eogan 1977). In this it is written that "the predominant type of pottery vessel in use during the Iron Age were (*sic*) bucket-shaped pots of coarse, gritty ware" (*ibid*. 238). More recently four further monographs on Irish prehistory have appeared (Harbison 1988; O'Kelly 1989; Mallory and McNeill 1991; Cooney and Grogan 1994). None of these refers to the problem of Iron Age pottery.

The problem is, however, far too important to be simply ignored. From the earliest appearance of ceramic containers in the fourth millennium BC pottery making undergoes continuous development through local initiative and external impulse. For at least three thousand years there was an unbroken tradition of pottery manufacture, both for domestic and funerary purposes, reaching at times no mean levels of technical and artistic excellence. The quality of the wares declines noticeably in the later phases of the Bronze Age and in the Late Bronze Age coarsely made, bucket-shaped vessels become the norm throughout the land. Decoration is virtually abandoned and the only criterion appears to have been crude utilitarianism (fig. 74).

Yet this pottery, despite its brittle and unprepossessing character, doubtless served the Late Bronze Age communities well. It must have been prone to frequent breakages but replacing the smashed containers was hardly a major task with clays and grits readily available and no advanced skills required. Every household probably had its own potter. These vessels served for the preparation, cooking and storage of foodstuffs and the same vessels were, on occasion, used as receptacles for the burnt remains of the dead (e.g. Raftery 1981: 173–7). As well as pottery containers there were also containers of wood used at this time and it is likely that these were as widespread as the vessels of clay. Inevitably, however, it is only in waterlogged sites such as the Rathtinaun, Co. Sligo crannóg (Raftery, J. forthcoming) that these survive.

Pottery making is thus well documented in the Irish

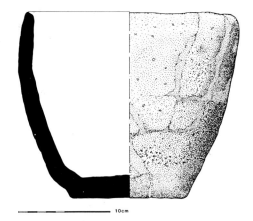

fig. 74. Coarse pottery container of Late Bronze Age date, Rathgall, Co. Wicklow. Scale 1:4.

Late Bronze Age and it seems clear that coarse wares of bucket or tub shape were the only forms of ceramic containers in use. The key question relevant to our Iron Age studies, therefore, is what happens to this pottery development as the Late Bronze Age draws to a close. Does it continue to be used into the Iron Age, as some commentators have suggested, or does it disappear? And if the latter, how can we explain such a change? It is in this context that the latest dating of coarse ware in Ireland must first be examined.

LATER COARSE WARES?

Iron Age, and even later, dating has in the past been claimed for a number of sites producing coarse pottery of the type under discussion. For many years, for example, there has been an implicit acceptance that pottery from an enclosure at Lugg, Co. Dublin (Kilbride-Jones 1950) dated to the Iron Age. However, apart from citing a few British sites producing vaguely comparable pottery, some of which *might* date to the Iron Age, no evidence was presented by the excavator to substantiate his statement that "the pottery was exclusively of early Iron Age date" (*ibid*. 325). A Late Bronze Age date is possible, even likely, but it could be earlier (Raftery 1981: 177).

Coarse pottery was found in association with a number of cremation deposits in and beside two ring barrows (Sites A and B) at Mullaghmore, Co. Down (Mogey 1949; Mogey and Thompson 1956). A tiny blue glass bead was found at the centre of Site A in possible association with a cremation deposit which was accompanied by coarse pottery (*op. cit.* 1949: 86). We are told, however, that the cremated bones and the sherds "formed a confused mass among and under the stones of the cairn" (*ibid.*) and later that the bead was "so small that it could have infiltrated from a higher level" (*op. cit.* 1956: 19). Proudfoot's, admittedly tentative, suggestion that the pottery "should be dated to a late rather than an early period" (in Mogey and Thompson *op. cit.* 27) was largely influenced by the presence of the bead. Later commen-

tators (e.g. Herity and Eogan 1977: 244), less cautiously, included Mullaghmore in the list of Iron Age burials.

Clearly the evidence for this is not strong. The present writer has, indeed, elsewhere suggested that the Mullaghmore burials, on the basis of analogies with the urn burial at Rathgall, Co. Wicklow, is likely to date to the Late Bronze Age (Raftery 1981: 173–6).

Sherds of coarse ware, described as of "undecorated Late Bronze Age or Iron Age type" (ASCD 179), also came from one of the hut sites on Scrabo Hill, Co. Down. Despite an Iron Age radiocarbon date for charcoal from the site (Mallory and McNeill 1991: 150) the context of the pottery remains uncertain and without further investigation cannot be regarded unequivocally as dating to this period.

A suggested date in the early historic period for coarse ware from a Fulacht Fiadh (cooking place) at Coarhamore, Valentia Island, Co. Kerry seems even less clearly founded. It is apparently based on an associated spindle whorl – hardly a diagnostic form – and the date sits uncomfortably with a radiocarbon determination of 2950±80 BP from the site (Sheehan 1990: 32, 35). Sheehan's attempt to explain away this early date is not entirely convincing.

The dating of a small quantity of coarse pottery uncovered in the earliest level at the monastic site of Reask, Co. Kerry is also unclear. Fanning could find no close parallels for it either in the prehistoric wares of the region or in the later forms of the historic period (1981: 112–3). He took a radiocarbon date in the fourth century AD as a chronological indicator but there were three other substantially earlier dates extending back into the later Bronze Age (*ibid*. 164). The earlier dates were, however, dismissed by the excavator as contaminated. It is, nonetheless, far from certain that the Reask pottery does not, in fact, belong to the prehistoric period.

FREESTONE HILL, CO. KILKENNY

This Co. Kilkenny hillfort was excavated by G. Bersu in 1948/9 but, owing to his death, it was another twenty years before the full publication report appeared (Raftery 1969). The site consisted of a univallate hillfort about 2ha in area, within which there was a series of hut platforms and a black occupation layer on the summit enclosed by a slight stone wall. The finds included a number of provincial Roman bronzes as well as a mid-fourth century copper coin of Constantine II. A quantity of coarse potsherds, evidently from flat-bottomed, bucket-shaped containers was found in this layer, and elsewhere on the site. A number of glass beads was also found.

The archival documentation left behind by the excavator left no room to doubt that most of these items came from the black occupation layer within the stone enclosure on the hilltop. Coarse pottery was also found in occupation debris immediately inside the bank, within and under the bank, in the fill of the hillfort ditch and

THE CONUNDRUM OF IRISH IRON AGE POTTERY

also associated with several of the hut platforms which occurred on the western slopes of the hill within the hillfort defences. The physical association of the pottery with the Roman bronzes seemed certain and the writer, in publishing the site, confidently pronounced that the construction and occupation of the hillfort dated to the late Iron Age. There appeared not the slightest doubt that the coarse pottery belonged to this same horizon (*ibid.* 91).

In a wide-ranging discussion of the pottery the writer sought to date coarse ware from other sites, especially that from several excavated Irish hillforts, to the Iron Age on the basis of the Freestone Hill evidence. By an ironic coincidence, when the Freestone Hill report was at the final page proof stage, the writer had commenced his excavations at the Rathgall, Co. Wicklow hillfort (Raftery 1976). There, in the first week, before any clear stratigraphy had been established, a second/third century AD bronze strap mount came to light (Raftery 1972) A quantity of coarseware fragments, indistinguishable in every way from the Freestone Hill sherds, even in the common presence at both sites of rims with a row of pin-prick perforations, was also found. Thus it was possible to insert a paragraph into the Freestone Hill report (p. 95) citing the Rathgall finds as apparent confirmation for the dating of the Freestone Hill coarse wares. The writer concluded with ringing confidence that "... at last in Freestone Hill we have a peg, a fixed chronological point, a base from which further research can be developed. It is this positive dating of a body of domestic material which gives Freestone Hill its great significance and the site may well be a milestone in future Iron Age research in Ireland (*ibid.* 96).

No sooner had the Freestone Hill report finally gone to press when the first doubts began to enter the writer's mind on the dating of the coarse pottery there. By the end of the 1969 season at Rathgall it had become evident that all the coarse pottery at the Wicklow site belonged unequivocally to the later Bronze Age. The decorated strap tag was from a disturbed layer and was not primarily associated with the pottery. The remarkable similarity between coarse wares from Freestone Hill and Rathgall thus presented a problem, one to which there were two possible solutions. The first possibility was that the Freestone Hill pottery represented an example of remarkable cultural conservatism whereby the pots used, in every detail of size, form and manufacturing technique, remained utterly unchanged for over a millennium despite the major transformations which evidently took place in other areas of material culture over the same period. The second possibility was that the pottery from Freestone Hill was wrongly dated, that the association with the Roman metalwork was spurious and that it was, in fact, contemporary with the Late Bronze Age wares from Rathgall.

The latter misgiving was mooted by the writer in 1977 when he expressed the view that a Late Bronze Age

level, undetected by the excavator, may have existed at Freestone Hill and that material from that level had become mixed with later occupation layers thus explaining the seeming association of pottery and Roman metalwork (Raftery 1977: 49). The writer was also struck by the decoration on one of the Freestone Hill glass beads which possessed raised concentric-circle inlays reminiscent of the decoration on late Hallstatt beads on the Continent (e.g. Kromer 1959: Taf. 9; 68; 120; Röhrig 1994: Taf. 58,6). Furthermore, the presence of a large collection of blue-green glass beads from Late Bronze Age Rathgall (Raftery 1987) also provided parallels for the simple blue beads from Freestone Hill. Henderson (1988), on the basis of spectrographical analysis, has more recently supported the early dating of these beads.

Thus there appeared to be increasingly strong grounds for a redating of the Freestone Hill coarse ware to the Late Bronze Age. Emphatic support for this contention has been recently supplied by a radiocarbon age determination produced in Groningen University for a charcoal sample labelled "Freestone Hill occupation layer" which was preserved in a sealed plastic bag for nearly fifty years in the National Museum. The date is 2565±35 BP (GrN – 21255) which, at 2 sigma calibration, converts to 810–550 Cal BC. The balance of probability must now be that the Freestone Hill pottery is, in fact, Late Bronze Age in date and, indeed, that the hillfort itself is a Late Bronze Age construction thus conforming to the escalating body of evidence in Ireland that the hillfort in this country is essentially a phenomenon of the Bronze rather than of the Iron Age (Raftery, 1994, 58–9).

If a Late Bronze Age date for the Freestone Hill pottery is accepted it seems evident that there is now no compelling reason for dating *any* coarse pottery to the Iron Age. Indeed, there are increasing indications to suggest that coarse pottery is one of the type fossils of the Irish Late Bronze Age and in fact the extent to which this pottery can be reliably dated to earlier periods is no longer as clear as it once was (e.g. Kelly 1978; Herity 1987: 153–4; Cleary 1993).

THE IRON AGE

Thus the wheel has turned full circle and we are back to the situation of sixty years ago. With an apparent cessation in the manufacture of coarse pottery sometime around the middle of the last pre-Christian millennium we come to an "Iron Age" seemingly devoid of pottery. But can this be true, or is this no more than an embarrassing gap in our knowledge? Perhaps, pottery was indeed being made through the centuries of the Iron Age but we simply have not recognised it. Or could it be that we have not discovered Iron Age pottery simply because of the great scarcity of secular, domestic settlements of the period?

At first glance the latter possibility must be taken

seriously. It is true that there is an unprecedented dearth of recognised Iron Age occupation sites in Ireland and it could thus legitimately be argued that the discovery and excavation of relevant habitations within the country will inevitably yield the missing Iron Age pottery. After all, it is certain that clay moulds were used for casting in Iron Age Ireland (see below), yet not a single fragment of a mould has ever been found in the country. Could not the same be said of Iron Age pottery?

Things are not, however, quite so simple. Some sites of that ill-defined period known as the Iron Age *are* known in Ireland but not one has yielded as much as a scrap of contemporary pottery. Iron Age occupation, for example, was undoubtedly present at Feerwore, Co. Galway (Raftery, J. 1944). A fibula of iron was found, some items of iron, stone, lignite and glass were recovered and a quantity of animal bones all of which seem to indicate normal domestic occupation. There was no pottery. Dún Ailinne, Co. Kildare, the great royal centre of Celtic Leinster, yielded evidence of a complex sequence of use. A series of timber-built enclosures was successively erected and dismantled on the hilltop, culminating in a final phase of events which involved annual open-air feasting on an extensive scale. Again no pottery was found (Wailes 1991). Navan Fort, Co. Armagh is less clear cut as there was a considerable quantity of coarse ware present not all of it in clearly recognisable archaeological contexts (Lynn 1986). It appears, however, to belong to the later Bronze Age layers and there are no indications that it was still in use there during the Iron Age (C. Lynn: pers. comm.). There was no pottery associated with the Iron Age activity at Lough Crew, Co. Meath (Raftery 1983: 250–63) and the hearth site in sandhills at Ballymacrae Lower, White Rocks, Co. Antrim, which yielded portion of a La Tène fibula, also failed to produce any Iron Age pottery (Collins 1977). A number of other hearth and midden sites of suggested Iron Age date from the northeast of Ireland are also devoid of pottery remains (Mallory and McNeill 1991: 150). The Rath of the Synods at Tara, Co. Meath, which was certainly in occupation in the early centuries AD, and probably earlier, similarly lacked any trace of locally made pottery (Raftery 1994: 212–3). The classic Irish La Tène site at Lisnacrogher, Co. Antrim was also unaccompanied by any contemporary pottery (Raftery 1983: 287–8).

Most telling of all is the recently excavated domestic enclosure at Lislackagh, Co. Mayo (Walsh 1995). The site was a ringfort-like structure comprising a bank with external ditch within which three small round houses occurred. It may be regarded as a simple, rural occupation site. There were three radiocarbon dates spanning the birth of Christ. The finds were few but once more the absence of any evidence for pottery was striking.

Thus, though occupation sites of the Iron Age in Ireland are, indeed, few in number it must be regarded as significant that they are consistently without any evidence for the use of pottery by the occupants. Could a ritual explanation help to solve this problem? After all, the classic Iron Age ritual site in Europe, La Tène itself, produced no pottery despite the great quantity and variety of the material found there (Vouga 1925). Lisnacrogher might be viewed in the same context and, indeed, Lough Crew, Dún Ailinne and Navan Fort are all reasonably to be seen as having had a ritual or ceremonial character. But Lislackagh is hardly ritual, as noted above, while Feerwore, too, and at least the later phases at the Rath of the Synods, are surely secular occupation sites. Moreover, the extensive feasting which took place over a number of years at Dún Ailinne, even if it was associated with one or more of the great Celtic festivals, still implies that significant numbers of people congregated there, eating and drinking over lengthy periods. Had pottery been in daily use by these people, it is difficult to imagine a situation in which some broken vessels would not have been left behind.

The absence of pottery from the admittedly few known Iron Age sites is given added importance by the even more striking absence of any native wares in the earlier ringfort and crannóg horizon. Garranes and Ballycatteen in Cork (Ó Ríordáin 1942; Ó Ríordáin and Hartnett 1943), Letterkeen, Co. Mayo (Ó Ríordáin and McDermott 1952), Garryduff, Co. Cork (O'Kelly 1963) represent but a small selection of excavated ringforts which produced extensive occupation evidence but no hint of the manufacture of native pottery. The same picture is supplied by the contemporary excavated crannógs. Lagore, Co. Meath, for example, a major royal residence of the early historic period, was once more without any ceramic containers (Hencken 1950). Several crannógs, such as Ballinderry 2, Co. Offaly (Hencken 1942) and Rathtinaun, Lough Gara, Co. Sligo (Raftery, J. 1972; Raftery, B. 1994: 32–5) have lower occupation layers of the later Bronze Age with reoccupation in each instance in the early historic period. In each instance the presence of coarse pottery in the early levels contrasts with the absence of any native domestic pottery in the upper layers.

All the available evidence thus conforms to the view that the coarse pottery of the Late Bronze Age gave way to a phase when the tradition of pottery making was abandoned. Ireland thus moved into an aceramic phase some time in the last half millennium BC and remained so for at least a millennium. Only with the appearance of the so-called souterrain ware in the latter part of the first Christian millennium did the country move again to the use of pottery but even this was a regionally confined phenomenon as such pottery was virtually unknown outside the extreme northeast of Ireland (Ryan 1973). It was not until medieval cooking pots begin to be made that Irish society becomes once more fully ceramic (Edwards 1990: 75).

The reasons for the abandoning of the manufacture of pottery making are as obscure as they are inexplicable. It seems inconceivable that an entire people should turn its back on this universally useful commodity. Late Bronze Age pottery must have broken frequently and was of poor quality but this is hardly a reason for giving up the entire process. The people of the Iron Age in Ireland cannot have been ignorant of the techniques involved since they certainly used clay moulds in the lost-wax and other bronze-casting processes. They presumably also used crucibles of clay. Thus they must have been acquainted with the properties of clay and the means to fashion it into functional shapes. In addition, in the later period, imported wares from Gaul and the East Mediterranean found their way to Ireland (Edwards 1990: 68–73). Yet there was no attempt to imitate them. The move away from pottery containers was thus conscious and deliberate. The change extended also to the burial practice. Whereas coarse pots did accompany or contain cremation deposits in the Late Bronze Age (e.g. Raftery 1981: 173–7) this appears never to have been the case in the succeeding Iron Age.

We can only assume that in the course of the Iron Age, for a reason as yet unknown to us, the occupants of Ireland decided that they could do without pottery containers. Metal, leather, basketry and, above all, wood must have been deemed adequate to fulfil the needs of the people. The change was doubtless gradual. During the Late Bronze Age containers of pottery and wood would have been in widespread use but bit by bit pottery might have declined in popularity as wood became the dominant substance for the manufacture of vessels. In time, pottery had completely disappeared. It is interesting to note, in this regard, the apparent absence from Old Irish of any indigenous word referring unequivocally to a ceramic container.

In a letter of the 21.8.1995 to the writer on this topic Professor Fergus Kelly of the Dublin Institute for Advanced Studies has written the following.

"The linguistic evidence emphatically supports that of archaeology in relation to the absence of poetry in Early Christian Ireland. The few Old Irish references to pottery are in foreign contexts. For example, one of the 9th century Milan Glosses on the Psalms refers to earthenware (créodae) vessels. This is an explanation of uas fictilis in the Latin commentary (W. Stokes and J. Strachan, Thesaurus Palaeohibernicus 1, 1901–3, 22.32).

Later in the same series glosses (op. cit. 23.30), the glossator refers to "the round wheel on which the potters make the vessels" (roth cruind forsa denat na cerda inna lestrai). It is significant that he does not use a special term for "potter" – cerd is a general word for craftsman, artisan, poet, etc.

More negative evidence is supplied by a passage in the 8th century law-text Bretha Nemed toísech (D. Binchy, Corpus Iuris Hibernici VI, 1978, 2219.32– 2220.16). This refers to the skills required of various craftsmen including the coppersmith, silversmith, blacksmith, comb-maker and builder. But no mention of a potter! Similarly, the text on rank Uraicecht Becc lists all sorts of craftsmen (Binchy, op. cit., 2332.8–2333.22) – boat-builders, millwrights, chariot-makers, etc. – but again no potters."

Beginning in the Iron Age, therefore, and continuing throughout most of the first Christian millennium, the people of Ireland did not make pots because they did not need pots. Whether this implies a different diet from earlier times, or different methods of food storage and preparation, we simply cannot say. The absence of ceramic containers is not, at any rate, a major handicap in a rural economy and organic or metal containers will readily fulfil most of the functions of a pottery vessel. Only the boiling of water becomes more difficult but this can be achieved in metal vessels and, indeed, also by using heated stones in leather containers. An aceramic society therefore, while it may be highly unusual, and in sharp contrast with most other contemporary societies outside the country, is not necessarily a backward one.

Nor should the seeming change from a pottery-using Late Bronze Age to a potteryless Iron Age be regarded as having wider cultural significance. Such a change was purely internal and is not in any way related to incoming influences. It can only have resulted from the pragmatic choice of the indigenous occupants of the country. Similarly, once abandoned, the continued rejection of pottery-making in Ireland over many centuries seems an impressive argument for an exceptional level of cultural continuity in the country from the Iron Age into the Early Historic Period, a continuity which is scarcely in keeping with recent suggestions of the arrival of intrusive population groupings in Ireland in the early centuries of the Christian era (e.g. Warner 1995).

IRON AGE CONTAINERS

Containers of varying kinds must, of course, have been in widespread use throughout Iron Age Ireland and into the Christian era. Some examples are known giving us an indication of what was in vogue. We have, for instance, a number of metal cauldrons of varying type and one or two examples of wood are also known (Raftery 1984: 226–36; Earwood 1993: 46–9). Handled and unhandled bowls of bronze also occur and a small group of wooden handled bowls, in each instance carved from a single piece, give us an inkling of the sort of "table ware" which may once have been widespread in the country (Earwood op. cit. 62–7). An elaborate bronze-bound, stave-built tankard from Carrickfergus, Co. Antrim is, on the other hand an imported piece, and was probably exceptional (Raftery op. cit. 223–5).

A recent discovery, however, supplies us for the first time with information of the sort of storage containers and general, all-purpose utility vessels which must have been common in all areas of Iron Age Ireland. The site is the massive wooden corduroy road in Corlea bog, Co. Longford which has been dated by dendrochronology to 148 BC (Raftery 1990; 1994: 98–104). Directly associated with it were fragmentary wooden vessels, portions of two wooden platters and the handles of two larger containers which may have been churns.

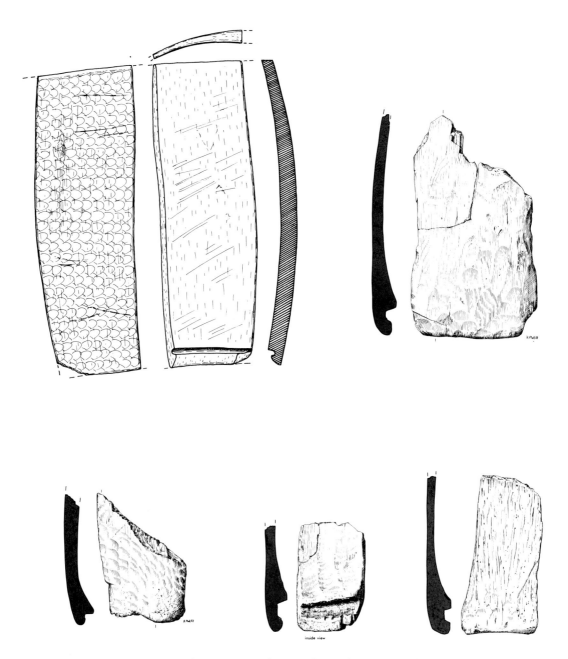

fig. 75. Fragments of Iron Age wooden vessels, Corlea, Co. Longford. Scale 1:4.

About 20 vessel fragments were found (fig. 75). These were predominantly of ash and a small percentage of alder specimens was also present. With a single possible exception, the vessels had originally been of two-piece construction consisting of a hand-carved cylindrical body, with a basal disc which fitted into a groove (croze) chiselled around the inner circumference of the body a short distance from its lower end. The vessels thus produced were either straight-sided or gently convex. One surviving piece may be a stave as it has straight, regular edges and there are transverse marks on its outer surface, which may be from binding strips (fig. 75 top left). Its uneven thickness, however, allows for the possibility that this fragment too may be from a two-piece con-

tainer which split regularly along the vertical grain. The only fragment which was complete from top to bottom indicated an original height of 33.5cm. Diameters could be roughly estimated at around 24–26cm.

Rims, where present, were, with one exception, either flat or internally bevelled. The exception is a vessel which had an expanded, clublike profile with a pronounced steplike hollow around its inner surface (fig. 76A).

This vessel is of considerable interest for it appears not to have close parallels in wood. It could be that this thickened, internally bevelled rim was intended to support a wooden lid. On the other hand, however, the form closely mirrors the sort of club rim which is not infrequently encountered on coarse pots of the Late Bronze

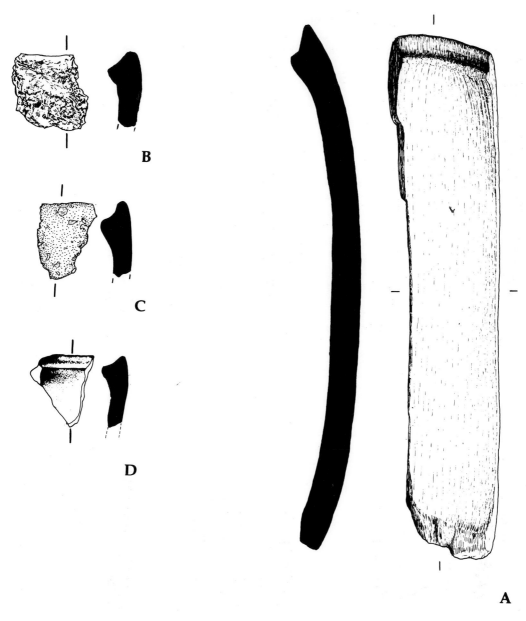

fig. 76. Late Bronze Age coarse pottery rims from Rathgall, Co. Wicklow (B, C) and Curraghator, Co. Tipperary (D) compared with rim portion of Iron Age wooden vessel from Corlea, Co. Longford (A). D after Doody 1987; fig. 3,6. Scale 1:2.

Age (fig. 76B–D). The possibility thus arises that this wooden vessel from Corlea preserves in wood the form of the Late Bronze Age coarse pots which by then had been abandoned. If this were indeed the case we would here have a striking illustration of the way in which the shape of the wooden container was influenced by that of the coarse pottery which it subsequently replaced.

The Corlea fragments, at any rate, provide us with an indication of the sort of domestic containers which were, in all probability, in widespread use throughout Iron Age Ireland. In them we may even see echoes of earlier ceramic forms. They show us, therefore, what was used: they do not, however, inform us as to why the manufac-

ture of ceramic wares ceased. This remains quite inexplicable. We can hardly, however, agree with Macalister when he wrote "There is no escape from the conclusion that this absence of pottery, more than anything else, makes it absolutely impossible to entertain the notion that the late Iron Age was a period of high civilization in Ireland" (1935: 99).

Acknowledgements
I am grateful to Dr. Jan Lanting of the Rijksuniversiteit Groningen, The Netherlands for arranging the radiocarbon dating of the Freestone Hill charcoal.

References

ASCD *An Archaeological Survey of County Down*. Belfast: HMSO 1966.

Cleary, R.M. 1993. The Later Bronze Age at Lough Gur: Filling in the Blanks. In *Past Perceptions: The Prehistoric Archaeology of South-West Ireland* (eds E. Shee Twohig and M Ronayne). Cork: Cork University Press, pp. 114–120.

Collins, A.E.P. 1977. A Sand-dune site at the White Rocks, Co. Antrim. *Ulster Journ. Archaeol.*, 40: 21–6.

Cooney, G. and Grogan, E. 1994. *Irish prehistory: a social perspective*. Dublin: Wordwell.

Doody, M.G. 1987. Late Bronze Age Huts at Curraghatoor, Co. Tipperary. In *Archaeological Excavations on the Cork–Dublin Gas Pipeline (1981–82)* (eds R.M. Cleary, M.F. Hurley and E.A. Twohig), Cork Archaeological Studies No. 1, pp. 36–40.

Earwood, C. 1993. *Domestic Wooden Artefacts in Britain and Ireland from Neolithic to Viking times*. Exeter: University of Exeter Press.

Edwards, N. 1990. *The Archaeology of Early Medieval Ireland*. London: Batsford.

Fanning, T. 1981. Excavation of an early Christian cemetery and settlement at Reask, County Kerry. *Proc. Roy. Irish Acad.*, 81C: 3–172.

Harbison, P. 1988. *Pre-Christian Ireland*. London: Thames and Hudson.

Hencken, H. O'N. 1942. Ballinderry Crannóg no. 2. *Proc. Roy. Irish Acad.*, 47C: 1–76.

Hencken, H. O'N. 1950. Lagore Crannóg: an Irish royal residence of the seventh to tenth century A.D. *Proc. Roy. Irish Acad.*, 53C: 1–248.

Henderson, J. 1988. Glass production and Bronze Age Europe. *Antiquity*, 62: 435–51.

Herity, M. 1987. The Finds from Irish Court Tombs. *Proc. Roy. Irish Acad.*, 87C: 5–281.

Herity, M. and Eogan, G. 1977. *Ireland in Prehistory*. London: Routledge and Kegan Paul.

Kelly, E.P. 1978. A reassessment of the dating evidence for Knockadoon Class II pottery. *Irish Archaeol. Res. Forum*, 5: 23–8.

Kilbride-Jones, H.E. 1950. The excavation of a composite Early Iron Age monument with "Henge" features at Lugg, Co. Dublin. *Proc. Roy. Irish Acad.*, 53C, 311–332.

Kromer, K. 1959. *Das Gräberfeld von Hallstatt*. Florence.

Lynn, C.J. 1986. Navan Fort: A Draft Summary of D.M. Waterman's Excavations. *Emania*, 1:1–19.

Macalister, R.A.S. 1928. *The Archaeology of Ireland*. London: Methuen. (Revised and rewritten: 1949).

Macalister, R.A.S. 1935. *Ancient Ireland*. London: Methuen.

Mallory, J.P. and McNeill, T.E. 1991. *The Archaeology of Ulster from Colonization to Plantation*. Belfast: Institute of Irish Studies, The Queen's University of Belfast.

Mogey, J.M. 1949. Preliminary Report on Excavations in Mullaghmore td., Co. Down. Ulster Journ. Archaeol., 12: 82–8.

Mogey, J.M. and Thompson, G.B. 1956. Excavation of Two Ring-Barrows in Mullaghmore Townland, Co. Down. *Ulster Journ. Archaeol.*, 19: 11–28.

O'Kelly, M.J. 1963. The excavations of two earthen ringforts at Garryduff, Co. Cork. *Proc. Roy. Irish Acad.*, 63C: 17–125.

O'Kelly, M.J. 1989. *Early Ireland*. Cambridge: Cambridge University Press.

Ó Ríordáin, B. and Waddell, J. 1993. *The Funerary Bowls and Vases of the Irish Bronze Age*. Galway: Galway University Press.

Ó Ríordáin, S.P. 1942. The excavation of a large earthen ringfort at Garranes, Co. Cork. *Proc. Roy. Irish Acad.*, 47C: 77–150.

Ó Ríordáin, S.P. and Hartnett, P.J. 1943. The excavation at Ballycatteen fort, Co. Cork. *Proc. Roy. Irish Acad.*, 49C: 1–43.

Ó Ríordáin, S.P. and MacDermott, M. 1952. The excavation of a ring-fort at Letterkeen, Co. Mayo. *Proc. Roy. Irish Acad.*, 53C: 89–119.

Raftery, B. 1969. Freestone Hill, Co. Kilkenny: an Iron Age hillfort and Bronze Age cairn. *Proc. Roy. Irish Acad.*, 68C, 1–108.

Raftery, B. 1972. A decorated strap-end from Rathgall, Co. Wicklow. *Journ. Roy. Soc. Antiq. Ireland*, 100: 200–211.

Raftery, B. 1976. Rathgall and Irish Hillfort Problems. In *Hillforts: Later Prehistoric Earthworks in Britain and Ireland* (ed. D.W. Harding). London: Academic Press.

Raftery, B. 1977. *The Irish Iron Age: Problems of Origin, Development and Chronology*. Doctoral dissertation. Department of Archaeology, University College, Dublin.

Raftery, B. 1981. Iron Age Burials in Ireland. *Irish Antiquity: Essays and Studies presented to Professor M.J. O'Kelly* (ed. D. O Córráin). Cork: Tower Books, pp. 173–204.

Raftery, B. 1983. *A Catalogue of Irish Iron Age Antiquities*. Marburg: Veröffentlichung des Vorgeschichtlichen Seminars Marburg.

Raftery, B. 1984. *La Tène in Ireland*. Marburg: Veröffentlichung des Vorgeschichtlichen Seminars Marburg.

Raftery, B. 1987. Some glass beads of the later bronze Age in Ireland. In *Glasperlen der Vorrömischen Eisenzeit* 2. Marburger Studien zur Vor- und Frühgeschichte, 9. Mainz: Phillip von Zabern, pp. 39–48.

Raftery, B. 1990. *Trackways Through Time*. Dublin: Headline.

Raftery, B. 1994. *Pagan Celtic Ireland*. London: Thames and Hudson.

Raftery, J. 1944. The Turoe Stone and the Rath of Feerwore. *Journ. Roy. Soc. Antiq. Ireland*, 74: 23–52.

Raftery, J. 1951. *Prehistoric Ireland*. London: Batsford.

Raftery, J. 1972. Iron Age and Irish Sea: Problems for Research. *The Iron Age in the Irish Sea Province* (ed. C. Thomas). Council Brit. Archaeol. 9: 1–10.

Raftery, J. forthcoming. Excavations at crannog 61, Rathtinaun. Lough Gara, Co. Sligo.

Röhrig, K.-H. 1995. *Das Hallstattliche Gräberfeld von Diefurt a.d. Altmühl = Archäologie am Main/Donau Kanal*, 1. Buch am Erlbach: Verlag Marie L. Leidorf.

Ryan, M. 1973. Native pottery in Early Historic Ireland. *Proc. Roy. Irish Acad.*, 73C: 619–645.

Sheehan, J. 1990. The excavation of a fulacht fiadh at Coarhamore, Valentia Island, Co. Kerry. In *Burnt Offerings: International Contributions to Burnt Mound Archaeology* (comp. V. Buckley). Dublin: Wordwell, pp. 27–37.

Vouga. P. 1925. *La Tène: Monographie de la station publiée au nom de la commission des fouilles de la Tène*. Leipzig: Karl W. Hiersemann.

Wailes, B. 1991. Dún Ailinne: A Summary Excavation Report. *Emania*, 7: 10–21.

Walsh, G. 1995. Iron Age Settlement in Co. Mayo. *Archaeol. Ireland*, 9, 2: 7–8.

Warner, R.B. 1995. Tuathal Techtmar: A Myth or Ancient Literary Evidence for a Roman Invasion? *Emania*, 13: 23–32.

Umbro-Celtica

Miklós Szabó

During my study trip to Italy in 1985, with P. Pelagatti's (then director of the Villa Giulia in Rome) authorization and his colleague, M.A. Rizzo's help, I had a chance to examine and to sketch the Gualdo Tadino shield fittings. This find has often been mentioned lately in connection with the study of the history of Celtic shields with spine and the Roman *scutum*. I believe this short paper will contribute to the clarification of certain ambiguous aspects of the problem and I also hope it will please our colleague celebrating his jubilee who has recently shown special interest in Iron Age shields (Stead 1991).

THE GUALDO TADINO FIND

The shield fittings were discovered in grave XII of Malpasso cemetery at Gualdo Tadino (prov. Perugia, ancient Tadinum), Umbria. They were acquired, together with other grave goods, by the Villa Giulia, Rome, in 1922. (cf. Shefton 1988: 144, no. A 12: in connection with grave IX.). As the find has not been published scientifically, one would normally refer to the museum guide that presents the goods on exhibition found in the three graves (VIII, IX and XII) without precisely indicating which grave they belong to and without illustrations (Moretti 1973: 336–338). M. Egg enumerates the goods found in grave XII in his monograph on helmets in which two Negau-type pieces discovered in this grave were published (Egg 1986: 202–3, no. 199–200, Taf. 121–2). It is important to add that the *Bronzestamnos* mentioned by Egg corresponds to Moretti's "stamnos in bronzo ... privo di decorazione", while the *zwei rotfigurige Gefässe* correspond to the "cratere a colonnette a figure rosse" (Inv. no. 44436) and probably to a red-figured kylix (not identical with the cup Pianu 1978: 164, no. 27, which belongs to a grave published by Stefani 1935: 163, fig. 10). The other bronze stamnos (Moretti 1973: 336–7) and the other red-figured kylix (Moretti 1973: 338: con Satiri et Menadi) was found in grave IX (Shefton 1988: *loc. cit.*).

The umbo itself (Inv. no. 44434: sketch to be found in Klindt-Jensen 1953: 48, fig. 26a; Bockius 1989: 272,

Abb. 3, 2; photograph: Eichberg 1987: Taf. 2a and 225, no. 4) was made of thin bronze sheet that was approximately 1mm in maximum thickness. The surface is in poor condition, much of it is damaged. Only one side panel is intact, the one that is represented as the upper part in fig. 77. One can clearly see a series of punched circles, situated some 2 to 3mm distant from one another, that also decorate the two undulated bindings. (They cannot be distinguished along the left because of corrosion.) The "lower" part of the umbo is damaged, mainly on the left, while on the right its edge is surprisingly even. The second and third rivets from the top of the right flange have been preserved and their size indicates that the umbo used to be attached to a piece of wood maximum 1cm thick.

This size corresponds to the thickness calculated on the basis of the rivets found in the 5 heart-shaped bronze fittings (Inv. no. 44443: fig. 78a) and in the rectangular appliqué equally made of bronze (Inv. no. 44443; fig. 78c). One should add that the heart-shaped fittings are of slightly different size (4.6×3; 3.9×2.6; 4.2×2.8; 4.5×3.2 and 4.9×2.9 cm). It is only a hypothesis that the two originally circular fittings (Inv. no. 44435; fig. 78b) and the fragmentary iron fitting (Inv. no. 44435; fig. 78d) also belonged to the shield. However, both the size and the rivets of the iron handle (Inv. no. 44435; fig. 78e) make it clear that it belonged to the same shield as the umbo.

If we take into consideration the material of the boss, that is the fact that it was made of extremely thin bronze sheet, it seems probable that its maker intended it as ornamentation.

Dating grave XII of Gualdo Tadino is rather problematic. Setting aside the two extremes, that is the dating of the grave from 500 BC (Stary 1981/a: 80) and from the 4th/3rd centuries BC (Klindt-Jensen 1953: 48–9 and 83), it seems obvious that it dates from the 5th century (Moretti 1973: 336; Egg 1986: 61) and also that it cannot be older than the mid 5th century (cf. Eichberg 1987: 47 and 225, no. 4, Taf. 2a; Bockius 1989: 272–4, Abb, 3/2: last third of 5th century BC). Nevertheless, only the

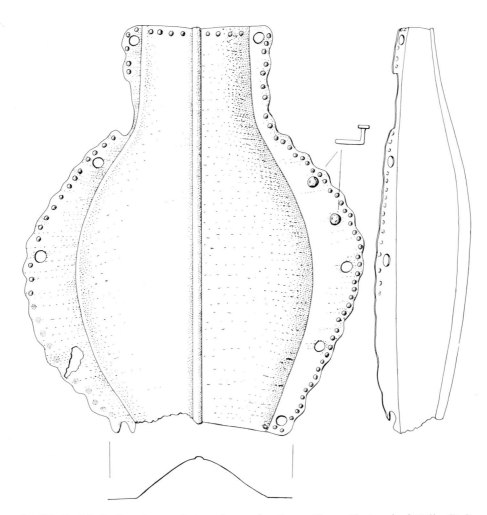

fig. 77. Gualdo Tadino: bronze fitting of an umbo. Rome, Museo Nazionale di Villa Giulia.

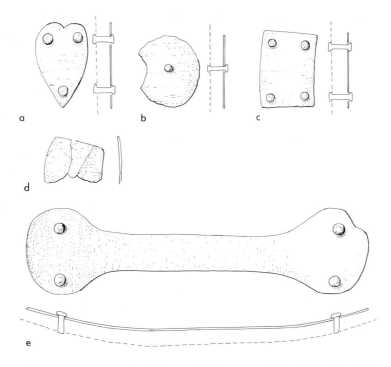

fig. 78. Gualdo Tadino: shield fittings (a, c: made of bronze; b, d: iron) and handle (e: iron). Rome, Museo Nazionale di Villa Giulia.

complete scientific publication of the finds will provide a definitive solution to the problem.

HISTORICAL AND ICONOGRAPHIC REMARKS

The Gualdo Tadino umbo is an argument in favour of the hypothesis according to which oval shields with spine, originating in the Early Iron Age Villanova Culture of Central Italy, continued to be used in peripheral areas mainly in the North – thus, for instance, by the Umbrii even after these objects had gone out of fashion under Greek influence in Etruria in the 7th century (Stary, 1981/a: 80–1; Stary 1981/b: 296–7). It is not by chance that the piece in question has also been used as one of the documents of the history of the Roman *scutum*, as it corroborates, at least indirectly, the fact that the *scutum* originated in Italy (cf. Eichberg 1987: 219–21; Bockius 1989: 278). Anyway, it provides, up to now, the unique archaeological evidence proving that the frequent Italian pictorial representations of shields of this type show, at least to a certain extent, local arms (cf. Stary 1981/a: 81, 433, W 18 and Taf. 70–4). A quasi contemporaneous representation of the Gualdo Tadino warrior is to be found on the Arnoaldi situla in Bologna (cf. Kruta 1992: 270–273, fig. 227–9; Pauli 1978: 245). We should add that the spear or spears were part of the weapons of the Umbrii (cf. Moretti: 1973, 337, graves VIII and IX; Eles Masi 1981: 375–7, 379). This proves the existence of local pictorial traditions that can only be interpreted in an Italian context, which, from a different point of view,

also means that one has to break away from the misleadingly generalized opinion that Italian representations of oval shields with umbo and spine are in all cases related to the Celts, either by depicting them, or by proving the diffusion and the use of a weapon of Celtic origin in Italy (cf. Adam 1986: 27; Adam-Jolivet 1986: 129 *et seq.*). That is, shields of this type were considered an almost absolute ethnicity marker and started to play a decisive role from the point of view of chronology. Thus their presence was often considered *terminus post quem*: finds having some connection to them had to be dated from the period following 390 BC, that is the Celtic invasion of Italy (see, for example, on Venetic *ex voto* sheet reliefs: Roth 1978: 179 *et seq.*, Beil 3.).

The scene decorating an Etruscan red-figured krater dated from the early 4th century BC (represented in fig. 79) used to be interpreted as the fight of a Gaul and a Roman because of the horseman with a shield (Etrusker 1989: 251–2, D 1.15; cf. Adam-Jolivet 1986: 139: "cavalier gaulois, face à un autre d'une autre nationalité"). E. Paul's brilliant paper has recently rejected this interpretation by proving that the scene does not depict a fight and also that the riders cannot be differentiated from an ethnic point of view (Paul 1990: 254–7). Should one "put back" the shield represented on the krater into an Italian context by referring to the Gualdo Tadino find or the Arnoaldi situla, one will find that the scene is certainly not to be interpreted as related to the Gauls and their arrival in Etruria.

Nevertheless, we have to point out that these remarks

fig. 79. Etruscan red-figured krater (side B). Leipzig Universität, Antikenmuseum

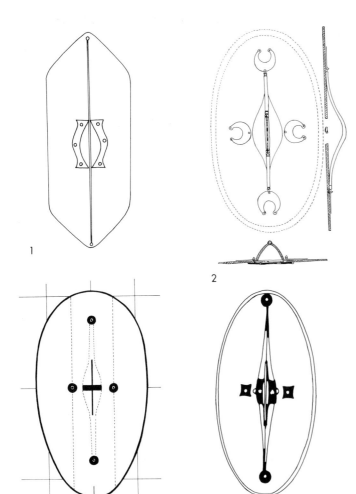

fig. 80.

1 *Franzhausen, grave no. 295: reconstruction of a shield. (J.W. Neugebauer)*
2 *Etréchy: reconstruction of a shield. (A. Rapin)*
3 *Ménföcsanak, grave no. 14: reconstruction of a shield. (A. Uzsoki)*
4 *Reconstruction of the La Tène B2 shield (boss consisting of two parts). (A. Rapin)*

do not contradict in general the well-known thesis according to which the big oval shield was part of the traditional image of the Celtic warrior in ancient art (cf. Stary 1981/a: 290–298; Adam 1986: 27). The interpretation of one particular scene, however, should be based on the analysis of the artistic and archaeological sources of the type of representation.

THE EARLY LA TÈNE SHIELD AND ITALY

The origin of the oval La Tène shield with spine has been subject to controversy for over half a century. The Italian or at least South-East Alpine (that is Venetic or, in other words, "Situlenkunst") origins of its prototypes were proved by such eminent scholars as P. Reinecke or O.H. Frey. Later P.F. Stary has followed in their footsteps. (On this subject: Stary 1981/b: 289–90). As far as the opponents of the thesis are concerned, one should above all take notice of L. Pauli's argument (Pauli 1978: 24–57). He brings up the question of priority that he considers insoluble; however, grave XII of Gualdo Tadino appears to corroborate in a rather unambiguous way the priority of Italy.

From this point of view it is worth taking early La Tène shields into consideration as well. The Franzhausen (Lower Austria) find that can probably be dated from the late La Tène A period (grave no. 295: Neugebauer-Gattringer 1987: 56, Abb. 16; Neugebauer 1992: 87–8, Abb, 33, 1–2 and 70) seems to indicate that in this case, in contrast to the primarily decorative role of the Gualdo Tadino shield fittings, the maker of the shield's approach to the problem was far more functional. The iron umbo is made of two parts which are held together by a long, stick-like spinal element to reinforce the shield along its whole vertical axis (fig. 80, 1). I would also like to mention a find very similar to this: a quasi contemporaneous umbo found in grave no. 39/2 of the cemetery at Dürrnberg bei Hallein (Pauli 1978: 239; cf. Bockius 1989: 276 Abb. 6,1). It is important to notice that both finds come from an area that had well-documented connections with the "Situlenkunst". We should add to our list the sword found in the same area, in grave no. 994 (dated from La Tène A) of the Hallstatt cemetery, the scabbard of which is decorated with a scene representing warriors with shields similar to the above mentioned pieces (Pauli 1978: 246–7, Abb. 34, 2). This group of early La Tène shields can be completed by the Branov example, almost identical with the Franzhausen umbo (Czech Republic: Filip 1956: 335, fig. 101; Sankot 1994: 431 *et seq.*, Abb. 1), and the Horath (Kr. Bernkastel-Wittlich) finds (Haffner 1976: 237 and 244, Abb. 72, Taf. 29,3); the latter is probably to be dated from La Tène B1.

In addition to these there is a great number of shield finds dated from late La Tène A and early La Tène B1 that show clearly that this period was not characterized by the working out and the perfecting of canonical forms but rather by experimenting (cf. recently: Bockius 1989: 27–68). The spine of the much debated Etréchy shield was secured by a vertical strap-fitting (fig. 80, 2; Rapin 1984: 10 *et seq.* pl. IV.). The Novy Bydzov (Czech Republic) find is characterized by an essentially similar solution (Moucha 1974: 445 *et seq.*). In contrast, the umbo of the La Tène B1 shield found in Ménföcsanak (fig. 80, 3) was protected by a vertical and a horizontal strap-fitting (Uzsoki 1970: 104–5, fig. 8–9). If we take also into consideration the fact that bronze umbo fittings were used on the territory of today's Czech Republic (Pauli 1978: 243–4, Abb. 33), the above mentioned experimental "program" appears to be even more colourful. Still it is important to add that in contrast to the last example, early La Tène workshops tended to reinforce shields with iron fittings, which can be interpreted eventually as a sign of preparing for an invasion. A canonical solution was not to be worked out until the end of the 4th century when – at the beginning of the La Tène B2 phase – bosses consisting of two parts were introduced. After this point in time development on the Continent followed mainly one direction (Rapin 1982–83: 70 *et seq.*; Rapin 1988: 12 *et seq.*).

On the basis of the above mentioned facts I believe the origins of the oval shield with spine are not to be found in the La Tène culture. Priority should be given to Italy and it was from there that the stimuli transmitted by the Venetic cultural sphere originated, and these induced the Celts to adopt and to perfect rapidly this useful defensive weapon. Later, however, as a result of the Gaulish incursions, La Tène shields produced in workshops situated north of the Alps were brought back to Italy (cf. Stary 1981/b: 296; 1986–7: 84, 97 *et seq.*).

References

Abbreviations

NSc   *Notizie degli Scavi*
MEFRA   *Melanges de l'Ecole Francaise de Rome Antiquite*

Adam, A.-M. 1986. Emprunts et échanges de certains types d'armement entre l'Italie et le monde non-méditerranéen aux Vᵉ et IVᵉ siècles avant J.-C. In *Guerres et sociétés en Italie. Vᵉ-IVᵉs. avant J.-C. (eds A.-M. Adam and A. Rouveret)*. Paris, pp.19–28.

Adam, A.-M. and Jolivet, V. 1986. A propos d'une scène de combat sur un vase falisque du musée du Louvre, in Adam and Rouveret, 1986: 129–144.

Bockius, R. 1989. Ein römisches Scutum aus Urmitz, Kreis Mayen-Koblenz, *Archäologisches Korrespondenzblatt*, 19: 269–282.

Egg, M. 1986. *Italische Helme*, Röm.-Germ. Zentralmuseum, Monographien 11, Mainz.

Eichberg, M. 1987. *Scutum. Die Entwicklung einer italisch-etruskischen Schildform von den Anfängen bis zur Zeit Caesars*. Europäische Hochschulschriften, Archäologie 14. Frankfurt am-Main-Bern-New York-Paris.

Eles Masi, P. von (ed.) 1981. *La Romagna tra VI e IV secolo a. C.* Bologna.

Etrusker 1988. *Die Welt der Etrusker*, Archäologische Denkmäler aus Museen der sozialistischen Länder. Berlin: Staatliche Museen zu Berlin.

Filip, J. 1956. *Keltové ve stredni Evrope*. Monumenta Archaeologica V. Praha.

Haffner, A. 1976. *Die westliche Hunsrück-Eifel-Kultur*. Röm.-Germ. Forsch. 36, Berlin.

Klindt-Jensen, 0. 1953. *Bronzekedelen fra Brå*. Jutland Arch. Soc. Publ. 3, Aarhus.

Kimmig, W. 1988. *Das Kleinaspergle*. Forsch. u. Ber. z. Vor- und Frühgesch. in Baden-Württemberg, 30: Stuttgart.

Kruta, V. 1992. *L'Europe des origines*. L'univers des formes, Paris.

Moretti, M. 1973. *Il Museo Nazionale di Villa Giulia*. Roma.

Moucha, V. 1974. Prispevek k poznani stitu z doby laténské v Cechach. *Archeologické rozhledy*, 26: 445–453.

Neugebauer, J.-W. 1992. *Die Kelten im Osten Österreichs*. St. Pölten-Wien: Niederösterreichisches Pressehaus.

Neugebauer, J.-W. and Gattringer, A. 1987. Rettungs-grabungen im Unteren Traisental im Jahre 1987. *Fundeberichte aus Österreich*, 26: 35–39.

Paul, E. 1990. Zum Bildprogramm und zu Gestaltung-selementen des Stangenhenkelskraters Maler Vatican G 111. In *Die Welt der Etrusker* (eds H.Heres and M.Kunze). Berlin, pp.254–258.

Pauli, L. 1978. *Der Dürrnberg bei Hallein III*. Münchner Beiträge zur Vor- und Frühgeschichte 18. München.

Pianu, G. 1978. Due fabbriche etrusche di vasi sovradipinti. *MEFRA*, 90: 161–95.

Rapin, A. 1982–83. Les umbos de bouclier celtiques décorés de Nogent-sur-Seine. *Antiquités Nationales*, 14–15: 70–77.

Rapin, A. 1984. Le bouclier d'Etréchy canton de Vertus (Marne). *Mémoires de le Société d'Agriculture, Commerce, Sciences et Arts du département de la Marne*, 99: 7–15.

Rapin, A. 1988. Gournay II: *Boucliers et lances. Dépôts et trophées*, (With J.-L. Brunaux), Revue Archéologique de Picardie. Paris.

Roth, H. 1978. Venetische Exvoto-Täfelchen aus Vicenza, Corso Palladio. *Germania*, 56: 172–189.

Sankot, P. 1994. Das La Tène-A Schildgrab von Branov. *Arch. rozhledy*, 46: 493–500.

Stary, P.F. 1981/a. *Zur eisenzeitlichen Bewaffnung und Kampfesweise in Mittelitalien*. Vorgesch. Seminar Marburg: Mainz.

Stary, P.F. 1981/b. Ursprung und Ausbreitung der eisenzeitlichen Ovalschilde mit spindelförmigem Schildbuckel. *Germania*, 59: 287–306.

Stary, P.V. 1986–7. Die militärische Rückwirkungen der

keltischen Invasion auf die Appenin-Halbinsel. *Hamburger Beitrage zur Archäologie*, 13–14: 65–117.

Stead, I.M. 1991. Many more Iron Age shields from Britain. *Antiq. Journ.*, 71: 1–35.

Stefani, E. 1935. Gualdo Tadino. *NSc.*, 155–73.

Uzsoki, A. 1970. A ménföcsanaki kelta pajzs rekonstrukciós kísérlete. *Archeologiai Értesítö*, 97: 97–108.

Some Comments on Swords with Dragon-Pairs

Otto-Herman Frey

Some ten years ago Ian Stead published two La Tène swords with surviving fragmentary scabbards from the old collections of the British Museum. Both came from the River Thames, one from Battersea, the other from the vicinity of Hammersmith Bridge.[1] Careful conservation work revealed representations of the dragon-pair motif on each scabbard, a motif hitherto unknown in the British Isles. Since J.M. de Navarro's work[2] this talismanic emblem *(Heilszeichen)* has been a recurring subject for archaeological research.[3] Stead too, in his publication of the two British examples, developed de Navarro's basic ideas and adopted his classification.

The decoration on the first scabbard is a characteristic version of de Navarro's Type II, that on the Hammersmith example is a variant of the latter's type I. The form of the two swords and their scabbards places them in the La Tène B2 (LT Ic) phase. The particular significance of these new discoveries is that they mark the chronological horizon when the La Tène style – characterised by the products of first rate craftsmen, working for an elite stratum of society and inventing and developing novel stylistic concepts which unified the Celtic world – established itself in the British Isles.[4]

Stead, benefitting from more recent investigations, significantly expanded de Navarro's list of dragon-pair scabbards. With his usual thoroughness, he dealt with the typology, chronology and distribution of these objects and clearly established the Continental background of the British examples. He showed that recent work has necessitated some modification of de Navarro's ideas. For example, Type II can be seen as the oldest version of the dragon-pair motif, on the basis of its presence in the princely grave of "le Catillon" – St Jean-sur-Tourbe.[5] This can now be augmented by well dated finds from Monte Bibele in Italy.[6] As far as the few closed deposits allow us to say, this type appears to have been current for the entire La Tène B phase, while Type I seems to appear only in the course of this phase continuing, like Type III, into La Tène C.

When de Navarro was compiling his list of dragon-pair swords the only discernible concentration of the type was in Hungary. Supported by P. Jacobsthal[7] he thus proposed an eastern origin for the motif. Today this assessment has changed. The griffon motif, from which the "dragons" are derived,[8] was taken over by the Celts from Italy.[9] In addition, Stead's distribution map demonstrated that the concentration of dragon-pair scabbards in France matched that in the Carpathian region so that discussion must focus on two major zones of dragon-pair scabbards. More recently, a third important zone of dragon-pairs has been recognised in north Italy (fig. 81).[10] These regional concentrations emerge even more clearly if only the oldest dragon-pair scabbards of Type II are plotted (fig. 82).

It is perplexing that in a broad intermediate zone, extending from the Mosel to the eastern border of Germany and beyond, dragon-pair scabbards are only rarely found. Is this no more than a product of the present state of archaeological research? After all, as the two British discoveries demonstrated, it is often only through conservation that the presence of dragon-pair motifs is recognised. In addition it may be argued that in the zone in question inhumation was normal in the La Tène B phase so that the protective burnt patina is absent from the scabbards. Both these factors could explain the scarcity of examples in this intermediate region.[11]

But there are other possible reasons for the noticeable gap in our distribution map. W. Krämer demonstrated convincingly for Bavaria south of the Danube[12] that settlement was significantly sparser there, in contrast to that in other regions, during the relevant period. Indeed, during this period we can scarcely reckon with a consistently even population cover in the central and west European areas. It seems simply that in some regions, because of local tribal expansion, greater concentrations of population occurred than in others. In the present state of our knowledge, however, we are hardly in a position to pursue this matter very far. Not only do we lack detailed regional analyses, it is, moreover, virtually impossible in certain regions, such as, for example, northeast Bavaria[13] or south-west Bohemia,[14] to achieve a proper overview of the relevant material culture.

While in some areas the association of the sword with the deceased became less common in the course of the Early/Middle La Tène period, in other areas a contrasting development is recognisable. For example, in the Hunsrück-Eifel region – where gold and Mediterranean imports in the "princely" graves appear to indicate a focus of culture during La Tène A – the custom of depositing weapons in the graves sharply decreased.[15] There are, thus, several varied factors which may have influenced the modern distribution map of the swords, specifically those with dragon-pair designs.

It may be, however, that our notion of wider regional developments is confused by such difficulties which hinder our understanding of the overall picture. For we must similarly reckon with specific cultural "zones of tradition" whose formation and development we are seeking to recognise. While Jacobsthal still regarded the Early La Tène culture as a unified phenomenon,[16] subsequent studies have repeatedly sought to emphasise its regional diversity.

Thus, apart from the systematic study of material in specifically defined regions it was, for example, the work of W. Dehn which sought to demonstrate in the grave material the presence of contrasting distributional emphases between La Tène A and La Tène B.[17] Following Dehn's ideas his students and others defined and interpreted these distributions with increased precision.[18] This led to a certain modification of his ideas. Today developments in the Champagne and in the Middle Rhine region in particular are seen as separate although, as Dehn stressed,[19] contacts did exist between the two culture zones. The investigations of H. Lorenz clearly demonstrated that the division between La Tène A and La Tène B types were not simply a product of simple regional differences, but rather of differing traditions, which manifested themselves in details of clothing and personal equipment, in weaponry and in burial ritual.[20]

The distributions of all these various elements overlap, to an extent, with those which place emphasis on figural representations and art styles. Let us firstly consider the former, which are, indeed, a reflection of a specific belief system.[21] In the La Tène A phase there is a wide range of varied figural representations – often with particular attributes – in a broad zone which extends from the Mosel, Saar and Middle Rhine areas far to the east. This area corresponds well with the distribution of the so-called *Maskenfibeln* (fig. 83).[22] In La Tène B this, the richest and most extensive documentation of the Celtic spiritual world, ends.[23] Only the representations of the human face continue, now for the most part in heavily stylised form. These are spread over the entire La Tène province, and at the end of La Tène B they are again enhanced and embellished by supplementary motifs.[24]

How can we explain this phenomenon? Is it possible that in the course of the Celtic migrations, which must have decisively influenced structures of power and society, the warrior ethos and so on, the leading role within the Celtic world passed to other regions with their own locally developed ideas? And does that mean that in the region referred to above, in which the La Tène A culture was so richly developed, significant elements of their belief system were displaced? Or were they only partly lost so that the manner of their presentation was diluted? Does not, indeed, the whole region disintegrate during La Tène B into individual units which, through differing contacts, undergo divergent development?

In the context of the figural representations of La Tène A the griffon figure in particular, i.e. the representation of a creature usually with a gaping beak and clearly accentuated "ears (or crest)", has a different, wider distribution. Convincing examples are also present in the zone outlined above.[25] But griffons are similarly encountered in Upper Italy and in France in the 5th century BC.[26]

This motif was popular on the ornate openwork buckles which secured the Celtic weapon-belt.[27] In Upper Italy and in the alpine regions there is a well defined group of buckles with antithetic griffons.[28] The fact that these are local products is indicated not only by their distribution but also by the incorporation of motifs into the local repertoire such as the "Lord of the Animals" or the "Birds at the Tree of Life".[29] On the other hand, for example, the "waders" *(Stelzvögel)* are more generally Antique in character and – more obviously – the little human figures *(Männchen)* are derivative of Upper Italian models.[30] Even before the great plantation of Central and Upper Italy by the larger Celtic tribes such as the Cenomanes(?), the Boii or the Senones,[31] there already exists in the Upper Italian and southern Alpine regions a typical version of the La Tène A culture. This also spread northwards across the Alps and appears particularly to have reached the eastern sector of the zone of *Maskenfibeln*).[32] In these regions influences from the south-east alpine situla art and from the area of Este are also recognisable in figural representations.[33]

Lyres with griffon heads are related to lyres with other animal heads, although in the main north of the Alps only water birds and "birds of prey" with closed, curved, hook-shaped beaks[34] occur. There are also other motifs which are also often mistaken for such animal heads.[35] More precise discussion of the various representations, which are often only hinted at, is for the most part, impossible. Bird and griffon ("dragon") motifs turn up again in the sword styles. Must we reckon here with directly linked traditions?

An examination of the development of early, non-figural, Celtic art reveals similar tendencies. Jacobsthal based his so-called Early Style principally on artifacts from the Rhine region.[36] Noteworthy among these is a progressive design of additional ornamental forms ("additive ornament") such as is present, for example, on the openwork gold decoration on the Schwarzenbach bowl[37] and in the engraving on the bronze flagon from Waldalgesheim.[38] Further east, where lavish metal artifacts rarely occur in graves, comparable though simpler motifs occur on La Tène A stamped pottery.[39] To the west there is only a handful of corresponding items.[40] Nonetheless in the French region we encounter the "*Premier Style Continu*" as defined by S. Verger.[41] For him typical representatives of this style are, for example, the decoration on the beaked flagon in the Besançon Museum,[42] the helmet from Berru[43] and other metal objects and painted pottery in the Marne region.[44]

Traditions developing from this style and further links with Mediterranean (italic) tendril patterns are likely to have stimulated the formation of the so-called Waldalgesheim Style (*"Style Végétal Continu"*).[45] A glance at Verger's distribution map of tendril types A 1–2 and B indicates their concentration in the Champagne (along with the central Swiss area) and in north and central Italy to which, in a doubtless somewhat later development, characteristic finds in the Carpathian basin may be added (fig. 84).[46]

Naturally these three tendril forms and their variants do not include everything which may be attributed to this stylistic phase. Among other elements, for example, ornamentation such as that which occurs on the *Scheibenhalsringe* might be added.[47] A survival of the "progressive additive" style in the decoration of the stamped pottery (the Braubacher bowls) was emphasised by Schwappach.[48] Their distribution is, of course, dependent on the custom of placing pots in graves, whereby a wide-ranging expansion eastwards is recognisable.[49] Similarly, a decorative bronze mount from Manching, recently published by S. Sievers, may be placed in the La Tène B phase.[50] On this object rows of opposed triskele motifs are recognisable. Here too an "additive" arrangement of ornament is evident. In contrast is the comparison with, for example, the tendril of whirligigs on the helmet from Amfreville in the lower Seine.[51] Yet it is scarcely possible to speak of a continuation into this period of the stylistic province outlined above. Rather does this cultural zone break up into discrete entities and the artistic development takes distinct and separate paths in the Hunsrück-Eifel zone, in the Rhine Valley, in Bavaria and further east at the end of the Early and at the beginning of the Middle La Tène period.

A comparison of the distribution map fig. 84 with the distribution of dragon-pair swords (figs 81, 82) reveals a noticeable overlap. Three clearly corresponding culture regions stand out: northern France as far as central Switzerland, north and central Italy and the Carpathian region. These areas are further emphasised by the developing Sword Style, the widely distributed products of which are closely related to one another and which represent one of the high points of Celtic art.[52] It is difficult to believe in a significant distortion of this picture through future research.[53] If one regards a vigorous art style as symbolic of a wider flourishing and potency in

other areas of life – a matter which cannot be further pursued here – it is likely that significant impulses emanated from these regions across the whole of the Celtic world.

Moreover, if the distribution of La Tène A griffon representations is included representations which are prominently present in Champagne and in north Italy before the expansion of the Celtic world to the east, and which reflect specific belief systems – it is evident that the dragon-pairs on the scabbards may be considered in this same tradition.[54] As A. Bulard indicated[55] the dragon motif moves from the sword belt to the weapon itself.

So we return once more to the form and content of the dragon motif. It is particularly noticeable that, despite certain variations and, in time, stylistic degeneration, it is, in general, produced in a rigid, almost formula-like manner. It thus contrasts with other representations in Early La Tène art. There is no subsequent development, rather it represents a particular stage of consciousness. It has become a "symbol" within a narrow time frame. The "dragon symbol" may thus be regarded as a *Heilszeichen* of the Celtic warrior class – doubtless linked with death.

Its wide and unified distribution may be explained by the interrelated social structures of the Celtic world, which similarly underlies the extended mercenary traditions.[56] Its presence even in Spain, on a La Tène sword carried in the Iberian manner, may probably also be explained by the movements of Celtic and Iberian mercenaries which were so common in the Mediterranean region.[57]

Similarly, the La Tène A belt hooks with griffon ornament, which secured the sword belt, may also be viewed in the context of corresponding beliefs on the part of the Celtic warrior. Despite the less formalised character of the griffon forms at this time, it is likely that already at this stage their talismanic nature had developed. Moreover, these belt hooks in all their manifestations represent, in all probability, a Celtic warrior elite which was accepted, beyond the narrow confines of the Celtic occupied zone, by the Veneti and Etruscans in Upper Italy.

One of the best indications of an early Celtic warrior class appears to the writer to be the concentration of belt hooks in Languedoc in Ensérune.[58] Some of the hooks are identical with Marnian types. Others belong to the Upper Italian group. In most cases, however, they are local products of which some forms derive from examples in Champagne. In addition, a number of Iberian belt hooks occur. In southern France this concentration of typical Celtic warrior equipment is totally isolated.[59] Are these finds not also in all probability to be regarded as early evidence of an early Celtic warrior grouping?

Following Ian Stead's cautious and sober investigations the foregoing pages represent some considerations of a more speculative nature which attempt to shed light on part of that which is hidden underneath the available evidence. The author offers his very best wishes to Ian

Stead and hopes that he will look kindly on these thoughts – also applicable to the British finds – even though they remain in some aspects provisional because of the many unanswered questions.

Translation: Barry Raftery

References

Binding, U. 1993. *Studien zu den figürlichen Fibeln der Frühlatènezeit.* Bonn.

Bretz-Mahler, D. 1971. *La civilisation de la Tène I en Champagne. Gallia, Suppl. 23e.* Paris.

Bulard, A. 1979. Fourreaux ornés d'animaux fantastiques affrontés découverts en France. *Études Celtiques,* 6: 27–52.

Bulard, A. 1982. A propos des origines de la paire d'animaux fantastiques sur les fourreaux d'épée laténiens. In *L'art celtique de la période d'expansion IVᵉ et IIIᵉ siècles avant notre ère.* Actes Colloque Paris 1978 (eds P.-M. Duval and V. Kruta). Genève-Paris: pp. 149–160.

The Celts. 1991. Catalogue Exhibition Palazzo Grassi, Venezia. Milano.

Charpy, J.-J. and Roualet, P. 1987. *La céramique peinte gauloise en Champagne. Exposition.* Epernay.

Dehn, W. 1950. Älter-latènezeitliche Marnekeramik im Rheingebiet. In *Reinecke-Festschr.* 1947 (eds G. Behrens and J. Werner). Mainz, pp. 33–50.

Dehn, W. 1964. Zu den Lenzburger Kannen. *Germania,* 42: 73–76.

Dehn, W. 1966. Die Doppelvogelkopffibel aus dem Val-de-Travers. In *Helvetia Antiqua.* Festschr. E. Vogt (eds R. Degen, W. Drack, R. Wyss). Zürich, pp. 137–146.

Drda, P. and Rybová, A. 1995. *Les Celtes de Bohême.* Paris: Errance.

Durante, A. 1987. Corredi tombali con elementi tipo La Tène dal sepolcretodi Ameglia. In *Celti ed Etruschi nell'Italia centro-settentrionale dal V secolo a.C. alla romanizzazione. Atti Colloqu. Internaz. Bologna 1985* (ed. D. Vitali). Imola: University Press Bologna, pp. 309–380.

Duval, A. 1989. *L'art celtique de la Gaule au Musée des antiquités nationales.* Paris.

Egg, M. 1986. Die "Herrin der Pferde" im Alpengebiet. *Arch. Korr.,* 16: 69–78.

Frey, O.-H. 1955. Au Musée de Besançon I. Eine etruskische Bronzeschnabelkanne. *Annales Litt. de l'Université de Besançon* (2ᵉ Série) II, 1 (Archéologie 2). Besançon – Paris.

Frey, O.-H. 1972. Die Goldschale von Schwarzenbach. *Hamburger Beitr. z. Arch.,* 1: 85–100.

Frey, O.-H. 1974. Durchbrochene Frühlatènegürtelhaken aus Slowenien. *Situla,* 14/15, (Opuscula I. Kastelic sexagenario dicata): 129–142.

Frey, O.-H. 1976. Du Premier Style au Style de Waldalgesheim. Remarques sur l'évolution de l'art celtique ancien. In *Celtic Art in Ancient Europe. Five Protohistoric Centuries. Proc. Colloquy Oxford 1972* (eds P.-M. Duval and Ch. Hawkes). London, pp. 141–159.

Frey, O.-H. 1984. Gräber mit keltischen Waffen aus dem Boiergebiet in Norditalien. *Die Kunde* N.F. 37 (Festschr. K. Raddatz): 85–92.

Frey, O.-H. 1987. Sui ganci di cintura celtici e sulla prima fase di La Tène nell'Italia del Nord. In *Celti ed Etruschi nell'Italia centro-settentrionale dal V secolo a.C. alla romanizzazione. Atti Colloqu. Internaz. Bologna 1985* (ed. D. Vitali). Imola: University Press Bologna, pp. 9–22.

Frey, O.-H. 1989. Zur "Kline" von Hochdorf. In *Gli Etruschi nord del Po. Atti Convegno Mantova 1986* (ed. E. Benedini). Mantova, pp. 129–145.

Frey, O.-H. 1991. Einige Bemerkungen zu den durchbrochenen Frühlatènegürtelhaken. In *Studien zur Eisenzeit im Hunsrück-Nahe-Raum. Symposium Birkenfeld 1987* (eds A. Haffner and A. Miron). Trier, pp. 101–111.

Frey, O.-H 1993. Die Bilderwelt der Kelten. In *Das keltische Jahrtausend* (eds H. Dannheimer and R. Gebhard). Landesausstellung Rosenheim 1993. Mainz, pp. 153–168.

Frey, O.-H. and Müller, U. 1994. Figürliche Kunst. In *Reallex. Germ. Altkde. (RGA)* 9: 20–24.

Frey, O.-H. 1995. The Celts in Italy. In *The Celtic World* (ed. M.J. Green). London – New York: Routledge, pp. 515–532.

Ginoux, N. 1994. Les fourreaux ornés de France du Ve au IIe siècle avant J.C. *Études Celtiques,* 30: 7–86.

Haffner, A. 1976. Die westliche Hunsrück-Eifel-Kultur. *Röm. Germ. Forsch.,* 36. Berlin.

Jacobi, G. 1982. Verzierte Schwertscheiden vom Frühlatèneschema aus den Flach-gräbern von Manching. *Germania,* 60: 565–8.

Jacobsthal, P. 1944. *Early Celtic Art.* Oxford. (reprinted 1969).

Jannoray, J. 1955. Ensérune. Contribution à l'étude des civilisations préromaines de la Gaule méridionale. *Bibl. Ecoles Franç. d'Athènes et de Rome* 181. Paris.

Joachim, H.-E. 1978. Die Verzierung auf der keltischen Röhrenkanne von Waldalgesheim. *Arch. Korr.,* 8: 119–125.

Krämer, W. 1985. Die Grabfunde von Manching und die latènezeitlichen Flachgräber in Südbayern. *Die Ausgrabungen in Manching 9.* Stuttgart: Franz Steiner Verlag.

Kruta, V. 1986. Le corail, le vin et l'arbre de vie: observations sur l'art et la religion des Celtes du Vᵉ au Iᵉʳ siècle avant J.-C. *Études Celtiques,* 23: 7–32.

Kruta, V. 1989. La fibule "à masques" du gué de Port-à-Binson (Marne). *Études Celtiques,* 26: 7–22.

Kurz, S. 1984. Figürliche Fibeln der Früh-latènezeit in Mitteleuropa. *Fundber. Baden-Württemberg,* 9: 249–278.

Lambot, B. and Verger, S. 1995. Une tombe à char de La Tène ancienne à Semide. Ardennes. *Mém. Soc. Arch. Champenoise,* 10.

Leconte, S. 1993. Les agrafes de ceinture ajourées de la Tène ancienne en Gaule. *Ant. Nat.,* 35: 51–79.

Lejars, T. 1994. *Gournay III. Les fourreaux d'épée. Le sanctuaire de Gournay-sur-Aronde et l'armement des Celtes de La Tène moyenne.* Paris: Errance.

Lenerz-de Wilde, M. 1980. Die frühlatène-zeitlichen Gürtelhaken mit figuraler Verzierung. *Germania,* 58: 61–103.

Lenerz-de Wilde, M. 1981. Keltische Funde aus Spanien. *Arch. Korr.,* 11: 315–319.

Lorenz, H. 1978 Totenbrauchtum und Tracht. Untersuchungen zur regionalen Gliederung in der frühen Latènezeit. *Ber. RGK,* 59: 1–380.

Meduna, J. and Peškař, I 1992. Ein latènezeitlicher Fund mit Bronzebeschlägen von Brno-Maloměřice (Kr. Brno-Stadt) (mit Beitr. O.-H. Frey). *Ber. RGK,* 73: 181–267.

Megaw, J.V.S. 1971. An unpublished early La Tène Tierfibel from Hallstatt, Oberösterreich. *Arch. Austriaca,* 50: 176–184.

Megaw, J.V.S. and Megaw, M.R. 1990. "Semper aliquid

novum" – Celtic Dragon-Pairs Re-Reviewed. *Acta Arch. Hung.*, 42: 55–72.

Megaw, J.V.S. and Megaw, M.R. 1991. The Earliest Insular Celtic Art: some unanswered questions. *Études Celtiques*, 28: 283–307.

Moosleitner, F. 1987. *Arte protoceltica a Salisburgo. Mostra Palazzo Pitti Firerize 1987.* Salzburg.

Müller, F. 1989. Die frühlatènezeitlichen Scheibenhalsringe. *Röm. Germ. Forsch.*, 46, Mainz.

de Navarro, J.M. 1959. Zu einigen Schwert-scheiden aus La Tène. *Ber. RGK*, 40: 79–119.

de Navarro, J.M. 1972. *The Finds from the Site of La Tène, I. Scabbards and the Swords found in them.* London: Oxford University Press.

Neugebauer, J.-W. *et. al.* 1992. *Die Kelten im Osten Österreichs.* St. Pölten-Wien. Niederösterreichisches Pressehaus, pp. 92–94.

Nortmann, H. 1990. Latènezeitliche Hügel-gräber bei Nittel, Kreis Trier – Saarburg. *Trierer Zeitschr.*, 53: 127–194.

Osterhaus, U. 1966. Die Bewaffnung der Kelten zur Frühlatènezeit in der Zone nördlich der Alpen. Unpublished doctoral dissertation. Vorgeschichtliches Institut Marburg.

Pauli, L. and Penninger, E. 1972. Ein verziertes Latèneschwert vom Dürrnberg bei Hallein. *Arch. Korr.*, 2: 283–288.

Rapin, A. 1985. Le fourreau d'épée à "lyre zoomorphic" des Jogasses à Chouilly (Marne). *Études Celtiques*, 22: 9–25.

Ruta Serafini, A. 1984. Celtismo nel Veneto: Materiali archeologici e prospettive di ricerca. *Études Celtiques*, 21, 7–33.

Ruta Serafini, A. and Serafini, M. 1994. Un nuovo gancio di cintura traforato da Montebello Vicentino (VI). In *Studi di Archeologia della X regio in ricordo di Michele Tombolani, a cura di B.M. Scarfi.* Roma, pp. 157–169.

Schaaff, U. 1965. Fibeln und Ringschmuck im westlichen Frühlatènekreis – Versuch einer Gruppengliederung. Unpublished doctoral dissertation. Vorgeschichtliches Institut, Marburg.

Schaaff, U. 1973. Frühlatènezeitliche Grab-funde mit Helmen vom Typ Berru. *Jahrb. RGZM*, 20: 81–106.

Schwappach, F. 1970. Die stempelverzierte Keramik der frühen Latènekultur und stempelverzierte Keramik von Armorica. Unpublished doctoral dissertation. Vorgeschichtliches Institut, Marburg.

Schwappach, F. 1972. Stempel des Waldalgesheimstils an einer Vase aus Sopron-Becsidomb (West-Ungarn). *Hamburger Beitr. z. Arch.*, 1: 131–172.

Schwappach, F. 1973. Frühkeltisches Ornament zwischen Marne, Rhein und Moldau. *Bonner Jahrb.*, 173: 53–111.

Schwappach, F. 1974. Zu einigen Tierdarstellungen der Frühlatènekunst. *Hamburger Beitr. z. Arch.*, 4: 103–140.

Schwappach, F. 1977. Die stempelverzierte Latène-Keramik aus den Gräbern von Braubach. *Bonner Jahrb.*, 177: 119–183.

Sievers, S. 1994. Zu einigen Waffen aus einem Manchinger Depotfund. In *Festschrift für Otto-Herman Frey zum 65. Geburtstag (ed. C. Dobiat). Marburger Stud. Vor- u. Frühgesch.*, 16. Marburg, pp. 595–602.

Stead, I.M. 1984. Celtic Dragons from the River Thames. *Antiq. Journ.*, 64: 269–279.

Stöllner, T. 1991. Neue Grabungen in der latènezeitlichen Gewerbesiedlung im Ramsautal am Dürrnberg bei Hallein – Ein Vorbericht. *Arch. Korr.*, 21: 255–269.

Szabó, M. 1979. La Gaule et les Celtes orientaux. In *Les mouvements celtiques du Vᵉ au Iᵉʳ siècle avant notre ère. Actes Colloqu. Internat. 1976,* (eds P.-M. Duval and V. Kruta). Paris, pp. 161–169.

Szabó, M. 1989. Beiträge zur Geschichte des keltischen Drachenpaarmotivs. *Communicationes Arch. Hung.*, 119–128.

Szabó, M. 1991. Le monde celtique au IIIᵉ siècle avant J.-C. *Études Celtiques*, 28: 11–31.

Szabò, M. and Petres, E.F. 1992. *Decorated Weapons of the La Tène Iron Age in the Carpathian Basin.* Budapest.

Verger, S. 1987. La genèse des rinceaux à triscèles. *Jahrb. RGZM*, 34. 287–339.

Vitali, D. 1984. Un fodero celtico con decorazione a lira zoomorfa da Monte Bibele (Monterenzio, Provincia di Bologna). *Études Celtiques*, 21: 35–43.

Vitali, D. 1987. Monte Bibele tra Etruschi e Celti: dati archeologici e interpretazione storica. In *Celti ed Etruschi nell'Italia centro-settentrionale dal V secolo a.C. alla romanizzazione. Atti Colloqu. Internaz.* Bologna 1985 (ed. D. Vitali). Imola: University Press Bologna, pp. 309–380.

Ulrich, R. 1914. *Die Gräberfelder in der Umgebung von Bellinzona.* Zürich.

Zachar, L. 1974. Datovanie posiev keltych mecov z Drne a Kosic. *Zbornik Slov. Narod. Miiz.*, 68: 55–80.

Notes

1. Stead 1984.
2. de Navarro 1959; 1972.
3. cf., for example, Megaw and Megaw 1990; Szabó 1989; Szabó and Petres 1992.
4. Most recently Megaw and Megaw 1991.
5. Most recently Duval 1989: 69ff.
6. Vitali 1984; 1987; see also Durante 1987. For discussion of chronological development see Szabó 1989; Szabó and Petres 1992: 29ff. It must be borne in mind that the relatively early dating of Type II is based on only a small number of sealed deposits. Nonetheless griffons are already present on a mount from the LT A "princely" grave at Bad Dürkheim (cf. Jacobsthal 1944: pls 103–4, no. 166), in each case displaying a "leg" and thus related to the "dragon" of Type I.
7. Jacobsthal 1944.
8. Bulard 1982.
9. Szabó 1969. Cf. also the references in Szabó and Petres 1992.
10. Cf. list below pp. 169ff., compiled courtesy of F. Stöllner, Marburg. To this should be added a sword from Medlesovice, Region of Strakonice, Bohemia, which will appear in *Bericht über das 4. Treffen der archäologischen Arbeitsgemeinshaft Ostbayern/West- und Südböhmen in Mariánská Tynice 1994* (Espelkamp 1995). I am indebted to P. Sankot, Rostoky for this information.
11. Cf., for example, Jacobi 1982.
12. Krämer 1985.
13. Cf. now the as yet unpublished Munich dissertation of W. Ender, completed in 1995, entitled *Studien zur Siedlungskeramik in Oberfranken.*
14. Most recent overview, Drda and Rybová 1995.
15. Haffner 1976.

16. Jacobsthal 1944.
17. Dehn 1964; 1966.
18. Cf. the unpublished Marburg dissertations, Schaaff 1965; Osterhaus 1966; Schwappach 1970. See also Frey 1976: 153.
19. Dehn 1950.
20. Lorenz 1978.
21. Summarised in Frey 1993; 1994.
22. The map is based on the synthesis of Kurz (1984), which lacks recent discoveries, especially in the east (e.g. Binding 1993). For extension westwards of zone with figural works see, for example Kruta 1986; 1989.
23. Worth mentioning, however, is the clearly LT B date of the figural ornament on the yoke mount from the grave at Waldalgesheim in the Hunsrück-Eifel-region, the core area of the LT A "princely" graves.
24. E.g. the representations on the container from Brno-Malměřice (Meduna and Peškař 1992).
25. E.g. the mount from the "princely" grave at Bad Dürkheim (see note 6).
26. For the region south of the Alps see griffons on belt hooks (Megaw and Megaw 1990). For France see now Lambot and Verger 1995.
27. These openwork belt hooks, along with belt rings (*Koppelringe*), are typically male equipment. In womens' graves such hooks are extremely rare (see Frey 1987:12; 1991: 103ff.).
28. See the distribution maps of Lenerz-de Wilde (1980: Abb. 14 and 16) and Frey (1991: Abb. 8). For a new find from Montebello, see Ruta Serafini and Serafini 1994.
29. Cf., for example, Kruta 1986.
30. Frey 1989: 137ff.; 1991: 109.
31. Most recent summary of Celtic invasion of Italy in Frey 1995.
32. Cf., for example, Megaw 1971; Pauli and Penninger 1972; Frey 1991. The belt hooks from Linz in Austria (Ruta Serafini 1984) and from Roseldorf (see the superb new illustration in the exhibition catalogue *The Celts* 1991: 142) illustrate particularly well the transalpine contacts with Italy. In addition, I am grateful to P. Sankot for informing me of a new study by him of the belt hook from Hosty in southern Bohemia which is currently in press. As a result of X-ray examination it has been possible to reconstruct extensively the ornament with its figural elements. The motifs particularly underline the connections with north Italy.
33. The best indication of this is the scabbard from Hallstatt Grave 994 (Jacobsthal 1944: pl. 59–60, no. 96). A summary of other figural representations is in Schwappach 1974.
34. For a lyre with ducks' heads see Jacobsthal 1944: pl. 169, no. 355a. Lyre designs with bird-of-prey heads see, for example Nortmann 1990: Abb. 20, 1 or Stöllner 1991: Abb. 51. The lyre with horseheads, engraved on the scabbard of a dagger from Bussy-le-Château (Schwappach 1974: Abb. 2–3) is a foreign element in Champagne where otherwise only griffons and birds, or birds' heads occur at this time. Although in the zone of the *Maskenfibeln* fibulae with horses' heads occasionally also occur, as for example at the Dürrnberg (Binding 1993), the best com-

parisons for the representation on the Bussy-le-Château piece are to be found in the Alpine/Upper Italian region (for some relevant belt hooks see Ruta Serafini and Serafini 1994). On the other hand horse motifs are especially common in the area of the Raeti (compare with the representations of the "Mistress of the Horses" – Egg 1986).
35. Cf., for instance, the examples brought together by Lambot and Verger (1995) or the neckrings from the Marne with heraldic bird motifs (Kruta 1986: fig.3). See also relevant fibulae (Binding 1993).
36. His work *Early Celtic Art* is based, to a very large extent, on the collection of illustrations assembled by E. Neuter, the long-serving director of the Rheinisches Landesmuseum, Bonn. This fact explains the greater emphasis on material from the wider Rhineland area.
37. Frey 1972.
38. Joachim 1978. A new publication of the entire find complex by H.-E. joachim, Bonn, in collaboration with other specialists, is in press.
39. Cf. numerous examples in Schwappach 1973.
40. See Jacobsthal 1944: pl. 20, no. 19; pl. 176, no. 376; pl. 177, no. 379.
41. Verger 1987.
42. Frey 1955.
43. Schaaf 1973.
44. Charpy and Roualet 1987; Verger 1987.
45. The various developments are summarised by Verger (1987).
46. The distribution map is largely based on Verger 1987: fig. 8. The additions are indicated in the new publication of the Waldalgesheim grave (see note 38).
47. Müller 1989.
48. Schwappach 1972: Abb.19; 1977.
49. Cf. the distribution map in Lorenz 1978: Beilage 2 (sic!).
50. Sievers 1994: Abb. 4.
51. Jacobsthal 1944: pl. 78–81, no. 140.
52. See, for example, de Navarro 1972; Szabó and Petres 1992; Lejars 1994.
53. In contrast to Germany where, in almost all regions, even if in varying degrees, information concerning graves is available (though the nature of the LT B horizon in northeast Bavaria remains unclear), France, for this period lacks, to a large extent, burials with characteristic gravegoods. Such gaps in our knowledge, however, do not affect the present argument, which is concerned with the region from Champagne as far as the Carpathians.
54. Szabó (1991: 18), however, considers the distribution of the dragon-motif more from the vantage point of the undoubtedly important influences from the Carpathian region in the west.
55. Bulard 1982; Megaw and Megaw 1990.
56. As emphasised, for example, by Szabó (1989) and Szabó and Petres (1992).
57. Lenerz-de Wilde 1981.
58. Jannoray 1955: 394ff; Frey 1991: Abb. 6.
59. There is only one other belt hook with a bird motif from Entremont (M. Willaume, Les objets de la vie quotidienne. *Catalogue: Archéologie d'Entremont au Musée Granet, Aix-en-Provence*, 1987:107, 141, fig. 155a.

List of Dragon-Motif Swords

(After I.M. Stead, J.V.S. and M.R. Megaw, O.-H. Frey, N. Ginoux, A. Rapin und A. Bulard, M. Szabó and E.F. Petres, and others.)

France

1. **Baron-sur-Odon**, Dép. Calvados, D. Bertin, *Gallia* 32, 1974, 243–248, Type I.
2. **Bouqueval**, Dép. Val. d'Oise, Rapin 1985, 19 (Grave 7, Var. Type II); Ginoux 1994, no. 68.
3. **Bussy-le-Chateau**, Dép. Mame, Type II, Bulard 1979, fig. 9–4.
4. **Corgnac-sur-l'Isle**, Dép. Dordogne, Type III, Ginoux 1994, no. 52, fig. 7.5.
5. **Chalon-sur-Saône**, Dép. Saône-et-Loire, Bulard 1979, 33, fig. 4.4, Ginoux 1994, no. 69, Type I.
6. **"Champagne"**, Type II, Ginoux 1994, pl.13.2.
7. **Chens**, Dép. Haute Savoie, Bulard 1979, fig. 9.15; Navarro 1972, pl. 123, Type III?
8. **Chouilly-les-jogasses**, Dép. Marne, Type II, Grave 53, Hatt and Roualet 1981, pl. 13; A. Rapin, *Etudes Celtiques* 22, 1985, 9–25, fig. 2.d.
9. **Gisy-les-Nobles**, Dép. Yonne, Bulard 1979, 42ff., fig. 7.2; Ginoux 1994, no. 53, Type I.
10. **Gourgancon**, Dép. Marne, Type I, Ginoux 1994, no. 54, fig. 7.2.
11. **Gournay-sur-Aronde**, Dép. Oise, Sanctuary, T. Lejars, Gournay III – *Les Fourreaux d'Epée* (Paris 1994) 169 (GSA 143, Type I), 250 (GSA 2524, Type III), 217 (GSA 2556, Type III), 224 (GSA 2693, Type I).
12. **Hauviné**, Dép. Ardennes, "Verboyon", Grave 6, Type I, P. Roualet, A. Rapin, P. Fluzin, L. Uran, Deux groupes de tombes de l'époque de La Tène au lieu-dit Verboyon à Hauviné. *Mem. Soc. Agr. Marne* 100, 1985, 7–28, pl. 7.
13. **Juvigny**, Dép. Marne, J.-J. Charpy, *Bull. Soc. Arch. Champ.* 79, 1989, 3–43, esp. 20.
14. **Lux**, Dép. Saône-et-Loire, Type I, Ginoux 1994, no. 56, pl. 20.2, fig. 7.1.
15. **Marnay**, Dép. Saône-et-Loire, Bulard 1979, 46ff., fig. 8.2; Ginoux 1994, no. 57, Type I.
16. **Meaux**, Dép. Seine-et-Marne, "La Mauve", Ginoux 1994, no. 58, pl. 12, Type II, Type. I.
17. **Michery**, Dép. Yonne, Ginoux 1994, pl. 12.1, 79, no. 59, Type I.
18. **Montigny-Lencóup**, Dép. Seine-et-Loire, Type II, Bulard 1979, 27–52, 36ff.; Ginoux 1994, no. 73, fig. 6.1.
19. **Népelier**, Dép. Ardennes, Rapin 1985, 19, Type I/III, Var.
20. **Nissan-lez-Ensérune**, Dép. Hérault, Ginoux 1994, no. 71, pl. 17.
21. **Ouroux-sur-Saône**, Dép. Saône-et-Loire, Type I, Bulard 1979, fig. 4.3, 50ff., fig. 8.3; Ginoux 1994, no. 60.
22. **Pontoux**, Dép. Saône-et-Loire, Type I, Bulard 1979, 46ff., fig. 8.1; Ginoux 1994, no. 61.
23. **Rives**, Dép. Isère, Bulard 1979, fig. 9.16, Ginoux 1994, no. 62, Type III?.
24. **Rungis**, Dép. Val de Marne, Ginoux 1994, pl. 18, fig.

6.1, Var. Type III.

25–26. **S. Benoit-sur-Seine**, Dép. Aube, Ginoux 1994, pl. 16, fig. 6.5 (Grave 8, no. 76, Type II, Var.) pl. 15, fig. 6.3 (Grave 31, no. 77, Type 11).
27. **S. Jean-sur-Tourbe**, Dép. Marne, Type II, Ginoux 1994, no. 75, pl. 13.1, fig. 6.4.
28. **Varennes-les-Macon**, Dép. Saône-et-Loire, Type II, Bulard 1979, 39ff., fig. 6.3; Ginoux 1994, no. 78.
29. **Vert-la-Gravelle**, Dép. Marne, Grave 3, Type I, J.-J. Charpy, *Bull. Soc. Arch. Champ.* 79, 1986, 3–43, fig. 11; Ginoux 1994, no. 63.
30. **Voreppe**, Dép. Isère, Bulard 1979, fig. 9.17; Ginoux 1994, no. 67, Type I/III.
31. **Villeperrot**, Dép. Yonne, "Le Haut des Longues", Grave W25, Type II, Ginoux 1994, no. 79, fig. 6.2.
32–33. **Villeperrot**, Dép. Yonne, Grave WC2: Bulard 1979, 42ff., fig. 7.1; Ginoux 1994, no. 64; Grave WD.1: Bulard 1979, 42ff., fig. 7.3, Type I; Ginoux 1994, no. 65.
34. **Villeseneux**, Dép. Marne, "La Barbière", Grave 10, Type I; A. Rapin, *Etudes Celtiques* 22, 1985, 9–25, fig. 4.a; Ginoux 1994, no. 66.

Britain

35. **London**, River Thames, Hammersmith Bridge, Type I. River find, Stead 1984, 276, pl. 32.
36. **London**, River Thames, Battersea, Type II. Water find, Stead 1984, fig. 1.1, fig. 2.5.

Spain

37. **Quintanas de Gormas**, prov. Soria, M. Lenerz-de Wilde, *Arch. Korr.* 11, 1981, 315; *idem*, Art celtiques et armes ibériques. *Rev. Aquitania* Suppl. 1, 1986, 273ff., fig. 1.6.

Italy

38–43. **Ameglia**, prov. Liguria, A. Durante, Corredi tombali con elementi tipo La Tène del sepoloreto di Ameglia, in: D. Vitali (ed.) *Celti ed Etruschi. Atti del Congr. Int. Bologna 1985* (Imola 1987) 415–436, esp. 426ff.
   – Grave 3, *op. cit.*, fig. 9.10, Type I,
   – Grave 8, *op. cit.*, fig. 11, Type II,
   – Grave 11–10, *op. cit.*, fig. 9–10, Type I,
   – Grave 11.11, *op. cit.*, fig. 9.11, Type I
   – Grave 22, *op. cit.*, fig. 10.1, Type III,
   – Grave 28, *op cit.*, fig. 14.1, Type I.
44. **Bologna**, tomba Benacci 176, D. Vitali, *Tombe e necropoli galliche di Bologna e del terretorio* (Bologna 1992) 176, 435, tav. 17.1 (Type II).
45. **Castel del Rio**, prov. Bologna, Type II/I, Megaw and Megaw 1990, 66f.; D. Vitali, Una tomba di guerriero di Castel del Rio. *Atti e Mem. Déput. di Storia di Romagna* 35, 1986, 9–35, esp. 12ff., fig. 2.b.
46. **Ciringhelli**, prov. Verona, L. Salzani and D. Vitali, Ein verziertes Latèneschwert von Ciringhelli (Verona,

Italien). *Arch. Korr.* 25, 1995, 171–179, Abb. 2.2, Abb. 3.

47–49. Monterenzio, Monte Bibele, prov. Emilia-Romagna, probably six graves in all with scabbards, Megaw and Megaw 1990, 67,
 – Grave 6, Type II, Megaw and Megaw 1990, fig. 6.3; D. Vitali, Monte Bibele (Monterenzio) und andere Fundstellen der keltischen Epoche im Gebiet von Bologna, *Kleine Schriften Vorgesch. Seminar* 16 (Marburg), 40ff., Abb. 28.
 – Grave 54, Vitali 1987, fig. 31.a, Type I.
 – Grave 70, Vitali 1987, fig. 35.a, Type I.

50. Piobbico, prov. Pesaro-Urbino, Marche, Type II D. Vitali, La necropoli di Piobbico (provincia di Pesaro-Urbino) in: D. Vitali (ed.) *Celti ed Etruschi. Atti del Congr. Int. Bologna 1985* (Imola 1987) 477ff., fig. 4.7.

51. Saliceta, S. Giulano, prov. Modena, Stead 1984, 278.

Switzerland

52. Bevaix, Kt. Neuchâtel, water find, Type I, Navarro 1972, pl. 113.1.

53–62. La Tène, Kt. Neuchâtel, Navarro 1972, no. 4, 359, pl. 2.2, pl. 72 (Var.), no. 7, 361, pl. 3, pl. 74.1 (Var.), no. 16, 368, pl. 9la–d (Var.), no. 7–11, 13–15, 361–368, pl. 6–8, pl. 74–75 (Type III).

63. Münsingen-Rain, Kt. Bern, Grave 138, Type I, Navarro 1972, pl. 121–122; Hodson 1968, pl. 134.

64. Neuenburger See/Region Neuenburg, Kt. Neuchâtel, Type III, after Stead 1984, 276, Navarro 1972, 66, pl. 143.2

65–66. Port, Kt. Neuchâtel, Navarro 1972, 66f., pl. 152.1 (Type III), pl. 154.5 (Type III, Var.).

67. Winterthur, Kt. Zurich, stray find, Type I Tanner, *Latènegräber* 4/8, 27, Taf. 103.A1, in contrast Navarro 1972, 66ff., fig. 20.

Germany

68. Aichach, Lkr. Aichach, Type III?, Krämer 1985, no. 4, Taf. 38.12.

69. Bad Nauheim, Wetteraukreis, S. Kunz, Die restaurierung eines keltischen Schwertes der Frühlatènezeit. *Denkmalpfl. Hessen* 1994/2, 41ff., Abb. S.42.

70. Ering, Lkr. Rottal-Inn, Grave 1, Type II, Krämer 1985, 147 (no. 110), Abb. 20.

71 74. Giengen a. d. Brenz, Kr. Heidenheim, J. Biel, *Arch. Korrb.* 4, 1974, 225ff., Taf. 53.1 (Type III, four swords).

75. Hesselberg, Lkr. Dinkelsbuhl, Krämer 1985, no. 166, Taf. 95. C4, Type ?(II).

76. Ludwigshafen, from the Rhine, Type III, Stead 1984, 276; Navarro 1972, 66, pl. 143.1b, pl. 144.1.

77. Manching, Hundsrucken, Lkr. Ingolstadt, Grave 1972, Type ?, Krämer 1985, Taf. 35.7, no. 96.

78. Singen, Kr. Konstanz, Type III?, Navarro 1972, 66ff., fig. 21.

Austria

79. Au am Leithagebirge, BH Bruck, Grave 13, S. Nebehay, Das latènezeitliche Gräberfeld von der kleinen Hutweide bei Au am Leithagebirge, *Arch. Austriaca Beih.* 11 (Vienna 1973) 14ff., Taf. 10–13 (Type I/III).

80. Dürrnberg, BH Hallein, Grave 102, SK 2, after Moos-leitner 1987, 94f., Abb. 47, cf. Abb., Type I.

81. Guntramsdorf, BH Mödling, R. Pittioni, La Tène in Niederösterreich, *Mat. Urgesch. Österreichs* 5 (Vienna 1930) Taf. 8.2, Taf. 4ab; Navarro 1972, pl. 78.1 (Var. Type I).

82–83. Pottenbrunn, Ratzersdorf, BH St. Pölten, Grave Verf. 400 (Type I), Grave 275 (Type I), Neugebauer *et. al.* 1992, Abb. 29.2–3; J.-W. Neugebauer and A. Gattringer, *Fundber. Österreich* 23; 1984, 97–128, Abb. 25.

84. Saak, BH Villach, "Förker Laas Riegel", "Gailtal", sanctuary, M. Fuchs, *Arch. Österreichs* 2/2, 1991, 19–24, U. Schaaff, *Keltische Waffen* (Mainz 1990) Abb. 6, esp. 14ff.

85. Wieselburg, G. Mossler, Schwert und Scheide der frühen Latènekultur aus Wieselburg, *NÖ. Mitt. Anthr. Ges. Wien* 92, 1962, 221ff., Taf. 17.1.

Czech Republic and Slovakia

86. Charváty, okr. Olomouc, Moravia, Navarro 1972, 67, pl. 139, Type III.

87. Drna, Slovakia, Zachar 1974, 58–61; Szabó and Petres 1992, no. 81, pl. 83.

88–91. Dubník, okr. Nove Zamky, Slovakia, J. Bujna, Das latènezeitliche Gräberfeld bei Dubník I. *Slov. Arch.* 37/2, 1989, 245–376, – Grave 14, *loc. cit.*, Taf. 12.B3 (Type I), – Grave 16, *loc. cit.*, Taf. 13.A2 (Type I), – Grave 30, *loc. cit.*, Taf. 32.3 (Type I), Grave 31, *loc. cit.*, Taf. 33.S (Type I).

92. Izkovice, okr. Trebisov, Slovakia, Grave 25, Type III, Szabó and Petres 1992, no. 93, pl. 93.1.

93. Kosice – Barka, okr. Kosice, Slovakia, Type I, Navarro 1972, 67ff., fig. 27.1a–1b; Szabó and Petres 1992, no. 95, pl. 94.

94. Nitra, okr. Nitra, Slovakia, Zachar 1974, fig. 10.9, Type II.

95. Ponetovice, Moravia, Grave 14, Navarro 1972, 67, pl. 140.1, *Pam. Arch.* 53, 1962, 99, fig. 7, 131.

96. Premysleni, okr. Praha-vychod, Bohemia, P. Sankot, Motifs zoomorphes dans l'art laténien de la Bohême au IIIe siècle avant J.C. *Etudes Celtiques* 28, 1991 (Actes IXe Congr. Int. d'études celt. Paris 1991), 401–433.

97. Sobcice, okr. Kolín, Bohemia, Navarro 1972, 67, pl. 138,4.a–d, Type I/III.

98. Velká-Mana, okr. Nove Zamky, Slovakia, Zachar 1974, fig. 2.3, Var. Type I/III.

Poland

99. Kreszów, A. Kunysz, Miecz celtyski z Rzeszowa. *Wiadimosci Arch.* 28, 1962, 86f., Abb. 3, Type I.

100. Zerán, arr. Warszaw, Z. Jakmowiczowa, Une épée celtique de Zerán, arrondt. de Varsovie, *Demstrykiezwicz Festschrift* (Poznán 1932) 291ff., fig. 3, Type I/III.

Hungary

101. Bonyhádvarasd, Kom. Tolna, Szabó and Petres 1992, no. 4, pl. 6, Type III.

102. Csabrendek, Kom. Veszprém, Szabó and Petres 1992, no. 8, pl. 10.1, Type II.

103. Gödöllo, Kom. Pest, Szabó and Petres 1992, no. 13, pl. 14, Type II (Var.).

104. Halimba, Kom. Veszprém, Szabó and Petres 1992, no.

15, Type I, fig. Suppl. 1.

105. Jutas, Kom. Veszprém, Szabó and Petres 1992, no. 23, fig. Suppl. 2.

106–113. Kosd, Kom. Nográd, Szabó and Petres 1992,
- Grave 1(?), no. 27, pl. 26, Type I,
- Grave 2, no. 29, pl. 28, Type I,
- Grave 15, no. 30, pl. 29–30, Type I,
- Grave 16, no. 31, pl. 31–32, Type I,
- Grave 31, no. 33, pl. 34–35, Type II,
- Grave 60, no. 34, pl. 36–37, Type I,
- Grave 63, no. 35, pl. 38, Type II,
- Stray find, no. 36, pl. 39, Type I.

114. Litér, Kom. Veszprém, Szabó and Petres 1992, no. 39, pl. 43–44, Type II.

115. Lovasberény-Alsotelek, Kom. Fejér, Szabó and Petres 1992, no. 41, pl. 46–47, Type I.

116. Magyarszerdahely, Kom. Zala, Szabó and Petres 1992, no. 42, pl. 48, Type III.

117. Muhi-Kocsmadomb, Kom. Borsod, Grave 23, Szabó and Petres 1992, no. 45, pl. 52.1, Type II.

118. Radostyán, Kom. Abaúj-Zemplén-Borsod, Grave 14, Szabó and Petres 1992, no. 51, pl. 55.1, Type I.

119. Rezi-Rezcseri, Kom. Veszprém, Grave 4, Szabó and Petres 1992, no. 55, pl. 57, Type I.

120–121. Szob, Kom. Pest, Szabó and Petres 1992, no. 65, pl. 68, no. 66, pl. 69, Type I, III.

122. Taliándárógd, Kom. Veszprém, Szabó and Petres 1992, no. 70, pl. 74, Type II.

123. Hungary, no. provenance, Szabó and Petres 1992, no. 74, pl. 77, Type I.

124. Veszprém Museum, no. provenance, Navarro 1972, 67, pl. 31, Type I.

Romania

125–126. Pişkolt, Distr. Satu Mare, Szabó and Petres 1992,
- Grave 40, no. 97, pl. 96, Type III
- Grave 124, unpublished, Type I.

127. Sanislau, Distr. Satu Mare, Grave 1, Szabó and Petres

1992, no. 98, pl. 95.1, Type II.

128. "Sibiu", Distr. Sibiu, Type II, Szabó and Petres 1992, no. 100, pl. 97.1.

129. Tarian-Giris, Distr. Oradea, Grave 34, Szabó and Petres 1992, no. 99, pl. 97.2, Type II.

Former Jugoslavia

130. Brestovik, Serbia, Grave 1, Szabó and Petres 1992, no. 103, pl. 100, Type III.

131. Brežice, Slovenia, Grave 47, Szabó and Petres 1992, no. 106, pl. 102. 1, Type III.

132–133. Dobova, Slovenia, Szabó and Petres 1992,
- Grave 6, no. 112, pl. 113, Type I/III.
- Grave 10, no. 114, pl. 110.1, Type III.

134. Dvorovi kod Bijeljine, Bosnia-Herzegovina, Szabó and Petres 1992, no. 117, pl. 117.1, Type II.

135–136. Karaburma, Serbia, Szabó and Petres 1992,
- Grave 29, no. 122, pl. 116, Type III.
- Grave 66, no. 123, pl. 117.2, Type II.

137. Mitrovica, Serbia, Szabó and Petres 1992, no. 127, pl. 119.1, Type II (Var.).

138. Mokronog, Slovenia, Szabó and Petres 1992, no. 129, pl. 120, Type III.

139. Negotin, vicinity of Serbia, Szabó and Petres 1992, no. 130, pl. 120.1, Type III.

140. Osijek, Croatia, Szabó and Petres 1992, no. 133, pl. 122.

141. Ritopek, vicinity of Belgrade, Serbia, Szabó and Petres 1992, no. 135, pl. 123.2.

142. Sremski-Karlovci, Voivodina, Serbia, Szabó and Petres 1992, no. 139, pl. 125.1, Type III.

Bulgaria

143–144. Plovdiv, two scabbards of Type II, information courtesy J.V.S. Megaw.

Representations of Heraldically Arranged Griffons

1. Bad Dürkheim, Kr. Neustadt a.d.W., Jacobsthal 1944, no. 166, pl. 203 (Decorative mount).

2. Balzers, Liechtenstein, J. Bill, Latènezeitliche Funde in Balzers (Fürstentum Liechtenstein). *Arch. Korr.* 12, 1982, 487ff., Taf. 52.1 (Belt hook).

3. Bussy-le-Château, Dép. Marne, "La Cheppe", Jacobsthal 1944, pl. 210.441; Bretz-Mahler 1971, pl. 124.1 (pottery ornament) .

4. Castaneda, Kt. Tessin, R. de Marinis, Il periodo Golasecca IIIA in Lombardia, *Studi Arch. I* (Bergamo 1981) 235ff., fig. 7 (Belt hook).

5. Castione, Kt. Tessin, Grave 64, Ulrich 1914, Taf. 7.3; Jacobsthal 1944, no. 361c (Belt hook).

6. Dolenjske Toplice, Slovenia, B. Terzan, Certoska fibula. *Arch. Vestnik* 27, 1976 (1977) Taf. 78.5 (Tum. 13/Grave 4).

7–8. Este, prov. Padua, Rebato, Grave 152, Megaw and

Megaw 1990, fig. 4.1; Benvenuti, Grave 116, *idem* fig. 4.3 (Belt hook).

9. Giubiasco, Kt. Tessin, Grave 29, Megaw and Megaw 1990, fig. 1.3, Jacobsthal 1944, no. 361b; Ulrich 1914, Taf. 47.3 (Belt hook).

10. Hauviné, Dép. Marne, Leconte 1993, 62ff., pl. 5.39 (Belt hook).

11. Lagole Calalzo, prov. Belluno, Megaw and Megaw 1990, fig. 1.1 (Belt hook).

12. Lothen, prov. Bozen, Ruta Serafini and Serafini 1994, fig. 4.9 (Belt hook).

13. Molinazzo d'Arbedo, Kt. Tessin, Grave 7, Megaw and Megaw 1990, fig. 1.4, Jacobsthal 1944, no. 361b, Ulrich 1914, Taf. 31.15.

14. Montebello, prov. Vicenza, Ruta Serafini and Serafini 157ff., fig. 2 (Belt hook).

15. Nissan-lez-Ensérune, Dép. Hérault, Frey 1991, Abb.

6.18 (Belt hook).

16. **Roseldorf**, BH Horn, Megaw and Megaw 1990, fig. 1.6 (Belt hook).

17. **San Polo d'Enza**, Campo di Servirola, prov. Reggio nell'Emilia, Megaw and Megaw 1990, fig.1.3 (Belt hook).

18. **S.Remy-sur-Bussy**, Dép. Marne, Leconte 1990, 62, pl. 5, no. 38 (Belt hook).

19. **Somme-Bionne**, Dép. Marne, Leconte 1990, pl. 5, no.

40 (Belt hook).

20. **"Val de Travers"**, Rochefort, Champ de Moulin, Kt. Neuchâtel, Kaenel 1990, pl. 3–1. decorated plate of fibula (uncertain),

21. **Waldalgesheim**, Kr. Kreuznach, Jacobsthal 1944, pl. 190, no. 387 (Handle element of LTA flagon).

22. **Vinica**, Slovenia, Jacobsthal 1944, pl. 230 g, openwork pendant.

Ornithomorphic Lyre Motifs

23. **Berlin – Wittenau**, Grave 11, "Mühlberg" (?), H. Seyer, Siedlungen und archäologische Kultur der Germanen im Havel- und Spree-Gebiet. *Schriften Ur.u.Frühgesch.* 34 (Berlin 1982) 65, Taf. 27.23 (Belt hook).

24. **Dürrnberg**, BH Hallein, Ramsautal, Stöllner 1991, Abb. 5.1 (Belt hook).

25. **Epernay**, Dép. Marne, Leconte 1993, 68, pl. 8, no. 61 (Belt hook, with water bird).

26. **Este**, prov. Padua, romba Palazzina, Frey 1974, Abb. 7.1–2 (Belt hook, with waterbird).

27. **Glauberg**, Kr. Büdingen, F.R. Herrmann, *Arch. Deutschland* 1995/1, Abb. S.55 (gold neck-ring).

28. **Hosty-Hladná**, okr. C. Budejovice, Benes, *loc. cit.* (see below) Abb. 2.1–2 (after J. Filip, Belt hook).

29. **Kobern**, Kr. Mayen-Koblenz, "Chorgesang", Tum. 33, H. Eiden, *Ausgrabungen an Mittelrhein und Mosel*

1963–1976. Tafelband. *Trierer Zeitschr.* Beih. 6 (Trier 1982) Taf. 39.2, Taf. 43.2 (Belt hook).

30. **Linz**, St. Peter, BH Linz-Stadt, Frey 1991, Abb. 8 (Belt hook).

31. **Nittel**, Kr. Trier-Saarburg, H. Nortmann, Latènezeitliche Hügelgräber bei Nittel, Kr. Trier-Saarburg. *Trierer Zeitschr.* 53, 1990, 127–194, 147, Abb. 8.2 (Tum. 4, Belt hook).

32. **Reinheim**, Kr. St. Ingbert, J. Keller, *Das keltische Fürstengrab von Reinheim 1* (Mainz 1965) Taf. 44.

33. **S. Denis-en-Palin**, Dép. Cher, *Gallia* 22, 1964, 233, Abb. 21.2–3.

34. **Ujezd nade Mzí**, okr. Plzen-sever, A. Benes, Der erste eiserne, durchbrochene Gürtelhaken aus Westböhmen. *Arch. Arbeitsgemeinschaft Ostbayern/West- und Südböhmen, Tagung 1993* (Deggendorf und Kelheim 1994) 124–129, Abb. 1.3 (Belt hook).

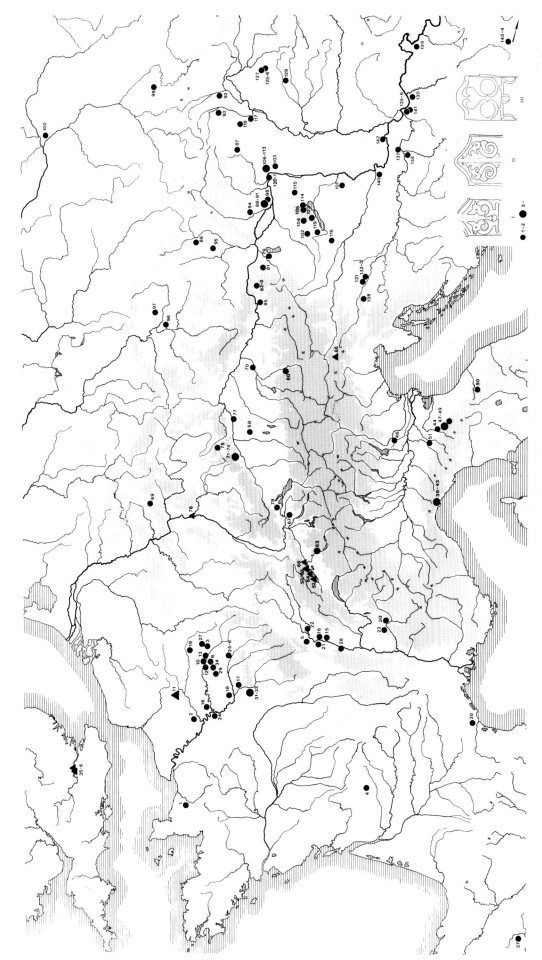

fig. 81 Distribution of swords with dragon-pair motifs of de Navarro Types I–III. Dots indicate grave finds or "individual" finds. Triangles indicate swords from other contexts (after Stöllner).

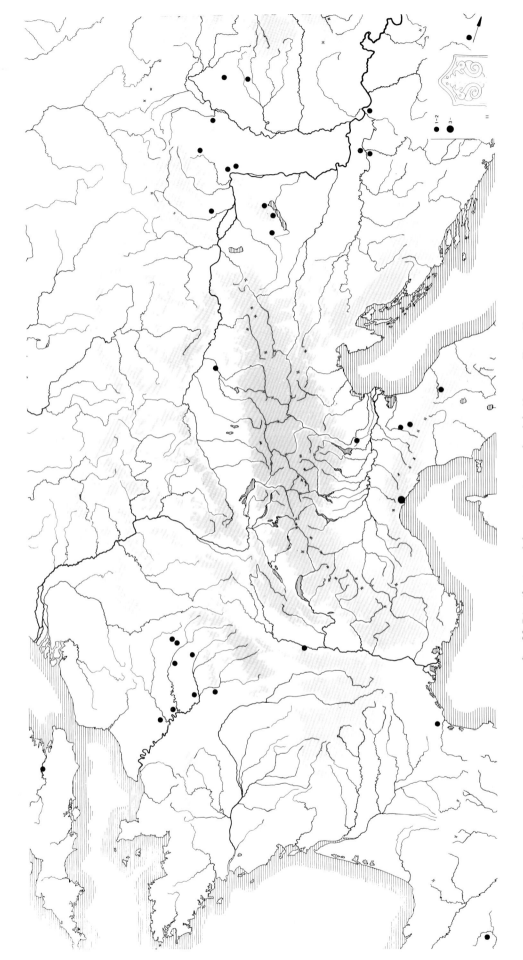

fig. 82 Distribution of dragon-pair swords of de Navarro Type II.

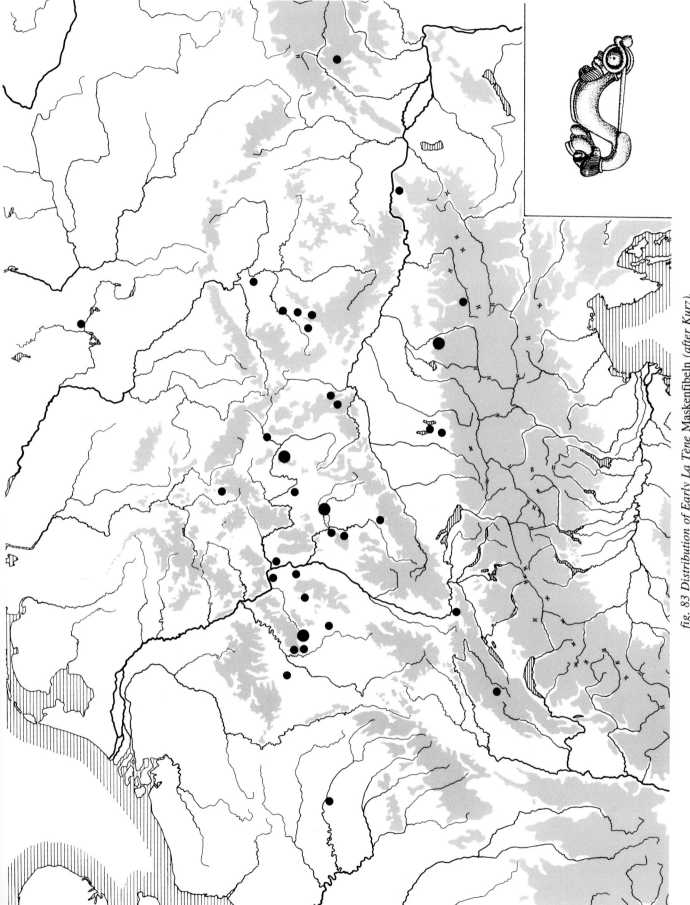

fig. 83 Distribution of Early La Tène Maskenfibeln (after Kurz).

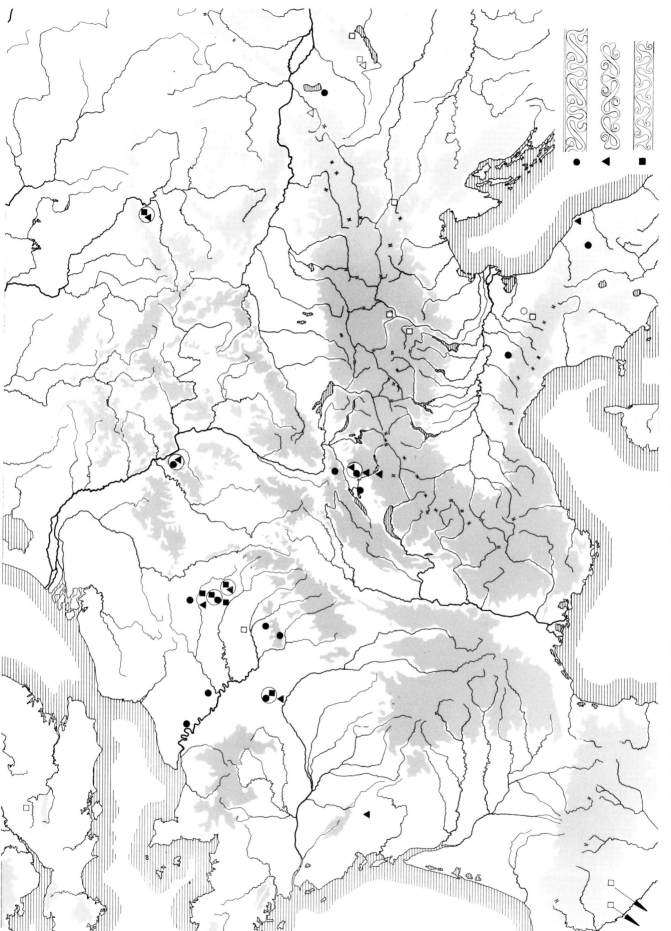

fig. 84. Distribution of Waldalgesheim-style tendril motifs of Verger's Types A 1–2 and B (after Verger 1987 with additions).

Index

(Numerals in *Italics* indicate illustration numbers)

Contributors

Dr Donald M Bailey
Department of Greek
  and Roman Antiquities
The British Museum
London WC1B 3DG
England

Dr. Andrew Burnett
Department of Coins and Medals
The British Museum,
London WC1B 3DG
England

Dr Jean-Jacques Charpy
Musee Municipal
13, Avenue de Champagne
51200 Epernay
France

Dr P.T. Craddock
Department of Scientific Research
The British Museum
London WC1B 3DG
England

Professor Barry Cunliffe
Institute of Archaeology
36 Beaumont Street
Oxford, OX1 2PG
England

John Dent
Borders Regional Council
Newtown St. Boswells
Melrose TD6 OSA
Scotland

Dr Jennifer Foster
Department of Archaeology
Saint David's University College
Lampeter
University of Wales
Wales SA48 7ED

Professor F.R. Hodson
26 Foxton Road
Barrington
Cambridge CB2 5RN
England

Ralph Jackson
Department of Prehistoric
  and Romano-British Antiquities
The British Museum
London WC1B 3DG
England

Dr Simon James
Education Department
The British Museum
London WC1B 3DG
England

Catherine Johns
Department of Prehistoric
  and Romano-British Antiquities
The British Museum
London WC1B 3DG
England

Professor E.M. Jope
1 Chalfont Road
Oxford
England

Professor J.B. Lambert
Department of Chemistry
Northwestern University
Evanston
Illinois 60201
U.S.A

Mrs Janet Lang
Department of Scientific Research
The British Museum
London WC1B 3DG
England

Dr Ian Longworth
Department of Prehistoric
  and Romano-British Antiquities
The British Museum
London WC1B 3DG
England

Professor W.H. Manning
School of History and Archaeology
University of Wales
PO Box 909
Cardiff CF1 3XU
Wales

Dr M. Ruth Megaw
Visiting Fellow
School of Cultural Studies
The Flinders University
  of South Australia
GPO Box 2100,
Adelaide
South Australia 5001

Professor J.V.S. Megaw
School of Cultural Studies
The Flinders University
  of South Australia
GPO Box 2100
Adelaide
South Australia 5001

Professor Stuart Piggott
The Cottage
West Challow
Wantage
Oxfordshire OX12 9TN
England

Professor Barry Raftery
Department of Archaeology
University College
Belfield
Dublin 4
Ireland

Valery Rigby
Department of Prehistoric
  and Romano-British Antiquities
The British Museum
London WC1B 3DG
England

Professor Miklós Szabó
Loránd Eötvös University
H-1364 Budapest
Egyetem ter 1–3, Pf. 109
Hungary

Em. Professor Otto-Herman Frey
Vorgeschichtliches Seminar
Philipps-Universität
D-35032 Marburg-Lahn
Germany